New SAT

Blue Math

Version 2.0

Letter to Parents

To Students and Parents

C2 Education's Redesigned SAT workbooks focus on curriculum that will help students build key foundation skills and learn problem-solving methods to tackle the new SAT to be released in 2016. We strongly recommend that students use these workbooks aligned with instructions and guidance from our tutors at a C2 Education center.

This book contains a number of exercises designed to guide the student through a careful, progressive process that will build layers of understanding and present problems with an increasing degree of difficulty. Each colored (belt) level will confront a variety of topics within the realms of Writing, Essay, Reading, and Math; some topics may re-appear in other workbooks of different difficulties while some topics may only appear once. The ultimate goal of C2 Education's workbooks is to cover the academic content in a comprehensive manner with sufficient practice sets and homework review.

Students will obtain the greatest benefit and improvement from these workbooks by following the workbooks from Lesson 1 to the end. Each lesson will contain the following:

- A diagnostic assessment designed to help our C2 tutors gauge the student's understanding prior to the lesson
- Instructional text and information focused on methodology and problem-solving thought processes
- Practice problems about the concepts presented and any connecting concepts from other lessons
- Test-like practice problems geared to emulate the real exam
- Homework problems to review academic information covered in class and the workbook

We wish you the best of luck in your academic endeavors and we hope that our workbooks will provide you with strong improvements, facilitated understanding, and expanded problem-solving skills. Thank you for being a part of the C2 family; we hope that you enjoy your time learning with us!

- C2 Education's Curriculum Team

SAT Blue Math
Table of Contents

SAT Blue Math
Table of Contents

BLUE MATH LESSON 1A: ONE- AND TWO-VARIABLE EQUATIONS AND INEQUALITIES
Getting Your Feet Wet

Directions: The problems below are intended as a short diagnostic exam.

1. If $3 - \frac{2}{x+5} = 0$, then x equals which of the following?

    A) $-\frac{17}{3}$

    B) $-\frac{9}{2}$

    C) $-\frac{13}{3}$

    D) 1

2. If $\frac{y-4}{y+3} = \frac{3}{5}$, then $\frac{y+3}{y-4} =$

$$x + 3y = 9$$
$$3x - 2y = 5$$

3. If the ordered pair (x, y) is a solution to the system of equations above, what is the value of xy?

4. If $x > y + 7$, then $3x - 3y > ?$

BLUE MATH LESSON 1A: ONE- AND TWO-VARIABLE EQUATIONS AND INEQUALITIES
Wading In

Directions: Read the explanation for each problem type mentioned below. Pay special attention to the methods and techniques used to solve the sample problems. Then, do the practice exercises that follow; use the appropriate method to solve each problem.

TOPIC OVERVIEW: ONE-VARIABLE EQUATIONS AND INEQUALITIES

Solving one-variable equations and inequalities is fairly straightforward: For the most part, we should follow the rules set forth by PEMDAS to simplify the expression to something manageable. Just remember that when dealing with inequalities and multiplying or dividing by a negative number, we flip the inequality sign (so, $<$ becomes $>$ and $\geq$ becomes $\leq$).

However, sometimes the SAT doesn't just ask us to solve for some variable like x. Instead of solving for x, we may have to solve for $3x$, $3x + 2$, or even $\frac{3x+2}{x-4}$! There are two big reasons for the extra complication: First of all, the makers of the SAT don't want us to be able to just plug in all of the answer choices to work backwards and find the answer without actually solving anything. Secondly, sometimes it's easier to manipulate the equation into what we're looking for than to actually solve everything out.
Let's look at a few examples of these below.

SAMPLE PROBLEM 1: ONE-VARIABLE EQUATIONS

If $3 - \frac{2}{x+5} = 0$, then x equals which of the following?

A) $-\frac{17}{3}$

B) $-\frac{9}{2}$

C) $-\frac{13}{3}$

D) 1

The first problem just asks us to solve for x. One thing makes this problem complicated to solve: The x is in the denominator of a fraction. As a rule, try to get rid of any fractions in the problem first. The easiest way to do this is to multiply each term by the denominator, $x + 5$.

$$3 - \frac{2}{x+5} = 0$$
$$3(x + 5) - \frac{2}{x+5}(x + 5) = 0(x + 5) = 0$$
$$3(x + 5) - 2 = 0$$
$$3x + 15 - 2 = 0$$
$$3x + 13 = 0$$
$$3x = -13$$
$$x = -\frac{13}{3}$$

So, our answer is **C**. Remember, on the SAT, it's always a good idea to plug the answer back into the equation to make sure it works if there is any time left over. Also, make sure that the answer is the correct answer and that it isn't extraneous.

SAMPLE PROBLEM 2: ONE-VARIABLE EQUATIONS

If $\frac{y-4}{y+3} = \frac{3}{5}$, then $\frac{y+3}{y-4} =$

Here we see a problem that's not just asking us to solve for our variable, y. Although we could certainly solve this for y by cross-multiplying, then plugging our value of y into the term we're looking for, there's a much easier solution to this problem:

Note that the left side of our equation, $\frac{y-4}{y+3}$, and the term we're looking for, $\frac{y+3}{y-4}$, are reciprocals of each other. Since $\frac{y-4}{y+3}$ is equal to $\frac{3}{5}$, its reciprocal would have to be equivalent to the reciprocal of $\frac{3}{5}$, or $\frac{5}{3}$. With one simple flip of a number, we've solved the problem.

On the SAT, always be on the lookout for ways to manipulate the equation to obtain what's needed. Some of the more common means of manipulation include:

- Adding to or subtracting from both sides of an equation
- Multiplying or dividing both sides of an equation by a number or variable
- Taking the reciprocal of both sides of an equation
- Squaring or taking the square root of both sides of an equation

TOPIC OVERVIEW: TWO-VARIABLE EQUATIONS

The SAT poses two types of problems containing two variables: those with one equation or inequality and those with two.

The problems with two equations are generally easier, as these problems just require solving a system of equations. Since most of these problems show up on the non-calculator portion of the test, graphing the lines in a calculator to find an intersection is usually not an option. Instead, use the elimination or substitution methods for solving systems of equations to solve these problems.

Other problems contain two variables, but only one equation or inequality. These questions are actually impossible to solve, as there are infinite solutions to the equation. Instead, these problems will involve the manipulation of both sides of the equation or inequality in order to turn an

expression like $\frac{y}{7} + \frac{x}{7}$ into one like $5x + 5y$ (In this case, the manipulation would just involve multiplying both sides by 35.)

Let's look at a few of these problems to understand how this works.

SAMPLE PROBLEM 3: TWO-VARIABLE EQUATIONS

$$x + 3y = 9$$
$$3x - 2y = 5$$

If the ordered pair (x, y) is a solution to the system of equations above, what is the value of xy?

One way to solve this system of equations is substitution: Solve one equation for a variable, like x, then plug that value into the other equation:

If $x + 3y = 9$, then $x = 9 - 3y$. Now we can plug that into the other equation.

$$3x - 2y = 5$$
$$3(9 - 3y) - 2y = 5$$
$$27 - 9y - 2y = 5$$
$$27 - 11y = 5$$
$$-11y = -22$$
$$y = 2$$

Now, as before, we can plug that value into one of our original equations to find x:

$$x + 3y = 9$$
$$x + 3(2) = 9$$
$$x + 6 = 9$$
$$x = 3$$

The solution is $x = 3$ and $y = 2$. So, our answer, xy, is 6.

SAMPLE PROBLEM 4: TWO-VARIABLE INEQUALITIES

If $x > y + 7$, then $3x - 3y > ?$

Since we only have one inequality but two variables, we can't actually solve for x or y. Instead, we have to figure out how to manipulate this equation to turn it into $3x - 3y$.

Let's start by getting both our x and our y terms on the same side:

$$x > y + 7$$
$$x - y > 7$$

So how do we turn $x - y$ into $3x - 3y$? Just multiply by 3! Since we multiply one side of the equation by 3, we have to multiply 3 to the other side as well.

$$3(x - y) > 3(7)$$

So, $3x - 3y > 21$.

WRAP-UP

When approaching SAT Algebra questions, always be aware of what to solve for. Some answers will be solved most easily via the methods included in Pre-Algebra or Algebra 1 classes, while others will require some sort of manipulation. As with anything, the more practice, the better, so try the methods we just discussed on the problems on the next few pages.

BLUE MATH LESSON 1A: ONE- AND TWO-VARIABLE EQUATIONS AND INEQUALITIES
Learning to Swim

Directions: Answer each question below.

PRACTICE SET 1 (NO CALCULATOR)

1. If $\sqrt{x-5} = 3$, what is $x - 2$?

2. If $x\frac{(y-4)}{(y+5)} = 2x$, $x \neq 0$, and $y \neq 4$ or -5, what is $\frac{(y+5)}{(y-4)}$?

3. If $x = y + 4$, what is $2x - 2y$?

4. If $x - 9 = y + 4$, what is $x - y$?

5. If $\frac{8}{x} - \frac{8}{y} = 8$, what is $\frac{3}{x} - \frac{3}{y}$?

BLUE MATH LESSON 1A: ONE- AND TWO-VARIABLE EQUATIONS AND INEQUALITIES
Diving into the Deep End

Directions: Answer each question below.

PRACTICE SET 2 (NO CALCULATOR)

6. If $-3|2x - 3| - 3 < 2$, then
   A) $\frac{2}{3} < x < \frac{7}{3}$
   B) $x < \frac{2}{3}$ or $x > \frac{7}{3}$
   C) A real value of x does not exist that satisfies this inequality.
   D) $-\infty < x < \infty$

9. If $\frac{2x(y-3)}{y+1} = 6x, y \neq -1$ or 3, and $x \neq 0$, then
   $\frac{y+1}{y-3} =$
   A) $\frac{1}{12}$
   B) $\frac{1}{3}$
   C) 3
   D) 12

$$x + y \geq 6$$
$$x < 3y$$

7. Which of the following ordered pairs does not satisfy the system of inequalities above?
   A) $(3, 3)$
   B) $(-1, 7)$
   C) $(-5, 11)$
   D) $(0, 5)$

$$\tfrac{1}{3}(x + 5) + 6 = \tfrac{2}{3}(2x + 4) - 4$$

10. In the equation above, what is the value of x?
    A) -1
    B) 1
    C) 9
    D) 11

11. If $\frac{3}{x} + \frac{3}{y} = 6$, then $\frac{2}{x} + \frac{2}{y} =$
    A) $\frac{1}{4}$
    B) 2
    C) 4
    D) 9

8. If $4x + 3y = 11$, what is the value of $\frac{2}{3}x + \frac{1}{2}y$?
   A) $\frac{11}{36}$
   B) $\frac{11}{6}$
   C) $\frac{22}{3}$
   D) 66

$$6x - 3y = 10$$
$$x + \frac{1}{3}y = 0$$

12. Which of the following points is a solution to the above system of equations?
    A) $(0, -\frac{10}{3})$
    B) $(1, -3)$
    C) $(\frac{2}{3}, -2)$
    D) $(2, \frac{2}{3})$

13. If $\frac{x}{3} = \frac{3}{x}$, then $x =$
    A) -3
    B) 3
    C) $\pm\sqrt{3}$
    D) ± 3

14. If $2x + 4y - x = x + 3$, then $y =$

15. If $\frac{1}{2} - x = y - \frac{1}{2}$, then $x + y =$

PRACTICE SET 3 (NO CALCULATOR)

$$\frac{1}{2}(4a - 3) + 3 = 1 - \frac{5}{2}(a - 2)$$

16. In the equation above, what is the value of a?
    A) -1
    B) 1
    C) $\frac{4}{3}$
    D) 9

$$-x + 2y = -y + 9$$
$$x + 2y = 2y - x$$

17. Based on the system of equations above, what is the value of y^2?
    A) 0
    B) 3
    C) 9
    D) 81

18. If $\sqrt{3x} - 5 = 2$, then $3x + 4 =$
    A) 25
    B) 33
    C) 45
    D) 53

19. If $-3x + 9y = -4$, then $2x - 6y =$
    A) $-\frac{64}{3}$
    B) $-\frac{8}{3}$
    C) $\frac{8}{3}$
    D) $\frac{64}{3}$

$$\frac{-(2z+5)+4}{3} = \frac{2+3(-z-2)}{4}$$

23. In the equation above, what is the value of z?
    A) -8
    B) $-\frac{8}{17}$
    C) 8
    D) 16

20. What is the solution to the equation $\frac{2}{x+2} = \frac{7}{x-3}$?
    A) -4
    B) -1
    C) $\frac{1}{5}$
    D) 4

24. If $\frac{1}{3}x < \frac{3}{2}$ and $\frac{3}{5}x \geq 2$, what is a possible value for x?

$$\sqrt{y-1} = \frac{5}{4}$$

25. In the equation above, what is the value of y?

21. If $-5 < 3x - 1 < -4$, what is one possible value of $2 - 6x$?
    A) 8
    B) 9
    C) 10
    D) 12

22. If $\frac{5y(x+3)}{x+5} = 3y$, $x \neq -5$ or -3, and $y \neq 0$, then $\frac{x+5}{-x-3} =$
    A) $-\frac{5}{3}$
    B) $-\frac{3}{5}$
    C) $\frac{3}{5}$
    D) $\frac{5}{3}$

BLUE MATH LESSON 1A: ONE- AND TWO-VARIABLE EQUATIONS AND INEQUALITIES
Race to the Finish

Directions: Answer each question below.

HOMEWORK SET (NO CALCULATOR)

1. If $\frac{4}{7}x + \frac{2}{3}y = -3$, what is the value of $12x + 14y$?
   A) −1323
   B) −63
   C) −7
   D) $-\frac{9}{7}$

2. If $-2x + 12y = 18$, then $5x - 30y =$
   A) −45
   B) −7.2
   C) 45
   D) 112.5

$$-x + 3y = 2x - 14$$
$$x + 6y = 14$$

3. Based on the system of equations above, what is the value of the product xy?
   A) $\frac{4}{3}$
   B) 6
   C) 8
   D) 24

$$\frac{2(k+1)-3}{5} = \frac{3-(k+2)}{3}$$

4. In the equation above, what is the value of k?
   A) $\frac{2}{11}$
   B) $\frac{8}{11}$
   C) $\frac{11}{8}$
   D) $\frac{11}{2}$

$$\frac{d-2}{3d} = \frac{2}{3}$$

5. In the equation above, what is the value of d?
   A) −2
   B) $-\frac{2}{5}$
   C) 0
   D) 2

$$\sqrt{y+3} = \frac{8}{5}$$

6. In the equation above, what is the value of y?
   A) $-\frac{139}{25}$
   B) $-\frac{11}{5}$
   C) $-\frac{11}{25}$
   D) $\frac{139}{25}$

$$14x - 4y = 6$$
$$-7x + 2y = -3$$

7. Which of the following ordered pairs is a valid solution to the system of equations above?

A) $(-2, 7)$

B) $(1, 4)$

C) $(3, 9)$

D) $(3, 12)$

8. If $\sqrt{4x + 1} = 16$, then $-4x =$

A) -257

B) -255

C) -5

D) -3

9. If $\frac{3}{x+2} - 2 = 5$, then $x =$

A) $-\frac{11}{7}$

B) $-\frac{3}{7}$

C) $\frac{1}{7}$

D) $\frac{3}{7}$

10. $3|x + 1| - 3 < 2$, then

A) $-\frac{8}{3} < x < \frac{2}{3}$

B) $x > \frac{2}{3}$ or $x < -\frac{8}{3}$

C) A real value of x does not exist that satisfies this inequality.

D) $-\infty < x < \infty$

11. If $\frac{(-3x)}{y-1} = 9$, $y \neq 1$, and $x \neq 0$, then $\frac{1-y}{x} =$

A) -3

B) $-\frac{1}{3}$

C) $\frac{1}{3}$

D) 3

12. If $-4y = 13 + x$, what is $4y + x$?

A) -13

B) $-\frac{13}{4}$

C) $\frac{13}{4}$

D) 13

13. If $\frac{1}{x} = \frac{y}{7}$, what is $xy + 2$?

A) 5

B) 7

C) 9

D) 10

14. If $\frac{4}{x} + \frac{4}{y} = 5$, what is $\frac{2}{x} + \frac{2}{y}$?

A) $\frac{2}{5}$

B) $\frac{4}{5}$

C) $\frac{5}{4}$

D) $\frac{5}{2}$

15. If $x\left(\frac{y-3}{y+4}\right) = 8x$ and $y \neq -4$ or 3, what is $\frac{y+4}{y-3}$?

    A) $\frac{1}{8}$

    B) $\frac{1}{4}$

    C) 2

    D) 8

16. If $(x-3)^2 = 9$, then $x =$

    A) 0

    B) 0 or 3

    C) 3 or 6

    D) 0 or 6

17. If $-\frac{3}{5} < \frac{x+2}{3} < \frac{1}{5}$, what is one possible positive integer value of $2x + 4$?

18. If $3x - 2y = 12$, what is the value of $\frac{1}{2}x - \frac{1}{3}y$?

19. If $\sqrt{x-3} = 4$, what is $x + 5$?

20. If $x = 3y + 11$, what is $4x - 12y$?

BLUE MATH LESSON 1B: INTERPRETING EQUATIONS AND INEQUALITIES
Getting Your Feet Wet

Directions: The problems below are intended as a short diagnostic exam.

1. Jackson wants to be able to store and edit documents on his smartphone, which has 3500 MB of free space. In order to do this, he needs to install an app which takes up 25 MB of space. If the average document he edits takes up 4.5 MB of space, and he needs to store d documents, which of the following equations could represent S, the amount of free space he has on his phone?

   A) $S = 3500 - 25d$
   B) $S = 3500 - 25 - d$
   C) $S = 3500 - 25 - 4.5d$
   D) $S = 3500 - (25 - 4.5d)$

2. Julie is performing an exit poll to try to determine the results of a city council election. She needs to poll at least 400 people. Every hour she waits outside the public library she polls 9 people, and every hour she waits outside the elementary school she polls 19 people. If she waits a hours outside the library and b hours outside the school, which of the following inequalities represents her time waiting at each location?

   A) $9a + 19b \leq 400$
   B) $9a + 19b \geq 400$
   C) $9a + 19b < 400$
   D) $9a + 19b > 400$

3. A major airline transports 13.4 million passengers each month, with an average ticket price of $380. The airline determines that for every $1 it decreases the ticket price, the airline can gain another 10,000 passengers. Which of the following functions models the number of passengers, P, in terms of the price of a ticket, t?

   A) $P(t) = 13{,}400{,}000 + 10{,}000(380)$
   B) $P(t) = 13{,}400{,}000 + 10{,}000(380 + t)$
   C) $P(t) = 13{,}400{,}000 + 10{,}000(t - 380)$
   D) $P(t) = 13{,}400{,}000 + 10{,}000(380 - t)$

BLUE MATH LESSON 1B: INTERPRETING EQUATIONS AND INEQUALITIES
Wading In

Directions: Read the explanation for each problem type mentioned below. Pay special attention to the methods and techniques used to solve the sample problems. Then, do the practice exercises that follow; use the appropriate method to solve each problem.

TOPIC OVERVIEW: INTERPRETING EQUATIONS AND INEQUALITIES

The last lesson showed us how to use algebra to solve equations and inequalities. Some questions on the SAT will simply provide an equation and ask for a solution, but most of the questions will present a short description of a situation and ask for an equation that best represents that situation. Some of the questions will require solving the equation (or system of equations), while some will simply ask us to pick the correct equation from a list of choices.

The fact that 75% of the test is multiple-choice is an advantage with problems like these. When approaching an Interpreting Equations and Inequalities problem, we can often select a number (based on the situation described in the problem) and use it to eliminate one or more of the answer choices. We can use this strategy in the first sample problem:

SAMPLE PROBLEM 1: INTERPRETING EQUATIONS

Jackson wants to be able to store and edit documents on his smartphone, which has 3500 MB of free space. In order to do this, he needs to install an app which takes up 25 MB of space. If the average document he edits takes up 4.5 MB of space, and he needs to store d documents, which of the following equations could represent S, the amount of free space he has on his phone?

A) $S = 3500 - 25d$
B) $S = 3500 - 25 - d$
C) $S = 3500 - 25 - 4.5d$
D) $S = 3500 - (25 - 4.5d)$

The equation needed should give us S, so start with the total amount of free space on Jackson's phone:

$$S = 3500$$

This is clearly not the answer, because it's (a) not one of the choices and (b) much too simple. The first thing to account for is the size of the app Jackson will use to edit the documents. Because this takes up 25 MB of space, subtract that from 3500:

$$S = 3500 - 25$$

This still doesn't match any of the answer choices because we still haven't subtracted the space that each of the documents will occupy on his phone. Choices A and B may look tempting because they include both the 25 MB and the variable d. But they don't account for the *size* of each document correctly. This is the trickier part, and here we'll use the "select a number" strategy. If Jackson stores 10 documents on his phone ($d = 10$) he needs to account for $10 \times 4.5 = 45$ MB of space. Choice A would subtract $25 \times 4.5 = 112.5$ MB, while Choice B would only account for $d = 10$ MB of space. Therefore we can eliminate choices A and B. The choices that multiply the number of documents (d) by the size of each document (4.5 MB) are C and D. Now we look at what makes C and D different. Notice in choice D that if we distribute the negative sign in front of the parentheses into the two terms inside, the $4.5d$ would become positive. This is not what we want, so the answer must be **C**.

SAMPLE PROBLEM 2: INTERPRETING INEQUALITIES

Julie is performing an exit poll to try to determine the results of a city council election. She needs to poll at least 400 people. Every hour she waits outside the public library she polls 9 people, and every hour she waits outside the elementary school she polls 19 people. If she waits a hours outside the library and b hours outside the school, which of the following inequalities represents her time waiting at each location?

A) $9a + 19b \leq 400$
B) $9a + 19b \geq 400$
C) $9a + 19b < 400$
D) $9a + 19b > 400$

Looking at the multiple-choice answers, it is obvious that the situation must describe an inequality (all the answer choices are inequalities). If this question were a grid-in, the key words "at least" would alert us to this. The next step to take is to notice that "at least" translates to "greater than or equal to" when used in a math problem. Now incorporate the rest of the information we are given: If Julie polls 9 people each hour, that would be 9 people in 1 hour, 18 people in 2 hours, 27 people in 3 hours, and so on. This clearly means that we need to multiply the number of hours she polls, a, by the number of people she polls each hour, 9, to get the total number of people she polls, $9a$. By the same logic, the number of people she polls at the school is $19b$. Therefore the total number of hours is: $9a + 19b$.

Putting this together with the words "at least" and the total number of people, we get the equation $9a + 19b \geq 400$, which is choice **B**.

Note: Once we realized that the inequality needed to be "greater than or equal to," we could have eliminated choices A and C.

SAMPLE PROBLEM 3: SIMPLE MODELING

A major airline transports 13.4 million passengers each month, with an average ticket price of $380. The airline determines that for every $1 it decreases the ticket price, the airline can gain another 10,000 passengers. Which of the following functions models the number of passengers, P, in terms of the price of a ticket, t?

A) $P(t) = 13,400,000 + 10,000(380)$
B) $P(t) = 13,400,000 + 10,000(380 + t)$
C) $P(t) = 13,400,000 + 10,000(t - 380)$
D) $P(t) = 13,400,000 + 10,000(380 - t)$

This problem asks for an equation that gives one variable in terms of another, which is often called a function. Using function notation, this would be:

$$P(t) = (something \ with \ t \ in \ it)$$

Our starting point for the number of passengers is 13,400,000. All the answer choices start with this number, so we can't eliminate any of them (but at least we know we're off to a good start!) As the airline decreases the ticket price, the number of passengers will increase, so check and see if any of the answer choices subtract something from that number—we'll be able to eliminate those choices as well. None of them do, so we have to do all the work on this one!

We want a function that will increase the number of passengers by 10,000 if the price of a ticket is $379. Looking at the choices, the expressions in parentheses in each choice are the "multipliers" of 10,000, which means that when t is equal to 379, we want this value to be 1; when t is equal to 378, we want this value to be 2; and so on. Clearly choice A won't work, because it's always equal to 380. When t is equal to 379, the multiplier in choice B is equal to 759, which is too large. Choice C is close, but it's equal to –1, not 1. Therefore the answer must be D, which works $(380 - 379 = 1)$.

A smart move is to try another number or two to make sure that the function picked doesn't only work for the case in which $t = 379$:

If $t = 370$, that's a $10 decrease, which means the number of passengers should increase by $10 \times 10,000 = 100,000$, so there should be $100,000 + 13,400,000 = 13,500,000$ passengers.

If we plug $t = 370$ into the function in choice D we get:

$$P(t) = 13,400,000 + 10,000(380 - t)$$

$$P(370) = 13,400,000 + 10,000(380 - 370)$$

$$P(370) = 13{,}400{,}000 + 10{,}000(10)$$

$$P(370) = 13{,}400{,}000 + 100{,}000$$

$$P(370) = 13{,}500{,}000$$

WRAP-UP

To begin these problems, first we must recognize that the problem is an Interpreting Equations and Inequalities problem. This is fairly easy because these problems have lots of words and rarely give us an equation in the problem, although we may see equations in the answer choices.

Notice that the solutions to the first and third sample problem began by finding a "starting point," which in this case was a piece of information we were given that is a base amount of the situation we're trying to model: in Sample Problem 1, it was the total amount of space on Jackson's smartphone and in Sample Problem 3 it was the number of passengers transported by the airline before any decrease in ticket price.

The next step in the solutions was to investigate the properties of the change that was occurring—in the three examples here, those changes were space being used up on a smartphone, the number of people being polled in an hour, and the number of passengers being transported at a given ticket price. With a little trial and error, writing the rules (functions) for these changes becomes pretty easy.

BLUE MATH LESSON 1B: INTERPRETING EQUATIONS AND INEQUALITIES
Learning to Swim

Directions: Answer each question below.

PRACTICE SET 1 (NO CALCULATOR)

1. At a water bottling plant, the volume of water placed in each bottle is about 1 liter (L). The quality control for the plant makes sure that the amount of water in each bottle is no more than 5 mL greater or less than 1 L. If the amount of water in a bottle is W, write an inequality that models the range of values of W, in mL (1 liter = 1000 mL).

2. Working in a luxury car dealership, employees make a monthly salary of $2,000 in addition to a commission of 3% of the dollar amount of the cars they sell. If an employee's sales for a month are c dollars, write an equation that could be used to find the monthly salary S of that employee.

3. The speed of sound is dependent on the temperature of the surrounding air. In order to find the speed of sound for a given temperature, you must add sixty percent of the Celsius temperature to the speed of sound at 0° C, which is 331 meters per second. Write an equation that can be used to find the speed of sound, v, at T degrees Celsius.

4. In order to qualify for a 10-kilometer charity run, a participant must acquire at least $500 in sponsorships. The sponsorships can be in the form of one-time donations or a pledge of a certain amount of money per km run by the participant. Write an inequality that expresses the relationship between d (dollars in one-time donations) and m (dollars per kilometer run) that a participant must have in order to qualify.

5. A zoologist tags x young bison and releases them into the wild. The number of bison who either die or are killed is y animals per year. The zoologist returns five years later and counts the number of tagged animals still alive. If the number of bison still alive is more than 80% of the number originally tagged, write an inequality that relates x and y.

BLUE MATH LESSON 1B: INTERPRETING EQUATIONS AND INEQUALITIES
Diving into the Deep End

Directions: Answer each question below.

PRACTICE SET 2 (NO CALCULATOR)

6. To calculate Body Mass Index (BMI), health professionals divide a person's weight by the square of his or her height and then multiply the result by 703 (if the measurements are in inches and pounds respectively). Which of the following equations models this calculation?

   A) $\frac{weight}{height^2} \times 703$

   B) $\frac{height}{weight^2} \times 703$

   C) $\frac{height}{\sqrt{weight}} \times 703$

   D) $\frac{\sqrt{weight}}{height} \times 703$

7. The molding used to create the border for a rectangular window costs $4 per foot. The height of the window is two less than twice the width of the window. If the window is w feet wide, what is the cost, in dollars, of the border of the window, in terms of w?

   A) $4(2w + 2h)$

   B) $4\left[2w + 2\left(\frac{w+2}{2}\right)\right]$

   C) $4[2w + 2(2w - 2)]$

   D) $4\left(\frac{w+2}{2}\right)$

8. Chicago cabs charge $3.25 for a "flag pull"—calling the cab off the street and the first $\frac{1}{9}$-mile of your trip. Each additional mile is $1.80. It is customary to tip the driver 15% of the total. Which expression gives the amount you would pay for a trip of m miles?

   A) $3.25 + 1.15(1.8m)$

   B) $1.15(3.25 + 1.8m)$

   C) $0.15\left[3.25 + 1.8\left(m - \frac{1}{9}\right)\right]$

   D) $1.15\left[3.25 + 1.8\left(m - \frac{1}{9}\right)\right]$

9. A farm in Kansas both raises cows and grows wheat. The farmer calculates that in each month, he can make $1500 per acre used for grazing his cows and $1200 per acre used for growing wheat. He can allow his cows to graze from the beginning of March until the end of October, but can only grow wheat from the beginning of April until the end of August. If he allots c acres for his cows and w acres for his wheat, which of the following represents the amount of money he can make in a year?

   A) $5 \times 1200 \times c + 8 \times 1500 \times w$

   B) $13 \times (1200 \times c + 1500 \times w)$

   C) $8 \times 1500 \times c + 5 \times 1200 \times w$

   D) $1200 \times c + 1500 \times w$

10. If the farmer in Problem 9 is required by federal law to allot twice as much acreage to wheat as to livestock and he must make at least $360,000 per year to keep his farm running, what is the minimum number of acres he must allot to livestock?

11. To get from the Vaca Muerta oil fields to Santiago, an engineer must travel in a helicopter for x kilometers and an ATV for a kilometers. If the helicopter's average speed is 120 km/h and the ATV's average speed is 40 km/h, which of the following gives the time in hours it takes the engineer to cover the entire distance?

    A) $\frac{x}{120} + \frac{a}{40}$

    B) $\frac{120}{x} + \frac{40}{a}$

    C) $120x + 40a$

    D) $40x + 120a$

12. Blue Bill Ice Cream Company makes two different flavors of chocolate ice cream—milk chocolate and dark chocolate. Milk chocolate ice cream costs a dollars per gallon to manufacture, and the company can sell it for b dollars per gallon. Dark chocolate costs c dollars per gallon to manufacture, and the company can sell it for d dollars per gallon. Which of the following is an expression for the monthly profit (cost subtracted from sales) for the company if it sells x gallons of milk chocolate and y gallons of dark chocolate in a month.

    A) $x(a-b) + y(c-d)$

    B) $x(b-a) + y(d-c)$

    C) $y(a-b) + x(c-d)$

    D) $y(b-a) + x(d-c)$

13. A parking garage charges a rate of a dollars for the first hour and b dollars for each additional hour the car is parked. When Jacqueline leaves this parking garage, she is charged c dollars. In terms of a, b, and c, what is the number of hours for which Jacqueline is charged?

    A) $\frac{a+b}{c}$

    B) $\frac{c-a}{b}$

    C) $a + cb$

    D) $1 + \frac{c-a}{b}$

14. The US Olympic Team has f members, and they will be distributed equally among g charter planes on their way to Rio in 2016. If the team decides to charter h more planes, how many fewer athletes will ride on each plane?

    A) $\frac{fg}{g(g+h)}$

    B) $\frac{fh}{g(g+h)}$

    C) $\frac{f}{g+h}$

    D) $\frac{f}{h}$

15. The BP oil rig Deepwater Horizon spilled approximately 780,000 cubic meters of oil into the Gulf of Mexico. As part of the cleanup process, the company used r oil recovery devices that each cleaned 80 cubic meters of oil per day and s oil recovery devices which each cleaned 40 cubic meters per day. Which of the following equations could be used to determine the number of days, d, that it would take to clean up the spill?

    A) $780{,}000 = 80 \times r + 40 \times s$

    B) $780{,}000 = d(80 \times s + 40 \times r)$

    C) $780{,}000 = d(80 \times r + 40 \times s)$

    D) $780{,}000 = rs(80 \times d + 40 \times d)$

16. When Chelsea starts her dentistry practice, she spends twenty percent of her startup funds on equipment and the first month's rent for her building. Then she spends one-fourth of her remaining funds on advertising in the local papers. If she started with F dollars, which of the following shows the amount of money, in terms of F, she had left over after these expenditures?
    A) $0.8F$
    B) $0.75F$
    C) $0.6F$
    D) $0.2F$

17. Two buses leave Asheville, NC at 6:30 a.m., for a school trip of 470 miles to Washington, D.C. Both buses drive at an average speed of 60 miles per hour for the first two and a half hours, and then one bus overheats. The repair is made thirty minutes later. Which equation will give the speed the overheated bus will have to average for the rest of the trip in order to be in D.C. at the same time as the other bus?
    A) average speed $= \dfrac{470-60\times2.5}{\frac{470-60\times2.5}{60}}$
    B) average speed $= \dfrac{470-60\times2.5}{\frac{320}{60}\frac{1}{2}}$
    C) average speed $= \dfrac{470-60\times2.5}{60}$
    D) average speed $= \dfrac{470+60\times2.5}{\frac{470-60\times2.5}{60}+\frac{1}{2}}$

18. A real estate investor "flips" a house by buying it for t dollars. She then invests 35% of that amount remodeling the bathroom and kitchen. At what price must she sell the house to realize a 25% profit on her investment?
    A) $1.25(1.35t)$
    B) $t + 0.6t$
    C) $1.25t + 1.35t$
    D) $t + 1.25(0.35t)$

19. In order to win the contest in her troop, Julie must sell more Girl Scout cookies than any other scout. Her friend Katie has sold 144 boxes already. If Julie sells 9 boxes per day for the first 6 days and then 8 boxes per day for the next x days, which of the following inequalities could be used to solve for x, assuming Katie doesn't sell any more boxes?
    A) $9 \times 6 + 8 \times x > 144$
    B) $9 \times 6 + 8 \times x \geq 144$
    C) $9 \times x + 8 \times 6 \geq 144$
    D) $9 \times 6 + 8 \times x \leq 144$

20. When planning a wedding, an event coordinator must ensure that she has the correct number of chairs. To ensure that enough people "mingle" over the course of an evening, the coordinator takes the number of people at the event and reduces it by 30%; this is the number of chairs that are required. If a banquet room hosts a wedding reception of 500 people and is then immediately followed by a reception for 350, how many chairs must be removed from the room?
    A) 350
    B) 245
    C) 150
    D) 105

21. A certain corporate coffee shop requires 4 bags of coffee for a day of normal operations, but an extra 2 bags if that day is a holiday. If a corporate district has 8 coffee shops, how many bags are required for all the shops in the month of July, which has 31 days, one of which is a holiday?

22. Paul's Pitch 'n' Putt runs batting cages, a putt-putt course, and a video arcade, which generate a, b, and c dollars of revenue per hour, respectively. In order to turn a profit on a Friday night, Paul must make at least $22,000 in total revenue. If the Pitch 'n' Putt is open for 6 hours on Friday, which of the following inequalities must be satisfied for Paul to turn a profit?

A) $a + b + c \leq 22{,}000$

B) $6(a + b + c) \geq 22{,}000$

C) $a + b + c \geq 132{,}000$

D) $6abc \geq 22{,}000$

23. A proposed tax system would tax the first $75,000 of a household's income at r%, and any additional income at q%. What would be the tax for a household with an income of $90,000?

A) $\frac{(r+q)}{100} * 90000$

B) $\frac{r}{100} * 75000 + \frac{q}{100} * 90000$

C) $\frac{r}{100} * 75000 + \frac{(r+q)}{100} * 15000$

D) $\frac{r}{100} * 75000 + \frac{q}{100} * 15000$

24. Cross A between two peas results in 19% of the offspring producing yellow, wrinkled seeds. Cross B results in 25% yellow, wrinkled seeds. If cross A produces a offspring and cross B produces b offspring, how many offspring do NOT have yellow, wrinkled seeds?

A) $0.19a + 0.25b$

B) $0.0475(a + b)$

C) $0.81a + 0.75b$

D) $0.44(a + b)$

25. A sweater that normally costs $42.00 is on sale for 30% off. If there is a storewide sale that applies an additional 20% off to everything, what will be the total price of the sweater and a belt that normally costs d dollars?

A) $0.5(42 + d)$

B) $0.56(42) + 0.8d$

C) $0.5(42) + 0.8d$

D) $0.14(42) + 0.2d$

BLUE MATH LESSON 1B: INTERPRETING EQUATIONS AND INEQUALITIES
Race to the Finish

Directions: Answer each question below.

HOMEWORK SET (NO CALCULATOR)

1. Alice, a car salesperson, gets paid $15 per hour plus a commission of 5% of the price of every car that she sells. She wants to make at least as much money as her friend Bahi, who gets paid the same way that Alice does. If Bahi works for 20 hours and has $34,000 in sales, which of the following values of h, Alice's number of hours worked, and s, Alice's sales in dollars, would allow her to make at least as much money as Bahi?
   A) $h = 10, s = \$35,000$
   B) $h = 30, s = \$30,000$
   C) $h = 15, s = \$36,000$
   D) $h = 40, s = \$27,500$

2. Many tropical fish require very specific water temperatures. The ideal water temperature for Betta fish is 76.8°F, and a variance of more than 3.1°F from that temperature will kill the fish. Which of the following equations best models the range of possible temperatures, t, of an aquarium that contains Betta?
   A) $|t - 76.8| \geq 3.1$
   B) $|t - 76.8| \leq 3.1$
   C) $|t - 3.1| \geq 76.8$
   D) $|t - 3.1| \leq 76.8$

3. A coffee maker is $34.99 at the corner store, which also carries ground bulk coffee for d dollars per pound. If sales tax, which does not apply to any kind of food or drink, is 7.25%, how much would a coffee maker and 2.5 pounds of coffee cost?
   A) $0.0725(34.99) + 2.5d$
   B) $1.0725(34.99) + 2.5d$
   C) $0.725(34.99 + 2.5d)$
   D) $34.99 + 0.0725(2.5d)$

4. In order to advance to the next round of a darts tournament, a player must score at least S points. A player gets 4 points for a bull's-eye, 3 points for a shot in the triple ring, 2 points for a shot in the double ring, and 1 point for every other shot. If a person makes $a, b, c,$ and d of these shots, respectively, which of the following inequalities can be used to determine if the player advances?
   A) $a + 2b + 3c + 4d \geq S$
   B) $a + 2b + 3c + 4d \leq S$
   C) $4a + 3b + 2c + d \leq S$
   D) $4a + 3b + 2c + d \geq S$

5. A ball was thrown upward into the air, and its height, in meters, can be modeled by the expression $h = -9.8t^2 + 8.2t + 2$, where t represents the time, in seconds, that have passed since the ball was thrown. What is the meaning of the '2' in the expression?
   A) The ball will reach its maximum height after 2 seconds.
   B) The ball will return to the ground in 2 seconds.
   C) The ball reaches a maximum height of 2 meters.
   D) The ball was thrown from an initial height of 2 meters.

Use the following information to answer questions 6 and 7.

The U.S. National Park Service has recently done some research into ticket prices in its parks in the Pacific Northwest. One park, Olympic National Park, currently charges $15 per multi-person vehicle to enter the park and expects 600,000 vehicles to enter each year. The U.S. National Park Service predicts that for each $1 increase in ticket price, 20,000 fewer vehicles will visit each year.

6. Suppose $V(x)$ is a function that gives the yearly revenue of the park, in dollars, based on x, the number of $1 price increases. Which of the following functions best models $V(x)$?
   A) $V(x) = (600,000 + 20,000x)(15 - x)$
   B) $V(x) = (600,000 - 20,000x)(15 + x)$
   C) $V(x) = (600,000 + 20,000x)(x - 15)$
   D) $V(x) = (600,000 - x)(15 + 20,000x)$

7. Which statement about $V(x)$ is true?
   A) Olympic Park will lose money during the first $1 price increase.
   B) The maximum revenue will be over $9,000,000.
   C) Increasing the price of a ticket by $7.50 will result in no visitors to the park.
   D) The maximum revenue will be obtained when the price of a ticket is $7.50.

8. Frederica drives s miles per hour for t hours, then increases her speed by 20%. She maintains her new speed for one-third longer than her original speed. Which expression gives the distance she traveled?
   A) $st + (1.2s)\left(\frac{4t}{3}\right)$
   B) $st + 1.2st$
   C) $st + (1.2s)\left(\frac{t}{3}\right)$
   D) $(1.2s)\left(\frac{4}{3}t\right)$

9. The population of Weaver, Alabama in 2000 was 2,736, but the population jumped to 3,036 by 2010. Which of the following linear equations best models the population of Weaver, $P(t)$, in terms of the number of years since 2000, t.
   A) $P(t) = 30t + 2736$
   B) $P(t) = -30t + 3036$
   C) $P(t) = 0.033t + 2736$
   D) $P(t) = -0.033t + 3036$

Year	Bison Population of Yellowstone National Park (in tens)
1980	192
1985	235
1990	302
1995	363

10. Which model, $P(y)$, the bison population of the park y years after 1980, best fits the data above?
   A) $P(y) = 120y + 1900$
   B) $P(y) = 12y + 190$
   C) $P(y) = 600y + 1900$
   D) $P(y) = 60y + 190$

Roberto is making a special window frame that consists of two distinct pieces: horizontal pieces, which cost $12.50 per foot, and vertical pieces, which cost $8.75 per foot. Roberto needs to make his frame h feet wide and wants his window frame to be twice as tall as it is wide.

11. Which equation can be used to determine the cost of Roberto's window frame, C, in terms of h?
   A) $C = 12.50h + 8.75h$
   B) $C = 2(12.50h + 8.75h)$
   C) $C = 12.50h + 8.75(2h)$
   D) $C = 2[12.50h + 8.75(2h)]$

12. Lindy currently has $25.00, and she wants to buy a new video game that costs $69.99. If she knows she can make $8.40 per yard she cuts, y, and $2.65 per car she washes, c, which of the following inequalities below can be used to show the number of cars she needs to wash and yards she needs to cut to save up enough money to buy the video game?
   A) $69.99 \geq 8.40y + 2.65c - 25.00$
   B) $69.99 \geq 25.00 + 8.40y + 2.65c$
   C) $69.99 \leq 8.40y + 2.65c - 25.00$
   D) $69.99 \leq 25.00 + 8.40y + 2.65c$

13. Death Valley's Badwater Basin is the point of lowest elevation in North America. It stays within 3 inches of 282 feet below sea level (−282 feet). Which of the following equations best models the possible elevations, h, of Badwater Basin, in feet?
   A) $|h - 3| \geq 282$
   B) $-|h - 282| \leq 3$
   C) $|h + 282| \leq 0.25$
   D) $-|h - 0.25| \leq -282$

14. Full-time in-state tuition at the University of Illinois is $6,018 per semester. In addition, there are service fees, not included in tuition, of $1,783 per student per semester. If there is an 8% tuition increase, what will be the cost of n semesters of college?
   A) $1.08(7,801n)$
   B) $1.08(6,018n) + 1,783$
   C) $n[1.08(6,018) + 1,783]$
   D) $n[1.08(1,783) + 6,018]$

15. Recording studio time is $75 per hour, but booking a six-hour block comes with a 10% discount. After the tracks are recorded, the sound engineer charges $60 for each hour of post-production mixing. What would be the total cost of a block of recording and h hours of mixing, if $h > 6$?

A) $0.90(75)(6) + 60h$
B) $0.10(75)(6) + 60h$
C) $0.10[75(6) + 60h]$
D) $0.90(75) + 60h$

16. A silk-screening company charges $150 to create a printing screen from your artwork and print 25 T-shirts; each additional shirt is $5. What is the cost of s shirts, if a 6.5% sales tax applies and $s > 25$?

A) $1.065(150 + 5s)$
B) $150(25) + 1.065(5s)$
C) $1.065[150 + 5(s - 25)]$
D) $1.065[150(25) + 5s]$

Year	Size of the Desert of Maine, in Acres
2001	37.5
2004	39.0
2007	40.5
2010	42.0

17. The data above shows the size of the Desert of Maine, in acres, over a span of several years. If the linear function $S(x)$ models the size of the desert based on how many years have passed since the year 2000, x, what would the size of the desert have been in 2000, in acres?

18. Parking at Hartsfield-Jackson Atlanta International Airport's three different lots is calculated at the following rates:

Hourly Lots	Time Length	Cost
	0 – 2 hours	$2 per hour
	3 – 6 hours	$3 per hour
	7 – 24 hours	$32
	Each Additional Day	$36 per day

Daily Lots	Time Length	Cost
	1 hour	$3 per hour
	1 day	$16 per day

Economy Lots	Time Length	Cost
	1 hr	$3 per hour
	1 day	$12 per day

If Martia needs to keep her car at the Atlanta airport for a total of 26 hours, what will be the price of her cheapest airport lot?

19. A ball is thrown upward into the air on the moon, and its height, in meters, can be modeled by the expression $h = -1.6t^2 + 12.8t + 1.86$, where t represents the time, in seconds, that has passed since the ball was thrown. From what height was the ball originally thrown?

20. Norway is one of the few countries that has filed an objection to the International Whaling Commission of 1986, which banned whaling worldwide. The Norwegians caught or killed an average of 650 whales per year over the past 30 years. If this is 25% of the total whales caught or killed per year, approximately how many whales are caught or killed each year by countries other than Norway?

BLUE MATH LESSON 2A: INTERPRETING RATIOS, RATES, PROPORTIONS, AND SCALE
Getting Your Feet Wet

Directions: The problems below are intended as a short diagnostic exam.

1. A map of your neighborhood is drawn to scale so that every 2 inches on the map represents the length of 1 city block. If every city block is perfectly square and 300 yards long, how many inches would the path be on the map from your home to the library, which is 1500 yards away?
   A) 2.5
   B) 5
   C) 10
   D) 50

2. A molecule of sucrose contains carbon, hydrogen, and oxygen atoms in the ratio of 12:22:11. If a pinch of table sugar contains 1800 total atoms, how many carbon atoms does it contain?

3. Cathy is mowing the lawn at a rate of 20 square feet per minute. Prentice is mowing the lawn three times as fast as Cathy is. If together they need to mow a 5000-square-foot lawn, write an expression that illustrates the time, x, it would take for them to do so.

4. Working at the same rate, 4 cowboys can build a square corral in 3 hours. How long will it take 6 cowboys to build the same corral?

BLUE MATH LESSON 2A: INTERPRETING RATIOS, RATES, PROPORTIONS, AND SCALE
Wading In

Directions: Read the explanation for each problem type mentioned below. Pay special attention to the methods and techniques used to solve the sample problems. Then, do the practice exercises that follow; use the appropriate method to solve each problem.

TOPIC OVERVIEW: INTERPRETING SCALE FACTOR

Our last lesson showed us how to turn word problems describing situations into algebraic equations. Sometimes, the SAT will require us to come up with equations or models to describe situations involving ratios, proportions, or scale factors. Of these, scale questions are the easiest, as the test generally tells us what the scale factor is (for example, 2 inches = 20 miles), and then requires us to convert one unit into another. Let's look at a question below:

SAMPLE PROBLEM 1: INTERPRETING SCALE FACTOR

A map of your neighborhood is drawn to scale so that every 2 inches on the map represents the length of 1 city block. If every city block is perfectly square and 300 yards long, how many inches would the path be on the map from your home to the library, which is 1500 yards away?
A) 2.5
B) 5
C) 10
D) 50

To solve a question like this, first set up two fractions, both with the same units in their numerators and denominators:

$$\frac{2 \text{ inches}}{1 \text{ city block}} = \frac{x \text{ inches}}{1500 \text{ yards}}$$

Our problem here is that our denominators do not have the same units. So, let's change 1500 yards to city blocks using a stoichiometry table:

$$\frac{1500 \text{ yards}}{1} \times \frac{1 \text{ city block}}{300 \text{ yards}} = 5 \text{ city blocks}$$

Now replace the 1500 yards above. Since we have the same units, we can cross multiply and solve our equation for our answer:

$$\frac{2 \text{ inches}}{1 \text{ city block}} = \frac{x \text{ inches}}{5 \text{ city blocks}}$$

$$2 \times 5 = 1 \times x$$
$$x = 10$$

So, our answer is **C**, 10 city blocks.

TOPIC OVERVIEW: INTERPRETING RATIOS AND PROPORTIONS

Ratio and proportion problems involving two numbers can always be solved by setting up a pair of equivalent fractions and cross multiplying, just as the previous scale factor problem did. However, ratio and proportion problems involving three numbers (for example, the ratio of 3:4:5) cannot be solved so easily. When faced with these, set up a ratio chart like we'll do in the problem below:

SAMPLE PROBLEM 2: INTERPRETING RATIOS AND PROPORTIONS

A molecule of sucrose contains carbon, hydrogen, and oxygen atoms in the ratio of 12:22:11. If a pinch of table sugar contains 1800 total atoms, how many carbon atoms does it contain?

First, let's set up a ratio chart:

	Carbon	Hydrogen	Oxygen	Total
Ratio:	12	22	11	
Real:				1800

Now that everything's set up, we're going to try to fill one column completely. We can add 12, 22, and 11 to get a total in the ratio column:

	Carbon	Hydrogen	Oxygen	Total
Ratio:	12	22	11	45
Real:				1800

Once we have a full column, look for the multiplier. To get from 45 to 1800, we must multiply by 40. Thus, we should multiply all of our numbers in the ratio row by 40 to obtain the numbers in the real row.

	Carbon	Hydrogen	Oxygen	Total
Ratio:	12	22	11	45
Real:	480	880	440	1800

So, our answer is **480**. Note that the ratio chart can be used on all ratio problems, not just the ones that have more than two quantities.

TOPIC OVERVIEW: INTERPRETING RATES

Rate questions on the SAT can be very challenging. The most basic rate problems involve the formula:

$$\text{distance} = \text{rate} \times \text{time}.$$

This formula can be rearranged to be an equation for time or an equation for rate:

$$\text{time} = \frac{\text{distance}}{\text{rate}} \qquad \text{rate} = \frac{\text{distance}}{\text{time}}$$

Keep in mind that a distance does not have to be a literal distance: A distance can refer to any amount of work that can be done. For example, if John can paint 3 walls in 15 minutes, 3 walls is his distance and 15 minutes is his time.

Many of the questions on the SAT using rates involve adding rates together. Let's look at a situation involving adding rates together:

SAMPLE PROBLEM 3: INTERPRETING RATES

Cathy is mowing the lawn at a rate of 20 square feet per minute. Prentice is mowing the lawn three times as fast as Cathy is. If together they need to mow a 5000-square-foot lawn, write an expression that illustrates the time, x, it would take for them to do so.

Let's look at our givens first: We have Cathy's rate of work, $\frac{20 \text{ square feet}}{\text{minute}}$, and Prentice's rate of work, which is 3 times Cathy's, or $\frac{60 \text{ square feet}}{\text{minute}}$. We are also given the distance they need to mow together, 5000 square feet. So, since we're combining our rates, let's just add them:

$$\frac{20 \text{ square feet}}{\text{minute}} + \frac{60 \text{ square feet}}{\text{minute}} =$$

Because we're adding two rates together, our answer must also be a rate, thus a distance divided by a time. Since they need to mow 5000 square feet in x minutes, let's write this as a fraction and insert it into our equation:

$$\frac{20 \text{ sq.feet}}{\text{minute}} + \frac{60 \text{ sq.feet}}{\text{minute}} = \frac{5000 \text{ sq.feet}}{x \text{ minutes}}$$

TOPIC OVERVIEW: INTERPRETING GROUP RATES

The last type of rate we're going to look at is group rate problems. These questions involve several people working together at the same rate to finish a task. Then the number of people working or time allowed to work is adjusted, and we'll be asked to find a new time to finish the task. Let's look at one of these below:

SAMPLE PROBLEM 4: INTERPRETING GROUP RATES

Working at the same rate, 4 cowboys can build a square corral in 3 hours. How long will it take 6 cowboys to build the same corral?

The easiest way to think of these problems is to draw a shape that is easy to divide into pieces, like a square, to represent the corral:

Since the work is divided among four cowboys, pretend that each cowboy is going to work on his own fourth of the corral:

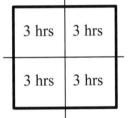

Each cowboy does 3 hours of work, so we can see that it will take 12 hours of work to finish the corral. This is true no matter how many cowboys work on the job. So, if we have 6 cowboys working on it, they will each have to do **2** hours of work.

WRAP-UP

Being able to recognize a word problem as a ratio, proportion, rate, or group rate problem is an important skill to have. Carefully review each of the above problems, and the problems in the following lessons, to figure out which category each belongs to. Then, use the appropriate method to solve each question. On the next page, list key words from each of the above sample problems that help indicate which type of problem it is. The first few have already been completed:

SCALE FACTOR	RATIO/PROPORTION
Scale	Ratio

RATE	GROUP RATE
Rate Distance Time	Work at the same rate

BLUE MATH LESSON 2A: INTERPRETING RATIOS, RATES, PROPORTIONS, AND SCALE
Learning to Swim

Directions: Answer each question below.

PRACTICE SET 1 (NO CALCULATOR)

1. Ricky and Julian need to buy C cases of chicken fingers to feed P people at their party. If F fewer people showed up than they expected, how many extra cases of chicken fingers do they have left, if they fed everyone at the original rate?

2. If 1 inch on a map represents y miles, how many miles are represented by x feet on the same map?

3. In order to mix mortar, water, sand, and cement mix must be mixed in the ratio of $a: b: c$ respectively. If Herschel uses $3b$ pounds of sand to make the mortar for a brick wall that he is building, how many pounds of mortar will he end up with in all?

4. If h hot dogs cost d dollars, what is the cost, in cents, of j hot dogs?

5. Set up an equation for the following scenario: A wedding reception needs 3 chairs for every 4 people. How many chairs, y, would be needed for x people?

BLUE MATH LESSON 2A: INTERPRETING RATIOS, RATES, PROPORTIONS, AND SCALE
Diving into the Deep End

Directions: Answer each question below.

PRACTICE SET 2 (NO CALCULATOR)

6. Christopher can make enough iced coffee for one person by mixing two teaspoons of espresso with 4 ounces of water. How many tablespoons of espresso would he need to make enough iced coffee for 24 people? (3 teaspoons = 1 tablespoon)
    A) 12
    B) 16
    C) 48
    D) 144

7. Christine is typing at a rate of 75 words per minute. Paula is typing at twice Christine's speed. If together they need to transcribe a 2000 word paper which of the following expressions would illustrate the time in minutes, x, it would take for them to do so.
    A) $150 = \frac{2000x}{75}$
    B) $\frac{75}{x} + \frac{150}{x} = 2000$
    C) $150 + 75 = \frac{x}{2000}$
    D) $x = \frac{2000}{(150+75)}$

$$7 + \frac{8}{x} = \frac{13}{x}$$

8. Two brothers are painting pictures. One of the brothers paints 7 pictures in a day. The other brother paints 8 pictures but it takes him x days to do so. Together they painted 13 pictures in x days. The expression above models this problem. What does $\frac{13}{x}$ represent?
    A) The number of days it takes the brothers to paint 13 pictures
    B) The rate at which the two brothers work together
    C) The rate at which the second brother paints
    D) The number of days it takes the first brother to paint 13 pictures

9. Three-fifths of the employees at Mac's Discount Grocery are female and one-fourth of the employees are under the age of 18. If one-third of the female employees are under the age of 18, what is the ratio of males over the age of 18 to males under the age of 18 who work at Mac's Discount Grocery?
    A) 7:4
    B) 3:1
    C) 4:1
    D) 7:1

10. Marco can paddle his canoe at a rate of 6 miles per hour on unmoving water. However, today Marco is canoeing down (with the current), and then back up (against the current), a river that's moving at a rate of 1 mile per hour, so the current affects his rate of speed. If it takes Marco 6 total hours to go x miles downstream and then return to his starting point, how far downstream does he travel?

    A) 1.25 miles
    B) 2.5 miles
    C) 5 miles
    D) 17.5 miles

11. Mr. Mullin's new house is being designed by an architect, who creates all of his blueprints with a scale factor of 1.5 inches to 16 feet. If the bottom floor of the house is rectangular and has an area of 27 square inches, what is the area of the bottom floor of the actual house, in square feet, provided that one of the walls is 4.5 inches long on the blueprint?

    A) 324
    B) 648
    C) 1440
    D) 3072

12. Three men, who work at equal rates, can set up a fence in ten hours. How many hours would it take four men, who work at the exact same rate, to set up the same fence?

    A) $1\frac{1}{5}$ hours
    B) $6\frac{2}{3}$ hours
    C) $7\frac{1}{2}$ hours
    D) $13\frac{1}{3}$ hours

13. The coastline of southern Florida receded 30 millimeters over the course of the 10 years from 1950 to 1959. What was the average rate, in centimeters per year, that the coastline receded during those years?

    A) 0.3
    B) 3
    C) 30
    D) 300

14. A printing press can print pages at a rate of 1,000 pages per hour. The printing press uses y gallons of ink in a half-hour. If the printing press has a completely-filled reservoir of x gallons of ink, how many gallons of ink will be left after the printing press has printed 2,250 pages?

    A) $x - 4.5y$
    B) $4.5y - x$
    C) $\frac{2x-y}{9}$
    D) $\frac{y-2x}{9}$

15. Kimberly drives at a rate of 50 miles per hour on her trip across the country. If it takes Kimberly 200 gallons of gasoline to drive 500 miles, how many minutes will it take her to use x gallons of gasoline?

    A) $20x$
    B) $\frac{3}{x}$
    C) $\frac{x}{20}$
    D) $3x$

PRACTICE SET 3 (NO CALCULATOR)

16. A rectangular garden measuring 10 feet by 15 feet needs to be expanded so that its new area becomes 16 times its original area. Which of the following changes would NOT result in the intended change?
    A) Expand the width by a factor of 16.
    B) Expand both the width and length by a factor of 4.
    C) Expand the width by a factor of 8 and the length by a factor of 2.
    D) Expand the width by a factor of 24 and the length by a factor of $\frac{1}{2}$.

17. If 15 chairs cost j dollars, which of the following equations would help determine the cost, k, of 3 chairs?
    A) $\frac{15}{j} = \frac{3}{k}$
    B) $\frac{15}{k} = \frac{3}{j}$
    C) $\frac{15}{3} = \frac{k}{j}$
    D) $\frac{k}{j} = \frac{15}{3}$

18. A prestigious university wants to make sure that exactly 1 of 20 students who apply to the school are accepted. The university also wants to make sure that the ratio of boys to girls accepted is 9 to 11. If 5600 boys and 6000 girls apply to the school, how many boys can be accepted this year?
    A) 249
    B) 261
    C) 319
    D) 331

19. Jamie is filling his y-gallon pool with water, and he has two hoses, each of which puts water into the pool at a different rate. If one hose can pump water into the pool at a rate of x gallons per minute, and the other hose is twice as fast as the first, which of the following equations shows that the two hoses can fill the pool in 4 hours?
    A) $x + 2x = \frac{y}{4}$
    B) $\frac{1}{x} + \frac{2}{x} = \frac{y}{4}$
    C) $60x + 120x = \frac{y}{4}$
    D) $\frac{1}{x} + \frac{1}{2x} = \frac{4}{y}$

20. A jelly factory can fill 300 jars an hour with jelly. Recently, the labeling machine has been running slowly and can only label 200 jars of jelly an hour. At this new rate of labeling, how many jars of jelly are unlabeled after k half hours?
    A) $100k$
    B) $\frac{100}{k}$
    C) $50k$
    D) $200k$

21. You are attempting to give your dog a bath. The faucet in your bathtub will fill the tub in 20 minutes. Unfortunately, the tub has a leak that will empty the bathtub in 35 minutes. Accounting for the leak, you can fill the bathtub in x minutes. What does $\frac{1}{x}$ represent in the expression that models this problem, $\frac{1}{20} - \frac{1}{35} = \frac{1}{x}$?
    A) The time it takes to fill the tub
    B) The rate at which the volume of water in the tub is increasing
    C) The rate at which water is leaking out of the tub
    D) The rate at which the height of the water is rising in the tub

22. Five people who work at the same rate can erect a treehouse in 3 hours. If only three of the people show up to help erect the treehouse, how many hours will it take them to finish?

A) $\frac{5}{9}$ hours

B) $\frac{9}{5}$ hours

C) 5 hours

D) 15 hours

23. If one subway train can travel 20 city blocks in 3 minutes, which of the following equations would help determine how many city blocks, x, the train can travel in 1 hour?

A) $\frac{20}{3} = \frac{x}{1}$

B) $\frac{60}{x} = \frac{3}{20}$

C) $\frac{3}{20} = \frac{x}{60}$

D) $\frac{1}{x} = \frac{20}{3}$

24. Steel is formed by combining masses of carbon and iron in the ratio of 1:49. How many pounds of iron would it take to create 10 pounds of steel?

A) 0.49

B) 0.98

C) 4.9

D) 9.8

25. Kevin's iPad has a data limit of 500 megabytes of data per day. If he uses 2.5 megabytes a minute, how many more minutes of iPad usage does Kevin have today if he has already used m megabytes?

A) $\frac{500m}{2.5}$

B) $200m$

C) $\frac{500-m}{2.5}$

D) $2.5m$

BLUE MATH LESSON 2A: INTERPRETING RATIOS, RATES, PROPORTIONS, AND SCALE
Race to the Finish

Directions: Answer each question below.

HOMEWORK SET (NO CALCULATOR)

1. You are watering a garden using two hoses. One of the hoses has a kink in it that causes it to release water at one-third the speed of the other. Together, the two hoses take 3 hours to water the garden. Which of the following expressions models this scenario, where x is the speed of the unkinked hose?
   A) $3x + x = 3$
   B) $\frac{x}{3} + \frac{1}{x} = \frac{1}{3}$
   C) $\frac{1}{x} + \frac{3}{x} = \frac{1}{3}$
   D) $x + \frac{x}{3} = 3$

2. A gardener can plant a garden at a rate of 100 flowers an hour. If a square foot holds 25 flowers, how many hours will it take to plant F square feet?
   A) $\frac{F}{4}$
   B) $4F$
   C) $2500F$
   D) $\frac{F}{2500}$

Use the following equation and information for questions 3 and 4.

$$M = \frac{h_i}{h_o} = -\frac{d_i}{d_o}$$

The magnification of a mirror, M, can be found based on the opposite of the ratio of the image distance, d_i, to the object distance, d_o, or by the ratio of the image height, h_i, to the object height, h_o, as shown by the equation above.

3. If the magnification of the mirror is quadrupled, which of the following effects could happen?
   A) The image distance and object distance would both be doubled.
   B) The image distance could be doubled while the object distance is halved.
   C) The image distance is halved while the object distance is doubled.
   D) The image distance is halved while the object distance is quartered.

4. If the object distance is doubled and the magnification remains the same, which of the following changes could NOT occur?
   A) The image distance is doubled.
   B) Both the image height and object height are halved.
   C) Both the image height and object height are tripled.
   D) The image distance is halved.

5. Randy has 800 baseball cards in his collection. He is selling 50 cards a month to make some money, but buys g new cards a month to replace the old ones. After t months, how many cards does he have in his collection?
    A) $800 - 50t$
    B) $800 + t(50 - g)$
    C) $800 - gt$
    D) $800 + t(g - 50)$

8. Under normal conditions, the members of a marching band are expected to take 8 steps to walk 5 yards. If the band can take 4 steps every 2 seconds, how long will it take the band to march up and down the length of a football field, which is 100 yards long?
    A) 2 minutes, 40 seconds
    B) 3 minutes, 20 seconds
    C) 4 minutes
    D) 5 minutes, 20 seconds

6. If there are 6.022×10^{23} molecules in 44 grams of carbon dioxide, how many molecules would there be in 110 grams of carbon dioxide?
    A) 2.409×10^{23}
    B) 1.506×10^{24}
    C) 2.409×10^{24}
    D) 2.915×10^{27}

    $$\frac{110 \text{ g } CO_2 \times 6.02 \times 10^{23} \text{ molecules}}{1 \qquad 44 \text{ grams}}$$

9. When a plant with a heterozygous dominant trait for flat leaves (Ff) is crossed with another plant with a heterozygous dominant trait for flat leaves, the ratio of homozygous dominant offspring (FF) to heterozygous dominant offspring (Ff) to homozygous recessive offspring (ff) is 1:2:1. If every plant with a capital F shows the trait for flat leaves, how many of the 124 offspring of a match between the two original plants would show the trait for flat leaves?
    A) 31
    B) 62
    C) 93
    D) 124

7. Marind and her 3 sons, each of whom works at the same rate, can paint a house in 12 hours. How much longer will it take them to paint the same house if 1 of her 3 sons is sick?
    A) 3 hours
    B) 4 hours
    C) 6 hours
    D) 16 hours

10. A map of the continental United States is produced such that every 3 inches on the map represents 1000 miles. If the widest point of the United States is 2,680 miles, and the map maker wants at least 3 inches of ocean on each side of the map, how many inches wide does the map need to be?
    A) 11.04
    B) 14.04
    C) 17.04
    D) 20.04

11. A student can type 100 words per minute. At this rate, how many hours will it take this student to type a $100x$ word document, if x is a positive integer?

   A) $\frac{x}{60}$

   B) $6000x$

   C) $100x$

   D) $\frac{5x}{3}$

12. A driver drives a car at 45 miles per hour, starting at mile marker 0, going west. A second driver drives at 60 miles per hour, going east, at mile marker t, which is directly west of mile marker 0. How many hours do both drivers have to drive in order to meet on the road?

   A) $105t$

   B) $60t - 45$

   C) $25t$

   D) $\frac{t}{105}$

13. A printer can scan and print 8 pages per minute. If the printer only has enough toner to print 1500 pages, how many minutes of printing will be left before the toner needs to be replaced, if a document of t pages is scanned and printed and t is less than 1500 pages?

   A) $1500 - 8t$

   B) $\frac{1500}{8t}$

   C) $8t$

   D) $\frac{1500 - t}{8}$

14. A 1050 page textbook needs to be typed in x hours. Lisa can type 15 pages in an hour and Whitney can type 12 pages in the same amount of time. Which of the following shows the expression that can be solved to determine x?

   A) $\frac{1050}{x} = \frac{12}{x} + \frac{15}{x}$

   B) $\frac{x}{12} + \frac{x}{15} = \frac{x}{1050}$

   C) $15 + 12 = \frac{x}{1050}$

   D) $27 = \frac{1050}{x}$

$$M = \frac{h_i}{h_o} = -\frac{d_i}{d_o}$$

15. If $d_i = 10$ inches and $d_o = -4$ inches for the equation above, which of the following sets of values are possible?

   A) $M = -2.5$, $h_i = 4$, $h_o = 1.6$

   B) $M = 2.5$, $h_i = 4$, $h_o = 1.6$

   C) $M = -2.5$, $h_i = -4$, $h_o = 1.6$

   D) $M = 2.5$, $h_i = -4$, $h_o = 1.6$

16. Wind-borne soil erosion has caused 2 centimeters of silt build-up on a local farm plot over the past 5 years. What was the average rate, in millimeters per year, of silt build-up over those 5 years?

   A) 0.04

   B) 0.4

   C) 4

   D) 40

17. A square-shaped plot of land with area of 32 square feet is expanded to become a rectangle with length twice as great as its original width. If the original width of the plot of land will not be changed, what is the new area, in square feet, of the plot of land?
    A) 48
    B) 64
    C) 96
    D) 128

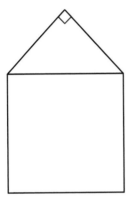

18. Jorge has a garden plot made out of a square piece of land. He wants to increase the size of his garden by placing an isosceles right triangle shaped piece of land adjacent to it, as shown in the picture above. After adding on the piece of land, the ratio of the area of his old garden to his new garden is:
    A) 3:4
    B) 4:5
    C) 5:4
    D) 4:3

Use the following information to answer Questions 19 and 20.

In 2013, the student-professor ratio at MIT was approximately 8:1.

19. Among MIT faculty, the ratio of male professors to female professors was approximately 3:1. If there were 225 female professors at MIT in 2013, approximately how many students were enrolled?
    A) 5400
    B) 6100
    C) 7200
    D) 8100

20. Among MIT faculty, there are 160 assistant professors, and the ratio of assistant professors to all professors is 8:45. What is the ratio of non-assistant professors to assistant professors?
    A) 37:45
    B) 45:37
    C) 37:8
    D) 45:8

BLUE MATH LESSON 2B: INTERPRETING PERCENTS
Getting Your Feet Wet

Directions: The problems below are intended as a short diagnostic exam.

1. John always tips his waiters and waitresses an amount equal to 20% of his meal's cost. One day, John's meal (with tax included) and tip amounted to a total of $32.40. However, before John added his tip to the meal, the restaurant's manager took 10% off of John's total bill, including tax. What was the original price of John's meal, after tax?
    A) $22.68
    B) $23.33
    C) $24.30
    D) $30.00

2. In 2000, 30% of the 150 faculty members at a local college were made up of full-time professors. In 2010, none of the original faculty members left, the number of faculty members increased by 10%, and 80% of the new faculty members are full-time professors. What was the approximate percent increase in full-time professors at the university from 2000 to 2010?

BLUE MATH LESSON 2B: INTERPRETING PERCENTS
Wading In

Directions: Read the explanation for each problem type mentioned below. Pay special attention to the methods and techniques used to solve the sample problems. Then, do the practice exercises that follow; use the appropriate method to solve each problem.

TOPIC OVERVIEW: INTERPRETING PERCENTS

Our last lesson showed us how to tackle word problems involving ratios, proportions, or scale factors. This lesson will be focused on something fairly similar: percents.

The most basic percent questions are those that refer to a percent as a part over a whole. For example, to solve something like 25% of 96, we can turn the problem into a proportion like this:

$$\frac{25\%}{100\%} = \frac{x}{96}$$

At this point, we can solve just as we did the proportions of our last lesson. After cross multiplying, our answer is 24.

Another way to think of percent problems is to turn every percent into a decimal and then set up an algebraic expression. To turn a percent into a decimal, we simply divide by 100 (or move the decimal point two spots to the left). So, 25% becomes 0.25. Since "of" means multiply in math, the expression "25% of 96" becomes:

$$0.25 \times 96$$

which equals 24.

On the SAT, many of the problems involving percents will involve interpreting situations and word problems similar to those in the last two lessons. Let's try one of these:

SAMPLE PROBLEM 1: INTERPRETING PERCENTS

John always tips his waiters and waitresses an amount equal to 20% of his meal's cost. One day, John's meal (with tax included) and tip amounted to a total of $32.40. However, before John added his tip to the meal, the restaurant's manager took 10% off of John's total bill, including tax. What was the original price of John's meal, after tax?
  A) $22.68
  B) $23.33
  C) $24.30
  D) $30.00

Since we're looking for the initial cost of the meal, let's call that cost x. Before John added his tip to the cost of the meal, the manager took 10% off of his meal:

$$x - 0.10x = 0.90x$$

So, the amount that John is going to consider when giving his tip is $0.90x$. Since John always adds 20% of the price of the meal as a tip, let's take 20% of that price, add it onto that price, and set it equal to the amount he paid, $32.40:

$$0.20(0.90x) + 0.90x = \$32.40$$
$$1.08x = \$32.40$$
$$x = \$30.00$$

So, our answer is **D**.

TOPIC OVERVIEW: PERCENT INCREASE AND DECREASE

Another common concept on the SAT is percent increase or decrease. Anytime we need to find the percent increase or percent decrease between two numbers, we should use the following formula:

$$\frac{\text{final value} - \text{initial value}}{\text{initial value}} \times 100\%$$

The formula is interchangeable for both percent increase and decrease; however, when looking for a percent increase, the final answer will be positive. A percent decrease, on the other hand, will have a negative final answer. Let's look at a sample question to clear this up:

SAMPLE PROBLEM 2: PERCENT INCREASE AND DECREASE

In 2000, 30% of the 150 faculty members at a local college were made up of full-time professors. In 2010, none of the original faculty members left, the number of faculty members increased by 10%, and 80% of the new faculty members are full-time professors. What was the approximate percent increase in full-time professors at the university from 2000 to 2010?

This problem has quite a few percentages we have to deal with, so let's start at the top. Since 30% of the 150 faculty members are full-time in 2000, this percentage accounts for 45 full-time members. So, we know that 105 of the members are part-time faculty.

In 2010, the number of faculty members increased by 10%. 10% of 150 is 15, so we now have 165 faculty members. Of the 15 new faculty members, 80%, 12, are full-time. So, our number of full-time faculty members increased from 45 to 57. Now we can plug these numbers into our percent increase formula and get our answer:

$$\frac{57-45}{45} \times 100\% = \mathbf{26.67\%}$$

That's it!

WRAP-UP

When approaching SAT percent questions, always be aware of what is given and what we are solving for. Understand how to set up both types of percent questions and how to identify the word problems and real-world situations given so that the correct problem set-up will be obvious. Make sure to memorize the percent increase/percent decrease formula.

BLUE MATH LESSON 2B: INTERPRETING PERCENTS
Learning to Swim

Directions: Answer each question below.

PRACTICE SET 1 (NO CALCULATOR)

1. A school has an enrollment of $120x$ students. If this a 60% increase from the year before, what was the number of students, in terms of x, enrolled in the previous year?

2. A student scored a 540 on the SAT in the mathematics section. If she wants her score to be a 650, by what percent, to the nearest tenth, should she increase her score?

3. A painter used 130 different paints to create a painting. If the painter increased the number of paints by $x\%$ for the second painting, how many paints did the painter use for the second painting?

4. A circle has diameter d. If the diameter decreases by 14%, what would the new area of the circle be, in terms of d?

5. A company sold $199x$ products for the month of July. If during the next month, sales decreased by $y\%$, how many products did the company sell in August?

BLUE MATH LESSON 2B: INTERPRETING PERCENTS
Diving into the Deep End

Directions: Answer each question below.

PRACTICE SET 2 (NO CALCULATOR)

6. A local clothing store has a 10% off sale on all sweaters so that it can clear out merchandise for the summer season. At the register, the clerk takes an additional 25% off of the already-discounted price. If the original price on the sweater is $39.95, and sales tax is 5%, what is the final price of the sweater?
   A) $25.62
   B) $27.27
   C) $27.97
   D) $28.31

7. The percent yield of a chemical reaction is given as the actual yield (the amount of product actually produced in the reaction), in grams, divided by the theoretical yield (the amount of product expected to be produced in the reaction), in grams. A new method increases the actual yield of the reaction by 20%. If the actual yield of the initial reaction was 60 grams and the percent yield of the initial reaction is 75%, what's the new percent yield after using the new method?
   A) 72%
   B) 90%
   C) 95%
   D) 100%

8. Over the course of a day, a restaurant manager wants at least 65% of the restaurant's customers to order soft drinks with their food orders. At the moment, 28 of the restaurant's 50 customers for the day have ordered soft drinks. What is the minimum number of new customers who must order soft drinks to bump the percentage up to 65%?
   A) 5
   B) 12
   C) 13
   D) 19

9. A new manufacturing process increases the rate of production of rubber tires by 13%. Previously, the factory could produce 1400 tires per hour. After implementation of the new process, how many tires can the factory produce in an 8-hour work day?
   A) 1,456
   B) 1,582
   C) 9,744
   D) 12,656

Problems 10 and 11 use the following information:

Marshall owns a business in which he buys in-demand toys from local retailers, marks up the price by 20%, and sells them to an online retailer. He uses 25% of the markup to pay for shipping and holding costs and pockets the rest.

10. How much will Marshall profit from the transaction if he buys $100 of toys and sells all of them to the online retailer?
    A) $15.00
    B) $20.00
    C) $22.50
    D) $25.00

11. In reality, Marshall only sells, by cost, 90% of the toys he buys. The remainder he holds until the next month. If Marshall buys $5,000 of toys in January, how much profit will he make from the sale of these toys in January?
    A) $625
    B) $675
    C) $750
    D) $1250

12. 24% of a circular petri dish is covered by a colony of paramecia. If the petri dish has a radius of 1 inch, how many square inches do the paramecia cover, to the nearest hundredth of a square inch?
    A) 0.24
    B) 0.48
    C) 0.75
    D) 1.50

$$A = \frac{1}{2}s^2$$

13. The area of an isosceles right triangle is given by the equation above. If each side length of the triangle, s, is increased by 40%, by what percent will the area, A, of the triangle increase?
    A) 40%
    B) 48%
    C) 96%
    D) 196%

14. A pair of shoes has an original price of x, but in June the shoes go on sale for 30% off and are priced at $126. If in July, the shoes go on sale for 35% off the original price, what is the sale price for July in dollars?

15. A driver is driving at a rate of 50 miles per hour for 200 miles. If he increases his speed by 12% on the return home, what will be the percentage decrease in time, to the nearest tenth, it takes him to travel the 200 miles?

PRACTICE SET 3 (CALCULATOR)

16. Jackson County has a countywide sales tax rate of 1.25%. In addition, the state charges a sales tax of 6%. Furthermore, the state legislature recently voted to implement an additional five-cent sales tax on each total cigarette purchase, which will go exclusively to fund anti-smoking campaigns. Which of the following represents the total amount, in dollars, that Charlie must pay to buy d dollars of cigarettes in Jackson County, including all taxes?
    A) $1.1225d$
    B) $(d + 0.05)(1.0725)$
    C) $1.725d + 0.05$
    D) $1.0725d + 0.05$

17. Every week, Roberto wants to increase the number of pushups he can do by 10%. If he wants to be able to do at least 100 pushups by the end of 6 weeks, how many must he be able to do at the start of his 6-week regimen?
    A) 57
    B) 60
    C) 62
    D) 63

Problems 18 and 19 use the following information:

A local real estate agent, Vic Vine, charges $500 plus a third of 1 percent commission to help sell your house, while the typical real estate agent charges a rate of 6 percent commission.

18. If your house sells for $130,000, how much will you save on commission by using Vic Vine to sell your house?
    A) $7800.00
    B) $6866.67
    C) $5571.00
    D) $933.33

19. What sell price would result in both real estate agents receiving the same commission?
    A) $8,823.53
    B) $10,713.52
    C) $88,235.30
    D) 107,135.20

20. A businessman is increasing his salary from $35,000 to $45,000. After that salary increase, he gets a bonus of 10% of his new salary. What was the percent increase from his previous salary to his new salary, including bonus?
    A) 28.6%
    B) 31.4%
    C) 38.6%
    D) 41.4%

21. A college Calculus class calculates grades by summing 70% of the average of the five regular exams and 30% of the score of the final exam. If Jennifer wants to get at least an 80 in the Calculus class and currently has an exam average of 76 over her five exams, what score must she get on her final exam? Each exam is out of 100 points and only whole number scores are possible.
    A) 84
    B) 89
    C) 90
    D) 92

Use the following information for Questions 22 and 23.

Customer Satisfaction with Sugar-Free Soft Drink

Customer	Approved	Disapproved	Total
Male	16	46	62
Female	24	22	46
Total	40	68	108

22. What percent of males surveyed approved of the new sugar-free soft drink?
   A) 26%
   B) 37%
   C) 40%
   D) 74%

23. Of the people surveyed who disapproved of the new soft drink, what percent were female?
   A) 32%
   B) 48%
   C) 59%
   D) 68%

For questions 24 and 25, use the information below.

The graph below represents the average rainfall in inches per month for the town of Jefferson Lake.

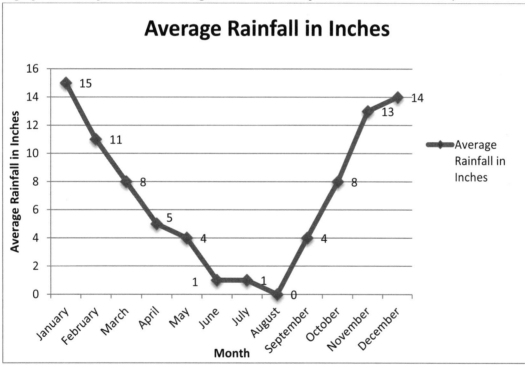

24. What is the greatest percent decrease between the average rainfall amounts of two consecutive months?

25. Next year, the average rainfall for February increases by 20% and the average rainfall for October increases by 30%. What is the positive difference between these two values, to the nearest tenth?

BLUE MATH LESSON 2B: INTERPRETING PERCENTS
Race to the Finish

Directions: Answer each question below.

HOMEWORK SET (NO CALCULATOR)

1. A grocery store is offering a pre-Thanksgiving sale in which you can buy a turkey, a disposable aluminum roasting pan, a turkey baster, and a carving knife for $36.00. The local 6.5% sales tax applies to everything but food. The turkey itself is priced at $24.99 before tax. Which of the following represents the cost, in dollars, for p people to buy this Thanksgiving package deal?
   A) $36p(1.065) - 24.99$
   B) $(11.01[1.065] + 24.99)p$
   C) $24.99 + (1.065)11.01p$
   D) $36p - 24.99(0.065)$

2. At the local Food Outlet, prices are deceptively low: the cashier adds 10% of the total cost to the bill before adding on tax. If tax is 6%, how much would a bill of $24.00 cost after tax and mark-up, to the nearest cent?
   A) $22.90
   B) $25.44
   C) $27.84
   D) $27.98

3. The foreman of a paper clip factory expects that 0.03% of all of the paper clips manufactured will be defective due to shape and 0.01% will be defective due to incorrect metal density. How many paper clips must be manufactured on average to produce 4 that are defective due to shape?
   A) 100
   B) 133
   C) 10000
   D) 13333

4. If 4 L of water is added to an 8 L mixture of HCl and water that is 2% HCl, what percent of the new mixture is HCl?
   A) 0.67%
   B) 1.33%
   C) 1.5%
   D) 2%

5. An electronics store offers a 4% discount if a customer pays with cash rather than paying with a credit card or check. If the cash price of an item is $24.00, how much would the credit card price be?
   A) $23.00
   B) $23.04
   C) $24.96
   D) $25.00

Use the following information for Questions 6 and 7:

Duluth Middle School recently surveyed its students on the topic of installing vending machines in the cafeteria. The results are shown below.

Student Survey on Vending Machines

Student	Yes	No	Total
7th Grade	632	100	732
8th Grade	234	475	709
Total	866	575	1441

6. Of the students who answered no to the survey, what percent were in the 8th grade?
   A) 17%
   B) 27%
   C) 67%
   D) 83%

7. Of the students surveyed, what percent in the 7th or 8th grade answered yes?
   A) 60%
   B) 66%
   C) 67%
   D) 86%

8. Brian's backyard is $\frac{2}{5}$ of an acre, and 30% of his backyard is covered in kudzu, an invasive vine. If Brian wants a garden that will cover half of the remainder of his backyard, what percent of his backyard will it cover?
   A) 14%
   B) 28%
   C) 35%
   D) 50%

9. Anna's commission for selling a car is 12% of the price of the car. She also makes a monthly salary of $1200 regardless of how many cars she sells. If Anna wants to make at least $3000 next month, what should be the total price of all of the cars that she sells?
   A) $10,000
   B) $12,000
   C) $15,000
   D) $25,000

10. A motorcycle dealership sells a certain brand-new vehicle for $8,250. On the 4th of July, the dealership has its Independence Day sale, which slashes the price of every bike by 17.76%. A customer buys this bike on the 4th of July, and the next day realizes that she wants a different model, which costs $7,982. What percent of the price (without the sale) of the second bike will she get if she returns the original bike and gets a full refund?
    A) 17.76%
    B) 79.57%
    C) 85.00%
    D) 96.75%

11. In 2012, there were 165 students at Happy Valley High School with driver's licenses, which was $9\frac{1}{6}\%$ of the total number of students at the school. In 2013, the number of students at the school increased by 15%, and the number of students with driver's licenses increased by 42. What percent of the students at HVHS had licenses in 2013?
    A) $9\frac{1}{6}\%$
    B) $9\frac{5}{6}\%$
    C) 10%
    D) $10\frac{1}{6}\%$

12. A certain type of concrete is made by using a mixture of 3 parts cement, 14 parts aggregate (stones and sand), and 3 parts water. A construction company changes the "recipe" for the concrete by tripling the amount of cement, doubling the amount of aggregate, but leaving the amount of water the same. What percent of the new cement is water?

A) 7.5%

B) $8\frac{1}{3}\%$

C) 10%

D) 15%

13. In order to join the wrestling team, Preethi needs to increase her weight by 15% so that she can wrestle at the maximum weight in the 100-108 pound weight class. What is her current weight, to the nearest pound?

A) 87 pounds

B) 90 pounds

C) 92 pounds

D) 94 pounds

14. The manager of a retail chain is offered a bonus of x dollars for every percent increase in sales his store achieves over the next month. Which of these scenarios would result in the largest bonus?

A) Initial Sales: $35,000, Final Sales: $50,000, x:$40

B) Initial Sales: $35,000, Final Sales:$60,000, x:$30

C) Initial Sales: $24,000, Final Sales: $50,000, x:$12

D) Initial Sales: $24,000, Final Sales: $60,000, x:$10

15. If the price of gas increases by 0.5% to $4.08 what was the initial price of gas, to the nearest cent?

A) $3.89

B) $4.00

C) $4.03

D) $4.06

16. A 32,000 KB file is downloading at a constant rate of 16 KB per second. When the file is 25% downloaded, how many seconds remain?

A) 500 seconds

B) 1500 seconds

C) 4000 seconds

D) 8000 seconds

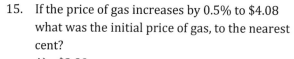

be smarter

For Questions 17 and 18 use the information below:

The average daily temperatures were recorded for one week in the two cities of Washington Township and North Valley and were graphed.

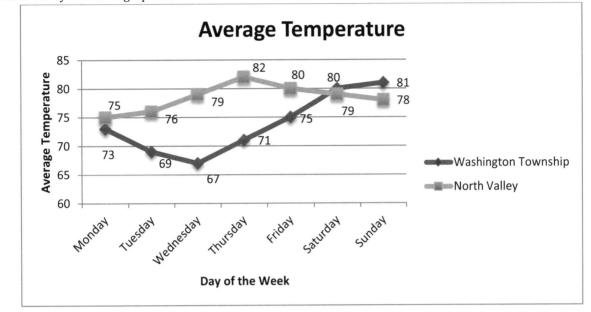

17. Based on the graph above, what is the greatest percent increase in temperature between two consecutive days in North Valley, to the nearest hundredth of a percent?

18. Because of errors in the weather recording software, North Valley's Monday temperature should have been 4% higher and Washington Township's Saturday temperature should have been decreased by 5%. If these values are updated to reflect their actual values, what is the difference between North Valley's Monday value and Washington Township's Saturday value?

19. A stock price increased by 15% on Tuesday, decreased by 13% on Wednesday, increased by 3% on Thursday, and closed that day at $58. At what price did the stock start?

20. A tennis player practices by serving 100 times a day, hitting 200 times a day, and volleying 50 times a day. She wants to increase her serving by 15% and decrease her hitting by 12%. If the number of total swings increases by 10%, how many times will she practice volleying a day?

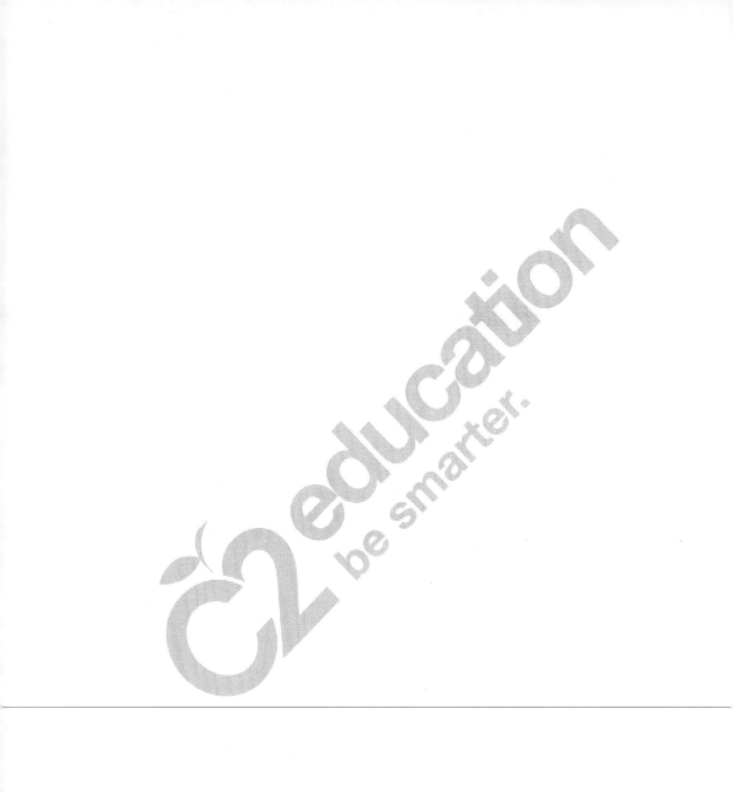

BLUE MATH LESSON 3A: MULTI-STEP UNIT CONVERSIONS
Getting Your Feet Wet

Directions: The problems below are intended as a short diagnostic exam.

1. If the speed of light in a vacuum is 983,571,056 feet per second, what is the speed of light in a vacuum in miles per hour?
   A) 11,176,943
   B) 223,538,876
   C) 299,792,458
   D) 670,616,629

2. Chemists use the constant Avogadro's Number, 6.022×10^{23}, to show how many molecules are in a mole of any substance. If a mole of bleach has a mass of 74.42 grams, how many molecules are in a 1 L bottle of bleach, if bleach has a density of 1.11 g/mL? (Note: Density is mass divided by volume.)
   A) 7.29×10^{21}
   B) 7.29×10^{24}
   C) 8.98×10^{24}
   D) 4.97×10^{25}

BLUE MATH LESSON 3A: MULTI-STEP UNIT CONVERSIONS
Wading In

Directions: Read the explanation for each problem type mentioned below. Pay special attention to the methods and techniques used to solve the sample problems. Then, do the practice exercises that follow; use the appropriate method to solve each problem.

TOPIC OVERVIEW: MULTI-STEP UNIT CONVERSIONS

Many questions on the SAT will involve changing one unit of measurement to another. These questions are relatively simple if we set up something we learn in chemistry called the bridge method. Look below for a picture of what the bridge will look like:

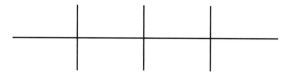

To use the bridge method, start by putting the initial unit of measure in the left-hand side of the chart. If the unit of measure is one term, like 8 km, put the term in the upper row. However, if the unit of measure is something more complicated, like $9.8 \frac{m}{s^2}$, put the 9.8 and the m in the upper row, but the s^2 in the bottom column, as shown below:

Our next task is to use unit conversion factors to change each unit into the required unit. Let's turn $9.8 \frac{m}{s^2}$ into $\frac{ft}{min^2}$: start by turning meters into feet. Since there are 3.28 feet in one meter, and we need to cancel out meters, be sure to put the feet on top in the next column.

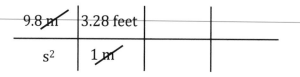

Now that we've gotten rid of our meters, we need to turn seconds into minutes. We know there are 60 seconds in a minute, so again we'll put our 60 seconds on top and our minute on bottom.

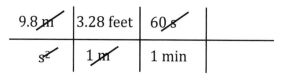

We're done, right? Not quite... As of right now, we've only gotten rid of one of the seconds units on bottom. We need to repeat the process to get rid of the other seconds units (after all, it's seconds squared).

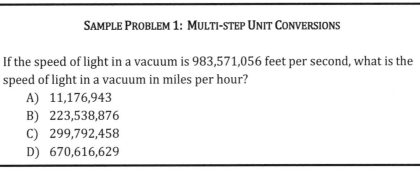

Now that we've gotten rid of all of our old units and replaced them with new ones, we're done. Just multiply the numbers on top, then divide by each number on bottom. Our final answer will be $115{,}718.4 \frac{\text{ft}}{\text{min}^2}$.

SAMPLE PROBLEM 1: MULTI-STEP UNIT CONVERSIONS

If the speed of light in a vacuum is 983,571,056 feet per second, what is the speed of light in a vacuum in miles per hour?

  A) 11,176,943
  B) 223,538,876
  C) 299,792,458
  D) 670,616,629

We're starting with an easier one, so let's set up our bridge first:

$$\frac{983{,}571{,}056 \,\text{ft}}{\text{s}} \cdot \frac{1 \text{ mile}}{5{,}280\,\text{ft}} \cdot \frac{3{,}600\,\text{s}}{1 \text{ hr}}$$

After multiplying across the top and dividing by the bottom, we get a final answer of 670,616,629 miles per hour, **D**.

Let's try one more problem. This one will be a little more difficult, though.

SAMPLE PROBLEM 2: MULTI-STEP UNIT CONVERSIONS

Chemists use the constant Avogadro's Number, 6.022×10^{23}, to show how many molecules are in a mole of any substance. If a mole of bleach has a mass of 74.42 grams, how many molecules are in a 1 L bottle of bleach, if bleach has a density of 1.11 g/mL? (Note: Density is mass divided by volume.)

  A) 7.29×10^{21}
  B) 7.29×10^{24}
  C) 8.98×10^{24}
  D) 4.97×10^{25}

This question is a bit harder because it's not immediately apparent what we're starting with and what we're ending with. However, we see that we

want to know how many molecules are in 1 L of bleach, so let's put 1 L in the top left-hand corner of our bridge and go from there, filling in conversion factors until we get to our final answer of molecules:

1 L	1000 mL	1.11g	1 mole	6.022×10^{23} molecules
	1 L	1 mL	74.42g	1 mole

After multiplying across the top and dividing by the numbers on bottom, we get a final answer of 8.98×10^{24}, or **C**.

WRAP-UP

When approaching SAT unit conversion questions, always be aware of what is given and what is being solved for. Always set up a bridge so that it's clear which unit conversion factors need to be multiplied and which need to be divided.

Below are some important unit conversions that show up frequently on the SAT. Memorize them!

Length:
1 mile (mi.) = 5280 feet (ft.)
1 mile (mi.) = 1760 yards (yd.)
1 yard (yd.) = 3 feet (ft.)
1 foot (ft.) = 12 inches (in.)

1 kilometer (km) = 1000 meters (m)
1 meter (m) = 100 centimeters (cm)
1 meter (m) = 1000 millimeters (mm)
1 millimeter (mm) = 1000 micrometers (μm)
2.54 centimeters (cm) = 1 inch (in)

Mass:
1 ton (T.) = 2000 pounds (lb.)
1 pound (lb.) = 16 ounces (oz.)

1 kilogram (kg) = 1000 grams (g)
1 gram (g) = 1000 milligrams (mg)
1 milligram (mg) = 1000 micrograms (μg)
1 kilogram (kg) = 2.2 pounds (lb.)

Volume:
1 gallon (gal.) = 4 quarts (qt.)
1 quart (qt.) = 2 pints (pt.)
1 pint (pt.) = 16 fluid ounces (fl. oz.)

BLUE MATH LESSON 3A: MULTI-STEP UNIT CONVERSIONS
Learning to Swim

Directions: Answer each question below.

PRACTICE SET 1 (CALCULATOR)

1. The world record ball speed for the game of jai alai is 302 km per hour. The fastest recorded baseball pitch in an MLB game was clocked at 105.1 miles per hour. If there are approximately 1.6 km in a mile, how much faster is the world record jai alai ball speed than the fastest recorded baseball pitch, in feet per second?

2. Dendrochronology is the study of counting tree rings to determine a tree's age. A particular tree found in the Amazon rainforest develops 3 rings every 2 years, and the distance from one ring to the next ring is approximately 0.5 inches. If the tree is 38 years old, what is its diameter, in inches?

3. Round your age to the nearest half-year. Approximately how many seconds have you been alive?

4. A sphere has a radius of x feet. What is the volume of the sphere in cubic inches, in terms of x? (The volume of a sphere is found by $V = \frac{4}{3}\pi r^3$).

5. One page of plaintext type contains 1,200 characters. If 1 MB of data is 1,024 KB, and 1 KB is 1,024 bytes. If 1 MB of data can hold 873 pages of plaintext type, how many bytes can be found in x pages of plaintext type?

BLUE MATH LESSON 3A: MULTI-STEP UNIT CONVERSIONS
Diving into the Deep End

Directions: Answer each question below.

PRACTICE SET 2 (CALCULATOR)

6. Each server at a pancake restaurant covers a section containing 11 tables for four. If there are five such sections in the restaurant, and five out of every eight customers order coffee, how many coffee orders are there when the restaurant is 80% occupied?
   A) 110
   B) 138
   C) 172
   D) 282

7. The white oak tree is an Illinois native that can grow 15 inches taller in one year, but only adds ¼ inch to its diameter each year. A tree that is 48 inches tall and ¾ inches in diameter when it is planted will have what circumference when it reaches 50 feet tall (to the nearest inch)?
   A) 9"
   B) 29"
   C) 31"
   D) 462"

8. Fish is offered for sale in a French coastal town for €12.86 per kg. How much will a British visitor pay for 1 pound 10 ounces of fish, in the more familiar units of British currency, £? (The euro may be exchanged for British pounds at a rate of €1.25 for £1.)
   A) £5.14
   B) £7.17
   C) £7.59
   D) £10.29

9. A recipe for vegetable frittata calls for 10 chard leaves for every 6 eggs. Eggs are available either by the dozen for $3.20 or by the half-dozen for $1.70. Marissa has gotten a bumper crop of 25 chard leaves at the farmer's market; how much will she have to spend on eggs to use them all?
   A) $3.20
   B) $4.00
   C) $4.90
   D) $5.10

10. A wooden fence that is 6 feet tall and 11 feet wide needs to be painted front and back. If two gallons of paint cover 5000 square inches, and a one-gallon can of paint costs $3.50, how much will it cost to paint the fence?
    A) $28.00
    B) $33.26
    C) $44.19
    D) $66.52

11. When a bicycle is in its highest gear, the wheels (radius 14") rotate 9 times for every 2 revolutions of the pedals. When Hildaur is pedaling at 60 revolutions per minute, how fast will his bicycle travel down the road in miles per hour?
    A) 1.11
    B) 3.58
    C) 5.00
    D) 22.49

12. One measure of the quality of fabric is the threadcount, the number of threads per inch in each direction of the weave. The threadcount for the warp (threads running along the length of the fabric) is the same as for the weft (threads running across the width of the fabric). A twin sheet is 5'10" in width and 8'9" in length. If it is made of 400 threadcount material, how many total threads does the sheet contain (ignore hems)?

A) 28,000
B) 42,000
C) 67,200
D) 70,000

13. Kavya has $200 in US dollars, which she will exchange for local currency at each stop as she travels to Ireland, India, Japan, Denmark, and Canada. On the dates she makes her transactions, she gets exchange rates of 2 Danish krone per 37 Japanese yen; 4 US dollars for 3 euros (used in the European Union, including Ireland); and 5.1 krone per Canadian dollar. 1000 Indian rupees may be exchanged for 12.2 euros or 1700 yen. How does her final cash-on-hand in Canadian dollars compare to what she would have gotten by travelling directly to Canada, getting $1.07 CAD for every $1 US? (Ignore transaction fees.)

A) $34.16 CAD less
B) $7.53 CAD less
C) $7.53 CAD more
D) $221.53 CAD more

14. One GB of data can hold, on average, 256 MP3 audio files, and 1 GB is equivalent to 2^{30} bytes. If 1 MB is equivalent to 1024^2 bytes, how many MB does each MP3 average?

15. One gram of fat is equivalent to 9 calories, 1 gram of protein is equivalent to 4 calories, and 1 gram of carbohydrates is equivalent to 4 calories. If a granola bar weighs 1.4 oz and is 37.5% fat by weight, 15% protein by weight, and 40% carbohydrates by weight, how many calories, to the nearest calorie, are in the granola bar, if 1 ounce is 28.34 grams?

PRACTICE SET 3 (CALCULATOR)

16. The density of dichloromethane, a commonly used solvent, is 1.326 g/mL at 20°C. A particular sample of dichloromethane has a volume of 1.28×10^5 mL at 20°C. What is the mass of the sample, in kg?
A) 169.728 kg
B) 1697.28 kg
C) 16972.8 kg
D) 169728 kg

17. A compact hybrid car gets 48 miles to the gallon (mpg), while a compact gas-only car gets 30 mpg. Lydia drives 12,000 miles per year; Alan drives only 8,000 miles per year. If gas averages $4.15 per gallon, how much more will Lydia save in one year by buying the hybrid than Alan?
A) $207.50
B) $345.83
C) $622.50
D) Lydia saves less than Alan does.

18. Immunoglobulin G is a therapy given intravenously; a dosage for severe infection is 1.8 g per kg of the patient's weight, which is to be administered in equal increments over the course of 36 hours. A patient who weighs 52 kg is diagnosed with a condition which requires him to be given immunoglobulin G. If a preparation of immunoglobulin G contains 50 mg of immunoglobulin per mL fluid, how many mL of the preparation should be given to the patient every hour?
A) 26
B) 52
C) 104
D) 1872

19. A car's turn signal turns on and off again in a cycle with a frequency of 1.6 hertz (1.6 cycles per second). How far, to the nearest whole foot, does the car travel at 55 miles per hour during 5 blink cycles?
A) 65
B) 252
C) 645
D) 2521

20. A mole is a unit used by chemists to describe a group of atoms or molecules. The reaction equation

$$2\ C_6H_6 + 15\ O_2 \rightarrow 16\ CO_2 + 18\ H_2O$$

states that 2 moles of benzene (C_6H_6) react with 15 moles of oxygen (O_2) to form 16 moles of carbon dioxide (CO_2) and 18 moles of water (H_2O). Given that each mole of oxygen has a mass of 32 g, 3 moles of benzene would react with how many grams of oxygen?
A) 12.8
B) 48.0
C) 720
D) 960

21. The cafeteria staff at Camp Quantitative knows that some campers want one sandwich for lunch, while other campers want two. The manager plans to make five sandwiches for every three campers. Each sandwich uses two pieces of bread; there are sixteen slices in a loaf. How many loaves of bread should the cafeteria have on hand for 243 campers?
A) 19
B) 31
C) 50
D) 51

22. A particularly speedy snail can move at 301 furlongs per fortnight, while his slower competitor manages only 252 furlongs per fortnight. By what margin will the faster snail win a 6-foot race? (Assume both snails glide on straight lines toward the finish. A furlong is equal to 201.168 meters; 2.54 centimeters is equal to one inch. A "fortnight" is an abbreviation for "fourteen-night," i.e. a period of 14 days.)
    A) 0.004 seconds
    B) 0.71 seconds
    C) 7.11 seconds
    D) 36.53 seconds

23. An ampere is a unit of electrical current equal to one coulomb of electrical charge flowing per second. One brand of smartphone draws 240 mA (a mA is 1/1000 of an ampere) of current when running its color screen at full brightness. Each electron carries a charge of 1.602×10^{-19} coulombs; how many electrons leave the phone's battery during five minutes of operation?
    A) 1.80×10^{-18}
    B) 4.49×10^{-18}
    C) 1.80×10^{20}
    D) 4.49×10^{20}

24. A student can read 1 page every 2 minutes. If every page has 80 words and the student reads for 3 hours, how many words will the student read?

25. Big Box Company, a company that recycles cardboard, uses three pieces of cardboard, each of which measures 1 square yard, to create 20 new smaller boxes. If it takes five minutes to make 10 new smaller boxes, how many pieces of cardboard are used after 8 hours of work?

BLUE MATH LESSON 3A: MULTI-STEP UNIT CONVERSIONS
Race to the Finish

Directions: Answer each question below.

HOMEWORK SET (CALCULATOR)

1. The density of gold is 19.3 g/cm³. A rectangular block of gold with dimensions of 0.1 m by 0.05 m by 0.3 m has what mass in kilograms?
   A) 0.02895
   B) 2.895
   C) 28.95
   D) 28,950,000

2. Lutein is a yellow pigment found in marigold petals and egg yolks. A 200 µL sample of a solution of 50 µg/mL lutein in ethanol contains how many µg of lutein?
   A) 0.1
   B) 0.4
   C) 4
   D) 10

3. A palletizer is a machine that takes cans coming from a canning production line and shakes them into a close-packed arrangement on a wooden pallet for storage. For a certain size of can, 132 cans will fit on each layer on the pallet, and cans are stacked 14 layers high. If cans come off the production line at 103 cans/minute, how many complete pallets can be produced during a 7½ hour shift?
   A) less than 1
   B) 25
   C) 26
   D) 118

4. A mole is a unit used by chemists to describe a group of atoms or molecules; one mole of nitrogen has a mass of 28.02 g, while a mole of silver has a mass of 107.87 g. A certain substance is composed of only the elements nitrogen and silver. If it is 28% nitrogen by mass, then a 25 g sample of this substance would contain how many moles of silver?
   A) 0.0649
   B) 0.1669
   C) 0.4996
   D) 1942

5. A dram is a unit of volume equal to $\frac{1}{8}$ of a fluid ounce. How many drams are there in 2½ quarts?
   A) 10
   B) 80
   C) 160
   D) 640

6. Jane is 5' 4" tall. This is equivalent to how many centimeters? (Note: 3 feet is equal to 91.44 cm.)
   A) 137.16
   B) 162.56
   C) 411.48
   D) 487.68

7. A certain brand of chocolate candies contains 6 grams of fat per 3-piece serving. Each piece has a mass of 15 grams. If Eric's dessert contains 10 grams of fat, how much chocolate does he get?
    A) 1.5 g
    B) 12 g
    C) 25 g
    D) 75 g

8. At an outdoor concert venue where attendees place their own lawn chairs, each person may occupy from 9 to 20 square feet. On a hot summer afternoon, it is wise for the venue to supply 8 ounces of water per person per hour. If the lawn is a rectangle of 70 yards by 80 yards, and the whole space is occupied at minimum density, how many gallons of water should the organizers have on hand for a 3-hour event?
    A) 157.5
    B) 350
    C) 472.5
    D) 1050

9. Dry-roasted peanuts contain 35 g of protein per serving; a serving is defined as 146 g. If Mya eats 200 g of peanuts as a snack, how much protein does she get?
    A) 0.0209 g
    B) 25.6 g
    C) 47.9 g
    D) 1022 g

10. Rishik's biology textbook is printed on paper that makes a stack 5.1 cm high when 1 ream (500 sheets) is piled up. If it takes him 5 minutes to read every 2 pages, to the nearest hour, how long will it take him to read the entire book, which is 4.8 cm thick not counting the covers (each sheet is printed on both sides)?
    A) 20 hours
    B) 39 hours
    C) 44 hours
    D) 2353 hours

11. Each phase of a pharmaceutical clinical trial involves dosing patients with a drug, then drawing a sample of their blood every hour for fifteen hours. An analytical chemist who tests the blood samples can pipet one sample every 15 seconds. How long will it take her to pipet the samples for two patients from a three-phase clinical trial?
    A) 7.5 minutes
    B) 22.5 minutes
    C) 25 minutes
    D) 27.5 minutes

12. Ellie is studying for her physics final by doing a problem set for each chapter that the class covered. If each problem set is 12 problems, and on average Ellie spends 15 minutes on each problem, how long will it take her to review 8 chapters?
    A) 6.4 hours
    B) 22.5 hours
    C) 24 hours
    D) 1440 hours

13. Diane is sprouting beet seeds that she will eventually transplant into her garden. She can sprout 4 seeds in each peat pot. The seedlings are transplanted one for every 2 inches in garden rows. To plant 6 rows, each 3 feet long, how many peat pots does Diane need?
    A) 2
    B) 3
    C) 27
    D) 144

14. SAT graders can spend no more than 2 minutes on each student essay they read. To read an essay of 4 paragraphs, if the paragraphs are 5 sentences each and sentences average 15 words each, what must be a reader's minimum reading rate?
    A) $\frac{2}{5}$ word/second
    B) 2.5 words/second
    C) 5 words/second
    D) 60 words/second

15. Human hair can grow 1/30th of an inch every day. If Becky's hair is 3" long, approximately how many weeks will it take to grow out to waist-length, 28" long?
    A) 5.8
    B) 12
    C) 107
    D) 5250

16. Ayesha is making a wood-chip path in her garden. The path will be a rectangle $4\frac{2}{3}$ yards long and $1\frac{1}{3}$ yard wide, and she wants the wood chips to be three inches deep. If wood chips come in bags of 2 cubic feet each, how many bags will Ayesha need to buy to have enough?
    A) 3
    B) 7
    C) 28
    D) 84

17. A summer camp is having an end of the year pizza party. Each group contains 4 children, and every group eats a total of 6 slices (some children eat one slice, while others eat two). If a pizza has 8 slices, and it costs $10 for one pizza, how much will it cost to feed 384 campers?

18. A cellphone company charges 25 cents per minute for calls. How many dollars will Maria pay this month if her phone calls equaled 1.5 days?

19. Suzy is driving to a destination that is 250 kilometers away. Unfortunately, she fills her gas tank with enough gas to allow her to drive only 100 miles. If she can drive 25 miles for every gallon, and gas costs $3.25/gallon, how much money will she pay for gas, in dollars, to reach her destination after the tank runs out? (1 mile is 1.6093 kilometers)

20. Silver has a density of 9.320 g/cm³. If a silver plaque has dimensions of 4 inches long, 3 inches wide, and 0.8 inches thick, how many grams of silver is the plaque, to the nearest gram? (1 inch = 2.54 cm)

BLUE MATH LESSON 3B: DIRECT AND INVERSE VARIATION
Getting Your Feet Wet

Directions: The problems below are intended as a short diagnostic exam.

1. Hooke's Law states that the force, F, needed to extend a spring by a distance varies directly with that distance, X, based on a constant factor for each spring, k, that measures its stiffness. If a certain spring needs 2200 N of force to extend the spring 3 meters, how much force will it need to extend the spring 2 meters?

2. The square of the mountain goat population of a certain volcanic island varies inversely with the wolf population on the same island. In 1900, the population of mountain goats on the island was 1000, while the population of wolves was 25. If the population of wolves in 2000 was 100, what was the population of mountain goats?
   A) 250
   B) 400
   C) 500
   D) 2000

3. The table below shows the voltage, V, resistance, R, and current, I, for a given circuit. Which of the following sentences best describes the relationship between I, R, and V?

I	R	V
3.85 Amperes	2.60 Ohms	10.0 Volts
1.99 Amperes	5.01 Ohms	10.0 Volts
5.20 Amperes	1.92 Ohms	10.0 Volts
3.13 Amperes	3.19 Ohms	10.0 Volts
1.12 Amperes	8.91 Ohms	10.0 Volts

   A) R varies directly with I for a constant value of V.
   B) R varies inversely with I for a constant value of V.
   C) There is no apparent relationship between I, R, and V.
   D) R varies inversely with I and directly with V.

BLUE MATH LESSON 3B: DIRECT AND INVERSE VARIATION
Wading In

Directions: Read the explanation for each problem type mentioned below. Pay special attention to the methods and techniques used to solve the sample problems. Then, do the practice exercises that follow; use the appropriate method to solve each problem.

TOPIC OVERVIEW: DIRECT VARIATION

When two quantities maintain a constant ratio, they are said to vary directly with each other. This relationship is called a direct variation, or the two variables are said to be directly proportional. The formula for this is given as $y = kx$, where k is known as the constant of variation. The graph of two variables that vary directly with each other will always be linear and pass through the origin. Also notice that as x increases, y must increase at the same rate; at the same time, if x decreases, then y must also decrease at the same rate.

Let's look at a sample problem to see how questions involving direct variation are given on the SAT:

SAMPLE PROBLEM 1: DIRECT VARIATION

Hooke's Law states that the force, F, needed to extend a spring by a distance varies directly with that distance, X, based on a constant factor for each spring, k, that measures its stiffness. If a certain spring needs 2200 N of force to extend the spring 3 meters, how much force will it need to extend the spring 2 meters?

To solve this question, we first need to set up our direct variation equation:

$$F = kX$$

Since we have initial values for F and X, plug them in and let's figure out our constant of variation first:

$$2200 = k(3)$$
$$k = 733.33$$

Now, we can plug in k and our second value for X and find our second value for F.

$$F = 733.33(2)$$

So, our answer is **1466.67 N**.

TOPIC OVERVIEW: INVERSE VARIATION

When two quantities vary inversely, they change in the opposite direction: as one increases, the other decreases. Inverse variation, also known as inverse proportionality, is shown by the formula:

$$k = xy$$

Let's look at a sample problem to see how inverse variation works:

SAMPLE PROBLEM 2: INVERSE VARIATION

The square of the mountain goat population of a certain volcanic island varies inversely with the wolf population on the same island. In 1900, the population of mountain goats on the island was 1000, while the population of wolves was 25. If the population of wolves in 2000 was 100, what was the population of mountain goats?

   A) 250
   B) 400
   C) 500
   D) 2000

Since we know the square of the goat population varies inversely with the wolf population, let's set up an equation to show this:

$$k = g^2 w$$

Notice how we squared the goat population to show that the wolf population varied inversely with the square of the goat population, not just the goat population. Now we should be able to plug in our values and solve:

$$k = (1000)^2(25) = 25,000,000$$
$$25000000 = (g)^2(100)$$
$$g = 500$$

So, our answer is **C**.

We'll do one more problem to make sure we understand the concept of variation.

SAMPLE PROBLEM 3: IDENTIFYING VARIATION

The table below shows the voltage, V, resistance, R, and current, I, for a given circuit. Which of the following sentences best describes the relationship between I, R, and V?

I	R	V
3.85 Amperes	2.60 Ohms	10.0 Volts
1.99 Amperes	5.01 Ohms	10.0 Volts
5.20 Amperes	1.92 Ohms	10.0 Volts
3.13 Amperes	3.19 Ohms	10.0 Volts
1.12 Amperes	8.91 Ohms	10.0 Volts

A) R varies directly with I for a constant value of V.
B) R varies inversely with I for a constant value of V.
C) There is no apparent relationship between , R, and V.
D) R varies inversely with I and directly with V.

The most noticeable thing about the data in the above table is that the values for V always remain constant. Since three of our answers hint at either direct or inverse variation, let's start by setting up both of those equations for every possible combination of variables, plugging in numbers, and figuring out which one works. We'll start with direct variation first.

$$I = VR \text{ clearly doesn't work, as } 10 \times 2.60 \text{ is not } 3.85.$$
$$R = VI \text{ doesn't work for the same reasons;}$$
$$10 \times 3.85 \text{ is not } 2.60$$

Now let's try inverse variation:

$IR = V$ seems to work for all 5 of the rows. Some of them are slightly off (9.98 instead of 10.0 exactly, but the question says best describes, not exactly describes.) So, our answer must be **B**.

WRAP-UP

Always be on the lookout for the phrases "direct variation" and "inverse variation" when working through any SAT questions and apply the formulas $y = xk$ and $k = xy$ appropriately. In addition, be aware that the graph of any variables that are directly related will be a linear function that passes through the origin, while the graph of two variables that are inversely related will never pass through the origin. As with anything, practice makes perfect, so try these next questions.

BLUE MATH LESSON 3B: DIRECT AND INVERSE VARIATION
Learning to Swim

Directions: Answer each question below.

PRACTICE SET 1 (CALCULATOR)

1. The amount of sugar needed for a cookie recipe varies directly with the amount of flour. If the standard recipe calls for $1\frac{2}{3}$ cups of sugar and $2\frac{1}{2}$ cups of flour, how much flour is needed if $2\frac{1}{3}$ cups of sugar are used?

2. The area of office space that a company needs varies directly with the number of employees working in that office. Company A, which has 30 employees, needs 3,750 square feet of office space. How much office space does Company B need if it has 12 more employees than Company A?

3. The cost per person of a catered event varies inversely with the number of people at the event. If a 30-person event costs $45 per person, how many fewer people attend the event if the price per person is raised to $50?

4. Two metal sheets are connected by 72 rivets along a seam that measures 225 centimeters long. If the number of rivets varies directly with the square root of the length of the seam, how many rivets would be needed to connect two sheets along a 12.25 meter seam?

5. Given a constant amount of engine force, the acceleration of a car varies inversely with its mass. If a car with mass m kilograms accelerates at 1.6 meters per second squared, what will be the acceleration, in meters per second squared, of a car with mass 1,200 kilograms?

BLUE MATH LESSON 3B: DIRECT AND INVERSE VARIATION
Diving into the Deep End

Directions: Answer each question below.

PRACTICE SET 2 (CALCULATOR)

6. The intensity of the Sun's radiation varies inversely with the square of the distance from the Sun. Earth is 2.6 times farther from the Sun than Mercury. If Earth receives r watts per square meter of radiation, which of the following best approximates how much radiation Mercury receives?

    A) $0.148r$ watts / square meter
    B) $0.385r$ watts / square meter
    C) $2.60r$ watts / square meter
    D) $6.76r$ watts / square meter

8. The amount of gold ore removed from a mine is directly proportional to the amount of rock removed from the mine. If a mine removes 71,250,000 pounds of rock and finds 950 pounds of gold, how much additional rock must be removed in order to increase the total amount of gold to 1,000 pounds?

    A) 3,750,000 pounds
    B) 7,500,000 pounds
    C) 37,500,000 pounds
    D) 75,000,000 pounds

7. The number of books on a shelf varies inversely with the average thickness of each book. If there are 40 books on a shelf, and those books have an average thickness of $1\frac{3}{8}$ inches, how many books can fit on the same shelf if the books have an average thickness of $1\frac{2}{3}$ inches?

    A) 29
    B) 33
    C) 48
    D) 55

9. An engineer is studying the relationship between a car's engine size and its top speed. Car G has a 2000 cubic centimeter engine and Car H has a 1600 cubic centimeter engine. Car G has a top speed of g kilometers per hour. If top speed varies directly with engine size, what is the top speed of Car H in terms of g?

    A) $0.6g$
    B) $0.8g$
    C) $1.25g$
    D) $1.6g$

10. The interest rate on a loan from the World Bank varies inversely with the length of the loan. If a loan has a length of 60 months, its interest rate is 2.4%. What is the interest rate on a loan of 72 months?
    A) 1.8%
    B) 2.0%
    C) 2.6%
    D) 2.9%

13. According to the information in the previous two questions, an immigrant who has a stress level of 50 and a vocabulary of 196 words after 2 years would have what stress level and vocabulary after 4 years?
    A) Stress level 25; vocabulary of 392 words
    B) Stress level 25; vocabulary of 784 words
    C) Stress level 12.5; vocabulary of 392 words
    D) Stress level 12.5; vocabulary of 784 words

Question 13 relies on the information given in questions 11 and 12.

11. A recent study of immigrants from non-English-speaking countries found that the immigrants' English vocabularies varied directly with the square of the number of years spent in the U.S. For instance, one immigrant knew 80 English words after one year and 320 after two years. How many words would the same immigrant know after five years?
    A) 400
    B) 1,280
    C) 2,000
    D) 2,880

14. The unemployment rate in the United States has historically varied inversely with the rate of inflation. When the inflation rate was 2%, the unemployment rate was 7%. If the unemployment rate is 10.5% today, what is the inflation rate, as a percentage?

15. In an electrical circuit, the current is directly proportional to the voltage. If the current through a conductor is 7 amperes and the voltage across that conductor is 126 volts, what is the current, in amperes, through a conductor that has a voltage of 270 volts?

12. The same study from the previous question found that the number of years spent in America varied inversely with reported levels of stress (on a 100-point scale, with 100 being highest). For example, immigrants who had spent 2 years in America reported an average stress level of 35. How many total years did it take this group's stress level to fall to 10?
    A) 5
    B) 6
    C) 7
    D) 8

PRACTICE SET 3 (CALCULATOR)

16. A study of hair loss in men found that the amount of hair on a man's head varies inversely with how many years older than 30 he is. If a 38-year-old man has 120,000 hairs, how many hairs will that man have when he is 50?
   A) 48,000
   B) 91,000
   C) 158,000
   D) 300,000

17. Troy and Abed are running in a race. Troy finishes the race in 12 minutes and Abed finishes the race in 7 minutes and 30 seconds. If Troy is running at an average speed of 3 miles per hour and speed varies inversely with time, what is Abed's average speed for the race?
   A) 1.6 miles per hour
   B) 1.875 miles per hour
   C) 4.8 miles per hour
   D) 6.4 miles per hour

18. The size of the United States economy (by Gross Domestic Product, or GDP) has varied directly with the number of years elapsed since 1940. If the GDP was $9 trillion in 2000, during what year did the GDP first become higher than $2 trillion?
   A) 1950
   B) 1952
   C) 1954
   D) 1956

19. A recent study estimated that, during the 19th century, the human population in the American West varied inversely with the number of wolves. If the human population was a when the wolf population was b, what was the human population when there were 550,000 wolves (in terms of a and b)?
   A) $\dfrac{550,000}{ab}$
   B) $\dfrac{550,000a}{b}$
   C) $\dfrac{a}{550,000b}$
   D) $\dfrac{ab}{550,000}$

20. In sociology, a rule of thumb states that the number of people who end up knowing a piece of information varies directly with the square of the number of people who initially know it. A study tracked the spread of two facts in the same population over a year. The first fact spread from 25 to 7,500 people in this time; if 3,888 people knew the second fact at the end of the year, how many people initially knew that fact?
   A) 14
   B) 18
   C) 35
   D) 45

C2 education
be smarter

Questions 21 through 23 use the following information:

A recent study of insect populations in a park found the following correlations:

- The number of mosquitoes varied directly with the temperature
- The number of moths varied inversely with the humidity.
- The number of beetles varied inversely with the number of mosquitoes.
- The number of bees varied directly with the number of mosquitoes.

21. Based on these correlations, if the temperature was highest in July, which of these insect species most likely was at its lowest population during that month?
    A) mosquitoes
    B) moths
    C) beetles
    D) bees

22. Which of these insect species' populations does NOT vary directly or inversely with temperature?
    A) mosquitoes
    B) moths
    C) beetles
    D) bees

23. On March 7th, the average temperature was 55 degrees, the average humidity was 40%, and 150 mosquitoes and 33 beetles were observed in the park. The next day, 165 mosquitoes were observed in the park. Which statement is true regarding March 8th?
    A) 30 beetles were observed.
    B) 36 beetles were observed.
    C) The average temperature was 50 degrees.
    D) The average humidity was 44%.

24. The flow rate through a cylindrical pipe is directly proportional to the pipe's cross-sectional area. If Pipe A has a cross-section radius of 2 feet and Pipe B has a cross-section radius of 5 feet, then the flow rate through Pipe B is how many times that of Pipe A?

25. An agricultural study found that the length of time between applications of a certain fertilizer for a field varied inversely with the number of crops that are rotated through that field. On one field, 4 crops are rotated through, and fertilizer needs to be applied every 6 months. On another field, 3 crops are rotated through. If fertilizer is applied to both fields this month, how many months will it be until fertilizer is applied to both fields at the same time again?

BLUE MATH LESSON 3B: DIRECT AND INVERSE VARIATION
Race to the Finish

Directions: Answer each question below.

HOMEWORK SET (CALCULATOR)

1. Popsicle A melts in 260 seconds in 85° F air temperature. Popsicle B melts 39 seconds faster. If there is an inverse relationship between air temperature and melting time, what is the air temperature around Popsicle B?
   A)   90° F
   B)   95° F
   C)   98° F
   D)   100° F

2. A recent study found that the number of bacterial colonies in a sample varied directly with the length of time that the samples were exposed to air. Which of the following could describe the data collected at two points during the study?
   A)   40 colonies observed after 3 hours; 20 colonies observed after 6 hours
   B)   20 colonies observed after 3 hours; 80 colonies observed after 6 hours
   C)   40 colonies observed after 3 hours; 40 colonies observed after 6 hours
   D)   20 colonies observed after 3 hours; 40 colonies observed after 6 hours

3. Every year, a polling company takes a survey of college graduates to determine what their degrees are in. In 1960, 3.8% of students were philosophy majors, while 1.2% of students were engineering majors. In 2010, however, 6% of students were engineering majors, and just 0.76% of students were philosophy majors. The percentage of philosophy majors varies:
   A)   directly with the percentage of engineering majors.
   B)   directly with the square of the percentage of engineering majors.
   C)   inversely with the percentage of engineering majors.
   D)   inversely with the square of the percentage of engineering majors.

4. In astronomy, the length of a planet's orbit around its star varies directly with its distance from the star. Planet A is 12 million miles from its star and Planet B is 21 million miles from the same star. If Planet A has an orbit of length 80 days, what is the length of Planet B's orbit?
   A)   140 days
   B)   160 days
   C)   180 days
   D)   200 days

5. There is a direct relationship between the number of rose bushes planted in a garden and the average number of bees spotted in the garden each day. If an average of b bees are spotted on 27 rose bushes during the spring, and an average of $b + 5$ bees are spotted on 39 bushes during the summer, what is the value of b?

A) 11.25
B) 12
C) 15
D) 20

6. The number of people visiting a ski resort on a given day is inversely proportional to that day's high temperature (in degrees Celsius). If 1,222 people visited on a day in which the high temperature was 25° C, and the high temperature the next day is one degree higher, what effect will this have on the number of visitors to the ski resort?

A) There will be 49 fewer visitors.
B) There will be 47 fewer visitors.
C) There will be 47 more visitors.
D) There will be 49 more visitors.

7. The cost of a cheese pizza varies directly with its area. If a pizza with diameter 10 inches costs $10, what does a pizza with diameter 12 inches cost?

A) $8.33
B) $10.50
C) $12.00
D) $14.40

8. There is an inverse relationship between the age of a television (in years) and its cost. If a 7-year-old television costs x, how much does a 2-year-old television cost, in terms of x?

A) $\frac{2}{7}x$
B) $\frac{2}{7x}$
C) $\frac{7}{2}x$
D) $\frac{7}{2x}$

9. The amount of fur that a cat sheds varies directly with its weight. If Cat A sheds 3 times as much fur as Cat B, and Cat B weighs 6 pounds, how much does Cat A weigh?

A) 2 pounds
B) 9 pounds
C) 12 pounds
D) 18 pounds

10. A small city has three parks. One park measures 16 acres in area and has 60 parking spots. Another park measures 4.8 acres and has 18 parking spaces. A third measures 20 acres and has 75 parking spaces. Which of the following best describes the relationship between park area and number of parking spots for these parks?

A) Area varies directly with number of parking spaces.
B) Square root of area varies directly with number of parking spaces.
C) Area varies inversely with number of parking spaces.
D) Square root of area varies inversely with number of parking spaces.

11. A small-business owner is trying to determine the best way to pay off two loans. In the end, she decides that she will pay each loan off in an amount directly correlated with the interest rate on the loan. One loan has an interest rate of 7%, and the other has an interest rate of 11%. If she pays a total of $6,300 between the two loans, how much does she pay on the 7% loan?
   A) $1,750
   B) $2,450
   C) $3,150
   D) $3,850

12. The energy released by wood as it is burned varies directly with its mass. A block of wood has a mass of 12 grams, and when it burns, it releases enough energy to power a light bulb for 1 minute and 15 seconds. What is the mass of a block of wood that powers the same bulb for t seconds when burned?
   A) $\frac{4}{25}t$
   B) $\frac{25}{4}t$
   C) $\frac{4}{25t}$
   D) $\frac{25}{4t}$

13. There is an inverse relationship between c and the square of d. When c is 40, d is 30. What is c when d is 60?
   A) 10
   B) 20
   C) 45
   D) 80

14. In a video game, the player's score varies directly with the number of battles won and inversely with the number of battles lost by the equation $S = \frac{kW}{L}$, where S is the player's score, W is the number of the player's wins, and L is the number of the player's losses. Liz wins 27 battles and loses 8 battles; her score is 135 points. If Tina wins 60 battles and loses 12 battles, what is her score?
   A) 40 points
   B) 90 points
   C) 200 points
   D) 450 points

15. At the beginning of a party, there are 5 more children than adults. An hour later, there are 9 adults and 24 children. If the number of adults varies directly with the number of children, how many adults were there at the beginning of the party?
   A) 3
   B) 5
   C) 8
   D) 15

16. At the start of a picnic, a cooler contains 64 ounces of ice and 4 ounces of water. By the end of the picnic, the cooler contains an equal amount of ice and water. If the amount of ice varies indirectly with the amount of water, how much ice is in the cooler at the end of the picnic?
   A) 8 ounces
   B) 16 ounces
   C) 30 ounces
   D) 34 ounces

Questions 17 and 18 use the following information:

A study of home prices in American cities found that the average price of a home in a city varied directly with the square root of that city's population density.

17. New York City has a population density of 24,000 per square mile and an average home price of $500,000. If another city has an average home price of $125,000, what is its population density, in people per square mile?

18. City A has an average home price that is 3 times higher than that of City B, and City A has a population density of 9,000 people per square mile. How many more people live in an average square-mile section of City A, compared to a similar section of City B?

19. A survey of televisions made in the past year found that the refresh rate (in hertz, Hz) correlated directly with the diagonal screen size (in inches). If a TV has a 60-inch screen size and a refresh rate of x Hz, what is the screen size, in inches, of a TV with a refresh rate of $\frac{x}{2}$ Hz?

20. Coulomb's law states that, for any two electrical charges, the electrostatic force between them is inversely proportional to the square of the distance between them. If two point charges have an electrostatic force of 0.4 newtons when they are 0.03 meters apart, what is the force between them (in newtons) when the same charges are 0.02 meters apart?

BLUE MATH LESSON 4A: ADVANCED FOILING AND FACTORING
Getting Your Feet Wet

Directions: The problems below are intended as a short diagnostic exam.

1. $3(x + 2)(x^2 - 2x - 3) =$

$$9xyz^2 - 15xy^4z + 36xz$$

2. The above expression is equivalent to which of the following expressions?
    A) $3xz(3yz - 5y^3 + 12)$
    B) $-3xz(3yz + 5y^4 + 12)$
    C) $3xz(3yz - 5y^4 + 12xz)$
    D) $3xz(3yz - 5y^4 + 12)$

$$25x^2 - 10xz + z^2$$

3. The above expression is equivalent to which of the following expressions?
    A) $(5x - z)^2$
    B) $(5x + z)^2$
    C) $(5x - z)(5x + z)$
    D) $5x(5x - 2z) - z^2$

4. Factor $8x^2 + 26x + 18$

BLUE MATH LESSON 4A: ADVANCED FOILING AND FACTORING
Wading In

Directions: Read the explanation for each problem type mentioned below. Pay special attention to the methods and techniques used to solve the sample problems. Then, do the practice exercises that follow; use the appropriate method to solve each problem.

TOPIC OVERVIEW: FOILING

In Algebra, we're often asked to multiply two algebraic expressions that have two or more terms, such as $(3x - 4)(2x + 9)$. In cases like these, we FOIL:

$F \rightarrow$ Multiply the _F_irst terms
$O \rightarrow$ Multiply the _O_uter terms
$I \rightarrow$ Multiply the _I_nner terms
$L \rightarrow$ Multiply the _L_ast terms

Then, add up all of the resulting products by combining like terms whenever possible. So, if we were to multiply the above expression, we would get:

$$(3x - 4)(2x + 9)$$

$F \rightarrow$ Multiply the _F_irst terms : $3x \times 2x = 6x^2$
$O \rightarrow$ Multiply the _O_uter terms : $3x \times 9 = 27x$
$I \rightarrow$ Multiply the _I_nner terms : $-4 \times 2x = -8x$
$L \rightarrow$ Multiply the _L_ast terms : $-4 \times 9 = -36$

After combining like terms, we get our final answer:

$$6x^2 + 19x - 36.$$

Sometimes, we'll be asked to multiply two or more terms that are not binomials. In this case, the FOIL acronym no longer holds entirely true, but the pattern does. Multiply each term in the first polynomial by each term in the second polynomial, then add them altogether! Let's try an example:

SAMPLE PROBLEM 1: FOILING
$3(x + 2)(x^2 - 2x - 3) =$

The first issue with this problem is the 3 multiplied on the outside. Since multiplication is commutative, the order of multiplication does not matter. Thus, we can multiply the 3 into the $(x + 2)$ term now, or hold off and wait until the end. For now, we'll multiply first:

$$(3x + 6)(x^2 - 2x - 3) =$$

Now, we can begin to FOIL:

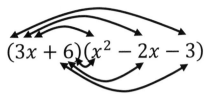

The arrows show each pair of terms that need to be multiplied. Since there are two terms in the first binomial and three terms in the second, we have a total of six multiplications to do before we can combine like terms:

$$3x \times x^2 = \mathbf{3x^3}$$
$$3x \times -2x = \mathbf{-6x^2}$$
$$3x \times -3 = \mathbf{-9x}$$
$$6 \times x^2 = \mathbf{6x^2}$$
$$6 \times -2x = \mathbf{-12x}$$
$$6 \times -3 = \mathbf{-18}$$

After combining like terms, we get $3x^3 - 21x - 18$

TOPIC OVERVIEW: FACTORING—GCFS

Before factoring anything, check to see if every term in the polynomial has a greatest common factor, or GCF. The GCF of a group of numbers or terms is the largest term that will go into each term evenly. The easiest way to find the GCF of a group of terms is to separate each term into its prime factors. Then, just see what each group of prime factors has in common. Let's try an example:

SAMPLE PROBLEM 2: FACTORING—GCFS

$$9xyz^2 - 15xy^4z + 36xz$$

The above expression is equivalent to which of the following expressions?
A) $3xz(3yz - 5y^3 + 12)$
B) $-3xz(3yz + 5y^4 + 12)$
C) $3xz(3yz - 5y^4 + 12xz)$
D) $3xz(3yz - 5y^4 + 12)$

Let's start by factoring each term into its prime factors:

$$9xyz^2 = 3 \times 3 \times x \times y \times z \times z$$
$$-15xy^4z = -1 \times 3 \times 5 \times x \times y \times y \times y \times y \times z$$
$$36xz = 2 \times 2 \times 3 \times 3 \times x \times z$$

Now that we've taken care of that, what do the prime factorings have in common? We'll bold everything that is in common to all three.

$$9xyz^2 = \mathbf{3} \times 3 \times \boldsymbol{x} \times y \times \boldsymbol{z} \times z$$
$$-15xy^4z = -1 \times \mathbf{3} \times 5 \times \boldsymbol{x} \times y \times y \times y \times y \times \boldsymbol{z}$$
$$36xz = 2 \times 2 \times \mathbf{3} \times 3 \times \boldsymbol{x} \times \boldsymbol{z}$$

So, the GCF is $3xz$. We can pull $3xz$ out from each term, and we'll have the non-bolded factors left:

$$9xyz^2 - 15xy^4z + 36xz = 3xz(3yz - 5y^4 + 12)$$

Thus, our answer is **D**.

TOPIC OVERVIEW: FACTORING—SPECIAL PRODUCTS

Factoring polynomials is like FOILing in reverse: We are given the end product and have to figure out which things were multiplied to get our result. There are a few common binomials and trinomials that show up frequently on the SAT, so be sure to memorize these patterns:

$$(a + b)(a - b) = a^2 - b^2$$
$$(a + b)^2 = a^2 + 2ab + b^2$$
$$(a - b)^2 = a^2 - 2ab + b^2$$
$$(a + b)(a^2 - ab + b^2) = a^3 + b^3$$
$$(a - b)(a^2 + ab + b^2) = a^3 - b^3$$

Keep in mind that on the SAT the a's and b's above won't necessarily be a's and b's...they could be $2x$'s or $-3y's$, instead. Focus on identifying the pattern.

SAMPLE PROBLEM 3: FACTORING —SPECIAL PRODUCTS

$$25x^2 - 10xz + z^2$$

The above expression is equivalent to which of the following expressions?
A) $(5x - z)^2$
B) $(5x + z)^2$
C) $(5x - z)(5x + z)$
D) $5x(5x - 2z) - z^2$

The answer is **A**. In this case, we used the pattern:

$$(a - b)^2 = a^2 - 2ab + b^2 \text{ with } a = 5x \text{ and } b = z.$$

TOPIC OVERVIEW: FACTORING QUADRATICS

Factoring quadratics of the form $ax^2 + bx + c$ can be tricky. When $a = 1$, use the guess-and-check method taught in most Algebra I classes. However, if $a \neq 1$, we should use a method of factoring known as Factoring by Grouping. We will explain how to do this with a sample problem:

SAMPLE PROBLEM 4: FACTORING QUADRATICS

Factor $8x^2 + 26x + 18$

Here, the guess-and-check method would take a long time—there are multiple factors of both the first and last numbers. So we'll factor by grouping:

(1) Find the product of the first and last numbers, and list all the factors of that product. We're looking for numbers whose sum or difference is the number in the middle (in this case, 26)

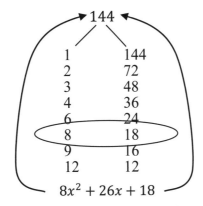

Because $8 + 18 = 26$, those are the factors we want.

(2) Rewrite the middle term as the sum (or difference) of the factors found in step (1):

$$8x^2 + \mathbf{26x} + 18 = 8x^2 + \mathbf{8x} + \mathbf{18x} + 18$$

(3) Group the first and last two terms, and then factor each set of parentheses:

$$8x^2 + 8x + 18x + 18 = (8x^2 + 8x) + (18x + 18)$$

$$(8x^2 + 8x) + (18x + 18) = 8x(x + 1) + 18(x + 1)$$

It's important that the two expressions in the parentheses match each other—they do in this case. We're on the last step!

(4) Factor the expression—one term will be whatever is in the parentheses, and the other will be the terms that are outside the parentheses:

$$\mathbf{8x}(x + 1) + \mathbf{18}(x + 1) = (8x + 18)(x + 1)$$

(5) Just to make sure, check the factoring before moving on:

$$(8x + 18)(x + 1) = 8x^2 + 8x + 18x + 18 = 8x^2 + 26x + 18$$

WRAP-UP

The SAT will very rarely ask us to FOIL or Factor an algebraic expression. For that reason, if something that can be FOILed or Factored ever shows up, that should be the first step. Always be on the lookout for ways to FOIL or factor out an expression and the work will become a lot simpler.

BLUE MATH LESSON 4A: ADVANCED FOILING AND FACTORING
Learning to Swim

Directions: Answer each question below.

PRACTICE SET 1 (NO CALCULATOR)

1. $(x + 4)(x - 3) =$

2. $(2x - 1)(3x - 1) =$

3. $(3y + z)(2z + 2y) =$

4. Factor $x^2 - 16$.

5. Factor $3x^2 - 11x + 6$.

BLUE MATH LESSON 4A: ADVANCED FOILING AND FACTORING
Diving into the Deep End

Directions: Answer each question below.

PRACTICE SET 2 (NO CALCULATOR)

6. $(x + 5)^2 =$
    A) $x^2 + 5x + 10$
    B) $x^2 + 5x + 25$
    C) $x^2 + 10x + 10$
    D) $x^2 + 10x + 25$

10. Factor $x^2 - 16x + 64$.
    A) $(x - 8)^2$
    B) $(x - 16)(x + 4)$
    C) $(x + 8)^2$
    D) $(x + 16)(x + 4)$

7. $(x + 7)(x - 4) =$
    A) $x^2 - 11x - 28$
    B) $x^2 - 3x - 28$
    C) $x^2 + 3x - 28$
    D) $x^2 + 11x - 28$

11. Factor $x^4 - 25$.
    A) $(x - 5)^4$
    B) $(x^2 - 5)^2$
    C) $(x - 5)^2(x + 5)^2$
    D) $(x^2 - 5)(x^2 + 5)$

8. $(5x + 2)(2x - 5) =$
    A) $10x^2 - 21x - 10$
    B) $10x^2 - 10$
    C) $10x^2 + 10$
    D) $10x^2 + 29x - 10$

12. What are the factors of $x^2 - 2$?
    A) $\left(x - \sqrt{2}\right)$ and $\left(x + \sqrt{2}\right)$
    B) $\left(x - \sqrt{2}\right)$ and $(x - 2)$
    C) $(x - 2)$ and $(x + 2)$
    D) $\left(x - \sqrt{2}\right)$ and $\left(x - \sqrt{2}\right)$

9. $(x + 6)(x - 6)(x + 1)(x - 1) =$
    A) $x^2 - 35x + 36$
    B) $x^4 - 37x + 36$
    C) $x^4 - 35x^2 + 36$
    D) $x^4 - 37x^2 + 36$

13. If one of the factors of $(x - 8)(x + 7) + 26$ is written as $(x + h)$, what is the smallest possible value for h?
    A) -7
    B) -6
    C) -5
    D) -4

14. If all of the factors of $3x^2 - 13x - 10$ are written as $(x + h)$, what is the larger of the two possible values for h?

15. $x^2 - qx + 16$ is equal to $(x - c)^2$. What is q?

PRACTICE SET 3 (NO CALCULATOR)

16. $(x + 4)(3x - 2) =$
    A) $3x^2 - 2x - 8$
    B) $3x^2 + 2x - 8$
    C) $3x^2 + 10x - 8$
    D) $3x^2 + 14x - 8$

17. $(3x - 2y)^2 =$
    A) $9x^2 - 12xy - 4y^2$
    B) $9x^2 - 12xy + 4y^2$
    C) $9x^2 + 4y^2$
    D) $9x^2 - 4y^2$

18. $(3x - y)(3x + y)(x - 3y)(x + 3y) =$
    A) $9x^4 - 9y^4$
    B) $9x^4 - 81x^4 - y^2 + 9y^4$
    C) $9x^4 - 80x^2y^2 + 9y^4$
    D) $9x^4 - 82x^2y^2 + 9y^4$

19. Factor $-x^2 + 10x - 21$.
    A) $(-x - 7)(x - 3)$
    B) $(-x - 7)(x + 3)$
    C) $(-x + 7)(x - 3)$
    D) $(-x + 7)(x + 3)$

20. What are the factors of $4x^2 - 17x - 15$?
    A) $(4x + 3)$ and $(x + 5)$
    B) $(4x + 3)$ and $(x - 5)$
    C) $(4x - 3)$ and $(x + 5)$
    D) $(4x - 3)$ and $(x - 5)$

21. How many distinct binomial factors are there for the expression $(x^2 - 2)(x^2 + 4x + 4)$?
    A) 1
    B) 2
    C) 3
    D) 4

22. If one of the factors of $(x + 6)(x - 1) + 12$ is written as $(x - h)$, what is the largest possible value for h?
    A) -6
    B) -3
    C) -2
    D) 1

23. If $(2x - 3d)(3x - 2) = 6x^2 + 23x - 18$ for all real values of x, what is the value of d?
    A) $-\frac{9}{2}$
    B) -3
    C) $\frac{2}{3}$
    D) 3

24. If $(x + 7)(x - 8) = ax^2 - bx - c$ for all values of x, what is the value of b?

25. If $(2x + s)(4x - 7) = 8x^2 + 2x - t$ for all values of x, what is the value of s?

BLUE MATH LESSON 4A: ADVANCED FOILING AND FACTORING
Race to the Finish

Directions: Answer each question below.

HOMEWORK SET (NO CALCULATOR)

1. $(x - 3)(x + 3) =$
   A) $x^2 - 6x - 9$
   B) $x^2 + 6x - 9$
   C) $x^2 - 9$
   D) $x^2 + 9$

2. $(x + c)(x + 8) =$
   A) $x^2 + (8 + c)x + 8c$
   B) $x^2 + (8 + c)x + 8$
   C) $x^2 + 8cx + 8c$
   D) $x^2 + 8cx + 8$

3. $(x + d)(2x - d) =$
   A) $2x^2 - dx - d^2$
   B) $2x^2 + dx - d$
   C) $2x^2 + dx - d^2$
   D) $2x^2 + 2dx - d^2$

4. Factor $x^2 + 3x - 4$.
   A) $(x - 4)(x - 1)$
   B) $(x - 4)(x + 1)$
   C) $(x + 4)(x - 1)$
   D) $(x + 4)(x + 1)$

5. Factor $x^2 - 8x + 12$.
   A) $(x - 6)(x - 2)$
   B) $(x - 4)(x - 3)$
   C) $(x + 4)(x + 3)$
   D) $(x + 6)(x + 2)$

6. Factor $4x^2 + 4xy + y^2$.
   A) $(x + 2y)^2$
   B) $(2x + y)^2$
   C) $(2x - y)^2$
   D) $(4x + y)(x + y)$

7. Factor $-5x^2 + 8xy - 3y^2$.
   A) $(5x + y)(-x + 3y)$
   B) $(5x - y)(-x + 3y)$
   C) $(5x + 3y)(-x + y)$
   D) $(5x - 3y)(-x + y)$

8. Factor $6x^2 + 20x + 14$.
   A) $(3x + 2)(2x + 7)$
   B) $(6x + 2)(x + 7)$
   C) $(3x + 7)(2x + 2)$
   D) $(6x + 7)(x + 2)$

9. What are all of the distinct factors of
   $x^2 - 12x + 36$?
   A) $(x - 9)$ and $(x - 4)$
   B) $(x - 12)$ and $(x - 3)$
   C) $(x + 6)$ only
   D) $(x - 6)$ only

10. How many distinct binomial factors are there for
    the expression $(x^2 - 6x + 9)(x - 3)$?
    A) 1
    B) 2
    C) 3
    D) 4

11. How many distinct binomial factors are there for
    the expression $(x^2 + 3x - 18)(x^2 - 4x + 3)$?
    A) 1
    B) 2
    C) 3
    D) 4

12. What are the factors of $(x - 3)(2x + 5) + 5$?
    A) $(x + 2)$ and $(2x - 5)$
    B) $(x + 2)$ and $(x - 5)$
    C) $(x - 3)$ and $(2x + 10)$
    D) $(x + 2)$ and $(2x + 5)$

13. If the factors of $6x^2 + px - 5$ are $(2x - 1)$ and
    $(3x + 5)$, what is p?
    A) −7
    B) −1
    C) 2
    D) 7

14. A rectangular yard is $x + 4$ meters long and
    $x - 5$ meters wide. What is the area of the yard,
    in terms of x?
    A) $(x^2 - 9x - 20)$ square meters
    B) $(x^2 - x - 20)$ square meters
    C) $(x^2 - x + 20)$ square meters
    D) $(x^2 + x - 20)$ square meters

15. A square block is placed on a rectangular sheet
    of paper. The paper's width is 6 inches greater
    than the block's side length; the paper's length is
    7 inches greater than the block's side length. If
    the block has side length s, what is the area of
    the sheet of paper, in terms of s?
    A) $13s$ square inches
    B) $42s^2$ square inches
    C) $s^2 + 13s + 42$ square inches
    D) $s^2 + 42$ square inches

16. There are $p + 3$ people working in an office. If
    each of the people contributes $2p - 7$ dollars to
    fund a holiday party, how much money is
    contributed in all?
    A) $\$(p^2 - 4p - 21)$
    B) $\$(p^2 - p - 21)$
    C) $\$(2p^2 - 4p - 21)$
    D) $\$(2p^2 - p - 21)$

17. If $(x - 4)(2x + 9) = ax^2 + bx - c$ for all values of x, what is the value of $a + b$?

19. If the factors of $15x^2 + rx - 4$ are $(5x + 4)$ and $(3x - 1)$ for all values of x, what is the value of r?

18. If $(4x - 2)(-3x + 7) = ax^2 + bx - c$ for all values of x, what is the value of $b - a$?

20. A class reads an entire short story out loud. Each of the $(v - 6)$ students in the class reads $(v + 10)$ paragraphs. If there are 161 total paragraphs in the story, how many students are in the class?

BLUE MATH LESSON 4B: SOLVING QUADRATICS
Getting Your Feet Wet

Directions: The problems below are intended as a short diagnostic exam.

1. If $x^2 - 5x + 6 = 0$, then $x =$

2. If $3x^2 - 6x + 2 = 0$, then $x =$

3. If $x^2 - 4x - 8 = 0$, then $x =$

BLUE MATH LESSON 4B: SOLVING QUADRATICS
Wading In

Directions: Read the explanation for each problem type mentioned below. Pay special attention to the methods and techniques used to solve the sample problems. Then, do the practice exercises that follow; use the appropriate method to solve each problem.

TOPIC OVERVIEW: SOLVING QUADRATIC FUNCTIONS

A quadratic function is a polynomial of the form $f(x) = ax^2 + bx + c$, where $a \neq 0$. The graph of a quadratic function will always appear to be a parabola, as shown below:

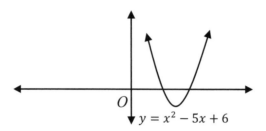

$$y = x^2 - 5x + 6$$

The places where the parabola intersects the x-axis are known as roots, zeros, or solutions of the quadratic. So, by that logic, one of the easiest ways to find the solutions to a quadratic function is to simply graph the function in a graphing calculator and use the root or solution command to find them. However, many of the questions on the SAT involving finding the solutions of a quadratic are not quite so easy or do not allow the use of a calculator. So, let's go through a few of the ways that these functions can be solved without a calculator.

SAMPLE PROBLEM 1: SOLVING QUADRATICS BY FACTORING
If $x^2 - 5x + 6 = 0$, then $x =$

Sometimes, we'll be able to solve a quadratic by factoring as we did in the previous lesson. In this case, our function turns into:

$$x^2 - 5x + 6 = 0$$
$$(x - 2)(x - 3) = 0$$
$$x - 2 = 0 \qquad x - 3 = 0$$
$$x = 2 \qquad\qquad x = 3$$

So, the solutions to our quadratic are 2 and 3, which we can verify by looking at the graph of the function above. Most quadratic functions will have two solutions, though a quadratic can never have more than two. Observe the next two quadratics: These have zero and one solution, respectively.

A quadratic with zero solutions: A quadratic with one solution:

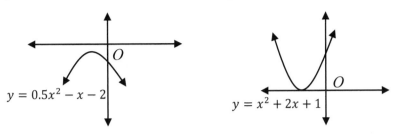

$y = 0.5x^2 - x - 2$ $y = x^2 + 2x + 1$

TOPIC OVERVIEW: SOLVING QUADRATICS BY THE QUADRATIC FORMULA

Unfortunately, not every quadratic function that shows up on the SAT will be factorable. For these unfactorable functions, we have two options: the quadratic formula and completing the square. We'll review the quadratic formula first. The solutions to a quadratic function of the format $f(x) = ax^2 + bx + c$ can be found by:

$$x = \frac{-b \pm \sqrt{b^2 - 4ac}}{2a}$$

SAMPLE PROBLEM 2: SOLVING QUADRATICS BY THE QUADRATIC FORMULA

If $3x^2 - 6x + 2 = 0$, then $x =$

Since the above function isn't factorable, let's use the quadratic formula:

$$x = \frac{-(-6) \pm \sqrt{(-6)^2 - 4(3)(2)}}{2(3)}$$

$$x = \frac{6 \pm \sqrt{36 - 24}}{6} = \frac{6 \pm \sqrt{12}}{6} = \frac{6 \pm 2\sqrt{3}}{6}$$

So, $x = \frac{3 + \sqrt{3}}{3}$ and $x = \frac{3 - \sqrt{3}}{3}$

TOPIC OVERVIEW: SOLVING QUADRATICS BY COMPLETING THE SQUARE

Another method for solving quadratics is known as "Completing the Square". To complete the square, rearrange the quadratic into an equation that's easy to solve by taking a square root. Ideally, it will involve turning an equation that looks like this:

$$x^2 - 4x - 8 = 0$$

into something that looks like this:

$$(x - 2)^2 = 12$$

We'll go through the steps for this below.

SAMPLE PROBLEM 3: SOLVING QUADRATICS BY COMPLETING THE SQUARE

If $x^2 - 4x - 8 = 0$, then $x =$

To start completing the square, first move the c term to the other side of the equation.

$$x^2 - 4x = 8$$

Next, take the b term, divide it by two, and square it. Add this value to both sides.

$$b = -4$$
$$\left(\frac{b}{2}\right)^2 = 4$$

So, after adding this term to both sides, we get:

$$x^2 - 4x + 4 = 8 + 4$$
$$x^2 - 4x + 4 = 12$$

Now, our expression on the left hand side is something that is easily factorable into the square of a binomial:

$$x^2 - 4x + 4 = 12$$
$$(x - 2)^2 = 12$$

At this point, we can take the square root of both sides to solve the equation.

$$(x - 2)^2 = 12$$
$$\sqrt{(x - 2)^2} = \pm\sqrt{12}$$
$$x - 2 = \pm 2\sqrt{3}$$
$$x = 2 \pm 2\sqrt{3}$$

We would have gotten the same answer by using the quadratic formula, but this method is faster for some functions. Solving quadratic equations by completing the square is a little bit more difficult when $a \neq 1$, but we'll go through one more example to reiterate the method. This question is the same as Sample Problem 2, so we'll be able to see the advantages and disadvantages of each method more clearly.

SAMPLE PROBLEM 4: SOLVING QUADRATICS BY COMPLETING THE SQUARE

If $3x^2 - 6x + 2 = 0$, then $x =$

$$3x^2 - 6x + 2 = 0$$
$$3x^2 - 6x = -2$$

Let's factor out the 3 from the left side and make our life a little easier:

$$3(x^2 - 2x) = -2$$
$$x^2 - 2x = -\frac{2}{3}$$

Now, we can complete the square as usual:

$$x^2 - 2x + 1 = -\frac{2}{3} + 1$$
$$x^2 - 2x + 1 = \frac{1}{3}$$
$$(x - 1)^2 = \frac{1}{3}$$
$$\sqrt{(x - 1)^2} = \pm\sqrt{\frac{1}{3}}$$
$$x - 1 = \pm\frac{\sqrt{3}}{3}$$
$$x = 1 \pm \frac{\sqrt{3}}{3}$$

WRAP-UP

When the SAT presents us with a quadratic function to solve, we should always attempt it via whichever method is easiest. Graphing will usually be the quickest way to find the solutions or roots, but calculators may not be available for every problem (the SAT has two math sections and one of them does not allow calculator use). If the quadratic is factorable, try to start there; otherwise, proceed with either the quadratic formula or completing the square. As always, practicing each method helps determine which method works best for each problem, so let's do some practice.

BLUE MATH LESSON 4B: SOLVING QUADRATICS
Learning to Swim

Directions: Answer each question below.

PRACTICE SET 1 (NO CALCULATOR)

1. If $m(m + 5) = 6$, what is the least possible value of m?

2. If $(n + 2)^2 = 9n$, what is the product of the two possible values of n?

3. What is the only possible value of p if $p^2 + 8p + 7 = 0$ and $3p^2 - p = 4$?

4. If $5p^2 + 7p - 10 = 3p^2 + 4p - 10$ and $p < 0$, what is p?

5. If $9z^2 + 24z + d = (3z + 4)(3z - 4)$ for all values of z, what is d in terms of z?

BLUE MATH LESSON 4B: SOLVING QUADRATICS
Diving into the Deep End

Directions: Answer each question below.

PRACTICE SET 2 (NO CALCULATOR)

6. Which of the following equations has the solutions $\frac{3}{4}$ and $-\frac{4}{3}$?
   A) $12y^2 + 7y - 12 = 0$
   B) $12y^2 - 7y + 12 = 0$
   C) $12y^2 - 12 = 0$
   D) $12y^2 + 12y - 7 = 0$

7. Which of the following equations has the solutions $\sqrt{2}$ and $3\sqrt{2}$?
   A) $z^2 + 4\sqrt{2}z + 6 = 0$
   B) $z^2 - 2\sqrt{2}z - 6 = 0$
   C) $z^2 + 2\sqrt{2}z + 3 = 0$
   D) $z^2 - 4\sqrt{2}z + 6 = 0$

8. If $4t^2 - t + 3 = 2(t + 5)$, t can be equal to which of the following?
   A) $-\frac{1}{4}$
   B) $\frac{1}{2}$
   C) 1
   D) $\frac{7}{4}$

9. If $7z^2 + 5z = z(6z - 24)$, what is the product of all the solutions for z?
   A) -5
   B) 0
   C) 12
   D) 29

10. If $6g^2 - 10g + 3 = -4g^2 + 7g$, which of the following integers is greater than one solution for g but less than the other solution for g?
    A) -1
    B) 0
    C) 1
    D) 2

11. If $4k^2 + 11k - 3 = 0$, what is the sum of all the solutions for k?
    A) -3.25
    B) -2.75
    C) 2.75
    D) 3.25

12. Given that $p^2 - 3p - 40 = 0$ and $6q^2 + 5q - 4 = 0$, which of the following is NOT a possible value of the product pq?
    A) -5
    B) $-\frac{5}{2}$
    C) $\frac{20}{3}$
    D) 4

13. Which choice lists all of the real solutions to the equation $x^2 - 8x + 11 = 0$?
    - A) $-4 - \sqrt{5}$ and $-4 + \sqrt{5}$
    - B) $-4 - \sqrt{5}$ and $4 - \sqrt{5}$
    - C) $-4 + \sqrt{5}$ and $4 + \sqrt{5}$
    - D) $4 - \sqrt{5}$ and $4 + \sqrt{5}$

14. What is the product of the two solutions to the equation $z^2 + 12z + 6 = 0$?

15. If $3k^2 - 19k + 8 = 0$, what is the sum of all the real solutions for k?

PRACTICE SET 3 (NO CALCULATOR)

16. Which of the following equations has the solutions -2 and $\frac{1}{2}$?
    - A) $2x^2 - 3x - 2 = 0$
    - B) $2x^2 + 3x - 2 = 0$
    - C) $2x^2 + 5x - 2 = 0$
    - D) $2x^2 + 2 = 0$

17. If $s + 18 = s^2 + 12$, what are all the possible values of s?
    - A) -3 and -2
    - B) -3 and 2
    - C) -2 and 3
    - D) 2 and 3

18. If $2(2x^2 + x) = 3x^2 + 8x - 9$, what are all the possible values of x?
    - A) -3 and 3
    - B) -3 and 1
    - C) 1 and 3
    - D) 3 only

19. Which choice lists all of the real solutions to the equation $v^2 + 6v + 2 = 0$?
    - A) $-3 - \sqrt{7}$ and $-3 + \sqrt{7}$
    - B) $-3 - \sqrt{7}$ and $3 - \sqrt{7}$
    - C) $-3 + \sqrt{7}$ and $3 + \sqrt{7}$
    - D) $3 - \sqrt{7}$ and $3 + \sqrt{7}$

20. Which of the following is one of the solutions to the equation $y^2 - 6y - 9 = 0$?
    A) -3
    B) $-3 + 3\sqrt{2}$
    C) $3 - 3\sqrt{2}$
    D) 3

23. What are the solutions to the equation $x^2 + 4x + 8 = 0$?
    A) -4 and -2
    B) $-2 - 2i$ and $-2 + 2i$
    C) $-2 - 2i$ and $2 - 2i$
    D) $2 - 2i$ and $2 + 2i$

21. If $c^2 - 4c + 4 = 0$ and $d^2 - 18d + 81 = 0$, which of the following could be equal to the product cd?
    A) -36
    B) -18
    C) 9
    D) 18

24. Given that $x^2 + 8x = -15$ and $y^2 + 10y = 24$, what is the greatest possible value for the expression $x - y$?

25. When $d^2 - 9d = -2$, what is the product of the two values of d?

22. What is the product of the two solutions to the equation $z^2 + 4z + 2 = 0$?
    A) -2
    B) $\sqrt{2}$
    C) 2
    D) 4

BLUE MATH LESSON 4B: SOLVING QUADRATICS
Race to the Finish

Directions: Answer each question below.

HOMEWORK SET (NO CALCULATOR)

1. Which of the following equations has the solutions 6 and –6?
    A) $w^2 - 12w - 36 = 0$
    B) $w^2 - 36 = 0$
    C) $w^2 + 12w - 36 = 0$
    D) $w^2 - 12w + 36 = 0$

2. If $q^2 + 6q + 8 = 2q^2 + 3q + 10$, which of the following is a solution for q?
    A) –3
    B) –2
    C) 1
    D) 6

3. The equation $r^2 + 5r + 4 = 3r^2 + 9r - 12$ is true if r is equal to which of the following?
    A) –4
    B) –1
    C) 1
    D) 4

4. If $16v - 5 = 8v^2 + 2v + 1$, which of the following fractions is greater than one solution for v but less than the other solution for v?
    A) $-\frac{3}{4}$
    B) $-\frac{1}{2}$
    C) $\frac{7}{8}$
    D) $\frac{3}{2}$

5. If $3y^2 + 5y + 2 = 0$, what is the sum of all of the solutions for y?
    A) $-\frac{5}{3}$
    B) $-\frac{1}{3}$
    C) $\frac{1}{3}$
    D) $\frac{5}{3}$

6. If $6d^2 - d + 5 = 4d(d - 2)$, d can be equal to which of the following?
    A) $-\frac{5}{2}$
    B) $-\frac{2}{5}$
    C) 1
    D) $\frac{5}{2}$

7. If $a^2 + 10a + 5 = 4a^2 - 6a - 7$, which of the following is a solution for a?
    A) –6
    B) –3
    C) 3
    D) 6

8. The equation $b^2 - 5b + 11 = 7b - 16$ is true if b is equal to which of the following?
    A) 1
    B) 5
    C) 9
    D) 11

9. If $2c^2 - 6 = c^2 + 10$, what are all the possible values of c?
   A) −4 and 4
   B) −4 and 2
   C) −4 only
   D) 4 only

10. If $3(h^2 - 2h - 3) = h^2 + 3h + 9$, what are all the possible values of h?
   A) $-\frac{3}{2}$ and −6
   B) $-\frac{3}{2}$ and 6
   C) $-\frac{2}{3}$ and −6
   D) $-\frac{2}{3}$ and 6

11. If $6n^2 - 4n = 3(3n - 2)$, what is the product of all the solutions for n?
   A) $\frac{2}{3}$
   B) 1
   C) $\frac{3}{2}$
   D) $\frac{13}{2}$

12. If $a^2 + 4a = -3$ and $b^2 - 3b = 10$, which of the following is NOT a possible value of $a + b$?
   A) −3
   B) −1
   C) 2
   D) 4

13. Given that $2m^2 + m = 15$ and $9n^2 - 6n = -1$, which of the following is the highest possible sum of m and n?
   A) $\frac{3}{2}$
   B) $\frac{13}{6}$
   C) $\frac{8}{3}$
   D) $\frac{17}{6}$

14. If $5r^2 + 3r - 2 = 0$ and $s^2 - 7s + 12 = 0$, how many distinct values of $r + s$ are there?
   A) 1
   B) 2
   C) 3
   D) 4

15. If $t^2 - t = 6$ and $u^2 + 2u = 24$, how many distinct values are there for the product tu?
   A) 1
   B) 2
   C) 3
   D) 4

16. What are the solutions to the equation $y^2 - 6y + 10 = 0$?
   A) $-3 - i$ and $-3 + i$
   B) $-3 - i$ and $-3 + 2i$
   C) $3 - i$ and $3 + 2i$
   D) $3 - i$ and $3 + i$

C2 education be smarter

17. If $a^2 - 6(a + 5) + 38 = 0$, what is the greatest possible value of a?

19. Given that $c^2 + 4c + 4 = 3c^2 - 12c + 36$, what is the greatest possible value of c?

18. If $b^2 + 6b = 16$, what is a possible value of value of $(b + 3)^2$?

20. If $5m^2 - 12m - 9 = 0$ and $2n^2 + 17n - 30 = 0$, what is the greatest possible product mn?

BLUE MATH LESSON 5A: SOLVING EQUATIONS WITH POWERS AND ROOTS
Getting Your Feet Wet

Directions: The problems below are intended as a short diagnostic exam.

1. If $\frac{\sqrt{x-3}}{3} - 2 = 4$, then $x =$
   A) 39
   B) 199
   C) 327
   D) 903

2. If $(3x - 3)^2 = 9$, then $x =$

BLUE MATH LESSON 5A: SOLVING EQUATIONS WITH POWERS AND ROOTS
Wading In

Directions: Read the explanation for each problem type mentioned below. Pay special attention to the methods and techniques used to solve the sample problems. Then, do the practice exercises that follow; use the appropriate method to solve each problem.

TOPIC OVERVIEW: SOLVING EQUATIONS WITH POWERS AND ROOTS

When solving equations, we should always do the opposite of what was being done to eliminate something troublesome: The equation $x + 4 = 18$ can be solved by the opposite of adding (subtracting) while the equation $3x = 21$ can be solved by the opposite of multiplying (dividing). Thus, if given an equation involving a square, cube, or higher-order root, the next step will involve raising both sides of the equation to that power to simplify things. Let's look at a few sample problems.

SAMPLE PROBLEM 1: SOLVING EQUATIONS BY POWERS

If $\frac{\sqrt{x-3}}{3} - 2 = 4$, then $x =$

    A) 39
    B) 199
    C) 327
    D) 903

Generally, when solving an equation that involves multiple steps (adding, multiplying, applying powers) do those steps in an order that's backwards from PEMDAS. So, here, we should add first:

$$\frac{\sqrt{x-3}}{3} - 2 = 4$$
$$\frac{\sqrt{x-3}}{3} = 6$$

Next, we should multiply both sides of the equation by 3.

$$\frac{\sqrt{x-3}}{3} = 6$$
$$\sqrt{x-3} = 18$$

Next, we can square both sides of the equation:

$$\sqrt{x-3} = 18$$
$$x - 3 = 324$$
$$x = 327$$

So, our answer is **C**.

TOPIC OVERVIEW: SOLVING EQUATIONS BY ROOTS

Solving equations by using roots is generally not much different from using powers to solve equations. The only real difference is when we take an even-powered root, we have to account for the positive and negative solutions. However, when we take an odd-numbered root, we do not have to worry about getting two different solutions. We'll go through a sample problem how to obtain both answers:

SAMPLE PROBLEM 2: SOLVING EQUATIONS BY ROOTS

If $(3x - 3)^2 = 9$, then $x =$

Start off the problem by taking the square root of both sides to get rid of the exponent:

$$(3x - 3)^2 = 9$$
$$\sqrt{(3x - 3)^2} = \pm\sqrt{9}$$
$$3x - 3 = \pm 3$$
$$3x = 3 \pm 3$$
$$3x = 6 \qquad 3x = 0$$
$$x = 2 \qquad x = 0$$

Notice that we get two different answers because we took an even-numbered root. Always check the answers by plugging them back into the original equation; sometimes, one or more of them will be extraneous solutions.

WRAP-UP

When the SAT presents us with an equation to solve, always attempt to solve it in reverse-PEMDAS order. Remember that PEMDAS stands for:

Parentheses
Exponents
Multiplying and **D**ividing (together, from left to right)
Adding and **S**ubtracting (together, from left to right)

Otherwise, always remember to plug the answers back into the original equation to check for correctness and to check for extraneous solutions. Good luck on these next problems.

BLUE MATH LESSON 5A: SOLVING EQUATIONS WITH POWERS AND ROOTS
Learning to Swim

Directions: Answer each question below.

PRACTICE SET 1 (NO CALCULATOR)

1. If $2(y - 5)^4 = 1250$, then y could equal

Questions 2 and 3 use the following information.

The electric power (P, in watts) in a circuit is equal to the square of that circuit's voltage (V, in volts) divided by its resistance (R, in ohms).

2. If a circuit has a resistance of 12 ohms and produces 48 watts of power, what is the voltage of that circuit?

3. Circuits A and B both have a resistance of 3 ohms; Circuit A's voltage is equal to k volts, where k is positive, while Circuit B's voltage is equal to $(k + 3)$ volts. If Circuit A's power is 300 watts, what is Circuit B's power?

4. If $x^2 - 18x + 81 = 121$ and $4x^2 + 4xy + y^2 = 0$, then y could equal

5. If $\frac{x^5}{27} = 8x^2$ and $x \neq 0$, what is x?

BLUE MATH LESSON 5A: SOLVING EQUATIONS WITH POWERS AND ROOTS
Diving into the Deep End

Directions: Answer each question below.

PRACTICE SET 2 (NO CALCULATOR)

6. What are all the possible values of a when $\frac{(a+1)^3}{7} = -49$?
   A) –6 and 8
   B) 6 and –8
   C) 6 only
   D) –8 only

7. If $(b-1)^4 = 16$, b could equal
   A) –1 or 3
   B) –1 or –3
   C) 3 or –3
   D) 1 only

Questions 8 through 10 refer to the following information and formula.

The kinetic energy (KE, in joules) of an object is related to the object's mass (in kilograms) and velocity (v, in meters per second) according to this formula: $KE = \frac{1}{2}mv^2$.

8. If an object has a kinetic energy of 200,000 joules when traveling at 20 meters per second, what is its kinetic energy when traveling at half that speed?
   A) 50,000 joules
   B) 100,000 joules
   C) 200,000 joules
   D) 400,000 joules

9. Two objects have the same kinetic energy. Object 1 is traveling at c meters per second, while Object 2 is traveling at $3c$ meters per second. Which statement is true?
   A) Object 1's mass is equal to 3 times Object 2's mass.
   B) Object 1's mass is equal to 9 times Object 2's mass.
   C) Object 2's mass is equal to 3 times Object 1's mass.
   D) Object 2's mass is equal to 9 times Object 1's mass.

10. What is the positive velocity of an object that has a mass of 8 kilograms and a kinetic energy of 256 joules?
    A) $2\sqrt{2}$ m/s
    B) $4\sqrt{2}$ m/s
    C) 8 m/s
    D) 16 m/s

11. If $\frac{108}{(x-4)^3} = 4$, what is one possible value for x?
    A) –3
    B) 1
    C) 3
    D) 7

C2 education
be smarter

12. If $(2y - 2)^4 = 256$, what are all the possible values for y?

    A) $2\sqrt{2}$ and $-2\sqrt{2}$

    B) 3 and –1

    C) 1 and –3

    D) –2 and 2

13. If $x^2 + 16x + 64 = 100$, then $x^2 - 16x + 64$ could equal

    A) –6

    B) 16

    C) 36

    D) 64

14. The potential energy a circuit is given by $U = \frac{1}{2}CV^2$, where C is the capacitance and V is the voltage. Given the values below, what is x if $x > 0$?

	Circuit A	Circuit B
Potential Energy (U)	810	2560
Capacitance (C)	20	20
Voltage (V)	x	$x + 7$

15. If $x^2 - 40x + 400 = 225$ and $x > 0$, then $3x$ could equal

Questions 16 through 18 use the following information and formulas.

When an object is attached to a particular spring in a frictionless system, the oscillation of the object can be expressed using two formulas. The angular frequency (ω, in radians per second) is given as $\omega = \sqrt{\frac{4}{m}}$, where m is the mass of the object (in kilograms). The period (T, in seconds) is given as $T = 2\pi\sqrt{\frac{m}{4}}$.

16. What is the mass of an object attached to the spring in terms of the period of its oscillation?

    A) $\dfrac{T^2}{\pi^2}$

    B) $\dfrac{T^2}{\pi}$

    C) $\dfrac{T^2}{4\pi^2}$

    D) $\dfrac{4T^2}{\pi}$

17. When each object is attached to the spring, a brick's motion has an angular frequency of $\frac{2}{7}$ radians per second, and a tile's motion has an angular frequency of 1 radian per second. What is the ratio of the brick's mass to the tile's mass?

    A) 49 to 1

    B) 49 to 4

    C) 7 to 1

    D) 7 to 4

18. What is the angular frequency of an object's oscillation if that motion has a period of $\frac{\pi}{4}$ seconds when the object is attached to the spring?
    A) 2 radians/second
    B) 4 radians/second
    C) 8 radians/second
    D) 16 radians/second

19. If $x^2 - 12x = -11$ and $y^2 - 6y = 0$, which of the following is a possible value of xy?
    A) 17
    B) 11
    C) 6
    D) 1

20. If $\frac{2}{\sqrt{x}} = 50$ and $\sqrt{y-1} = 3$, what is the value of the product xy?
    A) $\frac{2}{125}$
    B) $\frac{2}{5}$
    C) $\frac{8}{5}$
    D) $\frac{5}{2}$

Questions 21 and 22 use the following information.

The speed required to escape the gravity of a planetary body is called "escape speed" (v) and is measured in meters per second. The formula for escape speed is $v = \sqrt{\frac{4M \times 10^{-10}}{3R}}$, where M and R are the mass (in kilograms) and radius (in meters), respectively, of the planetary body.

21. A small moon has a radius of 120,000 meters and an escape speed of 100 meters per second. What is its mass?
    A) 9×10^8 kilograms
    B) 9×10^{12} kilograms
    C) 9×10^{16} kilograms
    D) 9×10^{17} kilograms

22. A planet has a mass of 2.25×10^{24} kilograms. What is the length of its radius, in terms of its escape speed?
    A) $\frac{3 \times 10^{10}}{v^2}$
    B) $\frac{9 \times 10^{14}}{v}$
    C) $\frac{3 \times 10^{14}}{v^2}$
    D) $\frac{9 \times 10^{24}}{v}$

23. What is one possible value of x if $-125x^2 = x^5$?
    A) -5
    B) $-5\sqrt{5}$
    C) 5
    D) $5\sqrt{5}$

24. If $25(x^2 + 8x + 16) = (x + 4)^4$ and $x > 0$, what is x?

25. The magnitude of an electric field due to an electric dipole is given by $E = k\frac{p}{z^3}$, where k is a constant, p is the dipole moment, and z is the distance to the midpoint of the dipole. If the dipole moment remains the same as the distance to the dipole's midpoint decreases from 1.2×10^{-7} meters to 3.0×10^{-8} meters, the magnitude of the electric field grows x times larger. What is x?

Blue Math Lesson 5A: Solving Equations with Powers and Roots
Race to the Finish

Directions: Answer each question below.

Homework Set (No Calculator)

1. What is a possible value of x if $x > 0$ and
   $(x - 1)^4 = x^2 + 10x + 25$?
   A) 0
   B) 2
   C) 3
   D) 4

2. If $6(2z - 2)^3 = 384$, what are all the possible
   values of z?
   A) 5 and –5
   B) 3 and –3
   C) 5 only
   D) 3 only

Questions 3 through 5 use the following information.

The force of gravity (in newtons) between a large asteroid and another object is given by $F = \frac{20,000m}{r^2}$, where m is the mass of the other object and r is its distance from the asteroid.

3. The force of gravity between an object and the asteroid is 5 newtons when it is 400 meters from the asteroid. What is the force of gravity when the same object is 100 meters from the asteroid?
   A) 20 newtons
   B) 40 newtons
   C) 80 newtons
   D) 160 newtons

4. How far away is a 100-kilogram object if the force of gravity between it and the asteroid is 50 newtons?
   A) 200 meters
   B) 800 meters
   C) 12,600 meters
   D) 40,000 meters

5. Objects X and Y both have a mass of 8 kilograms. The force of gravity between Object X and the asteroid is 400 newtons; the same force is 625 newtons between the asteroid and Object Y. If Object X is 4 meters farther from the asteroid than Object Y, how far away from the asteroid is Object Y?
   A) 4 meters
   B) 12 meters
   C) 16 meters
   D) 20 meters

6. If $4a^2 + 12a + 9 = 81$ and
   $a^2 + 12ab + 36b^2 = 0$, what are all the possible values of b?
   A) 1 or $-\frac{1}{2}$
   B) 3 or –6
   C) 1 only
   D) 3 only

7. If $16(x^2 - 4x + 4) = (x - 2)^4$, what is a possible value of x?
   A) −4
   B) −2
   C)   4
   D)   6

8. If $\frac{(z+7)^4}{144} = 144$ and $z > 0$, what is z^4?
   A)   125
   B)   625
   C) 2,401
   D) 20,736

Questions 9 through 11 focus on the following information.

A bank's loans use compound interest; this interest is compounded twice a year. The bank uses the following formula to determine the amount owed on a $1000 loan, where r is the interest rate and t is the number of years since the loan was taken out:

$$A = 1000(1 + \tfrac{r}{2})^{2t}$$

9. If Anne owes $1210 on her $1000 loan after 1 year, what is the interest rate on her loan?
   A) 11%
   B) 20%
   C) 21%
   D) 42%

10. How many years would it take the amount owed on a $1000 loan to reach $1340 if the interest rate is 10%?
    A) 3
    B) 4
    C) 5
    D) 6

11. Rudolph and Serena both have taken out $1000 loans at the same interest rate. However, Rudolph's loan was taken out 3 years ago, while Serena's was taken out 2.5 years ago. If Rudolph now owes $1194 and Serena owes $1159, what is the interest rate on their loans rounded to the nearest percent?
    A) 3%
    B) 4%
    C) 5%
    D) 6%

12. If $\frac{(a-2)^3}{64} = \frac{(a-3)^3}{125}$, which of the following choices could be a?
    A) −4
    B) −2
    C)   1
    D)   2

13. Which of the following could b equal when $(2b + 3)^6 = (4b + 5)^3$?

A) -1

B) $-\frac{\sqrt{2}}{2}$

C) $\frac{\sqrt{2}}{2}$

D) 1

14. What are all of the possible real values of c when $(c^2 - 9)^2 = c^4$?

A) $\frac{3\sqrt{2}}{2}$ and $-\frac{3\sqrt{2}}{2}$

B) 3 and -3

C) $\frac{3\sqrt{2}}{2}$ only

D) There are no possible real values for c.

Questions 15 and 16 use the following information.

In statistics, the standard error for a given statistic is equal to $\sqrt{\frac{p-p^2}{n}}$, where p is the proportion (a number between 0 and 1, often expressed as a percent) and n is the number in the sample. So if a survey of 2,400 people ($n = 2,400$) resulted in a proportion of 40% ($p = 0.4$) favoring soda over juice, the standard error would be $\sqrt{\frac{0.4-(0.4)^2}{2400}} = 0.01$, or 1%.

15. A 25% proportion of a people who take a poll say that they are afraid of snakes. If the standard error for this statistic is 0.5%, how many people took the poll?

A) 3,750

B) 5,000

C) 7,500

D) 10,000

16. If the sample size of a statistic increases by 16 times, but the proportion remains the same, what effect does this have on the standard error?

A) The standard error decreases by 75%.

B) The standard error decreases by 50%.

C) The standard error increases by 100%.

D) The standard error increases by 300%.

17. If $\frac{(2a-1)^4}{12} = \frac{1}{192}$, what is one possible value of a?

18. If z is equal to either -12 or 6 and $(z + 3)^4 = y^2$, what is the greatest possible value for y?

Questions 19 and 20 use the following information.

The square of a circuit's impedance (Z) is equal to the sum of the square of its resistance (R) and the square of its reactance (X).

19. If the resistance of a circuit is three times its reactance and $Z^2 = cR^2$, what is c?

20. A circuit's impedance remains constant at 30 ohms as its reactance increases from -5 ohms to 5 ohms. By how many ohms does the circuit's resistance decrease?

BLUE MATH LESSON 5B: BASIC EXPONENTIAL FUNCTIONS
Getting Your Feet Wet

Directions: The problems below are intended as a short diagnostic exam.

1. A bacteria culture doubles its population every 23 minutes. If the initial population of the culture was 1,200 bacteria, how many bacteria exist in the culture after 1 hour and 55 minutes?

2. In 2010, the population of the District of Columbia was 601,723. If the yearly population growth of the District of Columbia was 2.41%, how many people are expected to live in the district in 2015?

3. The half-life of Actinium-226 is 29 hours—this means that in 29 hours, one-half of the matter of a sample will undergo radioactive decay. If a quantity of 2000 mg of Actinium-226 disintegrates over a period of 87 hours, how much will remain?

4. If $2(4)^{3x} = 16^{x+1}$, then $x = ?$

BLUE MATH LESSON 5B: BASIC EXPONENTIAL FUNCTIONS
Wading In

Directions: Read the explanation for each problem type mentioned below. Pay special attention to the methods and techniques used to solve the sample problems. Then, do the practice exercises that follow; use the appropriate method to solve each problem.

TOPIC OVERVIEW: BASIC EXPONENTIAL FUNCTIONS

Exponential functions involve exponents, but not in a way that we've covered before. The general format for an exponential function is:

$$y = a \cdot b^x$$

For exponential functions, the variable, x, will always be in the power of the exponent, while b and a will be fixed constants. The graphs of exponential functions of the above format will typically have a horizontal asymptote at $y = 0$ and increase as the function moves from left to right, as shown below:

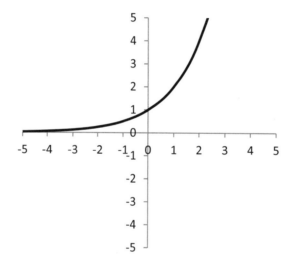

Most exponential function problems on the SAT will deal with exponential growth ($b > 1$) or exponential decay ($0 < b < 1$).

Some of the most basic exponential growth problems deal with something doubling or tripling every unit of time. In questions like this, 2 (for doubling) and 3 (for tripling) replace b in our equation above. Our initial amount is represented by a, while x represents the number of doubling or tripling periods. Let's look at one of these questions below:

SAMPLE PROBLEM 1: BASIC EXPONENTIAL FUNCTIONS

A bacteria culture doubles its population every 23 minutes. If the initial population of the culture was 1,200 bacteria, how many bacteria exist in the culture after 1 hour and 55 minutes?

Let's start by setting up an equation to model the situation. We will use the 1,200 initial bacteria as a. Since the population doubles every 23 minutes, we'll use $b = 2$. Our equation is $y = 1,200 \cdot 2^x$.

Now we have to figure out what x is. We know the population doubles every 23 minutes, so how many 23-minute intervals are there in 1 hour and 55 minutes? Five. So, plug 5 in for x and we have our answer.

$$y = 1,200 \cdot 2^5$$
$$y = 38,400$$

So, after 1 hour and 55 minutes, or five 23-minute intervals, our initial population of 1200 bacteria has turned into 38,400 bacteria.

Let's try another problem that deals with exponential modeling:

SAMPLE PROBLEM 2: BASIC EXPONENTIAL FUNCTIONS

In 2010, the population of the District of Columbia was 601,723. If the yearly population growth of the District of Columbia was 2.41%, how many people are expected to live in the district in 2015?

Since we have a population growth, let's define our variables and set up our exponential equation:

P = Population of the District of Columbia in 2015
C = Current population of the District of Columbia
t = Number of years since 2010

So, our equation is:

$$P = C(1.0241)^t$$

Let's plug in our values for our variables and solve for P.

$$P = 601,723(1.0241)^5$$

Thus, our answer (rounded to the nearest person) is **677,811**.

Many of the exponential functions found on the SAT show exponential decrease instead of exponential increase. For these functions, remember that the value of b will be between 0 and 1. A graph of one of these functions is shown on the next page:

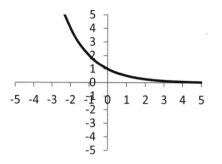

These functions still have a horizontal asymptote at $y = 0$, but note how the function decreases from left to right instead. Let's try an example:

SAMPLE PROBLEM 3: BASIC EXPONENTIAL FUNCTIONS

The half-life of Actinium-226 is 29 hours—this means that in 29 hours, one-half of the matter of a sample will undergo radioactive decay. If a quantity of 2,000 mg of Actinium-226 disintegrates over a period of 87 hours, how much will remain?

We know to use an exponential function for this problem because we're doing the same thing—multiplying by one-half—multiple times. So, let's start out by coming up with our equation:

$$Final = 2,000(0.5)^t$$

As of right now, we don't know what t is. Since we have a period of 87 hours, simple division tells us that we have 3 periods of 29 hours, so $t = 3$. Plug this in and solve.

$$Final = 2,000(0.5)^3$$
$$Final = 250$$

So, we end up with 250 mg of Actinium-226.

TOPIC OVERVIEW: SOLVING EXPONENTIAL EQUATIONS

Sometimes, we will see an exponential equation instead of a function. These equations will generally be of the form $3^x = 9^{x-1}$, but they're much easier to solve than they appear. To start with, manipulate both of these equations so that they have the same base. Once we've done that, the bases are largely irrelevant, so set the exponents equal to each other and solve for the variable. Let's try a problem like this:

SAMPLE PROBLEM 4: SOLVING EXPONENTIAL EQUATIONS

If $2(4)^{3x} = 16^{x+1}$, then $x = ?$

To start, analyze each exponent, as well any numbers out front, and see if they are all powers of a certain number. In this case, 2, 4, and 16 are all powers of 2. So, let's change them all to powers of 2 instead:

$$2^1(2^2)^{3x} = (2^4)^{x+1}$$

From our rules of exponents, we know that this expression is equal to:

$$2^{6x+1} = 2^{4x+4}$$

Next, set the two exponents equal to one another and solve.

$$6x + 1 = 4x + 4$$
$$2x = 3$$
$$x = \frac{3}{2}$$

As always, plug the answer back into the original equation after obtaining it to make sure that it's correct.

TOPIC OVERVIEW: LOGARITHMS

Every function in math has an inverse that can be used to help solve equations: Addition and subtraction are inverses, as are multiplication and division. The opposite of an exponential is a logarithm. In general, if $a^b = c$, then $\log_a c = b$.

In the logarithmic expression, a is called the base and c is called the argument. We will get more involved with the special functions of logarithms later, but for now, all we need to know is how to use logarithms to solve equations. Logarithms can be used to solve equations of the form:

$$136 = 10^x$$

To solve this, take the logarithm with base 10 of both sides of the equation.

$$136 = 10^x$$

$$\log_{10} 136 = \log_{10} 10^x$$

At this point, the logarithm and the 10 cancel out, leaving us with:

$$\log_{10} 136 = \log_{10} 10^x$$

$$\log_{10} 136 = x$$

The **log** button of all calculators can be used to solve logarithms with base 10. So, our answer is 2.134.

In addition to logarithms with base 10, most calculator cans also do logarithms with base e, an irrational number used in many interest problems. The shortcut button for these logarithms is the **ln** button.

Unfortunately, not every calculator has a button for logarithms with bases besides 10 or e. For these other bases, we use the change of base formula, which says:

$$\log_b a = \frac{\log_{10} a}{\log_{10} b} = \frac{\ln a}{\ln b}$$

Commit this formula to memory, as it will come up fairly frequently.

WRAP-UP

Many real-world situations are modeled by exponential functions; the most common of these include population increase or decrease, half-lifes, and repeated doubling, tripling, or halving. Always set up the equation $y = a \cdot b^x$ when dealing with any exponential equations and solving should be much easier.

BLUE MATH LESSON 5B: BASIC EXPONENTIAL FUNCTIONS
Learning to Swim

Directions: Answer each question below.

PRACTICE SET 1 (CALCULATOR)

1. If $6^x = 36^{x-1}$, what is x?

2. The annual rate of increase of the population of wolves in Roosevelt National Forest is 3.2%. If there were 600 wolves in the forest in 2009, how many wolves were there in 2014?

3. If $\left(\frac{1}{3}\right)^{3x} = 27^{x+4}$, what is x?

4. Jonas invests in a savings account that offers a 3% interest rate, compounded twice a year according to the formula $A = P\left(1 + \frac{r}{2}\right)^{2t}$, where r is the interest rate, written as a decimal, and t is the number of years. If Jonas invests a starting amount (P) of $1,000 in the account, how much money will it have after 10 years (rounded to the nearest dollar)?

5. The number of tickets sold by an opera company has been decreasing at an annual rate of 1.8%. If the company sold 315,000 tickets this year, how many tickets did it sell 8 years ago?

Blue Math Lesson 5B: Basic Exponential Functions
Diving into the Deep End

Directions: Answer each question below.

Practice Set 2 (Calculator)

6. What is z when $\left(\frac{1}{36}\right)^{2z} = 6^{-z+9}$?

    A) –6
    B) –3
    C) 3
    D) 6

7. A biologist compared the growth rates of two fungi. Fungus A increased in size (s) at a rate of $s(d) = 8^d$, while Fungus B increased in size at a rate of $s(d) = 2^{2d+6}$, where d in both equations is the number of days since the start of the experiment. After how many days will the two fungi be the same size?

    A) 3
    B) 4
    C) 5
    D) 6

8. The fastest-growing city in the United States is Raleigh, North Carolina. Since 2000, it has grown at an annual rate of 3.3%. What was Raleigh's population in 2005 if its population was 800,000 in 2000? Round to the nearest thousand.

    A) 826,000
    B) 911,000
    C) 941,000
    D) 1,064,000

9. A tree's volume increases at a rate of 8% annually. If the tree's volume was 6.5 cubic meters ten years ago, it has increased its volume by how much in that time (rounded to the nearest tenth of a cubic meter)?

    A) 3.7 cubic meters
    B) 7.5 cubic meters
    C) 11.7 cubic meters
    D) 14.0 cubic meters

Questions 10 through 13 use the following formula for compound interest.

$$A = P\left(1 + \frac{r}{n}\right)^{nt}$$

A = the final amount
P = the principal (starting amount)
r = interest rate
n = number of times the interest is compounded each year
t = number of years

10. A savings account pays a 2.4% interest rate, compounded monthly. If the principal amount is $500, how much will be in the account after 2 years?

    A) $512.00
    B) $524.56
    C) $576.95
    D) $664.61

11. Andrea's Tree Services took out a small business loan at an interest rate of 7%, compounded 4 times per year. If the loan amount is equal to $13,030 after 5 years, how much was the initial principal on the loan, rounded to the nearest dollar?
    A) $9,210
    B) $9,867
    C) $10,676
    D) $11,627

12. Jeffrey invests $1,200 in each of two savings accounts. The accounts are both compounded twice a year. If one account has an interest rate of 2% and the other has an interest rate of 1.6%, what is the difference between the values of the two accounts after 20 years?
    A) $56.36
    B) $96.00
    C) $115.77
    D) $136.19

13. How many years will it take a given amount of money to double if it is invested in a money market fund at 12% interest, compounded monthly?
    A) 4 years
    B) 5 years
    C) 6 years
    D) 8 years

14. A stream's flow rate today is 73 cubic feet per minute. If the stream's flow rate was 100 cubic feet per minute 3 years ago, what will its flow rate be 5 years from now (rounded to the nearest cubic foot per minute)? Assume the stream's flow rate declines at the same rate each year.

15. A biologist tests the competition between two microbial species by placing n individuals from both Species A and Species B in an enclosed environment. The biologist notices that every 8 hours, Species A's population increases by 25% and Species B's population declines by 25%. After a day has passed, the population of Species A is approximately how many times as large as the population of Species B, rounded to the nearest hundredth?

PRACTICE SET 3 (CALCULATOR)

16. If $16^6 = 2^{x+1}$, what is x?
    A) 11
    B) 17
    C) 20
    D) 23

17. If $5^p = \left(\frac{1}{625}\right)^q$, what is q in terms of p?
    A) $-4p$
    B) $-\frac{p}{4}$
    C) $\frac{p}{4}$
    D) $4p$

18. The price of a stock decreases by 2.3% each week. If the stock's price is $34 per share today, what was its price per share 6 weeks ago, rounded to the nearest dollar?
    A) $30
    B) $35
    C) $37
    D) $39

19. What is z when $\left(\frac{1}{81}\right)^{z+2} = 3^{-5z}$?
    A) -4
    B) 2
    C) 3
    D) 8

20. If $a^k = b^{2k}$, where a and b are both positive integers, what is b in terms of a?
    A) $\sqrt{a}$
    B) $\frac{a}{2}$
    C) $2a$
    D) a^2

21. The number of bacteria in a petri dish increases by 7.5% each hour during an experiment. If the dish initially holds b bacteria, how many does it hold one day into the experiment?
    A) $1.075b$
    B) $b(1.75)^{24}$
    C) $b(1.075)^{24}$
    D) $b(0.075)^{24}$

22. A farmer is planning to reduce the number of goats she owns by 25% each month. At this rate, how long will it take her to reduce the total number of goats by at least 75%?
    A) 3 months
    B) 4 months
    C) 5 months
    D) 6 months

23. The percentage of regular computer users in America increased at an annual rate of 8.2% over the last y years. If 8.0% of Americans used computers y years ago and 25.4% of Americans used computers $\frac{y}{2}$ years ago, what percentage of Americans use them today?
    A) 42.8%
    B) 68.2%
    C) 75.5%
    D) 80.6%

Questions 24 and 25 use the following information.

Atmospheric pressure (measured in atmospheres) decreases exponentially as height above sea level increases according to the equation $p = \left(1 - \frac{h}{45,000}\right)^n$, where h is the height above sea level (in meters) and n is a constant. The atmospheric pressure at 1,800 meters above sea level is equal to 0.815 atmospheres.

24. What is n, rounded to the nearest integer?

25. What is the approximate atmospheric pressure at 4,500 meters above sea level (rounded to the nearest tenth of an atmosphere)?

BLUE MATH LESSON 5B: BASIC EXPONENTIAL FUNCTIONS
Race to the Finish

Directions: Answer each question below.

HOMEWORK SET (CALCULATOR)

Questions 1 and 2 use the following information.

The half-life of a radioactive element in years is defined as the time required for exactly half of the element to decay. The amount of an element remaining t years into the decay process can be found using the equation $N(t) = N_0 e^{-\lambda t}$, where N_0 is the initial amount of the element and λ is a number known as the element's "decay constant."

1. A certain radioactive isotope has a decay constant of 0.0495. What is that isotope's half-life, rounded to the nearest year?
   A) 10 years
   B) 12 years
   C) 14 years
   D) 16 years

2. If one-fourth of a sample of an element remains after 4.2 years, which of the following best approximates the element's decay constant?
   A) 0.07
   B) 0.14
   C) 0.29
   D) 0.33

3. What is y when $12^{3y} = 12^{y+7}$?
   A) $\frac{7}{2}$
   B) 7
   C) 10
   D) 14

4. What is P, rounded to the nearest integer, if $(P)(1.1)^6 = 1506$?
   A) 228
   B) 703
   C) 850
   D) 941

5. The number of fruit flies in an experimental population doubles every 3 weeks. If there are 600 fruit flies today, how many will there be n weeks from now?
   A) $600(2)^{\frac{n}{3}}$
   B) $600(2)^{3n}$
   C) $600\left(\frac{n}{3}\right)^2$
   D) $600(3)^{2n}$

6. The number of coins in a fountain increases by 50% every day. If there are 64 coins in the fountain when Monday begins, how many coins are added to the fountain during the day Thursday?
   A) 72
   B) 96
   C) 108
   D) 216

7. If $64^{x-2} = 4^{12}$, what is x?
   A) 1
   B) 6
   C) 10
   D) 12

8. If $10^{y+2} = 100(10)^{2p}$, what is y in terms of p?

    A) $2p$

    B) $2p - 2$

    C) p

    D) $\frac{p}{2} + 1$

9. A chemist finds that, when exposed to a catalyst, two compounds decrease in mass exponentially. The first compound decays at a rate of $m(t) = 3(3)^{-2t}$ and the second decays at a rate of $m(t) = 9(3)^{-3t+3}$, where t is the number of seconds since exposure to the catalyst. After how many seconds are the two compounds equal in mass?

    A) 3

    B) 4

    C) 5

    D) 6

10. A restaurant served 8,751 customers in 2007 and 15,422 customers in 2012. What was the annual rate of increase in the number of customers, rounded to the nearest percent?

    A) 8%

    B) 12%

    C) 15%

    D) 20%

11. The number of major meteorite impacts on a planet t million years after its formation is given by $m(t) = 50(1.54)^{-4t}$. Which of the following best describes the rate of meteorite impacts over time?

    A) The rate slowly increases at first and then increases more rapidly later.

    B) The rate slowly decreases at first and then decreases more rapidly later.

    C) The rate rapidly increases at first and then increases more slowly later.

    D) The rate rapidly decreases at first and then decreases more slowly later.

12. During a chemical reaction, the amount of ammonium chloride in a sample increases at a rate of 9% per minute. If there is now twice as much ammonium chloride in the sample as there was to begin with, how much time has elapsed (rounded to the nearest minute)?

    A) 7 minutes

    B) 8 minutes

    C) 10 minutes

    D) 11 minutes

13. Years ago, Mario loaned his friend $500 with a simple interest rate of 20%. The debt had risen to $1,244 after $n - 2$ years. After $2n$ years, Mario's friend still had not paid back the loan, now owing Mario $6,420. What is n?

    A) 4

    B) 5

    C) 7

    D) 9

14. A machine's oil supply must be re-filled when it reaches one-fourth of its capacity. If the amount of oil in the machine is reduced by 13% each hour, how long should the machine go between oil refills, rounded to the nearest hour?

A)   8 hours
B)   10 hours
C)   12 hours
D)   14 hours

17. If $\left(\frac{1}{25}\right)^4 = 5^{-3c+1}$, what is c?

18. What is q when $4^{q+6} = 8^{2q}$?

Questions 15 and 16 use the following information.

A lab is testing two new anti-viral drugs by exposing them to viral cultures and measuring how long it takes the drugs to eliminate half of the viruses. Drug C reduces the virus by half every c hours; Drug D takes d hours to do the same.

15. Which equation best expresses the fraction of the original virus, v, left in a sample t hours after being treated with Drug C?

A) $v(t) = 2^{\frac{-t}{c}}$

B) $v(t) = 2^{\frac{-c}{t}}$

C) $v(t) = 2^{\frac{-t}{2}}$

D) $v(t) = t^{\frac{-2}{c}}$

19. The amount of money (in thousands of dollars) in Myeong-Wook's retirement account is given by the formula $m(t) = \frac{1}{81}(9^{5t})$, while the amount in Namond's retirement account is given by the formula $n(t) = 27^{3t}$. After how many years will the two accounts have the same amount of money?

20. The annual rate of growth of a vine is equal to 5% of the vine's length. In 2008, a vine was 6.4 meters long. What was the vine's length, rounded to the nearest meter, in 2015?

16. If $c = 2d$, which statement is true regarding the amount of viruses remaining in the culture after $4c$ hours?

A)   There is 4 times more virus remaining in Drug C's culture than in Drug D's.
B)   There is 16 times more virus remaining in Drug C's culture than in Drug D's.
C)   There is 4 times more virus remaining in Drug D's culture than in Drug C's.
D)   There is 16 times more virus remaining in Drug D's culture than in Drug C's.

BLUE MATH LESSON 6A: OPERATIONS ON RATIONAL FUNCTIONS
Getting Your Feet Wet

Directions: The problems below are intended as a short diagnostic exam.

1. Which of the following expressions cannot be expressed as a rational function?
    A) $5x^3 - 3x + 2$
    B) $\frac{x+2}{\sqrt{x+2}}$
    C) $3x^{-1}$
    D) $\frac{2x^2}{x+3}$

2. If $\frac{x+1}{x+3} - \frac{2x-1}{x-2} = \frac{Ax^2+Bx+C}{x^2+x-6}$, then $A - B - C =$

3. $\frac{3x^2+7x+4}{2x^2+5x+3} \div \frac{3x^2+10x+8}{2x^2+7x+6} =$
    A) $\frac{14}{15}$
    B) 1
    C) $\frac{(3x+4)^2}{(2x+3)^2}$
    D) $\frac{9x^2+24x+16}{4x^2+12x+9}$

4. If $\frac{x^2+3x}{x+1} = x + 2 - \frac{A}{x+1}$, then $A =$
    A) -4
    B) -2
    C) 2
    D) 4

BLUE MATH LESSON 6A: OPERATIONS ON RATIONAL FUNCTIONS
Wading In

Directions: Read the explanation for each problem type mentioned below. Pay special attention to the methods and techniques used to solve the sample problems. Then, do the practice exercises that follow; use the appropriate method to solve each problem.

TOPIC OVERVIEW: IDENTIFYING RATIONAL FUNCTIONS

In math, a rational number is simply one that can be written as a fraction or ratio. A rational function, then, is an expression written as the ratio of one polynomial to another polynomial. Look below for some examples of rational functions:

$$\frac{x^2+5}{x-1} \qquad \frac{1}{x+2} \qquad \frac{3x^2}{5}$$

Remember, to be a polynomial, the power of every term in the expression needs to be an integer greater than or equal to zero. Also note that, technically, every polynomial is itself a rational function, since it can be written with a 1 in the denominator. However, for our purposes, only expressions with polynomials in both the denominator and the numerator will be relevant. Let's try an example about identifying rational functions:

SAMPLE PROBLEM 1: IDENTIFYING RATIONAL FUNCTIONS

Which of the following expressions cannot be expressed as a rational function?

A) $5x^3 - 3x + 2$

B) $\frac{x+2}{\sqrt{x+2}}$

C) $3x^{-1}$

D) $\frac{2x^2}{x+3}$

Let's start out by looking at each individual term. Both A and D are ratios of polynomials (for A, the denominator is 1). Answer choice C looks like a compelling pick, but remember that negative exponents can be rewritten. So, $3x^{-1}$ can be rewritten as $\frac{3}{x}$. Thus, our answer must be **B**.

TOPIC OVERVIEW: ADDING AND SUBTRACTING RATIONAL FUNCTIONS

When adding or subtracting rational functions, one rule supersedes all others: Everything that is added or subtracted must have a common denominator. The process for getting common denominators of rational expressions is nearly identical for that of getting common denominators for regular fractions. Let's look at an example:

SAMPLE PROBLEM 2: ADDING AND SUBTRACTING RATIONAL FUNCTIONS

If $\frac{x+1}{x+3} - \frac{2x-1}{x-2} = \frac{Ax^2+Bx+C}{x^2+x-6}$, then $A-B-C =$

Any time we see a question involving adding and subtracting rational functions, we should begin by analyzing the denominators. Factor any denominator that can be factored: $x+3$ and $x-2$ are already completely factored, but we can factor $x^2 + x - 6$ into $(x+3)(x-2)$. Let's rewrite our rational expression:

$$\frac{x+1}{x+3} - \frac{2x-1}{x-2} = \frac{Ax^2+Bx+C}{(x+3)(x-2)}$$

Now, let's take all of our expressions on the left-hand side of the equation and get them to match the denominator of the right-hand side of the equation.

$$\frac{(x+1)(x-2)}{(x+3)(x-2)} - \frac{(x+3)(2x-1)}{(x+3)(x-2)} = \frac{Ax^2+Bx+C}{(x+3)(x-2)}$$

Next, FOIL out our expressions, then simplify things.

$$\frac{x^2-x-2}{x^2+x-6} - \frac{2x^2+5x-3}{x^2+x-6} = \frac{Ax^2+Bx+C}{x^2+x-6}$$

$$\frac{-x^2-6x+1}{x^2+x-6} = \frac{Ax^2+Bx+C}{x^2+x-6}$$

So, $A - B - C = $ **4**

TOPIC OVERVIEW: MULTIPLYING AND DIVIDING RATIONAL EXPRESSIONS

Multiplying and dividing rational expressions is relatively easy and uses the same rules as multiplying and dividing fractions does. First, factor out any expressions that can be factored to make our work a lot easier. Next, cross out any terms that appear on both the top and bottom. Finally, multiply the expressions on top by the other expressions on top and multiply the expressions on the bottom by the other expressions on the bottom. Remember to flip the second term if we're dividing instead of multiplying before we do anything else, though! Let's look at an example to see how this is done.

SAMPLE PROBLEM 3: MULTIPLYING AND DIVIDING RATIONAL EXPRESSIONS

$$\frac{3x^2+7x+4}{2x^2+5x+3} \div \frac{3x^2+10x+8}{2x^2+7x+6} =$$

A) $\frac{14}{15}$

B) 1

C) $\frac{(3x+4)^2}{(2x+3)^2}$

D) $\frac{9x^2+24x+16}{4x^2+12x+9}$

Since we're dealing with dividing, let's start by flipping our second term and changing our division sign to a multiplication sign:

$$\frac{3x^2+7x+4}{2x^2+5x+3} \times \frac{2x^2+7x+6}{3x^2+10x+8} =$$

Next, let's factor each of our quadratics:

$$\frac{3x^2+7x+4}{2x^2+5x+3} \times \frac{2x^2+7x+6}{3x^2+10x+8} = \frac{(3x+4)(x+1)}{(2x+3)(x+1)} \times \frac{(2x+3)(x+2)}{(3x+4)(x+2)}$$

At this point, cross out everything in common between the denominator and the numerator:

$$\frac{\cancel{(3x+4)}\cancel{(x+1)}}{\cancel{(2x+3)}\cancel{(x+1)}} \times \frac{\cancel{(2x+3)}\cancel{(x+2)}}{\cancel{(3x+4)}\cancel{(x+2)}}$$

So, since everything crosses out, our answer is **B**, 1.

Topic Overview: Synthetic Division

Sometimes, we'll be given a rational function that doesn't factor out easily. In cases like this, we use something called synthetic division, which is similar to long division. This process will be more easily explained with an example, so let's look at one below:

$$\frac{x^3+3x+9}{x+3}$$

When doing Synthetic Division, start by setting up half of a box:

Next, place the coefficient of each of the top polynomial's terms, in order, in a row. If a term is missing, treat zero as the coefficient.

$$\begin{array}{c|cccc} & 1 & 0 & 3 & 9 \\ \hline & & & & \end{array}$$

Synthetic division works best when the denominator is a binomial with order 1. Set that binomial equal to zero and put the solution to the left of the row of numbers in the box above.

$$\begin{array}{c|cccc} -3 & 1 & 0 & 3 & 9 \\ \hline & & & & \end{array}$$

Next, bring the number in the top left hand corner of the box, 1, down below the bar.

$$-3 \quad | \quad 1 \quad 0 \quad 3 \quad 9$$
$$\qquad\qquad 1$$

Now, multiply the number outside the box, –3, by the number we just moved, 1. Place this product below the zero in the next column.

Next, add down the column and place it below the bar. $0 + -3 = -3$.

$$-3 \quad | \quad 1 \quad 0 \quad 3 \quad 9$$
$$\qquad\qquad -3$$
$$\qquad\quad 1 \quad -3$$

Now, repeat the process with the next column. $-3 \times -3 = 9$. Place it below the 3, then add.

$$-3 \quad | \quad 1 \quad 0 \quad 3 \quad 9$$
$$\qquad\qquad -3 \quad 9$$
$$\qquad\quad 1 \quad -3 \quad 12$$

Let's repeat the process once more:

$$-3 \quad | \quad 1 \quad 0 \quad 3 \quad 9$$
$$\qquad\qquad -3 \quad 9 \quad -36$$
$$\qquad\quad 1 \quad -3 \quad 12 \quad \boxed{-27}$$

Place a box around this last number; we'll need it for the remainder of the expression.

And that's it. Take the numbers below the bar and use them as the coefficients of our answer. Since there are three numbers, our answer is a trinomial. Thus, its highest power is two. Our boxed in answer becomes our remainder, which we will place on top of the original divisor.

$$1x^2 - 3x + 12 + \frac{-27}{x+3}$$

Let's try another question:

SAMPLE PROBLEM 4: SYNTHETIC DIVISION

If $\frac{x^2+3x}{x+1} = x + 2 - \frac{A}{x+1}$, then $A =$

A) -4
B) -2
C) 2
D) 4

Since we have a division problem in which factoring doesn't help us, we'll start by setting up our synthetic division box:

$$
\begin{array}{c|ccc}
-1 & 1 & 3 & 0 \\
& & & \\
\hline
\end{array}
$$

Now, let's perform the synthetic division algorithm:

$$
\begin{array}{c|ccc}
-1 & 1 & 3 & 0 \\
& & -1 & -2 \\
\hline
& 1 & 2 & -2
\end{array}
$$

So, we get $x + 2 + \frac{-2}{x+1}$, and our answer is **C**.

WRAP-UP

As always, practice makes perfect, so a big part of working with rational expressions is getting used to the variety of ways that the SAT's test makers will ask these types of questions. To prepare for the worst case scenario, try to avoid using a calculator whenever possible.

BLUE MATH LESSON 6A: OPERATIONS ON RATIONAL FUNCTIONS
Learning to Swim

Directions: Answer each question below.

PRACTICE SET 1 (NO CALCULATOR)

1. What is the simplified form of $\frac{x}{x^2-1} \times \frac{x-1}{4x}$?

2. Simplify $\frac{2x^3+3x^2+x}{4x+2}$

3. What is the simplified form of $\frac{5x-10}{3x^2-3x-6}$ divided by $\frac{20x}{x^2+8x+7}$?

4. What is $\frac{5}{x-3} + \frac{6}{x+3}$?

5. Ruslan's Rugs sells x rugs every $(x - 8)$ days. The Floor Depot sells 2 rugs every $(x + 10)$ days. Compared to The Floor Depot, how many more rugs does Ruslan's Rugs sell each day, in terms of x?

BLUE MATH LESSON 6A: OPERATIONS ON RATIONAL FUNCTIONS
Diving into the Deep End

Directions: Answer each question below.

PRACTICE SET 2 (NO CALCULATOR)

6. Simplify $\frac{6x^2+3x}{6x^2+x-1}$.

   A) $\frac{3x-1}{3x}$

   B) $\frac{3x}{3x+1}$

   C) $\frac{3x}{3x-1}$

   D) $\frac{3x+1}{3x-1}$

7. $\frac{x^2-6x+9}{x+5} \times \frac{x^2+10x+25}{x^2+2x-15} =$

   A) $x - 3$

   B) $\frac{x-3}{x+5}$

   C) $\frac{x-3}{x^2+10x+25}$

   D) $\frac{x^2+2x-15}{x+5}$

8. What is the simplified form of $\frac{x^2-7x-18}{x^2-4x+4} \div \frac{x-9}{x^2-4}$?

   A) $\frac{x^2-4x+4}{x+2}$

   B) $\frac{x^2+4x+4}{x-2}$

   C) $\frac{x^2-18x+81}{x^2-4x+4}$

   D) $x + 2$

9. Mitch runs 4 miles in $2x + 3$ minutes, and Joy runs 7 miles in $5x - 1$ minutes. If each of them ran for 1 minute, how many miles would they run, combined (in terms of x)?

   A) $\frac{34x+17}{10x^2+13x-3}$

   B) $\frac{34x+2}{10x^2+13x-3}$

   C) $\frac{43x+5}{10x^2+13x-3}$

   D) $\frac{11}{7x+2}$

10. $\frac{x}{x-4} - \frac{4}{2x+8} =$

   A) $\frac{1}{x+4}$

   B) $\frac{x^2+6x-8}{x^2-16}$

   C) $\frac{x^2+2x+8}{x^2-16}$

   D) $\frac{x^2+16}{x^2-16}$

11. The equation $\frac{4}{x+3} \times \frac{5x+2}{2x} = \frac{10x+4}{x^2+3x}$ is true for all real values of x EXCEPT

   A) −3 and 0.

   B) 3 and 0.

   C) −3 only.

   D) 0 only.

12. Which of the following is a possible solution to the equation $\frac{3x^2+7x+2}{2x+1} \times \frac{2x^2-3x-2}{x^2-4} = 0$?

   A) -2

   B) $-\frac{1}{3}$

   C) $\frac{1}{3}$

   D) 3

13. If $\frac{x^2+1}{x^2+4x+3} = \frac{1}{x+1} + B$ for all real values of x other than $x = -3$ and $x = -1$, what is B in terms of x?

   A) $\frac{x+3}{x+1}$

   B) $\frac{x-3}{x+1}$

   C) $\frac{x-2}{x+3}$

   D) $\frac{x+1}{x+3}$

14. If $\frac{3y+1}{y+5} = \frac{3y}{y+1} - 1$, what is one possible real value of y?

15. Over $x + 3$ days, the state employment office in Duluth processed 18 applications for unemployment benefits. Meanwhile, another office in Conyers processed $3x$ applications in $3x + 4$ days. If the Duluth office processed an average of 3 more applications per day than the Conyers office, and x is positive, what is x?

PRACTICE SET 3 (NO CALCULATOR)

16. A horticulturist measures the growth of two varieties of corn plants. Plant A grows $2x$ inches in $x - 1$ days, while Plant B grows 5 inches in $x + 3$ days. The horticulturist determines that Plant A grew an average of 2 inches more per day than did Plant B. Which of the following could be x?

   A) $-\frac{11}{5}$

   B) 2

   C) $\frac{11}{3}$

   D) 4

17. Let $f(x) = \frac{3x}{x^2-7x+6}$ and $g(x) = \frac{x-6}{x^2-1}$. If $h(x)$ is equal to $f(x)$ divided by $g(x)$, what is the domain of $h(x)$?

   A) All real values of x except -1, 0, and 1.

   B) All real values of x except -1, 1, and 6.

   C) All real values of x except -1 and 1.

   D) All real values of x except 1 and 6.

18. What is the simplified form of $\frac{x-7}{2x+5} \times \frac{x^2+10x+21}{x^2-49} \times \frac{2x^2-9x-35}{x^2-9}$?

   A) $\frac{x+7}{x+3}$

   B) $\frac{x+7}{x-3}$

   C) $\frac{x-7}{x+3}$

   D) $\frac{x-7}{x-3}$

19. The domain of the rational function $f(x)$ is all real values of x except 2, –1, and 0. Which of the following could be $f(x)$?

    A) $f(x) = \dfrac{1}{x^3+x^2-2x}$

    B) $f(x) = \dfrac{x}{x^2-x-2}$

    C) $f(x) = \dfrac{1}{x^3-x^2-2x}$

    D) $f(x) = \dfrac{x}{x^2+x-2}$

20. If $\dfrac{1}{x+7} \times \dfrac{x^2+8x+7}{x^2+x} = 7$, what is x?

    A) $\dfrac{1}{7}$

    B) $\dfrac{6}{7}$

    C) 1

    D) 7

21. Which of the following lists all the real solutions of $\dfrac{x^2+5x+6}{x^2-4} \times \dfrac{x^2-5x+6}{x-3} = 1$?

    A) $x = 3$ only

    B) $x = 2$ or –2

    C) $x = -2$ only

    D) The equation has no real solutions.

22. If $\dfrac{4x+3}{2x^2+x-1} \div \dfrac{4x^2+7x+3}{4x^2-1} = 1$, what is a possible value of x?

    A) 0

    B) 1

    C) $\sqrt{2}$

    D) 2

23. If $\dfrac{2x}{x-2} = \dfrac{-3}{x^2-6x+8} + 3$, what are all the possible real values of x?

    A) 2 and 4

    B) 3 and 7

    C) 2 only

    D) 7 only

24. The functions f and g are defined as $f(x) = \dfrac{x^2-x+12}{x+2}$ and $g(x) = \dfrac{x-1}{x^2-5x+6}$. If $h(x)$ is defined as $f(x)$ divided by $g(x)$, what is a positive value of x that cannot be in the domain of $h(x)$?

25. What is x if $\dfrac{5}{x+4} + \dfrac{x}{x-2} = 1$?

BLUE MATH LESSON 6A: OPERATIONS ON RATIONAL FUNCTIONS
Race to the Finish

Directions: Answer each question below.

HOMEWORK SET (NO CALCULATOR)

1. Simplify $\dfrac{5x^2-35x+60}{x^2-16}$.

   A) $\dfrac{5x+2}{x-4}$

   B) $\dfrac{5x-15}{x-4}$

   C) $\dfrac{5x-15}{x+4}$

   D) $\dfrac{5x+15}{x-4}$

2. Simplify $\dfrac{3x^2+16x+16}{4x+16}$.

   A) $\dfrac{3x+4}{4}$

   B) $\dfrac{3x+4}{x+4}$

   C) $\dfrac{x+4}{4}$

   D) $\dfrac{3x+12}{4}$

3. What is the product of $\dfrac{4}{x+1}$ and $\dfrac{8x+8}{4x+3}$?

   A) $\dfrac{1}{2x+6}$

   B) $\dfrac{2}{x+3}$

   C) $\dfrac{32}{4x+3}$

   D) $\dfrac{x+3}{2x^2+4x+2}$

4. $\dfrac{x^2-5x}{x+8}$ divided by $\dfrac{x^2+8x}{x+1}$ is equal to

   A) $\dfrac{x^2+16x+64}{x^2-4x-5}$

   B) $\dfrac{x^3-5x^2}{x+1}$

   C) $\dfrac{x^2-4x-5}{x^2+16x+64}$

   D) $\dfrac{x^2-5x}{x+1}$

5. $\dfrac{4}{2-x}+\dfrac{x}{x+3}=$

   A) $\dfrac{7x+6}{x^2-x+6}$

   B) $\dfrac{7x+18}{x^2+x-6}$

   C) $\dfrac{x+6}{x^2-x+6}$

   D) $\dfrac{x^2-6x-12}{x^2+x-6}$

6. What is the sum of $\dfrac{x-1}{x+3}$ and $\dfrac{x+1}{x-3}$?

   A) 1

   B) $\dfrac{2}{x-3}$

   C) $\dfrac{6}{x^2-9}$

   D) $\dfrac{2x^2+6}{x^2-9}$

7. Marge makes $z^2 - 9$ cookies and $z^2 + 5z + 11$ cupcakes over the course of $4z^2 - 4z - 3$ days. How many combined cookies and cupcakes does she make each day on average, in terms of z?

A) $\dfrac{2z+1}{z+3}$

B) $\dfrac{2z-3}{z+2}$

C) $\dfrac{z+3}{2z+1}$

D) $\dfrac{z+2}{2z-3}$

8. Isaac wrote 16 pages in $y - 3$ days; Min wrote 12 pages in $y + 1$ days. Compared to Min's writing speed (in pages per day), how much faster was Isaac's writing speed, in terms of y?

A) $\dfrac{4y+52}{y^2-2y-3}$

B) $\dfrac{4y-20}{y^2-2y-3}$

C) $\dfrac{28y-20}{y^2-2y-3}$

D) $\dfrac{2}{y-1}$

9. What is $\dfrac{x-1}{x-5} - \dfrac{x-5}{x-1}$?

A) 1

B) $\dfrac{8x-24}{x^2-6x+5}$

C) $\dfrac{-12x+26}{x^2-6x+5}$

D) $\dfrac{4}{x^2-6x+5}$

10. What are all of the real solutions to $\dfrac{3x}{x-5} \times \dfrac{9x-45}{3x+6} = x + 2$?

A) 5 and –2

B) 4 and 1

C) 1 only

D) –2 only

11. A rectangular retaining wall is $\dfrac{b^2-9}{b+2}$ feet wide and $\dfrac{b^2+10b+16}{b^2-3b}$ feet high. If the area of the wall is 25 square feet, what is one possible value for b?

A) 2

B) 3

C) 8

D) 9

12. What is a possible solution to the equation $\dfrac{2x^2-7x+3}{x^2-4} \div \dfrac{x^2-5x+6}{x^2-4x+4} = x - 2$?

A) $x = -3$

B) $x = -1$

C) $x = 1$

D) $x = 2$

13. If the expression $\frac{9x^2}{3x+1}$ is written in the equivalent form $\frac{1}{3x+1} + A$, what is A in terms of x?

   A) $9x^2 - 1$
   B) $3x + 1$
   C) $3x - 1$
   D) $3x$

14. What is z if $\frac{z+3}{z+1} + \frac{z-2}{z-1} = 2$?

   A) -3
   B) 2
   C) 3
   D) 7

15. What is one possible solution to the equation $\frac{4}{x-3} - \frac{3}{x-2} = 1$?

   A) 1
   B) 2
   C) 3
   D) 4

16. An astronomer tracks the orbits of two of Jupiter's moons. Callisto needs $3y - 1$ days to orbit Jupiter $y - 5$ times, and Ganymede needs $y + 8$ days to orbit $y - 4$ times. If Callisto's average orbital period is 10 days longer than Ganymede's, what is a possible value for y?

   A) 3
   B) 6
   C) 7
   D) 17

17. What is the positive value of x that is not in the domain of the function $f(x) = \frac{5x^2+13x-7}{x^2-9}$?

18. If $\frac{x^2-x-6}{x^2+4x+4} \times \frac{x^2+2x-3}{x^2-9} = 0$, what is a possible value for x?

19. What is the possible positive value of x if $\frac{2x}{x-1} \times \frac{3}{x+2} = 3$?

20. If $\frac{z-1}{z-3}$ divided by $\frac{z-1}{3z}$ is equal to z, what is z?

BLUE MATH LESSON 6B: SYSTEMS OF EQUATIONS AND INEQUALITIES – LINEAR AND QUADRATIC
Getting Your Feet Wet

Directions: The problems below are intended as a short diagnostic exam.

$$y = 2x^2 - 3$$
$$x + y = 0$$

1. Which of the following sets of ordered pairs satisfies the system of equations above?

   A) $(1, -1), (\frac{3}{2}, -\frac{3}{2})$

   B) $(1, -1), (-\frac{3}{2}, \frac{3}{2})$

   C) $(-1, 1), (-\frac{3}{2}, \frac{3}{2})$

   D) $(-1, 1), (\frac{3}{2}, -\frac{3}{2})$

$$(y - 1)^2 = -x + 3$$
$$y = x + 1$$

2. Which of the following sets of ordered pairs satisfies the system of equations above?

   A) $(\frac{-1-\sqrt{13}}{2}, \frac{1-\sqrt{13}}{2}), (\frac{-1+\sqrt{13}}{2}, \frac{1+\sqrt{13}}{2})$

   B) $(\frac{1-\sqrt{13}}{2}, \frac{-1-\sqrt{13}}{2}), (\frac{1+\sqrt{13}}{2}, \frac{-1+\sqrt{13}}{2})$

   C) $(\frac{-1-\sqrt{13}}{2}, \frac{1+\sqrt{13}}{2}), (\frac{-1-\sqrt{13}}{2}, \frac{1-\sqrt{13}}{2})$

   D) $(-\frac{1+\sqrt{13}}{2}, \frac{1+\sqrt{13}}{2}), (-\frac{1-\sqrt{13}}{2}, \frac{1-\sqrt{13}}{2})$

$$(x - 1)^2 + (y + 1)^2 = 4$$
$$x = A$$

3. Which of the following values of A will cause the line $x = A$ to be tangent to the circle $(x - 1)^2 + (y + 1)^2 = 4$?

   A) -3

   B) -1

   C) 0

   D) 1

$$y > x^2$$
$$y < 3 - 2x$$

4. Which of the points is a valid solution to the system of inequalities above?

   A) $(0, 0)$

   B) $(0, 1)$

   C) $(1, 1)$

   D) $(-3, 9)$

BLUE MATH LESSON 6B: SYSTEMS OF EQUATIONS AND INEQUALITIES – LINEAR AND QUADRATIC
Wading In

Directions: Read the explanation for each problem type mentioned below. Pay special attention to the methods and techniques used to solve the sample problems. Then, do the practice exercises that follow; use the appropriate method to solve each problem.

TOPIC OVERVIEW: SYSTEMS OF EQUATIONS – LINEAR AND QUADRATIC

Solving systems of equations involving quadratics is different from solving linear systems of equations one major way: the presence of multiple solutions. Otherwise, we can solve these questions in the same way we solved those in Lesson 1A.

SAMPLE PROBLEM 1: SYSTEMS OF EQUATIONS – LINEAR AND QUADRATIC

$$y = 2x^2 - 3$$
$$x + y = 0$$

Which of the following sets of ordered pairs satisfies the system of equations above?

- A) $(1, -1), (\frac{3}{2}, -\frac{3}{2})$
- B) $(1, -1), (-\frac{3}{2}, \frac{3}{2})$
- C) $(-1, 1), (-\frac{3}{2}, \frac{3}{2})$
- D) $(-1, 1), (\frac{3}{2}, -\frac{3}{2})$

Typically, to solve a problem like this we should attempt to solve one of the equations for either variable. As the bottom equation is much simpler to solve than the top, let's do so:

$$x = -y$$

Now, we can plug $-y$ in for every x in the top equation. Then simplify and solve.

$$y = 2(-y)^2 - 3$$
$$y = 2y^2 - 3$$
$$2y^2 - y - 3 = 0$$
$$(y + 1)(2y - 3) = 0$$
$$y = -1, y = \frac{3}{2}$$

Now that we know both values of y, we can plug them back into the other equation to find two distinct values for x.

$$x = -y \qquad\qquad x = -y$$
$$x = -(-1) = 1 \qquad\qquad x = -\left(\frac{3}{2}\right)$$

So, our answer is **B**.

SAMPLE PROBLEM 2: SYSTEMS OF EQUATIONS – LINEAR AND QUADRATIC

$$(y - 1)^2 = -x + 3$$
$$y = x + 1$$

Which of the following sets of ordered pairs satisfies the system of equations above?

A) $(\frac{-1-\sqrt{13}}{2}, \frac{1-\sqrt{13}}{2}), (\frac{-1+\sqrt{13}}{2}, \frac{1+\sqrt{13}}{2})$

B) $(\frac{1-\sqrt{13}}{2}, \frac{-1-\sqrt{13}}{2}), (\frac{1+\sqrt{13}}{2}, \frac{-1+\sqrt{13}}{2})$

C) $(\frac{-1-\sqrt{13}}{2}, \frac{1+\sqrt{13}}{2}), (\frac{-1-\sqrt{13}}{2}, \frac{1-\sqrt{13}}{2})$

D) $(-\frac{1+\sqrt{13}}{2}, \frac{1+\sqrt{13}}{2}), (-\frac{1-\sqrt{13}}{2}, \frac{1-\sqrt{13}}{2})$

Looking at our answer choices, this sample is a little tougher than our previous sample. However, we should be able to solve the problem in much the same way as we did last time. Let's give it a shot. Since the bottom equation is already solved for y, we can plug this expression into the top equation, then simplify and solve:

$$(x + 1 - 1)^2 = -x + 3$$
$$x^2 = -x + 3$$
$$x^2 + x - 3 = 0$$

Since this expression can't be easily solved, we're forced to use either the quadratic formula or the completing-the-square method. Plugging these values into the quadratic formula, we get:

$$x = \frac{-1+\sqrt{13}}{2} \text{ and } x = \frac{-1-\sqrt{13}}{2}$$

Now, plug these expressions into the bottom equation to solve for y. So, our answer is **A**.

SAMPLE PROBLEM 3: SYSTEMS OF EQUATIONS – LINEAR AND QUADRATIC

$$(x - 1)^2 + (y + 1)^2 = 4$$
$$x = A$$

Which of the following values of A will cause the line $x = A$ to be tangent to the circle $(x - 1)^2 + (y + 1)^2 = 4$?

A) -3
B) -1
C) 0
D) 1

To solve a question like this, we have to know what the word tangent means. A line that is tangent to a circle touches it at exactly one place (i.e. it brushes the side of the circle instead of passing through the circle). Since we know the line $x = A$ must be a vertical line, we are forced to look at the points on the circle that are the farthest to the left or right. Let's start by looking at the graph of the circle to figure out where these points are:

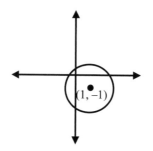

The general equation of a circle is $(x - h)^2 + (y - k)^2 = r^2$; its center will be $(h, \ k)$ and the length of its radius will be r. Above, we see the graph of the circle with its center labeled. Looking at the equation of the circle above, we see that the center is at $(1, -1)$. Thus, its horizontal end points must be $(-1, -1)$ and $(3, 1)$, since its radius is 2. So, the two vertical tangent lines are $x = -1$ and $x = 3$. Thus, our answer is **B**.

Topic Overview: Systems of Inequalities

Systems of inequalities can be solved in much the same way that systems of equalities can: the only difference is that many answers will fit the criteria in the problem. Many of these problems are easier to solve via graphing or plugging points back into the equation; these problems are far too time-consuming to solve algebraically as a rule.

Sample Problem 4: Systems of Inequalities

$$y > x^2$$
$$y < 3 - 2x$$

Which of the points is a valid solution to the system of inequalities above?

A) $(0, 0)$
B) $(0, 1)$
C) $(1, 1)$
D) $(-3, 9)$

The easiest solution to a problem like this is to plug all of the answer choices into both equations and see which one works. In this case, $(0, 0)$ ends up being the vertex of the parabola, while $(1, 1)$ and $(-3, 9)$ end up being the intersections of the two lines. Only the point $(0, 1)$ satisfies both inequalities, so **B** must be our answer.

WRAP-UP

Using a graphing calculator can be a big help on sections of the SAT that allow its use; otherwise, we may have to resort to strategies like plugging in numbers. Only practicing the varied problem types will help determine which method is fastest for which type of problem.

BLUE MATH LESSON 6B: SYSTEMS OF EQUATIONS AND INEQUALITIES – LINEAR AND QUADRATIC
Learning to Swim

Directions: Answer each question below.

PRACTICE SET 1 (NO CALCULATOR)

1. What is one set of ordered pairs that satisfies both $y = x^2 + 7$ and $y = 4(x + 1)$?

$$(x - 1)^2 + (y + 3)^2 = 25$$
$$y = x + 1$$

2. If the ordered pair (a, b) satisfies the system of equations above such that $a > 0$, what is $a + b$?

3. What is a value of K that will cause the line $x = K$ to be tangent to the circle $(x + 2)^2 + (y - 5)^2 = 16$?

4. If $y < -x^2 + 5$ and $y > 2x + k$, for what integer value of k does $(0, 0)$ satisfy both inequalities, but $(0, -1)$ does not?

5. A store sells fabric in square sheets of two sizes. Today, the store sold 4 sheets measuring x feet per side and 10 sheets measuring y feet per side; if all these sheets were put side by side, the total side length would be 40 feet. The total area of these sheets is 140 square feet. What is one possible ordered pair (x, y) that satisfies the situation above?

BLUE MATH LESSON 6B: SYSTEMS OF EQUATIONS AND INEQUALITIES – LINEAR AND QUADRATIC
Diving into the Deep End

Directions: Answer each question below.

PRACTICE SET 2 (NO CALCULATOR)

6. Which ordered pair satisfies both $(y + 3)^2 = x$ and $y = x - 5$?
   A) $(-1, -6)$
   B) $(1, -2)$
   C) $(4, -1)$
   D) $(9, 4)$

7. In physics, the equation for the distance traveled by an object that accelerates at a constant rate from a stationary position is $x = \frac{1}{2}at^2$, where a is the acceleration and t is the time elapsed. The equation for the object's velocity after the movement begins is $v = at$. If an object is traveling at 24 meters per second, and it has traveled a total of 96 meters, which of the following could be a and t?
   A) $a = 2 \text{ m/s}^2; t = 12 \text{ s}$
   B) $a = 3 \text{ m/s}^2; t = 8 \text{ s}$
   C) $a = 4 \text{ m/s}^2; t = 6 \text{ s}$
   D) $a = 12 \text{ m/s}^2; t = 4 \text{ s}$

$$(y + 2)^2 = x$$
$$y = x - 22$$

8. Which of the following sets of ordered pairs satisfies the system of equations above?
   A) $(-6, 16)$ and $(3, 25)$
   B) $(-4, 4)$ and $(9, -13)$
   C) $(9, -13)$ and $(16, -6)$
   D) $(16, -6)$ and $(25, 3)$

Questions 9 and 10 use the following information.

An object's potential energy due to gravity is approximated by $U = 10mh$, where m is its mass and h is its height. An object's kinetic energy is given by $K = \frac{1}{2}mv^2$, where v is its velocity. An object's total energy is the sum of its potential energy and kinetic energy.

9. A 10-kilogram object has total energy equal to 725 joules. The magnitude of its height, in meters, is one greater than the magnitude of its velocity, in meters per second. Which of the following could be its height and velocity?
   A) $h = 4 \text{ m}; v = 3 \text{ m/s}$
   B) $h = 5 \text{ m}; v = 6 \text{ m/s}$
   C) $h = 6 \text{ m}; v = 5 \text{ m/s}$
   D) $h = 8 \text{ m}; v = 7 \text{ m/s}$

10. A 12-kilogram object has total energy equal to 1134 joules. If its height is 9 feet, what is its velocity?
    A) 3 m/s
    B) 4 m/s
    C) 6 m/s
    D) 9 m/s

11. Which of the following lists all the possible values of K for which $y = K$ is tangent to the circle $(x - 2)^2 + (y - 6)^2 = 49$?
    A) -13 and 1
    B) -5 and 9
    C) -1 and 13
    D) 6 only

12. A parabola crosses the line $y = x + 1$ at the points $(3, 4)$ and $(-\frac{5}{2}, -\frac{3}{2})$. What is one possible equation for the parabola?

    A) $y = x^2 - 6$
    B) $y = 2x^2 - 14$
    C) $y = 3x^2 - 23$
    D) $y = -x^2 + 5$

13. Which of the following ordered pairs satisfies both $x^2 + (y - 5)^2 < 25$ and $y < 2x - 2$?

    A) $(1, 1)$
    B) $(2, 2)$
    C) $(3, 3)$
    D) $(5, 5)$

$$y < -x^2 - 2x + 5$$
$$y > 2x + 5$$

14. If a point $(-1, b)$ satisfies the system of inequalities above, what is a possible integer value for b?

$$x^2 + (y + 3)^2 < 25$$
$$y > 3x + 2$$

15. If the point $(a, 1)$ satisfies the system of inequalities above, what is a possible integer value of $-a$?

PRACTICE SET 3 (NO CALCULATOR)

$$y = 2x^2 + x$$
$$2x = y - 1$$

16. Which set of ordered pairs satisfies the system of equations above?

    A) $\left(-\frac{1}{2}, 0\right)$ and $(1, 3)$
    B) $\left(-\frac{1}{2}, 0\right)$ and $(2, 10)$
    C) $\left(\frac{1}{2}, 2\right)$ and $(1, 3)$
    D) $\left(\frac{1}{2}, 2\right)$ and $(2, 5)$

17. Which of the following values of C will cause the line $y = C$ to be tangent to the circle $(x + 4)^2 + (y - 3)^2 = 36$?

    A) -4
    B) -3
    C) 2
    D) 3

18. An engineer is designing two towers with square foundations. The total area covered by the towers' foundations is equal to 544 square meters. The sum of the two towers' perimeters is equal to 128 meters. What is the area of the larger foundation?

    A) 144 square meters
    B) 256 square meters
    C) 324 square meters
    D) 400 square meters

Questions 19 through 21 use the following equations.

A: $y = 3x^2 + 5x + 1$

B: $x + y = 10$

C: $(x + 3)^2 + (y + 1)^2 = 100$

19. Which set of ordered pairs satisfies equations **A** and **B**?

A) $(-5, 25)$ and $(-3, 13)$

B) $(-3, 13)$ and $(1, 9)$

C) $(-3, 13)$ and $(3, 7)$

D) $(1, 9)$ and $(3, 7)$

20. Which of these ordered pairs satisfies equations **B** and **C**?

A) $(-3, 9)$

B) $(3, 7)$

C) $(4, 6)$

D) $(6, 8)$

21. Which of the following lines is tangent to the circle represented by equation **C**?

A) $y = -9$

B) $y = 11$

C) $x = -7$

D) $x = 7$

22. Which of the following ordered pairs satisfies both $x < y$ and $(x + 1)^2 + y < 5$?

A) $(-1, 0)$

B) $(0, -1)$

C) $(1, 5)$

D) $(2, 1)$

$$x < 2y - 10$$
$$(x + 4)^2 + (y + 4)^2 < 121$$

23. Which of the following ordered pairs satisfies the system of inequalities above?

A) $(-9, 5)$

B) $(-6, -2)$

C) $(-3, 3)$

D) $(0, 5)$

Questions 24 and 25 use the information below.

Newton's law of gravitation states that for any two masses m_1 and m_2, the force of gravity between them is given by $F = \frac{Gm_1m_2}{r^2}$, where r is the distance between the objects' centers and G is a constant equal to 6.67×10^{-11}.

24. The Earth has a mass of 6.0×10^{24} kilograms. An asteroid's distance from Earth's center (in meters) is 10,000 times the asteroid's mass (in kilograms). What is a possible mass of the asteroid, in kilograms, if it has a force of gravitation with Earth equal to 1000 newtons? Round to the nearest 1000 kilograms.

25. Two objects have equal mass and are 13.34 meters apart. The force of gravitation between them is equal to 450 more than one-millionth the mass of one of the objects. What is the force, in newtons, of the gravitation between the objects?

BLUE MATH LESSON 6B: SYSTEMS OF EQUATIONS AND INEQUALITIES – LINEAR AND QUADRATIC
Race to the Finish

Directions: Answer each question below.

HOMEWORK SET (NO CALCULATOR)

$$y = 4x^2 - 2x - 1$$
$$x + y = 17$$

1. Which of the following ordered pairs satisfies the system of equations above?
   A) $(-2, 19)$
   B) $(-1, 7)$
   C) $(2, 15)$
   D) $(3, 14)$

2. If $y = x^2 - 4x - 10$ and $x = 3y$, what is a possible value for x?
   A) -6
   B) -2
   C) 2
   D) 6

3. Which ordered pair satisfies the equations $(x - 2)^2 + y^2 = 9$ and $y = 2x - 10$?
   A) $(0, 5)$
   B) $(2, 3)$
   C) $(5, 0)$
   D) $(7, 4)$

4. A line is parallel to the line $y = x$ and passes through the parabola $y = x^2 - 3$ at $(4, 13)$. What is the other point at which the two functions intersect?
   A) $(-3, 6)$
   B) $(-2, 1)$
   C) $(0, -3)$
   D) $(3, 6)$

$$(x - 5)^2 + (y + 3)^2 = 81$$
$$y - 1 = x$$

5. Which set of ordered pairs satisfies the system of equations above?
   A) $(-6, -5)$ and $(3, 4)$
   B) $(-5, -6)$ and $(4, 3)$
   C) $(-4, -3)$ and $(5, 6)$
   D) $(-3, -4)$ and $(6, 5)$

6. A state's economic development score is equal the sum of its unemployment rate and the square of its poverty rate. Texas' poverty rate is 0.13 higher than its unemployment rate, and its economic development score is 0.11. What is Texas' poverty rate?
   A) 0.07
   B) 0.12
   C) 0.20
   D) 0.24

7. Which system of equations is satisfied by the points $(-1, -5)$ and $(4, 10)$?

   A) $y = 3x - 2$
   $y = x + 6$

   B) $y = 3x - 2$
   $y = x^2 - 6$

   C) $y = x - 4$
   $y = x^2 - 6$

   D) $y = x + 6$
   $y = x^2 - 6$

8. Which system of equations is satisfied by the points $(4, 1)$ and $(0, 5)$?

   A) $x^2 + y^2 = 25$
   $y = -x + 5$

   B) $x^2 + (y - 1)^2 = 16$
   $y = 2x + 5$

   C) $x^2 + (y - 1)^2 = 16$
   $y = -x + 5$

   D) $(x - 1)^2 + y^2 = 16$
   $y = -x + 5$

9. A circle in the center of a soccer field has a radius of 10 yards. A player runs in a straight line due northeast, intersecting the circle 6 yards to the north and 8 yards to the east of its center. If an xy-coordinate plane is overlaid on the field so that the center of the field is the origin and north is the positive-y direction, which system of equations matches this description?

   A) $y = x - 2$
   $x^2 + y^2 = 100$

   B) $y = x + 2$
   $x^2 + y^2 = 100$

   C) $y = x - 2$
   $(x - 8)^2 + (y - 6)^2 = 100$

   D) $y = x + 2$
   $(x - 8)^2 + (y - 6)^2 = 100$

10. Which of the following sets of ordered pairs satisfies both $(y + 3)^2 = x - 2$ and $y = -2x + 2$?

   A) $(2, -1)$ and $(\frac{9}{4}, -\frac{5}{2})$

   B) $(2, -1)$ and $(\frac{5}{4}, -\frac{1}{2})$

   C) $(3, -4)$ and $(\frac{9}{4}, -\frac{5}{2})$

   D) $(3, -4)$ and $(\frac{5}{4}, -\frac{1}{2})$

$$y > 2x^2 - 3$$
$$y < 3x$$

11. Which of the following ordered pairs satisfies both of the inequalities above?

   A) $(-1, 2)$

   B) $(0, 1)$

   C) $(1, 2)$

   D) $(2, 1)$

Questions 12 and 13 use the following information.

Experts say that, when exercising, adults should try to achieve a heart rate of at least 200 minus their age. However, doctors consider it unsafe for people to raise their heart rate above a level equal to $190 - \frac{7A^2}{1,000}$, where A is their age.

12. Which of the following scenarios describes a healthy heartrate using both the criteria described above?

   A) A 20-year-old with a heart rate of 175.

   B) A 30-year-old with a heart rate of 185.

   C) A 40-year-old with a heart rate of 175.

   D) A 50-year-old with a heart rate of 145.

13. In which age range is a heart rate of 180 always acceptable under both criteria?
    A) 18 through 28
    B) 26 through 36
    C) 30 through 40
    D) 35 through 45

14. If $(x - 2)^2 + (y + 2)^2 < 16$ and $y > kx + 1$, which of the following could be the value of k if $(5, -1)$ satisfies both equations but both $(4, 2)$ and $(3, -1)$ do not?
    A) -2
    B) -1
    C) $-\frac{1}{2}$
    D) $\frac{1}{2}$

Questions 15 and 16 use the following information.

The path of a baseball hit to centerfield is modeled on a coordinate plane, with home plate being the point $(0, 0)$. The path of the baseball is graphed according to the parabola $h = -\frac{d^2}{160} + 2d + 3$, where h is the ball's height and d is its distance from home plate (both in feet). Two spotlights in the stadium situated above home plate shine towards the centerfield wall. The beam from spotlight A's position is given by $h = \frac{d}{4} + 100$; the beam from spotlight B's position is given by $h = -\frac{d}{4} + 100$.

15. A bird is flying over the field. At what combination of height and distance from home plate would the bird be higher than spotlight A's beam, but beneath the path of the baseball?
    A) $d = 80$ feet, $h = 100$ feet
    B) $d = 100$ feet, $h = 120$ feet
    C) $d = 120$ feet, $h = 140$ feet
    D) $d = 150$ feet, $h = 170$ feet

16. At which two distances from home plate is the ball lower than spotlight B's beam?
    A) 20 feet and 300 feet
    B) 40 feet and 320 feet
    C) 80 feet and 240 feet
    D) 120 feet and 320 feet

17. What is one possible x value that satisfies both $3x = y + 1$ and $y = \frac{1}{2}(x + 1)^2$?

$$(y - 3)^2 = x$$
$$y = 3x + 3$$

18. The ordered pair (a, b) satisfies the system of equations above. What is a possible value for a?

19. For what value of C is the line $y = C$ tangent to the parabola $y = 2x^2 + 4x + 3$?

20. What is a value of D that makes $x = 6$ tangent to the circle $(x - 3)^2 + y^2 = D$?

BLUE MATH LESSON 7A: GRAPHS OF NON-LINEAR FUNCTIONS
Getting Your Feet Wet

Directions: The problems below are intended as a short diagnostic exam.

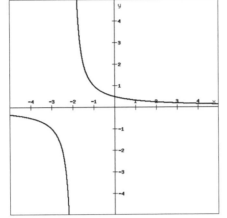

1. Which of the following equations represents the graph above?
    A) $y = \frac{1}{x+2}$
    B) $y = \frac{1}{x-2}$
    C) $y = \frac{1}{x^2}$
    D) $y = \frac{x-1}{x+2}$

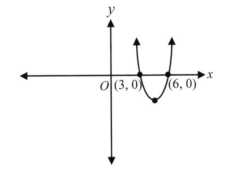

2. Which of the following is true about the above graph of the quadratic above?
    A) The inverse of the quadratic is a function.
    B) The vertex of the quadratic has an x-coordinate of 4.5.
    C) The quadratic is not a function.
    D) The quadratic has two imaginary roots.

3. Which of the equations below shows the graph of a circle with center $(-3, 2)$ and diameter of length 10?
    A) $(x - 3)^2 + (y + 2)^2 = 25$
    B) $(x + 3)^2 + (y - 2)^2 = 100$
    C) $(x + 3)^2 + (y - 2)^2 = 25$
    D) $(x - 3)^2 + (y + 2)^2 = 100$

BLUE MATH LESSON 7A: GRAPHS OF NON-LINEAR FUNCTIONS
Wading In

Directions: Read the explanation for each problem type mentioned below. Pay special attention to the methods and techniques used to solve the sample problems. Then, do the practice exercises that follow; use the appropriate method to solve each problem.

TOPIC OVERVIEW: GRAPHS OF NON-LINEAR FUNCTIONS

Many types of graphs are given on the SAT; below, we'll see some of the more common **parent functions**. These parent functions are standard shapes of graphs, each of which corresponds to a specific type of function. Memorizing these basic shapes will help us narrow down the answer choices on many of the graphing questions on the SAT.

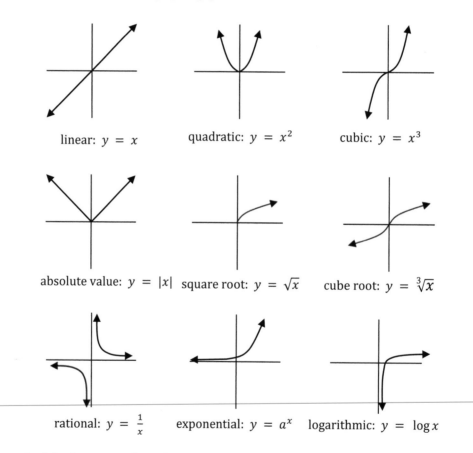

linear: $y = x$ quadratic: $y = x^2$ cubic: $y = x^3$

absolute value: $y = |x|$ square root: $y = \sqrt{x}$ cube root: $y = \sqrt[3]{x}$

rational: $y = \dfrac{1}{x}$ exponential: $y = a^x$ logarithmic: $y = \log x$

Let's look at a sample problem showing how questions dealing with non-linear graphs might be asked on the SAT.

SAMPLE PROBLEM 1: GRAPHS OF NON-LINEAR FUNCTIONS

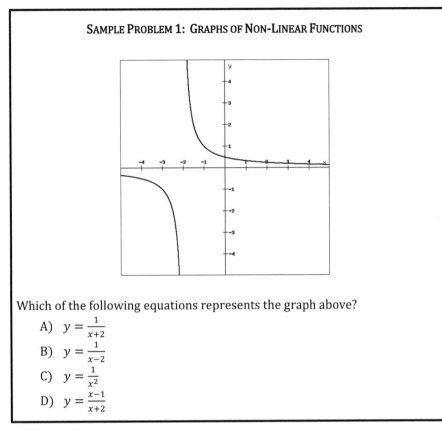

Which of the following equations represents the graph above?

A) $y = \dfrac{1}{x+2}$

B) $y = \dfrac{1}{x-2}$

C) $y = \dfrac{1}{x^2}$

D) $y = \dfrac{x-1}{x+2}$

The first step in solving a problem like this is to identify the parent function. The shape of the graph shows us that we have a rational function, so it must be of the form $f(x) = \dfrac{1}{x}$. So, we can eliminate answer choices C and D. Once we have those eliminated, try to find points that the graph passes through. For example, our graph above passes through the point $(0, 0.5)$. Plug this ordered pair into both A and B and we'll see that **A** must be the answer.

TOPIC OVERVIEW: PARABOLAS

There are two basic ways to write the equation of a parabola: **Vertex Form** and **Standard Form**. Below are the equations for both.

Vertex Form

$$y = A(x - h)^2 + k$$

The Vertex Form is named such because the form draws special attention to the **vertex**, the minimum or maximum point of the parabola. For a parabola in vertex form, the vertex is given by the coordinate pair (h, k).

The **axis of symmetry** is a line that passes through the vertex of any parabola. The two sides of the parabola on either side of the axis of symmetry are mirror images of each other.

The other form of the parabola is more common:

Standard Form

$$y = Ax^2 + Bx + C$$

The x-coordinate of the vertex of a parabola in standard form is $-\frac{B}{2A}$. To find the y-coordinate of the vertex, simply plug this number back into the x-values of the equation of the parabola.

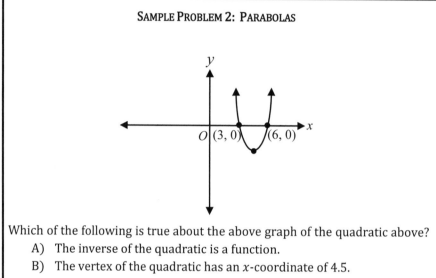

SAMPLE PROBLEM 2: PARABOLAS

Which of the following is true about the above graph of the quadratic above?
  A) The inverse of the quadratic is a function.
  B) The vertex of the quadratic has an x-coordinate of 4.5.
  C) The quadratic is not a function.
  D) The quadratic has two imaginary roots.

Since we're given the graph of the parabola, let's analyze the answer choices. To understand choices A and C, we have to remember what a **function** is. A function is a relationship between values. Each input value (x) gives back exactly one output value (y). An easy way to test if a graph is a function is the **vertical line test**: If we can draw a vertical line anywhere on the graph that touches the graph in more than one place, the graph is not a function. So, we can eliminate choice C.

To check the validity of choice A, we have to remember that an **inverse** function is one in which the x- and y-values are switched. If we're given the graph of a function, an easier way to find its inverse is to flip it over the line $y = x$. Let's show that below:

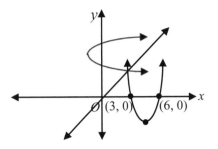

Since the inverse function does not pass the vertical line test, we know that it is not a function. So, we can eliminate choice A.

The **roots** (also known as **x-intercepts** or **zeros**) of a function are the points where the function crosses the x-axis. Since this function clearly crosses the x-axis at 3 and 6, it has two real zeros. We can cross out answer choice D.

So, our answer must be **B**. If a function is a parabola, its vertex is always exactly halfway between its zeros.

Topic Overview: Circles

A concept new to the SAT, but not to Algebra II students, is the equation of the graph of a circle. The general equation of a circle is:
$(x - h)^2 + (y - k)^2 = r^2$, where (h, k) represents the center of the circle and r is the length of its radius. Most questions involving the graph of a circle on the SAT will ask us to either construct the equation of the circle by looking at either its graph or its center and radius, or vice versa. Let's try one of these:

Sample Problem 3: Circles

Which of the equations below shows the graph of a circle with center $(-3, 2)$ and diameter of length 10?
- A) $(x - 3)^2 + (y + 2)^2 = 25$
- B) $(x + 3)^2 + (y - 2)^2 = 100$
- C) $(x + 3)^2 + (y - 2)^2 = 25$
- D) $(x - 3)^2 + (y + 2)^2 = 100$

Since we're given both the center and the diameter, let's figure out what h, k, and r are. $h = -3$, $k = 2$, and $r = 5$. So, plugging these into the equation of a circle, our answer must be **C**.

WRAP-UP

For questions involving graphs, our two biggest aids will be a graphing calculator and the ability to work backwards by plugging points into graphs. The SAT will never ask us to come up with the equation of a function without giving us options to choose from. In Lesson 8A, we will learn some additional ways to narrow down the graph of a function from a parent function to one of its transformations.

BLUE MATH LESSON 7A: GRAPHS OF NON-LINEAR FUNCTIONS
Learning to Swim

Directions: Answer each question below.

PRACTICE SET 1 (NO CALCULATOR)

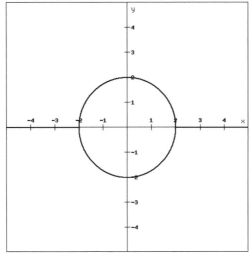

1.   Write the equation that represents the graph above.

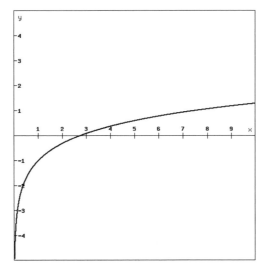

2.   Which parent function best describes the graph above?

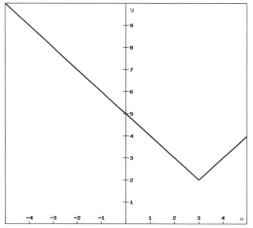

3.   Which parent function best describes the graph above?

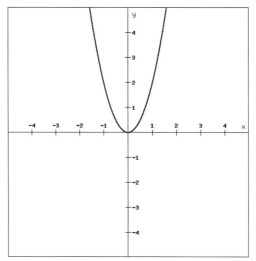

4.   Which parent function best describes the graph above?

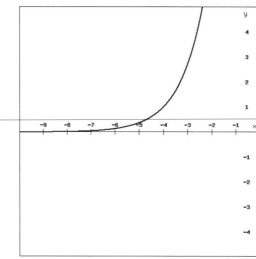

5.   Which parent function best describes the graph above?

BLUE MATH LESSON 7A: GRAPHS OF NON-LINEAR FUNCTIONS
Diving into the Deep End

Directions: Answer each question below.

PRACTICE SET 2 (NO CALCULATOR)

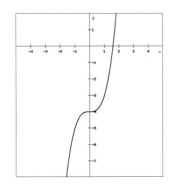

6. Which of the following equations represents the graph above?

A) $y = x^2 - 4$
B) $y = x^3 - 4$
C) $y = (x - 4)^3$
D) $y = (x + 4)^3$

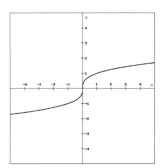

8. Which of the following equations represents the graph above?

A) $y = \sqrt{x}$
B) $y = e^x$
C) $y = \sqrt[3]{x}$
D) $y = \frac{1}{x}$

7. What is/are the x-intercept(s) of the equation $y = (x - 4)^4 - 1$?

A) $(4, 0)$
B) $(0, 3), (0, 5)$
C) $(1, 0)\ (2, 0)$
D) $(3, 0)\ (5, 0)$

9. Which of the following graphs represents the equation $f(x) = e^x$?

A) 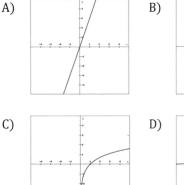 B)

C) 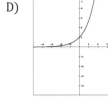 D)

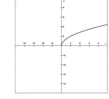

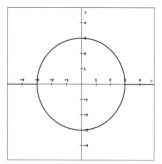

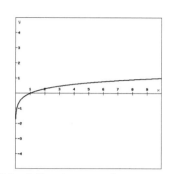

10. Which of the following equations represents the graph above?

    I. $y = \pm\sqrt{9 - x^2}$
    II. $x^2 + y^2 = 3$
    III. $y = \pm\sqrt{3 - x^2}$

A) I only
B) II only
C) II and III only
D) I, II, and III

12. Which of the following equations represents the graph above?
A) $f(x) = \log(x)$
B) $f(x) = \ln(x)$
C) $f(x) = e^x$
D) $f(x) = \sqrt{x - 1}$

11. Which of the following is the y-intercept of the equation $y = \frac{1}{3}(x)^3 - 3$?
A) $(3, 0)$
B) $(0, 3)$
C) $(0, -3)$
D) $(-3, 0)$

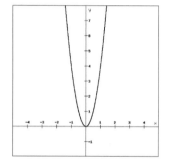

13. Which of the following equations represents the graph above?
A) $y = x^2$
B) $y = 4x^2$
C) $y = x^4$
D) $y = x^2$

14. In the function $f(x) = 3|-2x + 2| - 1$, what is the x-coordinate of the vertex?

15. What is the average of the two slopes produced by the function $f(x) = -2|3x - 9| - 7$?

PRACTICE SET 3 (NO CALCULATOR)

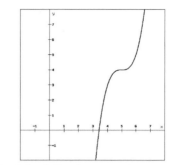

16. Which of the following equations represents the graph above?
    A) $y = x^3 + 4$
    B) $y = (x + 5)^3 + 4$
    C) $y = (x - 4)^3 + 5$
    D) $y = (x - 5)^3 + 4$

17. Which of the following represent the equation of a circle, with a center at the origin, and a radius of 4?
    A) $x^2 + y^2 = 4$
    B) $x^2 + y^2 = 16$
    C) $y^2 - x^2 = 16$
    D) $y^2 - x^2 = 4$

18. Which of the following represents a graph of a parabola, with a vertex at $(1, 0)$?
    A) $f(x) = x^2 + 1$
    B) $f(x) = (x - 1)^2$
    C) $f(x) = (x + 1)^2$
    D) $f(x) = x^2 - 1$

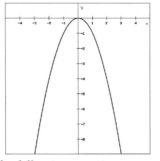

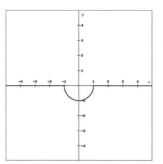

19. Which of the following equations represents the graph above?
   A) $y = x^2$
   B) $y = (-x)^2$
   C) $y = -x^2$
   D) $y = x^2 - 1$

21. Which of the following equations represents the graph above?
   A) $y = \sqrt{x}$
   B) $y = \sqrt{1 - x^2}$
   C) $y = -\sqrt{1 - x^2}$
   D) $y = \sqrt{x^2 - 1}$

20. Which of the following graphs represents the equation $f(x) = -\log(x)$?

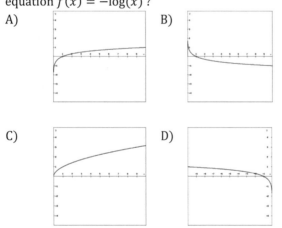

A)
B)
C)
D)

22. Which of the following equations represents a circle with radius of 1 and a center at $(-1, -1)$?
   A) $y = \pm\sqrt{1 - (x + 1)^2} - 1$
   B) $y = \pm\sqrt{1 - (x + 1)^2} + 1$
   C) $y = \pm\sqrt{1 - (x - 1)^2} + 1$
   D) $y = \pm\sqrt{1 - (x - 1)^2} - 1$

24. What is the y-intercept of the function
$f(x) = 2^{x+3} - 1$?

23. Which of the following equations represents the graph to the right?
A) $y = e^x - 4$
B) $y = e^{x-4}$
C) $y = e^{x+4}$
D) $y = e^x + 4$

25. A parabola has a vertex at $(3, -4)$ and a y-intercept of 5. What is a possible zero of the function?

BLUE MATH LESSON 7A: GRAPHS OF NON-LINEAR FUNCTIONS
Race to the Finish

Directions: Answer each question below.

HOMEWORK SET (NO CALCULATOR)

1. Which of the following equations passes through the points $(0, 0), (3, 27), (-2, -8)$?
   A) $y = 9x$
   B) $y = 4x$
   C) $y = x^3$
   D) $y = 3x^2$

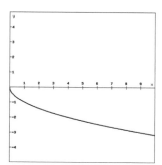

3. Which of the following equations represents the graph above?
   A) $f(x) = -\sqrt{x}$
   B) $f(x) = \sqrt{x} - 1$
   C) $f(x) = \sqrt{-x}$
   D) $f(x) = \sqrt{x}$

2. Which of the following equations represents the graph above?
   A) $y = \ln(x + 5)$
   B) $y = \log(x + 5)$
   C) $y = \log(x) + 5$
   D) $y = \ln(x) + 5$

4. Which of the following equations of a graph is equivalent to the graph of $f(x) = x^4$?
   A) $f(x) = x^2$
   B) $f(x) = -x^4$
   C) $f(x) = (-x)^4$
   D) $f(x) = x^6$

5. If a graph of $y = f(x)$ had all the y-values switch signs, what would happen to the graph of $f(x)$?
   A) It would be flipped over the x-axis.
   B) It would be flipped over the y-axis.
   C) It would be flipped over the line $y = x$.
   D) Nothing would happen to the graph.

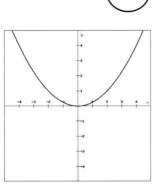

6. Which of the following equations represents the graph above?
   A) $y = 2x^2$
   B) $y = \frac{1}{4}x^2$
   C) $y = 4x^2$
   D) $y = x^2$

7. What is the radius of the graph of the equation $(x-3)^2 + (y-5)^2 = 5$?
   A) 5
   B) 2.5
   C) $\sqrt{5}$
   D) 1

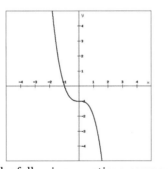

8. Which of the following equations represents the graph above?
   A) $y = x^3 - 1$
   B) $y = -x^3 - 1$
   C) $y = (x-1)^3$
   D) $y = -x^3 + 1$

9. Which of the following equations represents a graph that goes through the points $(0, 0)$, $(1, 1)$, and $(-4, 256)$?
   A) $y = x^6$
   B) $y = x^3$
   C) $y = x^4$
   D) $y = x^2$

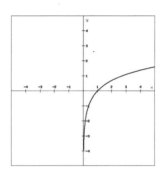

10. Which of the following equations represents the graph above?
    A) $f(x) = \log(x)$
    B) $f(x) = \ln(x)$
    C) $f(x) = e^x$
    D) $f(x) = \sqrt{x-1}$

11. Which of the following pairs of equations represents graphs that are reflections over the line $y = x$?
    A) $y = x^2$ and $y = \sqrt{x}$
    B) $y = x^4$ and $y = \sqrt{x}$
    C) $y = x^2$ and $y = x$
    D) $y = x^3$ and $y = \sqrt[3]{x}$

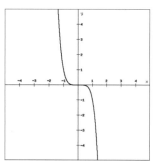

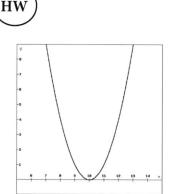

12. Which of the following equations represents the graph above?
   A) $f(x) = -x^{-5}$
   B) $f(x) = x^{-3}$
   C) $f(x) = x^3$
   D) $f(x) = -x^5$

15. Which of the following equations represents the graph above?
   A) $y = x^2 - 10$
   B) $y = (x - 10)^2$
   C) $y = (x + 10)^2$
   D) $y = x^2 + 10$

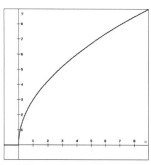

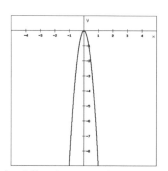

13. Which of the following equations represents the graph above?
   A) $f(x) = -\sqrt{x}$
   B) $f(x) = 2\sqrt{x}$
   C) $f(x) = 3\sqrt{x}$
   D) $f(x) = \sqrt{x}$

16. Which of the following equations represents the graph above?
   A) $y = x^2$
   B) $y = -x^2$
   C) $y = -(3x)^2$
   D) $y = -3x^2$

14. What is the radius of the graph of the equation $y = \pm\sqrt{16 - x^2}$?
   A) 4
   B) 16
   C) 8
   D) $\sqrt{8}$

17. What is the y-coordinate of the vertex of the parabola $y = 3x^2 - 6x + 18$?

19. A quadratic function has zeros of $(-3, 0)$ and $(8, 0)$. The axis of symmetry of the parabola is the equation $x = ?$

18. A circle is centered around the point $(3, 4)$ and passes through the point $(7, 7)$. What is the length of the radius of the circle?

20. What is the y-intercept of the rational function $f(x) = \frac{2}{x+3} + 5$?

BLUE MATH LESSON 7B: SOLVING FOR A VARIABLE

Getting Your Feet Wet

Directions: The problems below are intended as a short diagnostic exam.

1. If $\frac{ax+b}{cx-d} = a$, then $x =$

   A) $\frac{d-b}{1-c}$

   B) $\frac{d+b}{c-1}$

   C) $\frac{b-d}{a(1-c)}$

   D) $\frac{ad+b}{a(c-1)}$

2. Ohm's Law shows that the voltage, V, of a simple electrical circuit is equivalent to the product of its electric current, I, and its resistance, R. The power, P, of a resistor in a DC circuit is given by the product of the voltage of the circuit and its electric current. Find an expression for the electric current of the circuit in terms of its resistance and its power.

   A) $I = \pm\sqrt{RP}$

   B) $I = \pm\sqrt{\frac{P}{R}}$

   C) $I = \pm\sqrt{\frac{R}{P}}$

   D) $I = \frac{R}{IP}$

BLUE MATH LESSON 7B: SOLVING FOR A VARIABLE
Wading In

Directions: Read the explanation for each problem type mentioned below. Pay special attention to the methods and techniques used to solve the sample problems. Then, do the practice exercises that follow; use the appropriate method to solve each problem.

TOPIC OVERVIEW: SOLVING FOR A VARIABLE

Solving a complex equation for one variable is something that shows up often in many sciences classes, so it's no surprise that the new SAT will use the concept frequently. Let's look at an example to see how this is done:

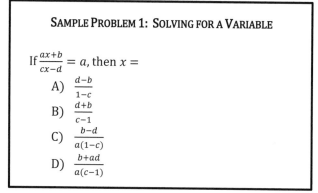

SAMPLE PROBLEM 1: SOLVING FOR A VARIABLE

If $\frac{ax+b}{cx-d} = a$, then $x =$

A) $\frac{d-b}{1-c}$

B) $\frac{d+b}{c-1}$

C) $\frac{b-d}{a(1-c)}$

D) $\frac{b+ad}{a(c-1)}$

This problem is fairly challenging, especially since there are not one, but two xs. Since this problem also features a fraction, let's get rid of that first by multiplying both sides by the denominator:

$$\frac{ax+b}{cx-d} = a$$

$$ax + b = a(cx - d)$$

Now that we've taken care of that, simplify everything as far as it can go. In this case, that means distribute the a.

$$ax + b = acx - ad$$

A new problem presents itself: we're trying to solve for x, but there are two xs. To fix this, let's get all of our terms that contain an x on one side and all the terms that do not on the other.

$$ax - acx = -b - ad$$

Now we can factor out our x. Once we've done that, it'll be relatively simple to solve for x.

$$x(a - ac) = -b - ad$$

$$x = \frac{-b-ad}{a-ac}$$

Unfortunately, this isn't one of our answer choices. Let's try to simplify this expression a little bit more by factoring other terms out.

$$x = \frac{-(b+ad)}{a(1-c)}$$

Another trick the SAT uses is eliminating negative signs. Notice that our answer looks very similar to answer choice D? Watch what happens when we pull a negative 1 out from the denominator:

$$x = \frac{-(b+ad)}{a(1-c)}$$

$$x = \frac{-(b+ad)}{-a(-1+c)}$$

$$x = \frac{(b+ad)}{a(c-1)}$$

And we're done. Our answer is **D**.

SAMPLE PROBLEM 2: SOLVING FOR A VARIABLE

Ohm's Law shows that the voltage, V, of a simple electrical circuit is equivalent to the product of its electric current, I, and its resistance, R. The power, P, of a resistor in a DC circuit is given by the product of the voltage of the circuit and its electric current. Find an expression for the electric current of the circuit in terms of its resistance and its power.

A) $I = \pm\sqrt{RP}$

B) $I = \pm\sqrt{\dfrac{P}{R}}$

C) $I = \pm\sqrt{\dfrac{R}{P}}$

D) $I = \dfrac{R}{IP}$

Let's start by figuring out our initial equations: Since V is the product of I and R, we have the equation $V = IR$. Since P is the product of V and I, we also have $P = IV$. We want to solve these two equations for I in terms of P and R, so we have to eliminate V as a variable. Since the first equation is already solved for V, let's plug that into the second equation:

$$P = IV$$
$$P = I(IR)$$
$$P = I^2R$$

Now we have to solve for I. Let's start by getting I by itself:

$$I^2 = \frac{P}{R}$$

To turn I^2 into I, we need to take the square root of both sides:

$$\sqrt{I^2} = \pm\sqrt{\frac{P}{R}}$$

$$I = \pm\sqrt{\frac{P}{R}}$$

So, our answer must be **B**.

Wrap-Up

When solving an equation or group of equations for a variable, it always helps to analyze the question beforehand to come up with a plan for solving the equation. Sometimes, finding the easiest method to solve for a variable isn't immediately obvious. In these cases, plug in a value for every value other than the variable that's being solved for. Simplify the expression to get a numerical solution for this variable. Then, plug in those same numbers for the variables in all of the answer choices. The choice that gives the same answer as the original equation will always be the answer. Remember, however, when using the plugging-in-numbers method to never pick 0 or 1 as the numbers: These choices can cause many mathematical inconsistencies that are best avoided. As always, plugging in numbers can be very time consuming, so avoid using it unless there are no better options.

BLUE MATH LESSON 7B: SOLVING FOR A VARIABLE
Learning to Swim

Directions: Answer each question below.

PRACTICE SET 1 (NO CALCULATOR)

1. The surface area S of a sphere is equal to $4\pi r^2$, where r is the radius. Solve for r in terms of S.

2. The volume V of a sphere is equal to $\frac{4}{3}\pi r^3$. Solve for V in terms of the surface area S. Do not use the radius r in your answer.

3. Solve for x in terms of y: $xy = 5 - 3x$.

    Matt divided both sides of the equation above to provide the following solution: $x = \frac{5-3x}{y}$. Is this a valid solution? Why or why not? If not, what is the correct answer?

4. A race car driver travels three laps around a one-mile track at speeds r_1, r_2, and r_3, respectively. Using the equation $d = rt$ (distance = rate × time), express the total time t that these three laps take in terms of r_1, r_2, and r_3.

5. The *Hardy-Weinberg Equation* in genetics relates the frequencies of two alleles (different versions of a gene) one of which is dominant and the other of which is recessive. The equation is $p^2 + 2pq + q^2 = 1$, where p is the frequency of the dominant version of the gene and q is the frequency of the recessive version. Given that p and q are both fractions between 0 and 1, solve for p in terms of q.

BLUE MATH LESSON 7B: SOLVING FOR A VARIABLE

Diving into the Deep End

Directions: Answer each question below.

PRACTICE SET 2 (NO CALCULATOR)

6. The *Reynolds number* is a quantity related to fluid in a tube that helps describe how it flows. A typical Reynolds number for human blood flow is 2000. The Reynolds number is calculated by the equation $R = \frac{\rho v L}{\mu}$, where ρ is the density of the blood, v is the mean velocity of the blood, L is the diameter of the vessel, and μ is the viscosity, or thickness, of the blood. If $R = 2000$, which of the following equations gives the velocity v of the blood in terms of ρ, μ, and L?

   A) $v = \frac{\rho L}{2000\mu}$

   B) $v = \frac{2000\rho L}{\mu}$

   C) $v = \frac{2000\mu}{\rho L}$

   D) $v = 2000\mu - \rho L$

7. The *flow rate* of a fluid in a tube is defined as the cross-sectional area of the tube (the shaded circle in the figure above), multiplied by the velocity of the moving fluid. The flow rate throughout a closed tube must be constant; that is, the product Av (Area × velocity) is the same at all points in the tube. If water enters a cylindrical pipe at a velocity of v centimeters per second, and the pipe's radius then decreases from R to r, what will be the velocity of the water in the narrower section, in terms of v, R, and r ?

   A) $\frac{vR}{r}$

   B) $\frac{vR^2}{r^2}$

   C) $\frac{vr}{R}$

   D) $\frac{vr^2}{R^2}$

8. A river is 60 feet wide and an average of 6 feet deep at its mouth. If the water at this point is flowing at a rate of f feet per second, how many cubic feet of water are discharged every minute, in terms of f?

   A) $6f$

   B) $216f$

   C) $360f$

   D) $21,600f$

9. *Ohm's Law* states that in an electric circuit, the voltage V in volts is equal to the current I in amperes times the resistance R in ohms. *Electric power*, measured in watts, is equal to the voltage times the current. If an electrical outlet is supplying 100 watts of power to a lamp, which of the following equations correctly expresses the current I in terms of the circuit's resistance?

   A) $I = \frac{0.8}{R}$

   B) $I = \frac{1.2\sqrt{R}}{R}$

   C) $I = 10\sqrt{R}$

   D) $I = \frac{10\sqrt{R}}{R}$

10. The gravitational force pulling two objects toward each other is given by the equation $F_G = \frac{Gm_1m_2}{r^2}$, where G is a constant, m_1 and m_2 are the masses of the two objects, and r is the distance between them. Which of the following equations correctly gives r in terms of G, F_G, m_1, and m_2?

A) $r = \frac{Gm_1m_2}{F_G}$

B) $r = \sqrt{\frac{Gm_1m_2}{F_G}}$

C) $r = \frac{F_G}{Gm_1m_2}$

D) $r = \sqrt{\frac{F_G}{Gm_1m_2}}$

11. If $\frac{3}{x} = \frac{y}{x+1}$, which of the following equations expresses x in terms of y?

A) $x = \frac{3}{y-3}$

B) $x = \frac{6}{y}$

C) $x = \frac{1}{3y}$

D) $x = 1 + \frac{1}{3y}$

12. A cannonball is fired from the edge of a cliff above the ocean. Its height h in meters above sea level at a time t seconds after firing is given by the equation $h = c + v_0t - 4.9t^2$, where c is the height of the cliff and v_0 is the cannonball's initial upward velocity. If the cliff is 120 meters high, which of the following expressions gives the initial velocity v_0 (in meters per second) for which the cannonball will take exactly x seconds to hit the water?

A) $v_0 = 4.9x$

B) $v_0 = \frac{4.9x^2 + 120}{x}$

C) $v_0 = \frac{4.9x^2 - 120}{x}$

D) $v_0 = 120 - 4.9x^2$

13. The volume V of a cone, in terms of the cone's radius r and height h, is given by $V = \frac{1}{3}\pi r^2 h$. Which of the following equations correctly expresses the radius in terms of the volume and the height?

A) $r = \sqrt{\frac{V\pi}{3h}}$

B) $r = \sqrt{\frac{3V}{\pi h}}$

C) $r = \frac{V}{3\pi h^2}$

D) $r = \sqrt{\frac{V}{3\pi h}}$

14. If $zx + 4 = \frac{y}{z}$, which of the following equations correctly expresses x in terms of y and z ?

   A) $x = \frac{y}{z^2} - 4$

   B) $x = \frac{y - 4z}{z^2}$

   C) $x = \frac{y - 4}{z}$

   D) $x = \frac{y - 4z}{z}$

15. A swimming pool must be designed to hold 64,000 cubic feet of water, and its length must be twice its width. The pool's depth in feet will equal $\frac{64000}{jw^k}$, where w is the pool's width, and j and k are constants. What is the value of $j + k$?

PRACTICE SET 3 (NO CALCULATOR)

16. If $r = \frac{1}{a} + \frac{1}{b}$ and $a + b = 1$, which of the following equations is a correct formula for the product ab in terms of r ?

   A) $ab = r^2 - r$

   B) $ab = r$

   C) $ab = \frac{2}{r}$

   D) $ab = \frac{1}{r}$

17. If $m = r\sqrt{\frac{np}{q}}$, solve for q in terms of m, r, n, and p.

   A) $q = \frac{rnp}{m^2}$

   B) $q = r\sqrt{\frac{np}{m}}$

   C) $q = \frac{r^2 np}{m^2}$

   D) $q = \sqrt{\frac{rnp}{m}}$

18. The area of a trapezoid is given by $A = \frac{1}{2}(b_1 + b_2)h$. Which of the following equations expresses the longer base, b_1, of a trapezoid in terms of its area A, its height h, and its shorter base b_2?

   A) $b_1 = \frac{2A - b_2}{h}$

   B) $b_1 = \frac{A - 2b_2 h}{2h}$

   C) $b_1 = 2Ah - b_2$

   D) $b_1 = \frac{2A - b_2 h}{h}$

19. If $b > a$ and $2a + \frac{4}{b} = b + \frac{a^2}{b}$, solve for b in terms of a .

   A) $b = a + 2$

   B) $b = a + 4$

   C) $b = (a + 2)^2$

   D) $b = (a + 4)^2$

20. Energy in physics is measured in joules. *Power*, in watts, is the rate at which energy is deployed per unit time; that is, $P = \frac{E}{t}$, where t is time in seconds. The power of an electric circuit is given by $P = VI$, where V is the voltage, in volts, and I is the current, in amps. How many volts must be delivered for 10 seconds with a current of I amperes to release E joules of energy, in terms of E and I ?

A) $\frac{EI}{10}$

B) $10EI$

C) $\frac{10E}{I}$

D) $\frac{E}{10I}$

21. If $\frac{a+1}{b+2} = \frac{3}{b+4}$, solve for a in terms of b.

A) $a = \frac{3(b+2)-1}{b+4}$

B) $a = \frac{2(b+1)}{b+4}$

C) $a = \frac{3(b+2)}{b+4}$

D) $a = \frac{3(b+1)}{b+4}$

22. If $y^2 = \sqrt{\frac{x^3}{y}}$, which of the following equations correctly expresses y in terms of x?

A) $y = x^{\frac{5}{3}}$

B) $y = x^{\frac{2}{3}}$

C) $y = x^{\frac{3}{2}}$

D) $y = x^{\frac{3}{5}}$

23. If $\frac{rs}{t} = 1 + rs - t$, and $t > 1$, which of the following equations is correct ?

A) $r = \frac{1-t}{s}$

B) $r = \frac{t}{s}$

C) $r = \frac{1-t}{st}$

D) $r = \frac{t(1-t)}{s}$

24. If $\frac{jk}{1-mnp} = \frac{1}{j^2}$, which of the following equations correctly expresses p in terms of j, k, m, and n?

A) $p = \frac{j^3 k}{mn}$

B) $p = \frac{j-k}{jmn}$

C) $p = -\frac{j^3 k}{mn}$

D) $p = \frac{1-j^3 k}{mn}$

25. If $a^2 - b^2 = \frac{-175}{a^2+b^2}$, $a > 0$, and $b = 4$, then $a =$

Blue Math Lesson 7B: Solving for a Variable

Race to the Finish

Directions: Answer each question below.

Homework Set (No Calculator)

1. The population P of a bacterial colony h hours after it is placed in a petri dish is given by $P = P_0(1 + r)^h$, where r is the population growth rate per hour and P_0 is the population at the start of the experiment. If a colony that begins with 10,000 bacteria is observed to grow to a population of x bacteria in 2 hours, which of the following expressions gives the growth rate r in terms of x?

   A) $r = \frac{100\sqrt{x}-1}{x}$

   B) $r = \frac{100\sqrt{x}-x}{x}$

   C) $r = \frac{\sqrt{x-1}}{100}$

   D) $r = \frac{\sqrt{x}}{100} - 1$

2. A sample of radioactive material from an experiment must be safely stored until the radiation it emits falls below the safe threshold for human exposure. Radioactive substances have an amount of time called a *half-life*; for each half-life, the radioactivity of the material decreases by 50%. If the amount of radioactivity deemed safe is B bequerels (the standard unit of radioactivity) and the material is considered safe after n half-lives, what was its initial radioactivity in bequerels, in terms of B and n?

   A) $B \times 2^n$

   B) $\frac{B}{2^n}$

   C) Bn

   D) Bn^2

3. In business, profit is equal to revenue minus costs, or $P = R - C$. Costs can be separated into the sum of fixed costs and variable costs: $C = C_F + C_V$. A sandwich shop owner's daily variable costs consist of ingredients (i dollars per sandwich sold) and employee wages ($100 per employee per day). The sandwiches are sold for $8 each. Which of the following equations represents the number of employees e that the shop must hire to make a daily profit of $500, in terms of sandwiches sold per day, s, dollars per sandwich sold, i, and fixed costs, C_F (such as rent for the building) ?

   A) $e = 0.01((8 - i)s - C_F - 500)$

   B) $e = (8 - i)s - C_F - 500$

   C) $e = (8 - i)s - C_F + 500$

   D) $e = 0.01(8s + 500 - C_F)$

4. *Body mass index* (BMI) is defined as a person's weight in kilograms divided by the square of his or her height in meters. Which of the following equations gives the height m in meters of a k kg person who has a BMI of 25, in terms of k?

   A) $m = \frac{\sqrt{k}}{5}$

   B) $m = \sqrt{\frac{k}{5}}$

   C) $m = \frac{k^2}{25}$

   D) $m = \frac{k}{5}$

5. A cylindrical disc of pure copper to be used in an experiment on electrical conductivity needs to have a diameter of d cm and a thickness of h cm. If copper costs c dollars per gram and has a density of 9 g/cm³, which of the following equations gives the total cost, C, of the copper disc in terms of d and h?

A) $C = \dfrac{4\pi cd^2h}{9}$

B) $C = \dfrac{\pi cd^2h}{36}$

C) $C = \dfrac{9\pi cd^2h}{4}$

D) $C = \dfrac{9\pi cd^2h}{2}$

6. Two students designed water balloon launchers for a science competition. The first student's launcher can fire a balloon straight forward at a feet per second; the second student's launcher can fire one at a faster speed of b feet per second. If they fire simultaneously at a target from which they are each 50 feet away, student 2's balloon will hit the target t seconds before student 1's balloon does. Which of the following equations correctly gives t in terms of a and b ?

A) $t = \dfrac{b-a}{50}$

B) $t = \dfrac{50}{b} - \dfrac{50}{a}$

C) $t = \dfrac{50}{a} - \dfrac{50}{b}$

D) $t = 50(b - a)$

7. When a moving bicycle's wheels make one complete revolution, the bicycle moves forward a distance equal to the circumference of the wheel. If a cyclist is pedaling at such a speed that the wheels make 3 revolutions per second, and the wheels have diameter d inches, it will take s seconds to travel one mile (5280 feet). Which of the following equations gives s in terms of d?

A) $s = 190080\pi d$

B) $s = \dfrac{21120}{d}$

C) $s = \dfrac{7040}{\pi d}$

D) $s = \dfrac{21120}{\pi d}$

8. A group of scientists is investigating how the speed of sound varies in different substances. A digital tone produced by a computer is found to travel through air at a rate of a feet per second, through water at w feet per second, and through soil at s feet per second. If a microphone is set up separated from the computer by 100 feet of air, 100 feet of water, and 100 feet of soil, which of the following expressions represents the time t in seconds that it will take for the sound wave to be detected by this microphone?

A) $t = \dfrac{100}{a} + \dfrac{100}{w} + \dfrac{100}{s}$

B) $t = \dfrac{a+w+s}{100}$

C) $t = 100(a + w + s)$

D) $t = \dfrac{300}{a+w+s}$

9. The internationally standard scientific unit of temperature is the kelvin (K), equal in magnitude to the degree Celsius but defined so that 0 K is absolute zero, the lowest theoretically possible temperature. The Fahrenheit temperature of an object can be determined from the kelvin temperature by the formula $F = \frac{9}{5}K - 459.67$. Which of the following equations gives the kelvin temperature of an object in terms of the Fahrenheit temperature?

A) $K = \frac{9}{5}(F + 459.67)$

B) $K = \frac{9}{5}F + 459.67$

C) $K = \frac{5}{9}(F + 459.67)$

D) $K = \frac{5}{9}K + 459.67$

10. The frequency of the note produced by a vibrating string on a musical instrument depends on the tension T in the string and the mass m and length L of the string, according to the equation $F = \frac{1}{2L}\sqrt{\frac{TL}{m}}$. Which of the following expressions gives the length of a string with tension T and mass m which, when plucked, plays a low A (frequency 110 Hz) ?

A) $\frac{T^2}{12100m^2}$

B) $\sqrt{\frac{T}{110m}}$

C) $\frac{T}{12100m}$

D) $\frac{T}{48400m}$

11. The velocity of a wave v is equal to the product of its wavelength λ and its frequency, f. The *period* (T) of a wave, or the time it takes for one oscillation, is the reciprocal of the frequency, or $Tf = 1$. An observer on a beach measures the distance between whitecaps (i.e. the wavelength of the waves rolling ashore) to be 3.6 meters. Which of the following formulas gives the period of these waves in terms of the velocity v at which they are moving?

A) $T = \frac{v}{3.6}$

B) $T = \frac{1}{3.6v}$

C) $T = 3.6v$

D) $T = \frac{3.6}{v}$

12. An electric car requiring W watts of power to operate is powered by n identical lithium-ion batteries. If the number of batteries is decreased by 1, how much additional power, in terms of n and/or W, will each remaining battery need to provide?

A) $\frac{W}{n(n-1)}$

B) $\frac{W}{n}$

C) $\frac{W}{n-1}$

D) W

13. To keep a car moving at a constant speed, the engine must supply enough power that the force pushing the car forward compensates for all forces (air resistance and friction) that slow the car down. The required power roughly quadruples with a doubling of the car's velocity; that is, $P = kv^2$ for some constant k. If a car has 225 horsepower (a measure of the maximum power capable of being supplied by the engine), what is the greatest velocity it is capable of attaining, in terms of k?

A) $15k^{\frac{1}{2}}$

B) $15k^{-\frac{1}{2}}$

C) $\frac{15}{k}$

D) $15k$

14. The Ideal Gas Law states that for a gas in a closed container, $PV = nRT$, where P is the pressure of the gas in pascals, V is the volume in cubic meters, n is the number of molecules of the gas, R is a constant called the ideal gas constant, and T is the temperature in Kelvin. Which of the following expressions is equal to the temperature of such a gas in a $2 \times 2 \times 2$ meter sealed box in terms of n, R, and P ?

A) $\frac{8nR}{P}$

B) $2PnR$

C) $\frac{2P}{nR}$

D) $\frac{8P}{nR}$

15. If the gas in problem 14 is heated by 50 K (degrees Kelvin) while kept in the same $2 \times 2 \times 2$ meter cubical container without removing or adding any mass, the pressure will increase proportionally so that the relationship $PV = nRT$ continues to hold. By how many pascals will the pressure increase, in terms of n, R, and/or the initial temperature T?

A) $\frac{nRT+50}{nrT}$

B) $\frac{25nRT}{4}$

C) $\frac{25nR}{4}$

D) $50nR$

16. The *root-mean-square speed* (average speed, in meters per second) of the individual molecules in a gas, labeled v_{rms}, is given by the formula

$v_{rms} = \sqrt{\frac{3RT}{M_m}}$, where R is the ideal gas constant (about 8.31), T is the temperature in kelvin, and M_m is the *molar mass*, the mass in kilograms of one mole (6.02×10^{23} molecules) of the gas. The molar mass of nitrogen is 0.028 kg. If the nitrogen molecules in air are moving at a speed of 500 m/s, what is their temperature to the nearest kelvin?

A) 281

B) 349

C) 842

D) 890

17. The amount of money A in an account with interest compounded monthly after t years is given by $A = P\left(1 + \frac{r}{12}\right)^{12t}$, where P is the principal, or initial amount deposited into the account, and r is the annual interest rate. If John's goal is to have \$100,000 after 50 years, and he makes no other deposits or withdrawals after putting the initial principal in, which of the following equations gives the principal P that John must deposit, in terms of the interest rate r?

A) $P = 100{,}000\left(1 + \frac{r}{12}\right)^{600}$

B) $P = \dfrac{\left(1 + \frac{r}{12}\right)^{600}}{100{,}000}$

C) $P = \dfrac{100{,}000}{\left(1 + \frac{r}{12}\right)^{50}}$

D) $P = \dfrac{100{,}000}{\left(1 + \frac{r}{12}\right)^{600}}$

18. If the world's population is growing exponentially, it can be modeled by the equation $P = P_0 e^{rt}$, where P_0 is the population at some starting year, e is a constant (≈ 2.71828), r is the growth rate, and t is the number of years since the chosen starting year. If the world population was 7 billion in 2011, which of the following expressions is equal to the estimated population in billions in 2050, in terms of r?

A) $7e^{39r}$

B) $7e^{2050r}$

C) $\dfrac{e^{39r}}{7}$

D) $7e^{39+r}$

19. Force, in physics, is defined as mass times acceleration, or $F = ma$, meaning that F is the force in newtons required to apply an acceleration of a m/sec² to an object of mass m kg. An object beginning from a standstill with constant acceleration a will be traveling at a velocity of at m/sec after t seconds. This is represented by the equation $v = at$.

What is the force in newtons required to accelerate a 1000 kg car to a speed of 30 m/s in 10 seconds?

20. Boyle's Law states that for a gas in a closed container, the product of the pressure and the volume will always be constant; that is, $P_1 V_1 = P_2 V_2$. Ten moles (1 mole $= 6.02 \times 10^{23}$ molecules) of helium are in a 25 liter tank with a pressure of 300 kPa (kilopascals). If the same helium is transferred to a 10 L tank, what will its pressure be in kPa?

BLUE MATH LESSON 8A: FUNCTIONS – TRANSFORMATIONS AND COMPOSITIONS
Getting Your Feet Wet

Directions: The problems below are intended as a short diagnostic exam.

1. How is the graph of $f(x) = -(2x - 2)^3$ changed from the graph of
   $f(x) = x^3$?

   A) A horizontal compression by a factor of 2, a horizontal shift to the
      right 2, and a reflection over the x-axis.
   B) A horizontal compression by a factor of 2, a horizontal shift to the
      right 1, and a reflection over the y-axis.
   C) A horizontal compression by a factor of 2, a horizontal shift to the
      right 2, and a reflection over the y-axis.
   D) A horizontal compression by a factor of 2, a horizontal shift to the
      right 1, and a reflection over the x-axis.

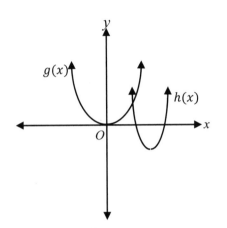

2. The graphs of $g(x) = x^2$ and $h(x)$ are shown above. Which of the
   following functions could possibly represent $h(x)$?
   A) $h(x) - 2 = 3(x + 4)^2$
   B) $h(x) + 2 = 3(x - 4)^2$
   C) $h(x) + 2 = \frac{1}{3}(x - 4)^2$
   D) $h(x) - 2 = \frac{1}{3}(x + 4)^2$

3. If $f(x) = x - 2$ and $g(x) = x^3$, which of the following represents
   $g(f(x))$?
   A) $x^3 - 8$
   B) $x^3 + 8$
   C) $x^3 + 6x^2 + 4x + 8$
   D) $x^3 - 6x^2 + 12x - 8$

BLUE MATH LESSON 8A: FUNCTIONS – TRANSFORMATIONS AND COMPOSITIONS
Wading In

Directions: Read the explanation for each problem type mentioned below. Pay special attention to the methods and techniques used to solve the sample problems. Then, do the practice exercises that follow; use the appropriate method to solve each problem.

TOPIC OVERVIEW: PARENT FUNCTIONS AND TRANSFORMATIONS

Most of the graphs that we'll be exposed to on the SAT involve parent functions and their transformations. We already went through the major parent functions in Lesson 7A, but here they are again as a reminder:

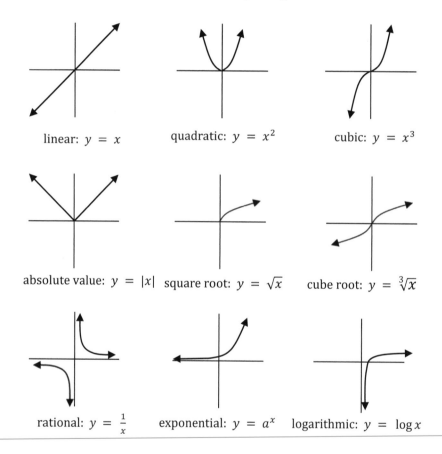

linear: $y = x$ quadratic: $y = x^2$ cubic: $y = x^3$

absolute value: $y = |x|$ square root: $y = \sqrt{x}$ cube root: $y = \sqrt[3]{x}$

rational: $y = \frac{1}{x}$ exponential: $y = a^x$ logarithmic: $y = \log x$

Transformations are what we use to get graphs that look similar to those above but vary in certain ways. These graphs may be shifted, stretched, shrunk, or reflected by adding, subtracting, multiplying, or dividing numbers to the equations of these functions. First, let's talk about translations:

A translation involves sliding a function in a specific direction. These functions always involve adding or subtracting a number to the function. Let's look at these on the next page:

Translation	Function notation	Example ($b = 3$)
Up b units	$f(x) + b$	$x^2 + 3$
Down b units	$f(x) - b$	$\log x - 3$
Left b units	$f(x + b)$	2^{x+3}
Right b units	$f(x - b)$	$\dfrac{1}{x - 3}$

Reflections involve reflecting the graph across either the y- or x-axis. To reflect a function over an axis, multiply by –1.

Reflection	Function notation	Example
Over the x-axis	$-f(x)$	$-x^2$
Over the y-axis	$f(-x)$	$\sqrt{-x}$

Stretches and compressions involve making the graph look thinner or wider. To obtain a stretch or compression, multiply by a number other than –1. Note that for the scenarios below, $b > 1$.

Stretch or Compression	Function notation	Example ($b = 3$)
Horizontal stretch by a factor of b	$f\left(\dfrac{x}{b}\right)$	$\left(\dfrac{x}{3}\right)^2$
Horizontal compression by a factor of b	$f(bx)$	$\ln 3x$
Vertical stretch by a factor of b	$bf(x)$	$3e^x$
Vertical compression by a factor of b	$\dfrac{1}{b}f(x)$	$\dfrac{1}{3}x$

When performing multiple transformations on a single function, use the following order:

1. Stretches or compressions
2. Horizontal shifts
3. Reflections
4. Vertical shifts

So, let's try an example using all of these transformations.

SAMPLE PROBLEM 1: TRANSFORMATIONS

How is the graph of $f(x) = -(2x - 2)^3$ changed from the graph of $f(x) = x^3$?

A) A horizontal compression by a factor of 2, a horizontal shift to the right 2, and a reflection over the x-axis.

B) A horizontal compression by a factor of 2, a horizontal shift to the right 1, and a reflection over the y-axis.

C) A horizontal compression by a factor of 2, a horizontal shift to the right 2, and a reflection over the y-axis.

D) A horizontal compression by a factor of 2, a horizontal shift to the right 1, and a reflection over the x-axis.

Since we know the parent function, let's start with the inside part of $f(x) = x^3$. Since the x is being multiplied by 2, let's first factor the two out. We now have: $f(x) = -[2(x - 1)]^3$. Since the number that we factored out is 2, we know it must be a horizontal compression by a factor of 2. We see that we have $x - 1$, so we know we have a horizontal shift to the right 1 unit. Lastly, the entire function is multiplied by –1, so we have a reflection over the x-axis. Thus, our answer is **D**.

SAMPLE PROBLEM 2: TRANSFORMATIONS

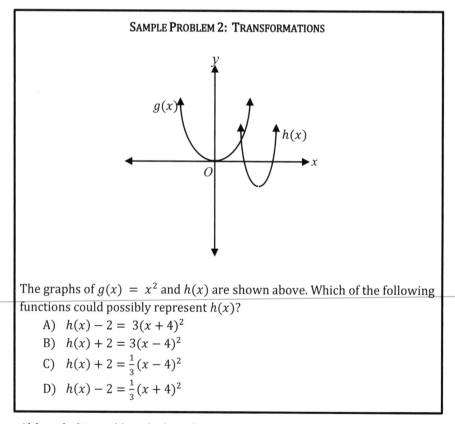

The graphs of $g(x) = x^2$ and $h(x)$ are shown above. Which of the following functions could possibly represent $h(x)$?

A) $h(x) - 2 = 3(x + 4)^2$

B) $h(x) + 2 = 3(x - 4)^2$

C) $h(x) + 2 = \frac{1}{3}(x - 4)^2$

D) $h(x) - 2 = \frac{1}{3}(x + 4)^2$

Although this problem deals with transformations, and we're given the equation of the graph of $g(x)$, we're not given any exact values. Without numbers we have to focus on the types of transformations instead of the size of the transformation. We clearly see that $g(x)$ has been moved to the

right and down. We can also see that the graph of $g(x)$ is wider than that of $h(x)$, indicating either a horizontal compression or a vertical stretch. Since all of the answer choices indicate a vertical stretch or compression, we must choose between choices A and B. Looking more carefully at the numbers inside and outside of the parentheses, our answer must be **B**.

TOPIC OVERVIEW: COMPOSITIONS

Composition is a special operation that can be done to functions. Effectively, it involves applying one function to the results of the other function. There are generally two ways to write the composition of two functions: $g(f(x))$ and $(g \circ f)(x)$, both of which indicate that the function $f(x)$ is to be plugged into the x of $g(x)$.

One especially important use of compositions is to determine whether or not two functions are inverses of each other. If two functions are inverses of each other, then $f(g(x)) = g(f(x)) = x$. Use this property to prove whether or not two functions are inverses of each other. Let's try a problem involving compositions:

SAMPLE PROBLEM 3: COMPOSITIONS

If $f(x) = x - 2$ and $g(x) = x^3$, which of the following represents $g(f(x))$?
A) $x^3 - 8$
B) $x^3 + 8$
C) $x^3 + 6x^2 + 4x + 8$
D) $x^3 - 6x^2 + 12x - 8$

Since we know what $f(x)$ and $g(x)$ are, we can start this problem off by plugging $f(x)$ into $g(x)$:

$$g(f(x)) = (x - 2)^3$$

$$g(f(x)) = (x^2 - 4x + 4)(x - 2)$$

$$g(f(x)) = x^3 - 6x^2 + 12x - 8$$

Thus, our answer is **D**.

WRAP-UP

Although transformations and compositions seem like two completely different topics, the two are actually very closely aligned—many of the questions involving compositions can be thought of as multiple transformations without the graph to provide visual aid.

BLUE MATH LESSON 8A: FUNCTIONS – TRANSFORMATIONS AND COMPOSITIONS
Learning to Swim

Directions: Answer each question below.

PRACTICE SET 1 (NO CALCULATOR)

Identify the parent equation and graph the given equation in the space provided.

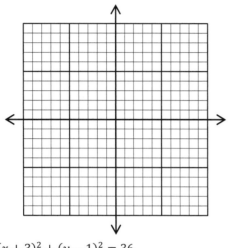

1. $(x + 3)^2 + (y - 1)^2 = 36$

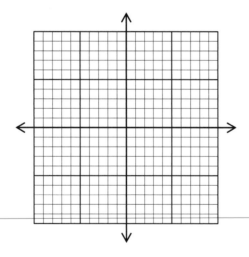

2. $f(x) = 2|x| - 4$

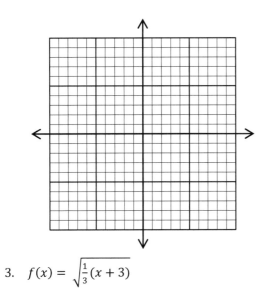

3. $f(x) = \sqrt{\frac{1}{3}(x+3)}$

Identify the parent equation and state an equation for the given graph.

4.

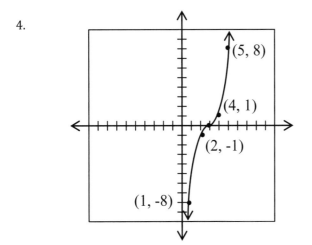

5.

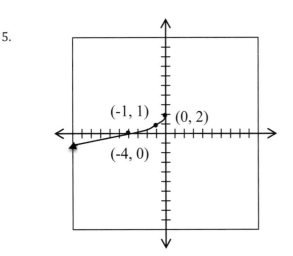

Blue Math Lesson 8A: Functions – Transformations and Compositions
Diving into the Deep End

Directions: Answer each question below.

Practice Set 2 (No Calculator)

6. What is the resulting function when you shift the graph of $f(x) = x^2$ left 3 units and up 5 units?
   A) $x^2 + 3x + 5$
   B) $(x + 3)^2 + 5$
   C) $(x - 3)^2 + 5$
   D) $x^2 + 3x + 5$

7. The function $f(x) = 2|x - 3| + 2$ is translated from its parent function $f(x) = |x|$ by which of the following transformations?
   A) Shifts 3 units left and 2 units up
   B) Vertical stretch of 2, shift left 3 units, and up two units
   C) Vertical shrink of 2, shift right 3 units, and up two units
   D) Vertical stretch of 2, shift right 3 units, and up two units

8. If the function $f(x) = \frac{1}{x}$ has an asymptote at $x = 0$, then the graph $f(x) = \frac{1}{x-4}$ has an asymptote at which of the following places?
   A) $x = 0$
   B) $y = 4$
   C) $x = 4$
   D) $x = -4$

9. If $f(x) = 2x + 3$ and $f(g(x)) = 2x^2 + 1$ then which of the following could be $g(x)$?
   A) x^2
   B) $2x^2$
   C) $(x - 2)^2$
   D) $x^2 - 1$

10. What is the resulting function when you horizontally stretch the graph of $f(x) = x^3$ by a factor of 2, shift it right 4 units, and then down 1 unit?
    A) $(2x - 4)^3 - 1$
    B) $(\frac{1}{2}x - 4)^3 - 1$
    C) $(\frac{1}{2}x - 2)^3 - 1$
    D) $(2x - 8)^3 - 1$

11. The function $f(x) = -|3x + 6|$ is translated from its parent function $f(x) = |x|$ by which of the following transformations?
    A) Horizontal shrink by a factor of 3, shift 2 units to the left, and a reflection over the x-axis
    B) Horizontal shrink by a factor of 3, shift 2 units to the right, and a reflection over the x-axis
    C) Horizontal stretch by a factor of 3, shift 2 units to the left, and a reflection over the x-axis
    D) Horizontal stretch by a factor of 3, shift 2 units to the right, and a reflection over the x-axis

12. If $g(x) = 2x^2 + 2$ and $f(g(1)) = 3$ then which of the following could be $f(x)$?
    A) $x + 1$
    B) x^2
    C) $(x - 2)^2$
    D) $x^2 - 4x + 3$

13. If $f(g(x)) = x$, and $f(x) = 5x^3 + 5$, then which of the following is equal to $g(x)$?

    A) $\sqrt[3]{\dfrac{x}{5}} - 5$

    B) $\sqrt[3]{\dfrac{x-5}{5}}$

    C) $\sqrt[3]{\dfrac{x}{5}} + 5$

    D) $\sqrt[3]{\dfrac{x+5}{5}}$

14. Let $f(x) = x^2 + 1$. Let $g(x)$ be the function $f(x)$ after translating the entire function 3 units to the right and 2 units down. If $g(a) = 0$, what is a possible value of $f(a)$?

15. The function $f(x) = x^2$ is translated 3 units to the right and 2 units down. The entire graph is then reflected over the x-axis. What is the x-coordinate of the new vertex?

PRACTICE SET 3 (NO CALCULATOR)

16. The graph of a circle has a radius of 4, and a center at $(3, -2)$. Which of the following is the equation of that circle?
    A) $(x^2 + 3) + (y^2 - 2) = 16$
    B) $(x^2 - 3) + (y^2 + 2) = 16$
    C) $(x + 3)^2 + (y - 2)^2 = 16$
    D) $(x - 3)^2 + (y + 2)^2 = 16$

17. You have a circle centered on the origin with a radius of 5. You wish to move the circle so that the circle passes through the origin. What is a possible equation of your new circle?
    A) $(x + 3)^2 + (y - 4)^2 = 25$
    B) $(x + 5)^2 + (y - 1)^2 = 25$
    C) $(x + 4)^2 + (y + 4)^2 = 25$
    D) $(x - 5)^2 + (y - 5)^2 = 25$

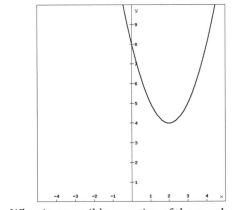

18. What is a possible equation of the graph above?
    A) $y = (x - 2)^2 + 4$
    B) $y = (x + 2)^2 + 4$
    C) $y = (x - 2)^2 - 4$
    D) $y = (x + 2)^2 - 4$

19. The graph of $f(x) = \frac{1}{x^2+3x-4}$ has two vertical asymptotes, one at $x = -4$ and the other at $x = 1$. If you wish to shift both asymptotes 2 units to the right, and the entire graph 2 units up, what should be the equation of the new graph?

A) $f(x) = \frac{1}{x^2+3x-2} + 2$

B) $f(x) = \frac{1}{x^2+x-6} + 2$

C) $f(x) = \frac{1}{x^2-x-6} + 2$

D) $f(x) = \frac{1}{x^2+3x+2} + 2$

20. What is the resulting function when you stretch the graph of $f(x) = |x|$ horizontally by a factor of 3, shift it right 3 units, and then down 3 units?

A) $|3x - 3| - 3$

B) $|3x - 6| - 3$

C) $|\frac{1}{3}x - 1| - 3$

D) $|\frac{1}{3}x - 3| - 3$

21. Let $h(x) = 3x^2 + 15x + 18$. Let $f(x)$ be the result of $h(x)$ after it is shifted 2 units to the right, 3 units upward, and 6 units to the left. If $f(a) = 3$, what is the product of the possible values of a?

A) 6

B) 8

C) 40

D) 42

22. The function $f(x) = \frac{1}{2}|-x-4| - 1$ is translated from its parent function $f(x) = |x|$ by which of the following transformations?

A) Stretch vertically by a factor of $\frac{1}{2}$, shifted left 4 units, down 1 unit, and reflect over the x-axis

B) Stretch vertically by a factor of $\frac{1}{2}$, shift right 4 units, down 1 unit, and reflect over the x-axis

C) Stretch vertically by a factor of $\frac{1}{2}$, shift left 4 units, down 1 unit, and reflect over the y-axis

D) Stretch vertically by a factor of $\frac{1}{2}$, shift right 4 units, down 1 unit, and reflect over the y-axis

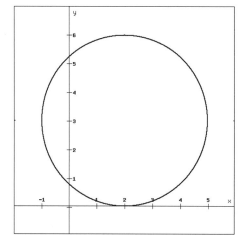

23. What is the equation of the graph of the circle above?

A) $(x - 2)^2 + (y - 3)^2 = 9$

B) $(x + 2)^2 + (y - 3)^2 = 3$

C) $(x - 2)^2 + (y + 3)^2 = 9$

D) $(x - 2)^2 + (y + 3)^2 = 3$

24. The function $f(x) = x^4 - 81$ is shifted upward 65 units. After the function is shifted, if $x \geq 0$, what value of x will make $f(x) = 0$?

25. If the function $f(x) = \frac{1}{x}$ has an asymptote at $y = 0$, then the graph $f(x) = \frac{1}{x-1} + 3$ has an asymptote at the line $y = ?$

Blue Math Lesson 8A: Functions – Transformations and Compositions
Race to the Finish

Directions: Answer each question below.

Homework Set (No Calculator)

1. The graph of $f(x) = x^3$ crosses the y-axis at the point $(0, 0)$. At which point will the graph $y = 2(x - 1)^3 - 1$ cross the y-axis?
   A) $(0, 1)$
   B) $(1, 0)$
   C) $(0, -3)$
   D) $(-1, 0)$

2. The definition of $f^{-1}(x)$ is that $f^{-1}(f(x)) = x$. If $f(x) = \frac{(x-5)}{3}$, then which of the following is equal to $f^{-1}(x)$?
   A) $5x + 3$
   B) $5x - 3$
   C) $3x + 5$
   D) $3x - 5$

3. The graph of a circle has a radius of 2, and a center at $(-4, -6)$. Which of the following is the equation of that circle?
   A) $(x + 4)^2 + (y - 6)^2 = 2$
   B) $(x - 4)^2 + (y + 6)^2 = 2$
   C) $(x - 4)^2 + (y - 6)^2 = 4$
   D) $(x + 4)^2 + (y + 6)^2 = 4$

4. The graph of $f(x) = \frac{1}{x}$ has a vertical asymptote at $x = 0$ and a horizontal asymptote at $y = 0$. What would be the equation of the function with a vertical asymptote at $x = -3$ and a horizontal asymptote at $y = 2$?
   A) $\frac{1}{x-3} + 2$
   B) $\frac{1}{x+3} + 2$
   C) $\frac{1}{x-3} - 2$
   D) $\frac{1}{x+3} - 2$

5. What is the resulting function when you vertically stretch the graph of $f(x) = x^3$ by a factor of ¼, shift it left 3 units, up 2 units, and reflect it over the y-axis?
   A) $\frac{1}{4}(-x - 3)^3 + 2$
   B) $\frac{1}{4}(-x + 3)^3 + 2$
   C) $\frac{1}{4}(x - 3)^3 + 2$
   D) $-\frac{1}{4}(x + 3)^3 + 2$

6. You have a circle centered on the origin with a radius of 6. You wish to move the circle so that the edge of the circle is tangent to both the x- and y-axis. What is a possible equation of your new circle?
   A) $(x + 3)^2 + (y - 3)^2 = 6$
   B) $(x + 6)^2 + (y - 6)^2 = 6$
   C) $(x + 6)^2 + (y + 6)^2 = 36$
   D) $(x - 3)^2 + (y - 3)^2 = 36$

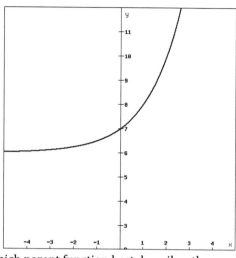

7. Which parent function best describes the graph of the function above?

    A) $y = a^x$
    B) $y = \ln x$
    C) $y = \sqrt[3]{x}$
    D) $y = a^{\frac{1}{x}}$

8. If $f(x) = 2x^2 + 2$, and $g(x) = x - 1$, then which of the following is equal to $f(g(x))$?

    A) $2x^2 + 4$
    B) $2x^2 - 2x + 4$
    C) $2x^2 - 4x + 3$
    D) $2x^2 - 4x + 4$

9. A function $f(x)$ has the form $x^2 + bx + c$. Reflecting $f(x)$ across the y-axis yields the same translation as shifting $f(x)$ 8 units to the right. What value must c hold if $f(x) = 0$ has only one solution?

    A) 2
    B) 4
    C) 8
    D) 16

10. Which of the following functions best describes the graph above?

    A) $f(x) = \left(-\frac{1}{3}x + 1\right)^2 + 3$
    B) $f(x) = -3(x + 1)^2 + 3$
    C) $f(x) = 3(-x - 1)^2 + 3$
    D) $f(x) = -3(x - 1)^2 - 3$

11. Let $f(x) = x + 3$ and $g(x) = 2x - 2$. First, $g(x)$ is halved. Then, $f(x)$ is shifted up 2 units and left 3 units. What is the product of the roots of the transformations of both functions?

    A) -8
    B) $-\frac{9}{2}$
    C) $\frac{9}{2}$
    D) 8

12. Let $h(x + 3) = 3x - 15$ and $g(x) = 4x^2$. If $h(x)g(x - 2) = 0$ what one possible value of x?

    A) -3
    B) -2
    C) 0
    D) 8

13. The function $f(x) = -2(x + 1)^2 - 2$ is translated from it parent function $f(x) = x^2$ by which of the following transformations?
   A) Shift 1 unit to the right, 2 units down, and reflect it over the x-axis
   B) Shift 1 unit to the left, 2 units down and reflect it over the x-axis
   C) Stretch it vertically by a factor of 2, shift 1 unit to the right, 2 units down, and reflect it over the x-axis
   D) Stretch it vertically by a factor of 2, shift 1 unit to the left, 2 units up, and reflect it over the x-axis

14. The graph of the parent function $y = x^3$ is transformed by a reflection across the x-axis, then a reflection across the y-axis. Which of the graphs best shows those transformations?
   A)   C)

   B)   D)

15. Let $f(x) = x^2$. First, $f(x)$ is translated 2 units to the left and 1 unit downward. Then, $f(x)$ is reflected across the x-axis. If c and d are both distinct roots of $f(x)$ after the transformations, what is $(c + d)^2$?
   A) −4
   B) −3
   C) −1
   D) 16

16. If $f(x) = x^2$ and $g(x) = \sqrt{x}$, which of the following could be the graph of $g(f(x))$?
   A)   C)

   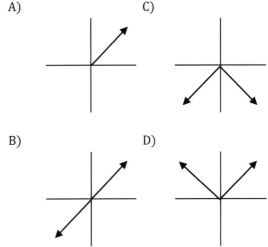

   B)   D)

17. The vertex of $f(x) = |x|$ is located at the point $(0, 0)$. What is the x-coordinate of the vertex of $f(x) = 2|x - 3| + 2$?

18. Let $f(x) = x - 2, g(x) = x^2$. What is a possible value of x for which $f(x) = g(f(x))$?

19. If the graph of $f(x) = -(x - 3)^2 + 6$ is shifted 3 units to the right and 2 units up to form $g(x)$, what is the y-coordinate of the vertex of $g(x)$?

20. What is the y-intercept of the graph of $f(x) = 3(2^{x-2})$?

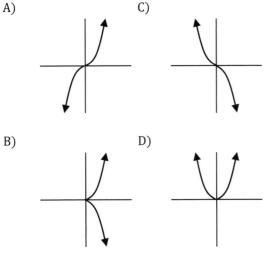

BLUE MATH LESSON 8B: SECTOR AREA AND ARC LENGTH
Getting Your Feet Wet

Directions: The problems below are intended as a short diagnostic exam.

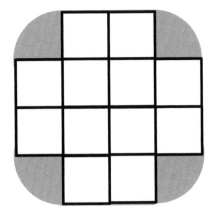

1. The sidewalk design above is made of 12 square concrete slabs, and the length and width of the entire figure are both 12 meters. If each of the four shaded areas represents part of a circular area of grass with center at the juncture of three different concrete slabs, what is the total area of the grass above?
    A) 6π
    B) 9π
    C) $24 + 6\pi$
    D) $72 + 9\pi$

2. Minor arc $\overset{\frown}{AB}$ of Circle O has an arc length of 3π. If the circle has an area of 16π, what is the measure of Angle AOB?
    A) 90
    B) 135
    C) 180
    D) 225

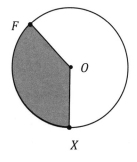

3. Minor arc $\overset{\frown}{FX}$ above has a length of 15. If the shaded part of Circle O above has an area of $\frac{350}{\pi}$, what is the radius of Circle O?

A) $\frac{5\sqrt{14}}{\pi}$

B) $\frac{140}{3\pi}$

C) $5\sqrt{14}$

D) 20

BLUE MATH LESSON 8B: SECTOR AREA AND ARC LENGTH
Wading In

Directions: Read the explanation for each problem type mentioned below. Pay special
attention to the methods and techniques used to solve the sample problems. Then, do the
practice exercises that follow; use the appropriate method to solve each problem.

TOPIC OVERVIEW: SECTOR AREA

A **sector** of a circle is a very specific piece of a circle, one that resembles a
slice of pizza. The pointed end of the pizza is known as the **central angle**—
this angle will always be between 0 and 360 degrees. The crust of the slice
of pizza is called the **arc** of a circle, but we'll talk more about that later in the
lesson.

Finding the area of a circle is easy if we do it the same way we would find
the area of a slice of pizza. If one slice of pizza is one-eighth of the pizza,
then that slice's area must be one-eighth the area of the entire pizza. There
always exists a ratio between the central angle of the sector and the whole
circle: 360°. This ratio is equivalent to the ratio of the area of the sector to
the area of the circle:

$$\frac{\text{central angle}}{360} = \frac{\text{sector area}}{\text{area of circle}}$$

Use this formula whenever there is a problem dealing with sector areas.
Let's try one on the next page:

SAMPLE PROBLEM 1: SECTOR AREA

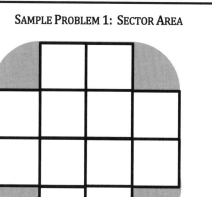

The sidewalk design above is made of 12 square concrete slabs, and the length and width of the entire figure are both 12 meters. If each of the four shaded areas represents part of a circular area of grass with center at the juncture of three different concrete slabs, what is the total area of the grass above?

A) 6π
B) 9π
C) $24 + 6\pi$
D) $72 + 9\pi$

Since each concrete slab is a square, we know that the central angle of each of the four sectors is 90°. We also know that the length of the entire sidewalk is 12 meters. Since 4 slabs make up the entire length of the sidewalk, each slab has a length of 3 meters. Thus, the radius of each sector is 3. Now, we can use our sector formula to find each area:

$$\frac{\text{central angle}}{360} = \frac{\text{sector area}}{\text{area of circle}}$$

$$\frac{90}{360} = \frac{\text{sector area}}{9\pi}$$

Thus, the sector area of each piece is 2.25π. Since there are 4 pieces, our total area is 9π, and our answer is **B**.

TOPIC OVERVIEW: ARC LENGTH

We used the slice of pizza example earlier to describe the shape of a sector of a circle. Remember that the crust of the slice of pizza is called the **arc** of a circle. To find the length of an arc of a circle, use a formula very similar to the one we used for the sector area:

$$\frac{\text{central angle}}{360} = \frac{\text{arc length}}{\text{circumference}}$$

Use this formula whenever presented with a problem dealing with arc length. Let's try one:

SAMPLE PROBLEM 2: ARC LENGTH

Minor arc $\overset{\frown}{AB}$ of Circle O has an arc length of 3π. If the circle has an area of 16π, what is the measure of Angle AOB?

   A) 90
   B) 135
   C) 180
   D) 225

Since we know the length of the circle already, let's start by setting up our equation:

$$\frac{\text{central angle}}{360} = \frac{\text{arc length}}{\text{circumference}}$$

$$\frac{\text{central angle}}{360} = \frac{3\pi}{\text{circumference}}$$

Since we don't know the circumference of the circle yet, let's look at the rest of the problem for more information. We know the circle has an area of 16π, so its radius must be 4. Thus, the circumference of the circle is 8π. Now we can solve our equation for the central angle.

$$\frac{\text{central angle}}{360} = \frac{3\pi}{8\pi}$$

So, the central angle must be 135, and our answer is **B**.

Let's try one problem that involves both sector area and arc lengths:

SAMPLE PROBLEM 3: SECTOR AREA AND ARC LENGTH

Minor arc $\overset{\frown}{FX}$ above has a length of 15. If the shaded part of Circle O above has an area of $\dfrac{350}{\pi}$, what is the radius of Circle O?

A) $\dfrac{5\sqrt{14}}{\pi}$

B) $\dfrac{140}{3\pi}$

C) $5\sqrt{14}$

D) 20

This problem is a little trickier. In this case, we have both the length of the minor arc of one segment and the area of the sector that includes that minor arc. Let's set up a few equations:

$$\frac{x}{360} = \frac{\frac{350}{\pi}}{\pi r^2} \qquad\qquad \frac{x}{360} = \frac{15}{2\pi r}$$

Next, we'll cross multiply both equations to attempt to simplify them:

$$\pi^2 x r^2 = 126{,}000 \qquad\qquad 2\pi x r = 5400$$

Since we know that $\pi x r = 2700$ from the second equation, let's plug that into the first equation:

$$\pi^2 x r^2 = 126{,}000$$
$$\pi x r (\pi r) = 126{,}000$$
$$2700(\pi r) = 126{,}000$$
$$r = \frac{140}{3\pi}$$

WRAP-UP

When working with circles, always be aware of what information is given. There are many equations that we must commit to memory to do well on this section of the test, so these upcoming problems will help us prepare for these problems that will show up frequently on the SAT.

BLUE MATH LESSON 8B: SECTOR AREA AND ARC LENGTH
Learning to Swim

Directions: Answer each question below.

PRACTICE SET 1 (NO CALCULATOR)

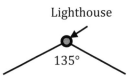

Lighthouse

135°

1. A lighthouse is stationed on the tip of an island before the ocean, as shown above. For night sailing, an observer must be at most 20 miles away from the lighthouse to see land. If the angle of the tip of the island measures 135 degrees, what is the total area of ocean a boat can sail at night if the island must be visible at all times? Leave your answer in terms of π.

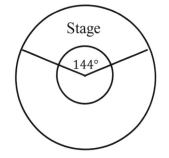

Stage

144°

2. An amphitheater is represented above by two concentric circles. The amphitheater's stage is represented by the smaller region of the area between the two concentric circles. The diameter of the amphitheater is 200 feet, and the angle shown above is 144 degrees. If the area of the stage is 3,840π, what is the diameter of the smaller circle in feet?

3. Mambo, a dog, is tied to a post in a yard with his bowl and doghouse. Mambo's doghouse and bowl are both the same distance from the post. From the post, the angle between Mambo's doghouse and his water bowl is 225 degrees, and the length of Mambo's leash is 5 feet. If the length from Mambo's bowl to the post is the same as the length of the leash, what is the length of the shortest arc Mambo can travel to reach his bowl and doghouse (to the nearest foot) (Use $\pi = 3.14$)?

4. A standard turntable rotates vinyl records at a rate of 45 complete rotations per minute. A vinyl record 12 inches in diameter is placed on this turntable and a fly lands on the outer edge of the record. If the fly sticks to the spinning record, to the nearest tenth of a inch, how far along the arc would the fly travel in 1.5 seconds (Use $\pi = 3.14$)?

5. A windshield wiper is 24 inches long and can clean an area equivalent to the sector of a circle with a 60° angle. The wiper is to be replaced with one 30 inches long. How much more area can the new wiper clean, in square inches? Leave your answer in terms of π.

BLUE MATH LESSON 8B: SECTOR AREA AND ARC LENGTH
Diving into the Deep End

Directions: Answer each question below.

PRACTICE SET 2 (NO CALCULATOR)

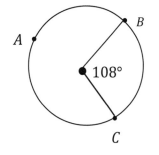

6. If the circle in the figure above has an area of 25π, what is the length of arc BAC?
    A) 3π
    B) 7π
    C) $\frac{15\pi}{2}$
    D) $\frac{35\pi}{2}$

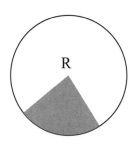

8. Circle R has a radius of $\frac{9}{2}$ m. The arc bordering the shaded region is $\frac{5\pi}{4}$ m long. What is the area of the shaded region?
    A) $\frac{45\pi}{16}$
    B) $\frac{31\pi}{4}$
    C) $\frac{279\pi}{16}$
    D) 50

7. Sector Q has an area of 27 cm². What is the radius of the circle?
    A) $\frac{3\sqrt{3\pi}}{\pi}$
    B) $\frac{6\sqrt{\pi}}{\pi}$
    C) $\frac{27}{2\pi}$
    D) 6

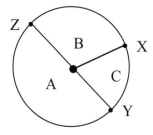

9. Sector B has an area of 12π and diameter ZY is 12 units long. What is the length of the arc bordering sector C?
    A) 2π
    B) 6π
    C) 12π
    D) 18π

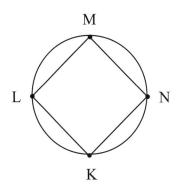

10. Square *KLMN* is inscribed in a circle as shown. Minor arc *LK* is $\frac{3\pi}{2}$ units long, what is the radius of the circle?

    A) $\frac{3}{4}$

    B) $\sqrt{6}$

    C) 3

    D) It cannot be determined from the information provided.

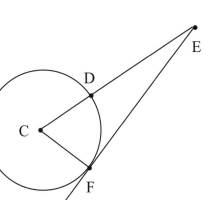

11. Line *EF* is tangent to circle *C* at *F*. If *CF* is 9 units long and arc *DF* is 3π, what is the length of *CE*?

    A) 18

    B) $9\sqrt{3}$

    C) 27

    D) It cannot be determined from the information provided.

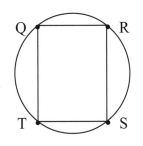

12. Rectangle *QRST* is inscribed in a circle of radius 8. If side *QT* is $8\sqrt{3}$ units long and side *ST* is 8 units long, what is the length of minor arc *QT*?

    A) $\frac{16\pi}{3}$

    B) 8π

    C) 16π

    D) $\frac{64\pi}{3}$

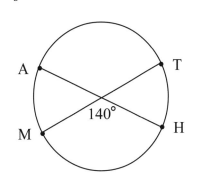

13. Arc *MA* has length 2π. Segments *AH* and *MT* intersect at the center of the circle. What is the length of the circle's radius?

    A) $\frac{1}{9}$

    B) $\frac{18}{7}$

    C) 3

    D) 9

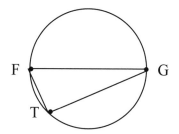

14. An engineer is designing a fountain for a public park. The fountain is a perfect circle and inscribed within is a square. Assuming each edge of the square measures $\sqrt{50}$ feet, what is the circumference of the fountain, to the nearest tenth of a foot (Use $\pi = 3.14$)?

16. Radius QT is 3 cm long and segment QP is $3\sqrt{3}$ cm long. What is the area of the unshaded region?
    A) π cm²
    B) 3π cm²
    C) 6π cm²
    D) 9π cm²

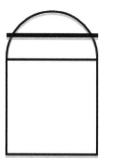

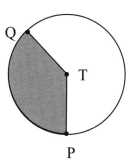

15. The Arc de Triomphe is one of the most famous monuments in Paris; the inside takes the shape of a semi-circle on top of a rectangle. The rectangle portion of the arc is 50 meters tall and 45 meters wide. In the semi-circle of the arc, a string of lights is hung parallel to the diameter of the semi-circle. If the string of lights is $\frac{1}{3}$ the length of the diameter, what is the shortest distance between the string of lights and the diameter of the semicircle, to the nearest tenth of a foot?

17. Triangle TFG is inscribed in a circle as shown. If segment FT is 18, GT is 24, and FG is 30, what is the length of arc FG?
    A) 12π
    B) 15π
    C) 30π
    D) It cannot be determined from the information provided.

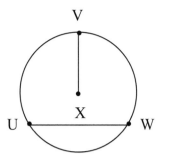

18. If segment XV is 5 m long and arc UVW of circle X is $\frac{15\pi}{2}$ m, what is the length, in meters, of segment UW?

A) 5

B) $5\sqrt{2}$

C) $5\sqrt{3}$

D) 10

19. Pluto's moon Charon orbits a center of motion in a circular path. Charon is located 19,573 km from this center, and travels at an angular speed of 56.4°/Earth day. What linear distance does it travel in an hour?

A) 128 km

B) 803 km

C) 19,267 km

D) 73,594 km

20. Circle U has a diameter of 64 units and a sector area of 256π square units. What is the measurement of the central angle of the sector?

A) 45°

B) 90°

C) 135°

D) 180°

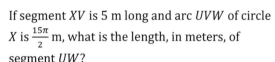

21. A square barn 40 feet on a side sits against a fence as shown. If a goat is tethered in the corner formed by the fence and one side of the barn on a rope 50 ft long, how much area will the goat have to graze?

A) 100π ft²

B) 625π ft²

C) 650π ft²

D) 2500π ft²

22. The ferris wheel on Chicago's Navy Pier takes riders from the boarding platform to the top, 140 ft above the platform, in 3 ½ minutes. It never stops, so riders must hop into a moving gondola. Which of the following is closest to the linear speed of the gondolas along the boarding platform?

A) 0.667 feet/sec

B) 1.05 feet/sec

C) 40.0 feet/sec

D) 62.8 feet/sec

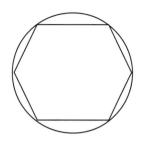

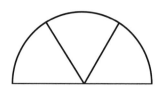

23. A cook is paring a cylindrical broccoli stem by trimming segments to form a regular hexagon, as shown. What percent of the stem will be discarded? (Hint: Compare the area of sectors of the circular cross-section to areas of triangles.)
    A) 13.8%
    B) 17.3%
    C) 41.3%
    D) 82.7%

24. In St. Patrick's Cathedral, there is a stained glass window in the shape of a semicircle. This window contains three congruent panes of stained glass. The diameter of the semicircle is 12 feet; what is the area of each pane of stained glass, to the nearest tenth of a square foot (Use $\pi = 3.14$)?

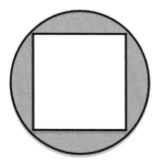

25. A scientist is designing a learned helplessness experiment, which uses a square of dry land surrounded by a circle of water. The corners of the square lie on the circumference of the circle. If the square has sides with a length of 2 cm each, what is the area of the shaded region, to the nearest hundredth of a square cm (Use $\pi = 3.14$)?

BLUE MATH LESSON 8B: SECTOR AREA AND ARC LENGTH
Race to the Finish

Directions: Answer each question below.

HOMEWORK SET (NO CALCULATOR)

Questions 1 through 4 use the following information.

Center pivot irrigation is a common farming technique that involves watering a circular field by means of a rotating pipe with spray nozzles along its length. A typical pipe is 400 m long; the wheels at the outer end are motor-driven at 2.1 m/min.

1. Through what angle will the pipe rotate in twelve hours (to the nearest degree)?
    A) 22°
    B) 36°
    C) 217°
    D) 360°

2. Which of the following is closest to the area in square meters that will be watered as the pivot turns 120°?
    A) 419
    B) 838
    C) 167,552
    D) 201,061,930

3. If the flow rate is set at 800 gallons/minute, how much water will be used as the pivot turns 135° (to the nearest hundred gallons)?
    A) 51,400 gal
    B) 114,300 gal
    C) 359,000 gal
    D) 754,000 gal

4. If each spray nozzle covers a band 1 m wide, what is the ratio of the area covered by the outermost nozzle (outer radius 400 m) to the area covered by a nozzle very close to the pivot (outer radius 5 m)?
    A) 80:1
    B) 799:9
    C) 399:4
    D) 6400:1

Questions 5 through 7 use the following information.

To investigate the depletion of underground aquifers, a student is making a pie chart showing how freshwater is used in the USA. According to the U.S. Geological Survey freshwater was removed from aquifers during 2005 for the following uses (all values are in millions of gallons per day):

Irrigation	Livestock/ Aquaculture	Industrial Uses	Domestic/ Public Supply
53,500	3200	7600	18,340

5. The sector for irrigation will have what degree measure?
    A) 33
    B) 65
    C) 127
    D) 233

6. The student revises the chart to show separate sectors for private domestic wells and public water supplies. If the sector for private wells measures 16°, how many million gallons of groundwater per day went into public water systems?
   A) 3673
   B) 5118
   C) 14,667
   D) 17,525

7. The chart is printed for display so that the circle is 20" wide. What will be the area of the industrial sector (to the nearest square inch)?
   A) 29
   B) 116
   C) 203
   D) 309

8. What is the linear speed of the tip of the minute hand (14 ft long) on Big Ben, the clock on the tower of the Palace of Westminster in London?
   A) 0.23 ft/min
   B) 0.73 ft/min
   C) 1.47 ft/min
   D) 87.96 ft/min

9. Big Ben's hour hand is 9 ft long. What is the area of the sector, in square feet, that it sweeps out between 12:10 PM and 4:40 PM the same day?
   A) 63.6 ft²
   B) 84.8 ft²
   C) 91.2 ft²
   D) 95.4 ft²

10. A sector is divided into two sectors, one with area of 36 and the other with area of 72. What is the circumference of the circle, to the nearest hundredth?
    A) 3.684
    B) 7.368
    C) 18.42
    D) 36.84

11. Three 45° slices of a 14" diameter pizza is approximately what percent larger a serving than two 45° slices of a 16" pizza?
    A) 15%
    B) 33%
    C) 115%
    D) The two slices of 16" pizza is a larger server

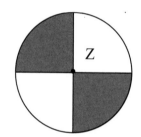

12. If the perimeter of the shaded region is $3\pi + 12$, what is the area of the shaded region?
    A) 3π
    B) 4.5π
    C) 9π
    D) 12π

13. What is the perimeter of a 30° sector of a 3-inch diameter circle?
    A) $3 + \frac{\pi}{4}$ inches
    B) $3 + \frac{\pi}{2}$ inches
    C) $6 + \frac{\pi}{4}$ inches
    D) $6 + \frac{\pi}{2}$ inches

(HW)

Questions 14 through 16 use the following information.

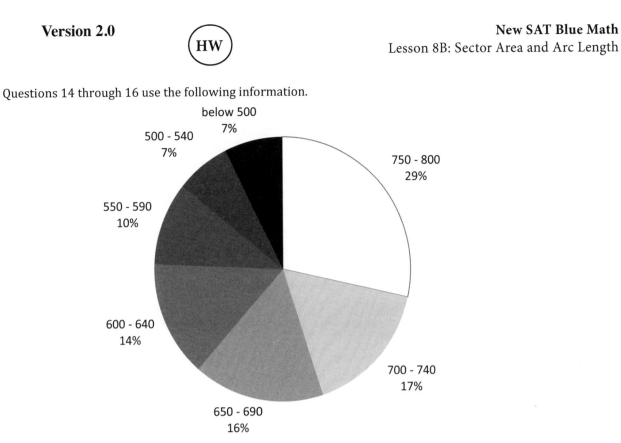

The chart above shows scores for the 52,300 students who took the SAT II subject test in Physics in 2013.

14. Students scoring in the 600 to 690 range account for what degree measure?
   A) 30
   B) 50.4
   C) 108
   D) 273.6

15. If 1308 students achieved a perfect score of 800, a new sector for perfect scores would measure how many degrees?
   A) 0.15
   B) 2.5
   C) 9
   D) 31

16. A new pie chart is made for scores above 600. The sector for the 600 to 640 range measures how many degrees?
   A) 50.4
   B) 66.3
   C) 93.3
   D) 168.0

17. You order a large pineapple pizza with a diameter of 18 inches that is cut into 8 equal slices. What is the area of two slices of pizza to the nearest square inch?

18. A biologist applies an antibiotic to a large portion of a perfectly circular petri dish that has a diameter of 9 centimeters. The section of the petri dish without antibiotics, which has an arc length of 4 centimeters, is the only section to grow *E. coli*. What is the area of the sector in which the *E. coli* flourished?

19. A neuroscientist is studying a subject's visual field, which can be represented as a circle. Assuming the visual field has a diameter of 6 meters, and a person's angle of view is a sector of that circle with central angle measure of 90°, what is the arc length of that person's visual field, to the nearest tenth of a meter?

20. An engineer designs a bicycle with a certain number of spokes. If the arc length created by each spoke is 10 cm, and the length of half a spoke is 14 cm, what is the interior angle of one section of the bike to the nearest degree?

BLUE MATH LESSON 9A: VOLUME

Getting Your Feet Wet

Directions: The problems below are intended as a short diagnostic exam.

1. A cylindrical container of height 2 m and radius 1 m contains a spherical ball of radius 1 m. What is the volume of the empty space contained within the container in cubic meters?
    A) $\frac{\pi}{3}$
    B) $\frac{2\pi}{3}$
    C) π
    D) 2π

2. The line $y = 2$ is drawn from $x = 0$ to $x = 3$. If this line is rotated around the x-axis, what is the volume of the cylinder created by the rotation?
    A) 12π
    B) 18π
    C) 24π
    D) 48π

3. A steel bar in the shape of a regular triangular prism is 175 cm long and weighs 8700 g. Each side of the base is 4 cm. What is the density of the bar, in g/cm^3? Round your answer to 2 decimal places.

BLUE MATH LESSON 9A: VOLUME
Wading In

Directions: Read the explanation for each problem type mentioned below. Pay special attention to the methods and techniques used to solve the sample problems. Then, do the practice exercises that follow; use the appropriate method to solve each problem.

TOPIC OVERVIEW: VOLUME

Figures that the SAT asks the volume of usually can be broken down into three categories, as shown below:

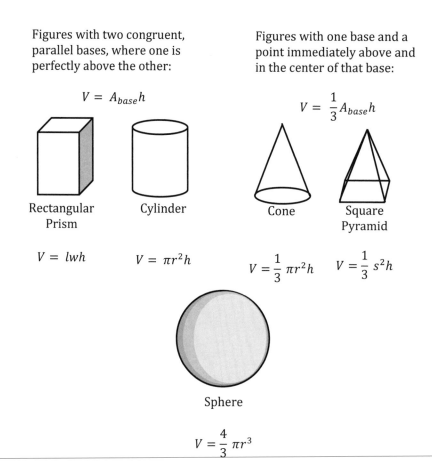

Figures with two congruent, parallel bases, where one is perfectly above the other:

$$V = A_{base}h$$

Rectangular Prism

Cylinder

$$V = lwh$$

$$V = \pi r^2 h$$

Figures with one base and a point immediately above and in the center of that base:

$$V = \frac{1}{3} A_{base}h$$

Cone

Square Pyramid

$$V = \frac{1}{3}\pi r^2 h$$

$$V = \frac{1}{3}s^2 h$$

Sphere

$$V = \frac{4}{3}\pi r^3$$

Now that we know the basic volume formulas, let's try a problem:

SAMPLE PROBLEM 1: VOLUME

A cylindrical container of height 2 m and radius 1 m contains a spherical ball of radius 1 m. What is the volume of the empty space contained within the container in cubic meters?

A) $\frac{\pi}{3}$

B) $\frac{2\pi}{3}$

C) π

D) 2π

Drawing a picture before starting a Geometry problem will help a lot on the SAT:

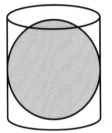

So, to find the volume of the space remaining after inserting the sphere, we simply need to subtract the volume of the sphere from the volume of the cylinder. Since the radius of the sphere is equivalent to the radius of the cylinder, we'll use one variable, r, to designate both of them:

$$V = \pi r^2 h - \frac{4}{3}\pi r^3$$

$$V = \pi(1)^2(2) - \frac{4}{3}\pi(1)^3$$

$$V = 2\pi - \frac{4}{3}\pi = \frac{2}{3}\pi$$

Our answer must be **B**.

SAMPLE PROBLEM 2: VOLUME

The line $y = 2$ is drawn from $x = 0$ to $x = 3$. If this line is rotated around the x-axis, what is the volume of the cylinder created by the rotation?

A) 12π

B) 18π

C) 24π

D) 48π

Again, this problem will be much easier if we can draw a picture to help visualize what's going on:

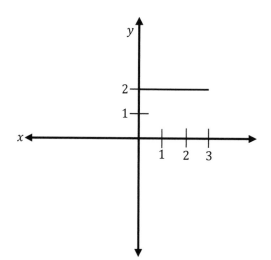

Now that we've drawn our line, let's rotate it around the x-axis to form a cylinder:

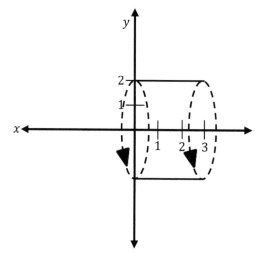

As we see from our image, we simply have a cylinder with a height of 3 and a radius of 2. Thus, our volume is 12π and our answer is **A**.

TOPIC OVERVIEW: DENSITY

Another topic that coincides with volume on the SAT is density. The density of a substance is its mass per unit volume. So,

$$\text{Density} = \frac{\text{mass}}{\text{volume}}.$$

Many of the density questions on the SAT will require finding the mass of a solid figure. For questions like this, we usually have to find the volume of the figure, then multiply it by the substance's given density. Let's try a problem to see how this works:

SAMPLE PROBLEM 3: DENSITY

A steel bar in the shape of a regular triangular prism is 175 cm long and weighs 8700 g. Each side of the base is 4 cm. What is the density of the bar, in g/cm³? Round your answer to 2 decimal places.

As always, let's start by drawing a picture of our figure:

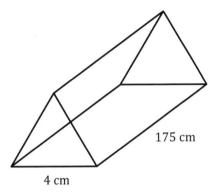

175 cm

4 cm

Since this figure has two congruent, parallel bases, and one is perfectly above the other, we know its volume must be $V = Ah$. There are many ways to find the area of an equilateral triangle, but the easiest one is $A = \frac{\sqrt{3}}{4}s^2$. So, the area of the base must be $4\sqrt{3}$ cm², and its volume will thus be $700\sqrt{3}$ cm³. Since we have the figure's mass, we can easily find its density:

$$\text{Density} = \frac{\text{mass}}{\text{volume}} = \frac{8700 \text{ g}}{700\sqrt{3} \text{ cm}^3} = \mathbf{7.18} \frac{\mathbf{g}}{\mathbf{cm^3}}.$$

WRAP-UP

When dealing with any volume problem, or any geometry problem in general, the first step should always be to draw a picture. Once we've drawn a picture of the figure, it should be very easy to figure out which general volume formula we will have to use. Always be on the lookout for problems that involve adding or taking away two or more different shapes; these problems will be the trickiest by far.

BLUE MATH LESSON 9A: VOLUME
Learning to Swim

Directions: Answer each question below.

PRACTICE SET 1 (CALCULATOR)

1. A lollipop is made of a stick and a solid chunk of candy. The stick is considered to be a solid cylinder with a height of h, radius r, and density c. The candy is considered to be a sphere with radius $6r$ and density $2c$. What is the mass of one lollipop?

2. An aluminum cube with length 10 cm is cut to form one regular octagonal prism with a base side length of 2 cm. What is the volume of aluminum in the prism?

3. A right cylinder has a height $6r$ and radius r and is filled with a gas. The density of the gas is d. If the cylinder is compressed such that the density is now $2d$, what is the new volume? (Note: the mass of gas doesn't change!) (Density is mass divided by volume)

4. A right cylinder with a base radius 3.00 inches and height 9.00 inches is filled halfway with water. A metal ball is dropped with a density of 2.00 grams per cubic inch and mass 5.00 grams. What is the height, in inches, of the water after the ball is dropped? (Density is mass divided by volume)

5. A model house is made with 2,000 toy bricks. 80% of the bricks used were large rectangular bricks and the rest were small rectangular bricks. The large brick has a length of 32mm, width of 16mm, and a height of 10mm. The small brick has the same dimensions but half the length. What is the volume of the bricks used to build the house, in cubic mm?

BLUE MATH LESSON 9A: VOLUME
Diving into the Deep End

Directions: Answer each question below.

PRACTICE SET 2 (CALCULATOR)

6. A bowling ball is a sphere with a diameter of 8 inches. Three cylindrical holes are drilled for the fingers, each with a radius of 0.5 inch and a height of 3 inches. The density is 3 grams/cubic inch; what is the mass of the bowling ball to the nearest cubic inch? (Density is mass divided by volume.)
    A) 87
    B) 89
    C) 783
    D) 797

7. A paint can has a height of 8 inches and a diameter of 6 inches. What is the volume, in cubic inches, of paint with which it can be filled?
    A) 56.55
    B) 207.35
    C) 226.19
    D) 904.78

8. A scientist places a cylindrical beaker with a radius of 4 cm inside a cylindrical beaker with diameter of 18 cm. Both beakers are 22 cm high. What is the volume of the space between the two beakers in cm^3?
    A) 1,105.84
    B) 4,423. 36
    C) 4,492.48
    D) 21,287.48

9. One version of a smart phone is 6 inches tall by 4 inches wide by 1 inch high. The newer model is 8 inches tall by 5 inches wide by 0.5 inch tall. What is the difference in volume, in cubic inches, between the phones?
    A) 3
    B) 4
    C) 5
    D) 6

10. A soccer ball has a surface area of 64π square inches. How many inches long is the diameter of the soccer ball?
    A) 4
    B) 8
    C) 33.51
    D) 268.08

11. A cylindrical glass with a diameter of 4 inches and a height of 7 inches is filled to the brim with soda. If the density of the soda is 2 grams/cubic inch, what is the mass of the soda in grams? (Density is mass divided by volume).
    A) 43.98
    B) 87.96
    C) 175.93
    D) 703.72

12. A washer is a small, cylindrical piece of metal through which a cylindrical hole is cut. The diameter of the washer is 4 inches, and the thickness is 2 inches. If the radius of the inner hole is 1 inch, what is the volume of the metal in the washer in cubic inches?
    A) 18.85
    B) 31.41
    C) 376.99
    D) 395.84

13. A rectangular bathtub is 0.75 meters deep by 2 meters long and 1 meter wide. If the density of water is 99 kg/cubic meter, how many kilograms of water can fill the tub? (Density is mass divided by volume.)
    A) 45
    B) 66
    C) 148.5
    D) 198

14. A ream of 8.5 inch by 11 inch paper is 2 inches thick. Three circular holes of equal diameter are punched along one edge of the entire ream causing the volume of paper to decrease by 0.1575% of the original volume. What is the diameter, in inches, of each hole that was punched?

15. An ice cream cone can be considered to be half a sphere on top of a cone. The height of the cone is 4 inches and the radius of the cone and sphere are both 1.5 inches. If the cone and sphere are completely filled with ice cream, what is the volume, to the nearest tenth of a cubic inch, of ice cream present?

PRACTICE SET 3 (CALCULATOR)

16. A cube-shaped footrest has a surface area of $24y^2$. What is its volume?
    A) $2y$
    B) $4y^2$
    C) $8y^2$
    D) $8y^3$

17. A megaphone is shaped like a cone with a radius of 7 inches and a height of 8 inches. What is the volume of the megaphone in cubic inches?
    A) 56.00
    B) 102.63
    C) 410.50
    D) 1231.50

18. A carpenter builds a box with three different sizes of wood panels—one set of the panels is 4 inches by 5 inches; another set is 3 inches by 4 inches, and the last is 3 inches by 5 inches. What is the volume of the box, in cubic inches?
    A) 47
    B) 60
    C) 83
    D) 94

19. A school fundraiser is wrapping gifts. If a box has a volume of 24 cubic feet, with sides equaling 2 feet, 3 feet, and x feet, what is the surface area, in ft², of the box that needs to be wrapped?
    A) 4
    B) 24
    C) 26
    D) 52

20. A circular stage at the local performing arts center has a circumference of 22 feet and a height of 4 feet. What is its volume, in ft³?
    A) 88.00
    B) 154.06
    C) 176.00
    D) 615.75

21. A marble is a sphere with a radius of 1 inch. The material it is made out of has a density of 5 grams per cubic inch. What is the mass of five marbles? (Density is mass divided by volume.)
    A) 4.19 g
    B) 20.95 g
    C) 104.72 g
    D) 167.55 g

22. An original design for a rectangular bus stop was not big enough, so each side was doubled in length. Assuming the bus stop looks exactly like a cube, by what factor was the volume increased?
    A) 2
    B) 4
    C) 6
    D) 8

23. A cone-shaped carrot has a volume of 6 cubic inches with a radius of 1. What is the height of the carrot?
    A) 1.43 in
    B) 5.73 in
    C) 6.28 in
    D) 22.92 in

24. A right circular cylinder with a height of 6 inches and a base radius of 1 inch is filled $\frac{3}{5}$ths of the way with water. The water is then frozen causing the volume of water to expand by 9% of the original volume. What is the volume of the frozen water to the nearest tenth of an in³?

25. A dumbbell is made by taking two identical regular hexagonal prisms and attaching one to each end of a right circular cylinder. The cylinder is 6 inches long with a radius of 0.5 inches and both hexagonal prisms have a side of length 1.5 inches and a thickness of 2.65 inches. If a dumbbell is made of iron with a density of 0.28 pounds per inch cubed, what is the mass of the dumbbell to the nearest pound? (Density is mass divided by volume)

BLUE MATH LESSON 9A: VOLUME
Race to the Finish

Directions: Answer each question below.

HOMEWORK SET (CALCULATOR)

1. A six-sided die has a volume of 8 cubic centimeters. What is its surface area in square centimeters?
   A) 2
   B) 9
   C) 24
   D) 43

2. An Egyptologist is studying a square pyramid, which is made up of four equilateral triangles and a base with a perimeter of 120 feet. What is the volume of the pyramid in cubic feet?
   A) 3600
   B) $4500\sqrt{2}$
   C) 9000
   D) $10,000\sqrt{2}$

3. An rectangular in-ground pool has a depth of 8 feet, a length of 26 feet, and is 9 feet wide. How many cubic feet of water will it take to fill the pool?
   A) 208
   B) 234
   C) 676
   D) 1872

4. A section of an oil pipeline is created by taking a solid cylindrical block of steel and boring a hole through the center. One of the sections is 5 yards long with a 4-yard diameter, and a hole with a diameter of 3.5 yards is bored into the cylinder. If the density of the metal is 5 kilograms per cubic yard, what is the mass of this pipe? (Density is mass divided by volume.)
   A) 4.08
   B) 7.54
   C) 73.6
   D) 188.5

5. The circumference of a sphere is 6π. What is its volume?
   A) 113.1
   B) 904.78
   C) 3501.4
   D) 28,011.17

6. An outdoor rectangular pond has a length of 5 meters, a depth of 2 meters, and a width of 3 meters. The density of water is 99 kilograms per cubic meter. What is the mass of the water of the pond in kilograms? (Density is mass divided by volume).
   A) 3.3
   B) 30
   C) 1485
   D) 2970

7. A spherical snow globe with a surface area of 16π is made. How much fluid will it take to fill the snow globe? (The thickness of the globe is negligible.)
    A) 25.12
    B) 33.51
    C) 200.96
    D) 268.08

8. A young woman buys a hexagonally-shaped jewelry box. The box is 6 inches tall, and the length of each side of a hexagonal face is 4 inches. What is the volume of her box?
    A) 24√3
    B) 48
    C) 216
    D) 144√3

9. A cylindrical can has a volume of 64π and a height of 4; what is its diameter?
    A) 4
    B) 6
    C) 8
    D) 16

10. The surface area of a cubical cardboard box used for shipping is 96 inches squared. What is the volume of the box in cubic inches?
    A) 64
    B) 90
    C) 96
    D) 912.6

11. An ice cream cone has a diameter of 4 inches and a height of 5 inches. What is the maximum amount, in cubic inches, of ice cream that can fit inside the cone?
    A) 10.5
    B) 20.93
    C) 62.8
    D) 83.7

12. A gardener builds a greenhouse that is a triangular prism. It is 10 feet long and the base of the equilateral triangle is 7 feet long. What is the volume of the greenhouse?
    A) 21.22
    B) 35
    C) 212.2
    D) 245

13. A metal cube-shaped bracelet charm with a side length of 3 cm has a cylinder of diameter 2 cm drilled through it. What is the remaining volume of the charm?
    A) 8.16
    B) 17.58
    C) 35.16
    D) 36.42

14. A softball has a diameter of 6 inches. If the material it is made out of has a density of 8 grams per cubic inch, what is the mass of the softball in grams? (Density is mass divided by volume).
    A) 14.14
    B) 301.44
    C) 904.78
    D) 7238.24

15. At the grocery store, a smaller size can of beans has a volume of 10. The larger size has a doubled radius; what is the volume of the larger can of beans? (Assume that the heights of the cans are the same.)
    A) 20
    B) 30
    C) 40
    D) 50

16. A chocolatier is making a large sphere-shaped chocolate with a radius of 5 inches, with a sphere-shaped caramel filling in the middle that has a diameter of 4 inches. Solid chocolate has a density of 3 grams/cubic inch; what is the mass of the solid chocolate in the treat in grams?
    A) 163.36
    B) 1470.27
    C) 1570.80
    D) 1671.33

17. Copper pipe is commonly used to move water around a home. A thin-walled pipe is hollow with an inside diameter of 0.450 inches and an outside diameter of 0.500 inches. To the nearest hundredth of a pound, what is the mass of 15 feet of copper pipe if the density of copper is 0.323 pounds per cubic inch? (Density is mass divided by volume.)

18. A rectangular prism with a height of 12 inches, width of 4 inches, and length of 6 inches is cut into tiny pieces that are each in the shape of a pyramid. The pyramid pieces are identical with a height of 4 inches and square base with side length 2 inches. If 24.07% of the volume of the rectangular prism is uncut and wasted, how many pyramid pieces can be made from the volume that is not wasted?

19. A rectangular pendant is made with a height of 5.08 cm, width of 1.27 cm, and thickness of 0.508 cm. The pendant is made with red gold, which is 75% gold and 25% copper by volume. If the density of gold is 19.32 grams per cubic cm and the density of copper is 8.96 grams per cubic cm, what is the mass of the pendant to the nearest tenth of a gram? (Density is mass divided by volume)

20. Babies are often fed a puree of food. A typical can of baby food is 2 inches tall with a 0.5 inch base radius. Density of the puree is 100 grams per cubic inch. If the puree gives 1.25 calories of energy per gram of puree, how many calories are in one can of baby food, to the nearest calorie? (Density is mass divided by volume)

Blue Math Lesson 9B: Complex Numbers
Getting Your Feet Wet

Directions: The problems below are intended as a short diagnostic exam.

1. The expression i^{23} is equivalent to which of the following expressions?
   A) i^{17}
   B) i^{25}
   C) $-i^{27}$
   D) $-i^{29}$

2. The expression $(3 - 4i) - (-4i - 3)$ is equivalent to what?

3. The product $(3 - 2i)(6 + 4i)$ is equivalent to what?

4. $\frac{3+6i}{2-4i}$ is equivalent to which of the following?
   A) $\frac{12i-9}{10}$
   B) $\frac{9-12i}{10}$
   C) $\frac{12i+15}{10}$
   D) $\frac{12i-15}{10}$

BLUE MATH LESSON 9B: COMPLEX NUMBERS
Wading In

Directions: Read the explanation for each problem type mentioned below. Pay special attention to the methods and techniques used to solve the sample problems. Then, do the practice exercises that follow; use the appropriate method to solve each problem.

TOPIC OVERVIEW: INTRODUCTION TO IMAGINARY NUMBERS

For much of math, we are taught that the square root of a negative number does not exist. In actuality, the square root of a negative number has many uses, many of them in the field of electrical engineering. Since $\sqrt{-1}$ is rather cumbersome to write, we represent it as i, the **imaginary number**, to make things easier. Since $i = \sqrt{-1}$, it can easily be proven that $i^2 = -1$, $i^3 = -i$, and $i^4 = 1$. From that point onwards, the pattern repeats. So, $i^5 = i = \sqrt{-1}$ and $i^6 = i^2 = -1$. Let's try a problem:

SAMPLE PROBLEM 1: INTRODUCTION TO IMAGINARY NUMBERS

The expression i^{23} is equivalent to which of the following expressions?
A) i^{17}
B) i^{25}
C) $-i^{27}$
D) $-i^{29}$

The easiest way to simplify an imaginary number is to divide 4 into its power. The remainder will be the power of the equivalent expression. Since 4 will divide into 23 a total of 5 times, and leave a remainder of 3, we know that $i^{23} = i^3$. By the same process, we know that $i^{17} = i$, $i^{25} = i$, $-i^{27} = -i^3$, and $-i^{29} = -i$. Since $i^3 = -i$, our answer must be **D**.

TOPIC OVERVIEW: ADDING AND SUBTRACTING COMPLEX NUMBERS

A **complex number** is the sum or difference of an imaginary number and a real number, represented in the form $a + bi$. The imaginary solutions to quadratic functions are always represented as complex numbers, so adding and subtracting them comes up fairly regularly. Adding and subtracting complex numbers is no different from adding algebraic expressions: We can only add terms like terms. So, we can only add real numbers to other real numbers and imaginary numbers to other imaginary numbers. Let's try an example to see how this works:

SAMPLE PROBLEM 2: ADDING AND SUBTRACTING COMPLEX NUMBERS

The expression $(3 - 4i) - (-4i - 3)$ is equivalent to what?

Since we're given two expressions to subtract, let's start by distributing our negative sign throughout the second term:

$$(3 - 4i) - (-4i - 3) = (3 - 4i) + (4i + 3) = 6$$

So, our answer is **6**.

TOPIC OVERVIEW: MULTIPLYING COMPLEX NUMBERS

Multiplying complex numbers is not much different from multiplying any other binomials. We still want to use the usual FOIL algorithm while keeping in mind the fact that $i^2 = -1$. Let's try a sample problem:

SAMPLE PROBLEM 3: MULTIPLYING COMPLEX NUMBERS

The product $(3 - 2i)(6 + 4i)$ is equivalent to what?

Let's start by FOILing:
$$(3 - 2i)(6 + 4i)$$
$$18 + 12i - 12i - 8i^2$$
$$18 - (-8) = 26$$

So, our answer is **26**.

TOPIC OVERVIEW: DIVIDING COMPLEX NUMBERS

When dividing complex numbers, keep in mind that imaginary numbers are still radicals, so any denominators that contain imaginary numbers will need to be simplified. To simplify a complex denominator, multiply both the denominator and the numerator by the imaginary denominator's **conjugate**. The conjugate is a binomial identical to the complex number, but contains the opposite of the bi term. So, the conjugate of $3 - 2i$ is $3 + 2i$. Let's look at an example involving dividing complex numbers:

SAMPLE PROBLEM 4: DIVIDING COMPLEX NUMBERS

$\frac{3+6i}{2-4i}$ is equivalent to which of the following?

A) $\frac{12i-9}{10}$

B) $\frac{9-12i}{10}$

C) $\frac{12i+15}{10}$

D) $\frac{12i-15}{10}$

Let's start by finding the conjugate of $2 - 4i$: $2 + 4i$. So, we'll first multiply both the numerator and denominator by that conjugate.

$$\frac{3+6i}{2-4i} \times \frac{2+4i}{2+4i} = \frac{6+24i+24i^2}{4-16i^2} = \frac{6+24i+(-24)}{4-(-16)} =$$

$$\frac{24i-18}{20} = \frac{12i-9}{10}$$

So, our answer is **A**.

WRAP-UP

Complex numbers show up fairly frequently on the SAT, so understanding how they work is extremely important. Always be prepared to deal with complex numbers when working with quadratics, but they show up in other situations just as frequently.

BLUE MATH LESSON 9B: COMPLEX NUMBERS
Learning to Swim

Directions: Answer each question below.

PRACTICE SET 1 (NO CALCULATOR)

1. If $Z_1 = 3 + 5i$; $Z_2 = 7 - 2i$; and $Z_3 = -10 - 85i$, then $\frac{Z_3}{3Z_1 - Z_2} = ?$

2. $((i^2)^3)^4 = ?$

3. What is the value of $\frac{10}{3-i}$, as a complex number in the form $a + bi$?

4. What is the value of $(11 + 7i)^2$, as a complex number in the form $a + bi$?

5. What is the value of $(11 - 7i)^2$, as a complex number in the form $a + bi$?

BLUE MATH LESSON 9B: COMPLEX NUMBERS
Diving into the Deep End

Directions: Answer each question below.

PRACTICE SET 2 (NO CALCULATOR)

6. What is the value of $i + i^2 + i^3 + i^4$?
   A) 0
   B) 1
   C) i
   D) $-i$

7. Which of the following is equal to $-i \cdot (4 - 5i)$?
   A) $-5 - 4i$
   B) $-5 + 4i$
   C) $5 - 4i$
   D) $5 + 4i$

8. Provided that a, b, and c are real constants, if
   $Z_1 = a + i$, $Z_2 = 4 - 4i$, and
   $Z_1 + Z_2 = b - ci$, which of the following MUST
   be true?
   A) $a = b + 4$
   B) $c = -3i$
   C) $c = 3$
   D) $b = a - 4$

9. $(5 + 12i)(5 - 12i) = ?$
   A) 10
   B) 25
   C) 169
   D) $169 - 120i$

10. $\frac{1}{2-i} \times \frac{1}{2+i} = ?$
    A) $\frac{1}{3}$
    B) $\frac{1}{4}$
    C) $\frac{1}{5}$
    D) $\frac{1}{4-i}$

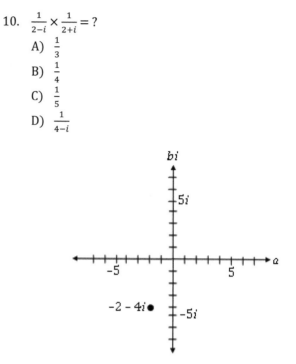

11. The graph of $-2 - 4i$ in the complex coordinate
    plane is depicted above. The *magnitude* of a
    complex number $a + bi$, written as $|a + bi|$, is
    equal to the distance in the coordinate plane
    between the point $a + bi$ and the origin. What
    is $|-2 - 4i|$?
    A) $2\sqrt{3}i$
    B) 2
    C) $2\sqrt{5}$
    D) 6

12. Which of the following expressions gives the
    magnitude (as defined in problem 11 above) of a
    complex number $a + bi$?
    A) $\sqrt{a^2 - b^2}$
    B) $\sqrt{a^2 + b^2}$
    C) $\sqrt{(a - b)^2 - (ai - bi)^2}$
    D) $\sqrt{a^2 + (bi)^2}$

PRACTICE SET 3 (NO CALCULATOR)

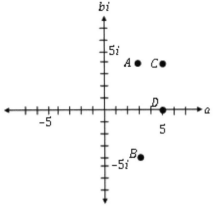

16. What is the value of i^{89} ?
    A) 1
    B) −1
    C) i
    D) −i

13. On the complex coordinate plane above, which point represents the complex number equal to $(-2-i)^2$?
    A) A
    B) B
    C) C
    D) D

17. $(3-2i)(4+i) = ?$
    A) $10-5i$
    B) $14-5i$
    C) $10-11i$
    D) $14-11i$

14. The expression $\frac{1}{20-13i}$ simplifies to $\frac{20+13i}{k}$, where k is an integer. What is the value of k?

15. The expression $i + 2i^2 + 3i^3 + 4i^4 + 5i^5 + 6i^6 + 7i^7 + 8i^8$ is equal to $a - ai$ for some integer a. What is the value of a?

18. $-\dfrac{5}{-3+4i} = ?$

    A) $\dfrac{15-20i}{7}$

    B) $\dfrac{3+4i}{5}$

    C) $\dfrac{4+2i}{3}$

    D) $\dfrac{-3+4i}{5}$

19. $i^{72} + i^{48} =$

    A) -2

    B) -1

    C) 1

    D) 2

20. Which of the following is equal to $(1 + i)^3 \cdot (-2 + 2i)^3$?

    A) -64

    B) -10

    C) $8 - 8i$

    D) 64

21. If $\dfrac{n}{1+3i} = 4 - 12i$, what is the value of n?

    A) $\dfrac{1}{4}$

    B) 4

    C) $4 - 4i$

    D) 40

22. If b is a real number, which of the following is an expression for $(1 + bi)^3$?

    A) $1 - b^3 i$

    B) $1 - 3b^2 + 3bi - b^3 i$

    C) $1 + 2bi - b^2$

    D) $1 + 2bi - b^3 i$

23. $(i^5)^5 - i^{24} = ?$

    A) $-i - 1$

    B) $i - 1$

    C) $1 + i$

    D) $1 - i$

24. The *magnitude* $|Z|$ of a complex number $Z = a + bi$ is defined as follows: $|Z| = \sqrt{a^2 + b^2}$. What is the magnitude of $24 - 7i$?

25. What is the value of $i \cdot (-1 + i)^2$?

HW

Blue Math Lesson 9B: Complex Numbers
Race to the Finish

Directions: Answer each question below.

Homework Set (No Calculator)

1. $i^{312} =$
   A) $-i$
   B) i
   C) -1
   D) 1

2. If $i^x = 1$, which of the following could be the value of x ?
   A) 6
   B) 21
   C) 44
   D) 50

3. Which of the following values of x satisfies the equation $x^3 = -8i$?
   A) $2i$
   B) $-2i$
   C) $8i$
   D) $-8i$

4. If $Z_1 = 2 - i$ and $Z_2 = -1 + 2i$, then $Z_1 + Z_2 = ?$
   A) $3 + i$
   B) $3 - i$
   C) $1 - 3i$
   D) $1 + i$

5. If $x = 6 + 7i$ and $y = 5 - 5i$, then $12x + 17y = ?$
   A) 158
   B) $157 + 169i$
   C) $157 - i$
   D) $29 + 2i$

6. $(-12 + 11i)^2 = ?$
   A) $144 - 121i$
   B) $265 - 264i$
   C) $23 - 264i$
   D) $144 + 121i$

7. Which of the following expressions is equal to 13?
   A) $(2 + 3i)(2 - 3i)$
   B) $9 + 4i^2$
   C) $-13i^4$
   D) $(2 - 3i)^2$

8. If $x^2 = -16$, then $x = ?$
   A) $\pm 4i$
   B) $-4i$
   C) $4 \pm i$
   D) $4 - i$

9. $\frac{1-i}{4-7i} = ?$

    A) $\frac{5+6i}{8}$

    B) $\frac{2}{65}$

    C) $\frac{-3-11i}{65}$

    D) $\frac{11+3i}{65}$

10. If $Z_1 = 6 - i$, and $Z_2 = 5 + 2i$, then
    $Z_1^2 - Z_2^2 = ?$
    A) 10
    B) 20
    C) $11 + 9i$
    D) $14 - 32i$

11. $3(i - 3) + 2(i + 3) =$
    A) $5i - 3$
    B) $5i + 3$
    C) $6i - 3$
    D) $6i + 3$

12. If $x^2 = -1$, then $x = ?$
    A) ± 1
    B) -1
    C) $\pm i$
    D) $-i$

13. If $x = 42 + 22i$ and $y = -12 + 6i$, then
    $x - 4y = ?$
    A) $30 + 28i$
    B) $90 - 2i$
    C) $-6 + 28i$
    D) 88

14. $\frac{1-i}{1+i} \times \frac{1}{i-1} =$
    A) $\frac{-1-i}{2}$

    B) $\frac{-1+i}{2}$

    C) $\frac{1-i}{2}$

    D) Undefined

15. The graph of a quadratic function with two imaginary roots crosses the x-axis in how many places?
    A) 0
    B) 1
    C) 2
    D) More than 2

16. If a, b and $\sqrt{(a - bi)(a + bi)}$ are each integers, then the ordered pair (a, b) could equal which of the following?
    A) $(1, 1)$
    B) $(1, 2)$
    C) $(3, 4)$
    D) $(4, 4)$

17. If $X = 3 + i$, and $Y = 4 - 3i$, what is the value of $3X + Y$?

19. The equation $(x - 5)(x + 5) = -74$ has two solutions, both of which are complex numbers. What is the product of these two solutions?

$$2i^2 + 4i^4 + 6i^6 + 8i^8 + 10i^{10}$$

18. The above expression is equal to an integer x. What is the value of $-x$?

20. The product $(7 - 2i)(6 + 3i) = a + bi$, where a and b are real numbers. What is the value of $a + b$?

BLUE MATH LESSON 10A: NON-LINEAR LINES OF BEST FIT – SCATTERPLOTS
Getting Your Feet Wet

Directions: The problems below are intended as a short diagnostic exam.

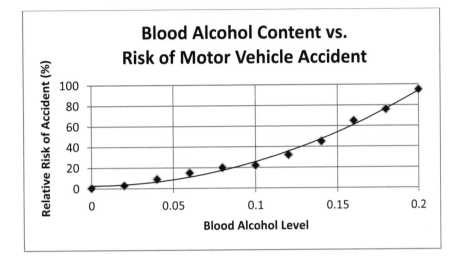

1. The scatterplot above shows a computer model comparing the relative risk of accident at various blood alcohol levels. Every U.S. state defines driving with a Blood Alcohol Level above 0.08 as a crime. Georgia is creating new laws that ban any driving with accident risk greater than 10%. Under the new law, what should Georgia's legal Blood Alcohol Level for drivers be?
    A) 0.02
    B) 0.06
    C) 0.10
    D) 0.15

2. Which of the following equations of a line of best fit would best represent the data above?
    A) $y = 470x - 13$
    B) $y = 2600x^2 - 53x + 0.5$
    C) $y = -2355x^3 + 1911x^2 + 0.51x + 1.33$
    D) $y = -1.56(1.06 \times 1010)^x$

BLUE MATH LESSON 10A: NON-LINEAR LINES OF BEST FIT – SCATTERPLOTS
Wading In

Directions: Read the explanation for each problem type mentioned below. Pay special attention to the methods and techniques used to solve the sample problems. Then, do the practice exercises that follow; use the appropriate method to solve each problem.

TOPIC OVERVIEW: INTERPOLATING AND EXTRAPOLATING

A **scatterplot** is a graph which plots two variables along the x- and y-axes. The pattern of the points sometimes strongly resembles a function. The graph of that function is called a **line of best fit**, and can be used to predict other data points that follow the same pattern. Look below for several examples of scatterplots and their lines of best fit:

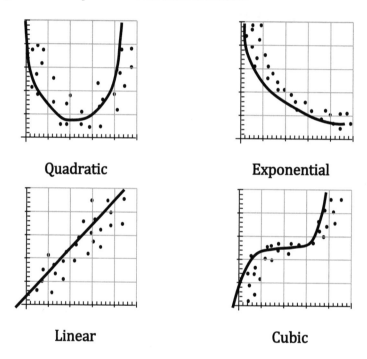

Quadratic   Exponential

Linear   Cubic

The most common type of questions involving scatterplots are those which ask us to predict a value based on the other information in the graph. There are two main types of predictions that we'll be asked to do on the SAT: interpolating and extrapolating. **Interpolating** involves predicting a data point on the line of best fit that is within the range of the graph, while **extrapolating** involves following our line of best fit to a point outside the range of the graph to predict the coordinates of our data point. Let's look at an example of this below:

SAMPLE PROBLEM 1: INTERPOLATING AND EXTRAPOLATING

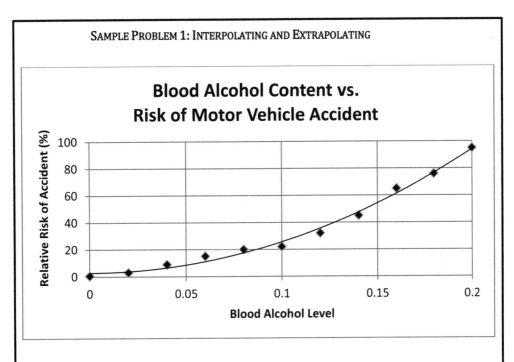

Blood Alcohol Content vs.
Risk of Motor Vehicle Accident

The scatterplot above shows a computer model comparing the relative risk of accident at various blood alcohol levels. Every U.S. state defines driving with a Blood Alcohol Level above 0.08 as a crime. Georgia is creating new laws that ban any driving with accident risk greater than 10%. Under the new law, what should Georgia's legal Blood Alcohol Level for drivers be?

A) 0.02
B) 0.06
C) 0.10
D) 0.15

This is a good example of an interpolation question; we're given our data, our line of best fit, and asked to find a Blood Alcohol Level based on a Relative Risk of Accident of 10%. So, all we have to do is find 10% on our y-axis and follow that point to the line of best fit. The x-coordinate of that point on the line of best fit must be our answer. Thus, our answer is **B**.

TOPIC OVERVIEW: EQUATION OF THE LINE OF BEST FIT

Many questions on the SAT give us the graph and line of best fit and ask for a function that best resembles the line of best fit. There is a set of steps we can work through to find the line of best fit when time is an issue:

1. Determine if the line of best fit of the graph is Linear, Quadratic, Cubic, or Exponential. Sometimes, the graph may fit more than one of these (for example the right-half of a quadratic function could resemble an exponential function), but eliminate any functions that don't resemble the choices we picked.

2. Pick at least two of the points on the line of best fit. Plug these points into all of the answer choices we did not eliminate. The correct graph should be a close match for all of the points.

There are many ways to get the equation of a graph that do not involve plugging in numbers; however, they are all very time-consuming. We may have to use some of these in our school classes or on other tests, but don't worry about them for the SAT unless plugging-in numbers isn't working. Let's try a problem like this, based on the graph from Sample Problem 1.

SAMPLE PROBLEM 2: EQUATION OF THE LINE OF BEST FIT

Which of the following equations of a line of best fit would best represent the data above?

    A) $y = 470x - 13$
    B) $y = 2600x^2 - 53x + 0.5$
    C) $y = -2355x^3 + 1911x^2 + 0.51x + 1.33$
    D) $y = -1.56(1.06 \times 1010)^x$

The first thing to notice is the curve of the graph—it can't be a linear function, so let's eliminate choice A. If we look closely at the exponential function, choice D, we'll see that every obtainable y-value is negative. Since our graph only contains positive y-values, we can eliminate D as well.

Theoretically, the graph could be quadratic or cubic, so let's see which one works best. Let's start with the easiest point to plug in: $x = 0$.

Plugging in 0 for B gives us 0.5, while plugging 0 in for C gives us 1.33. Both of these seem like reasonable answers, so let's try another point: $x = 0.1$.

Plugging in 0.1 for B gives us 21.2, while plugging 0.1 in for C gives us 18.136. B is looking like a better choice so far, but we'll try another point just to make sure.

Plugging in 0.2 for B gives us 93.9, while plugging 0.2 in for C only gives us 59.032. Clearly, **B** is our answer.

WRAP-UP

When asked about scatterplots and their lines of best fit on the SAT, it's imperative that we know the basic shapes of the four most common graphs. Always pick numbers to save time and we'll be able to get through these questions with more than enough time to tackle the rest of the time.

BLUE MATH LESSON 10A: NON-LINEAR LINES OF BEST FIT – SCATTERPLOTS
Learning to Swim

Directions: Answer each question below.

PRACTICE SET 1 (CALCULATOR)

1. The four scatterplots below can each be matched with a different one of four types of best-fit curves: linear, quadratic, cubic, and exponential. Label each plot with the type of function that best fits the data.

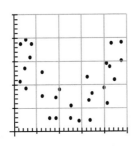

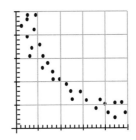

_____

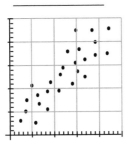

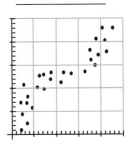

_____

_____

Questions 2 and 3 use the following information.

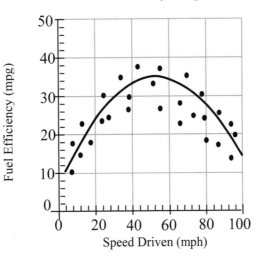

Fuel Efficiency vs. Speed

2. The scatterplot above shows the fuel efficiency of a car manufacturer's fleet in a variety of tests conducted at different speeds. Write an equation for the best-fit curve shown, expressing e (efficiency in mpg) in terms of s (speed in mph).

3. The cars above all have 12-gallon fuel tanks. Based on the best-fit curve shown, you are likely to be able to go more than 300 miles on a single tank of gas as long as you are traveling between which two speeds, in miles per hour?

Questions 4 and 5 use the following information.

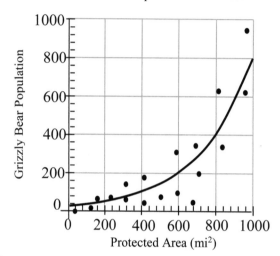

Large animals at the top of the food chain need a sufficiently large habitat in order to maintain a breeding population that can survive for multiple generations. The scatterplot shows the area and estimated population of grizzly bears in several national parks and wildlife preserves that provide grizzly habitat.

4. Based on the data and best-fit curve, what is the statistically expected population density (bears per square mile) of grizzly bears in a(n):
   A) 200 mi² preserve?
   B) 800 mi² preserve?

5. List the y-values (bear population) on the best-fit curve above for $x = 200, 400, 600, 800,$ and 1000. Based on this, is the best-fit curve a quadratic or exponential function? How do you know? What is its equation?

BLUE MATH LESSON 10A: NON-LINEAR LINES OF BEST FIT – SCATTERPLOTS
Diving into the Deep End

Directions: Answer each question below.

PRACTICE SET 2 (CALCULATOR)

Questions 6 and 7 use the following information.

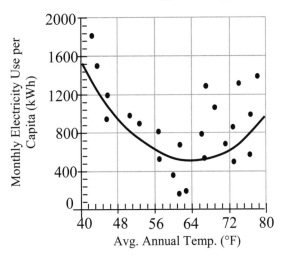

Home Energy Consumption

The scatterplot above shows the average monthly home energy in a variety of cities situated in different climates. Per capita monthly energy use in kilowatt hours is plotted against the average annual temperature in each city.

6. If energy use per capita is E and temperature is T, which of the following is closest to the equation of the best-fit curve shown in the graph above?
   A) $E = 1.75(T + 64)^2 + 500$
   B) $E = 1.75(T - 64)^2 + 500$
   C) $E = 0.25(T - 64)^2 + 500$
   D) $E = 0.25(T + 64)^2 + 500$

7. Based on the scatterplot and best-fit curve above, the average resident of Tampa (average annual temperature 76°) could be expected to use about how many times as much energy in his or her home as the average resident of San Francisco (average annual temperature 56°) ?
   A) 1.3
   B) 1.6
   C) 2.0
   D) 3.0

Questions 8 through 10 use the following information.

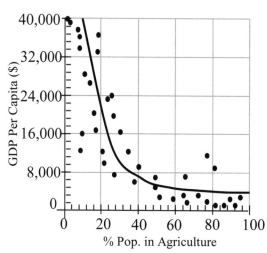

Industrialization and GDP

The scatterplot above shows the gross domestic product (GDP) per capita for a number of countries relative to how industrialized those countries are, as measured by the percentage of their populations working in the agricultural sector.

8. Which of the following equations, where G = per capita GDP and A = percent of work force involved in agriculture, is closest to that of the best-fit curve shown in the graph above?

A) $G = 2000 \cdot 2^A + 4000$

B) $G = 2000 \cdot 2^{0.1A} - 4000$

C) $G = 2000 \cdot 2^{5-0.1A} + 4000$

D) $G = (A - 100)^2 + 4000$

9. A decline from 40% to 20% of workers in the agricultural sector, according to the best-fit curve above, can be expected to lead to roughly what percent increase in a country's per capita GDP?

A) 80

B) 200

C) 18,000

D) 40,000

10. Botswana has 30% of its work force employed in agriculture, but has a GDP per capita of $17,000, in large part due to its large diamond mining industry. By how many dollars does Botswana's GDP per capita exceed what the best-fit model above would predict it to be?

A) 5000

B) 9000

C) 10,000

D) 17,000

Questions 11 through 13 use the following information.

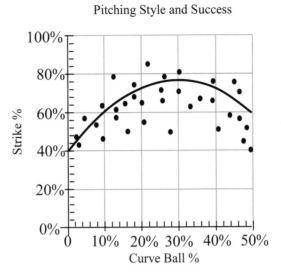

Pitching Style and Success

The scatterplot above shows an analysis of the frequency with which 34 professional baseball pitchers throw curve balls as opposed to other types of pitches and how that frequency correlates with their success in striking out opposing hitters.

11. The best-fit curve to the data shown above suggests that the most successful pitcher will throw curve balls what percent of the time, on average?
     A) 22
     B) 30
     C) 40
     D) 50

12. Which of the following statements is most strongly supported by the data presented above?
     A) A pitcher who throws a curve ball 10% of the time is predicted to be less successful than one who throws one 50% of the time.
     B) For all pitchers in the study, throwing a curve ball led to a strike between 40% and 88% of the time.
     C) A pitcher who throws curve balls with 60% frequency is predicted to strike out batters 10% of the time.
     D) Pitchers who used a particular technique with moderate frequency were more successful than those who relied upon it heavily or very rarely.

13. Based on the best-fit curve to the data shown above, if a pitcher not included in the study were to throw curve balls on 70% of his pitches, he would be likely to strike out opposing batters closest to what percent of the time?
     A) 20
     B) 30
     C) 40
     D) 45

Questions 14 and 15 use the following information.

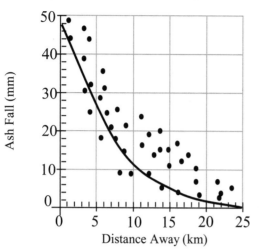

The scatterplot above shows the depth of ash that fell from a volcanic eruption on various monitoring sites within a 25 kilometer radius of the blast.

14. The best-fit curve shown above has the equation $y = a \cdot 2^{-0.2x}$, where a is an integer constant. Based on the graph, what is the value of a?

15. A farmer calls in from his home 12.5 km from the eruption site to report that 15.5 mm of ash fell on his crops. This exceeds the depth predicted by the best-fit equation by how many millimeters?

PRACTICE SET 3 (NO CALCULATOR)

Questions 16 through 18 use the following information.

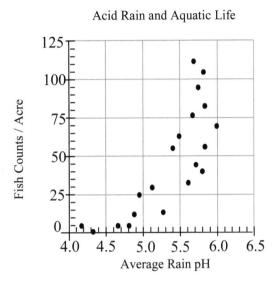

Acid Rain and Aquatic Life

The scatterplot above shows fish counts per acre in a number of lakes in Eastern Canada, where acid rain has been a known problem for several decades. The pH (a measure of acidity) of the water in each lake was also measured.

16. Which type of function provides the most appropriate best-fit line or curve to match the data shown above?
    A) Constant
    B) Linear
    C) Exponential
    D) Periodic

17. Which of the following equations provides the most appropriate best-fit line or curve to the data shown above? (Let y = fish per acre and x = pH of the lake.)
    A) $y = 6.25x^2$
    B) $y = (x - 4)^2$
    C) $y = 5 \cdot 9^{x - 4.5}$
    D) $y = 5 \cdot 4^{x - 4.5}$

18. A pH of 7.0 is neutral; anything below 7 is acidic, while anything above 7 is alkaline. Pure water has a pH of 7, while uncontaminated rainwater (and thus lake water) typically has a pH around 5.7 because carbon dioxide in the air naturally forms carbonic acid, a weak acid. Given this information and the data presented above, for a lake of which pH is a best-fit curve to the data LEAST likely to accurately predict the lake's fish population?
    A) 4.0
    B) 5.0
    C) 5.7
    D) 7.5

Questions 19 and 20 use the following information.

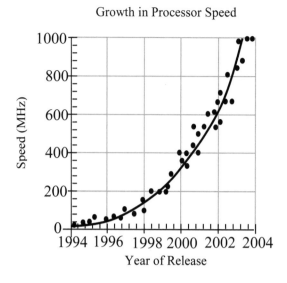

Growth in Processor Speed

The scatterplot above shows the release date and core processor speed in megahertz (MHz) of various personal computer models that went on sale between January 1994 and January 2004.

19. On average, during this ten-year period, processing speed doubled every m months. Which of the following is closest to the value of m?
A) 2
B) 12
C) 24
D) 30

20. In 2007, a state-of-the-art laptop had a processor speed of 2.16 gigahertz (1 GHz = 1000 MHz). Compared to what would be predicted by the best-fit curve to the data above, this actual speed was
A) lower by about 45%.
B) lower by about 60%.
C) higher by about 45%.
D) higher by about 85%.

Questions 21 through 23 use the following information.

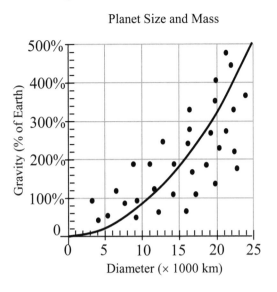

The scatterplot above depicts the diameter in kilometers and gravitational pull (an indirect way of measuring mass) of a number of recently discovered planets orbiting other stars.

21. Which of the following equations is closest to that of the best-fit curve depicted in the graph above, where g = gravity (as a percent of Earth's) and d = diameter in thousands of kilometers?
   A) $g = 20d$
   B) $g = 0.8d^2$
   C) $g = 0.08d^3$
   D) $g = 20 \cdot 2^{0.2d}$

22. Earth has a diameter of roughly 12,500 kilometers. If a planet of diameter 25,000 kilometers had the same density (mass / volume) as Earth, its mass (and thus its gravity) would be approximately
   A) 200% of Earth's.
   B) 300% of Earth's.
   C) 400% of Earth's.
   D) 800% of Earth's.

23. The graph above and the result of question 22 support the statement that
   A) planets larger than Earth tend to be more dense than Earth.
   B) planets larger than Earth tend to be less dense than Earth.
   C) planets larger than Earth tend to be about as dense as Earth.
   D) no conclusion can be drawn from this data about the density of other planets.

Questions 24 and 25 use the following information.

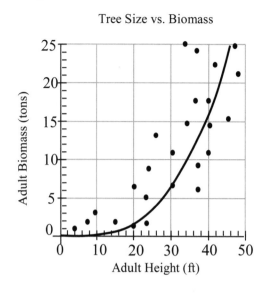

Tree Size vs. Biomass

The scatterplot above shows the average height and weight (when full-grown) of various species of tree.

24. The best-fit curve shown above has equation $m = 0.5h^b$, where m is the tree's weight in pounds (1 ton = 2000 lbs.) h is its height in feet, and b is an integer. What is the value of b?

25. One tree in the study had a weight that exceeded its expected weight (according to the best-fit equation) by more than that of any other tree. By how many tons did the tree's actual weight exceed the expected weight for its height?

BLUE MATH LESSON 10A: NON-LINEAR LINES OF BEST FIT – SCATTERPLOTS
Race to the Finish

Directions: Answer each question below.

HOMEWORK SET (CALCULATOR)

Questions 1 and 2 use the following information.

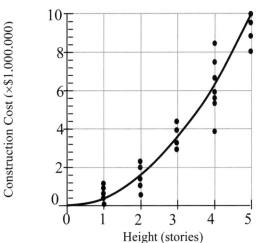

The cost of construction of every new building constructed in a seaside resort town over a two-year period was recorded and graphed in the scatterplot above, relative to the height of each of the buildings.

1. Which of the following equations, where C = cost in dollars and h = height in stories, is closest to that of the best-fit curve depicted above?
    A) $C = 0.4h^2$
    B) $C = 0.2h^3$
    C) $C = 400,000h^2$
    D) $C = 200,000h^3$

2. If the trend observed in the data above continues, about how many millions of dollars is the construction of an 18-story building in the same town likely to cost?
    A) 9
    B) 36
    C) 45
    D) 129

Questions 3 through 6 use the following information.

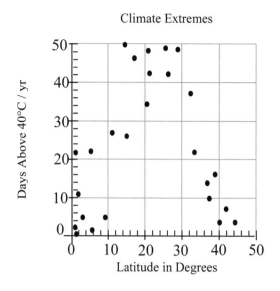

Climate Extremes

The scatterplot above shows the latitude (north or south of the equator) of a number of world cities and the average number of days per year in each city on which the temperature rises above 40°C (104°F).

3. Which type of function provides the most appropriate best-fit line or curve to match the data above?
    A) Constant
    B) Linear
    C) Quadratic
    D) Exponential

4. Which of the following equations provides the most appropriate best-fit curve for the data above? Let
    $y =$ the number of days exceeding 40°C, and $x =$ latitude.
    A) $y = 50 - 2^{0.125x}$
    B) $y = 50 - 0.125(x - 22)^2$
    C) $y = 2x$
    D) $y = 90 - 2x$

5. The highest temperatures on Earth are recorded in deserts, because the lack of cloud cover and humidity allows the sun to heat the land surface much more rapidly during the day than in areas where there is more precipitation to moderate the climate. The scatterplot above suggests that Earth's deserts are primarily found
    A) near the equator.
    B) near 15° latitude.
    C) near 25° latitude.
    D) near 45° latitude.

6. Based on their latitudes, for which of the following cities is the best-fit curve to the data above LEAST likely to yield in a reasonable estimate of the number of 40°C days per year?
    A) Jakarta, Indonesia (latitude 6° S)
    B) Cairo, Egypt (latitude 30° N)
    C) Montreal, Canada (latitude 45° N)
    D) Bergen, Norway (latitude 60° N)

Questions 7 and 8 use the following information.

Age vs. Cancer Incidence

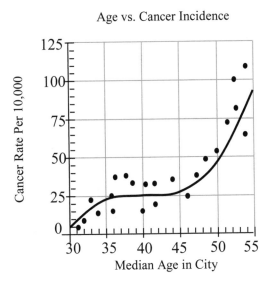

The scatterplot above charts the annual incidence of cancer in various cities (per 10,000 people) relative to the median age of their populations.

7. Which of the following equations is closest to that of the best-fit curve shown in the graph above? Let y = cancer cases per 10,000 people and a = median age.
    A) $y = 0.125(a - 25)^3 + 40$
    B) $y = 0.125(a + 40)^3 + 25$
    C) $y = 0.02(a - 40)^3 + 25$
    D) $y = 0.02[(a - 40)^3 + 25]$

8. According to the best-fit curve in the graph above, the expected number of cancer cases per year in a retirement community of population 20,000 and median age 60 is closest to
    A) 125
    B) 185
    C) 250
    D) 370

Questions 9 and 10 use the following information.

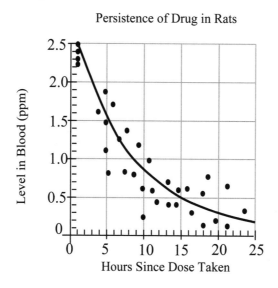

Persistence of Drug in Rats

The scatterplot above shows the results of a study in which a number of rats were given an experimental drug to test how long it remained in their system after dosing. The dose was fully absorbed by 1 hour after administration. During the following 24 hours, the rats were tested at random times for the amount of the drug still circulating in their bodies, measured in parts-per-million (ppm).

9. Which of the following equations is closest to that of the best-fit curve shown in the graph above, where y = blood concentration of the drug in ppm, and h = hours elapsed since the dose was administered?

A) $y = 0.004(h - 25)^2 + 0.2$

B) $y = 2.5 - 0.5^{\frac{h-1}{6}}$

C) $y = 2.5 \times 0.5^{\frac{h-1}{6}}$

D) $y = 0.5^{\frac{2h}{3}} + 2.5$

10. The *half-life* of a decaying substance is the amount of time necessary for half of the amount of substance to decay. What is the half-life of this drug in a rat's circulatory system, in hours?

A) 6

B) 9

C) 11

D) 12.5

Questions 11 through 13 use the following information.

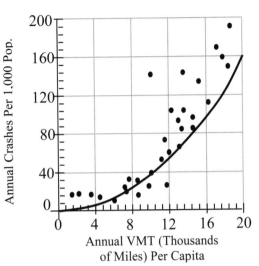

The scatterplot above depicts the rate in various cities of car and other motor vehicle collisions per capita per year, relative to the average annual number of miles that a resident of each city drives (VMT, or vehicle miles traveled).

11. Which of the following equations is closest to that of the best-fit curve shown in the graph above, where C = annual crashes and V = annual VMT per capita in thousands of miles?
    A) $C = 0.4V^2$
    B) $C = 0.16V^2$
    C) $C = (V - 4)^2$
    D) $C = V^2 - 240$

12. The city in the scatterplot with the highest rate of crashes per mile traveled has an annual VMT per capita of about how many miles?
    A) 1.5
    B) 18
    C) 1500
    D) 18,000

13. Which of the following conclusions is supported by the data and best-fit curve in the scatterplot above?
    A) Cities in which residents drive more miles tend to be have fewer crashes per capita and fewer crashes per mile.
    B) Cities in which residents drive more miles tend to be have more crashes per capita but fewer crashes per mile.
    C) Cities in which residents drive more miles tend to be have fewer crashes per capita but more crashes per mile.
    D) Cities in which residents drive more miles tend to be have more crashes per capita and more crashes per mile.

Questions 14 through 16 use the following information.

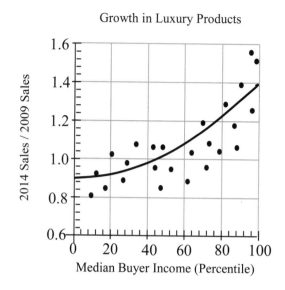

The scatterplot above shows the change in national sales of various products as a ratio of units sold in 2014 to units sold in 2009. This change is plotted against the median income of a buyer of that product (as a percentile—i.e. the 80th income percentile is that of people who earn more income than 80% of the population).

14. Which of the following equations is closest to that of the best-fit curve shown in the graph above, where S = sales ratio, and I = buyer income?

A) $S = \dfrac{I^2 + 0.9}{16,000}$

B) $S = \dfrac{I^2}{10,000} + 0.9$

C) $S = \dfrac{I^2}{20,000} + 0.9$

D) $S = \dfrac{I^2}{800,000} + 0.9$

15. Which of the following overall statements is NOT supported by the data and/or best-fit curve above?
A) Most products in the study saw their sales increase from 2009 to 2014.
B) Most products in the study whose median buyer had below-average income saw their sales decrease from 2009 to 2014.
C) All products in the study whose median buyer was in the top income bracket (above the 80th percentile) saw their sales increase from 2009 to 2014.
D) All products in the study whose median buyer was in the bottom income quartile (below the 25th percentile) saw their sales decrease from 2009 to 2014.

16. The manufacturer of a product not included in the study whose median buyer has an income of $75,000 (the 68th percentile) reports that in 2009, this product sold 600,000 units. In 2014, the best-fit curve to the data shown predicts that this product most likely sold about how many units?
A) 450,000
B) 600,000
C) 660,000
D) 880,000

Questions 17 and 18 use the following information.

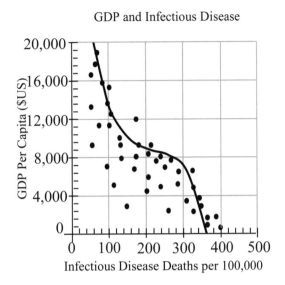

The scatterplot above plots the per capita GDP (gross domestic product) of various countries versus their annual death rates (per 100,000 people) from infectious diseases.

17. Based on the data and best-fit equation shown above, above what per capita GDP, to the nearest $1000, does the expected disease death rate drop below 0.2%?

18. An increase of $4000 in per capita GDP is likely to yield the greatest reduction in infectious disease deaths if it occurs in a country with what current per capita GDP, rounded to the nearest $4000?

Questions 19 and 20 use the following information.

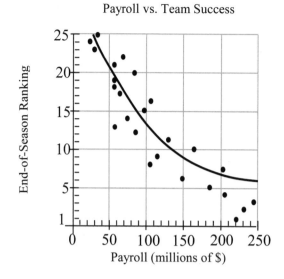

The scatterplot above charts the total payroll of the 25 teams in a professional sports league versus the rank that each team finished out of 25 in the most recent season.

19. According to the best-fit curve graphed above, if a team were to increase its payroll from $100 million to $200 million, it could expect its ranking to improve by how many places?

20. The team that finished in nth place underperformed expectations by a greater margin than any other team—that is, it finished the greatest number of places behind where its payroll and the best-fit curve would have predicted it to finish. What is the value of n?

BLUE MATH LESSON 10B: TWO-WAY TABLES
Getting Your Feet Wet

Directions: The problems below are intended as a short diagnostic exam.

	Cotton Candy	Moose Tracks	Vanilla	Mint Chocolate Chip	Total
Age 3-7	87	41	35	4	167
Age 8-12	34	55	40	38	167
Age 13-17	14	60	44	48	166
Total	135	156	119	90	500

A survey was conducted to determine the ice cream preferences of children and young people. The data collected from 500 youths is summarized in the table above.

1. Which group of people who preferred a particular ice cream flavor had the greatest percentage of youths in the 13-17 age range?
    A) Cotton Candy
    B) Moose Tracks
    C) Vanilla
    D) Mint Chocolate Chip

2. Based on the summary in the table, which of the following is most likely true about the groups sampled in the survey?
    A) A young person who likes Cotton Candy ice cream is more than twice as likely to be age 7 or under than any other age.
    B) A young person is roughly equally likely to prefer one of Cotton Candy or Vanilla as they are to prefer one of Moose Tracks or Mint Chocolate Chip.
    C) A child's preference is most likely to shift from Cotton Candy to Moose Tracks as he grows up.
    D) Because the number of children surveyed in each demographic is not proportional to the number of children in those demographics in the population at large, the survey is not representative of the population it surveys.

BLUE MATH LESSON 10B: TWO-WAY TABLES
Wading In

Directions: Read the explanation for each problem type mentioned below. Pay special attention to the methods and techniques used to solve the sample problems. Then, do the practice exercises that follow; use the appropriate method to solve each problem.

TOPIC OVERVIEW: TWO-WAY TABLES

A two-way table is a means of presenting data that allows us to easily examine the relationship between two different categorical variables. Look at the example of a two-way frequency table below:

Ice Cream Flavor Preference by Age Group

	Cotton Candy	Moose Tracks	Vanilla	Mint Chocolate Chip	Total
Age 3-7	87	41	35	4	167
Age 8-12	34	55	40	38	167
Age 13-17	14	60	44	48	166
Total	135	156	119	90	500

A survey was conducted to determine the ice cream preferences of children and young people. The data collected from 500 youths is summarized in the table above.

For this table, our two categorical variables are **age** and **ice cream flavor preference**. All of the values for age are listed in the horizontal rows, while all of the values for ice cream flavor preference are listed in the vertical columns. Each box in the table gives us a specific number—the number of people in a certain age range who like a specific flavor of ice cream. Some of the easier two-way table questions give us a partially filled in two-way table and ask us to fill in the rest based on the total amounts in the far-right column and bottom row. However, most questions will ask about comparing different segments of the population based on the information gathered above. Let's try a question based on the above data:

SAMPLE PROBLEM 1: TWO-WAY TABLES

Which group of people who preferred a particular ice cream flavor had the greatest percentage of youths in the 13-17 age range?

    A) Cotton Candy
    B) Moose Tracks
    C) Vanilla
    D) Mint Chocolate Chip

To answer this question, we first need to look at the total number of people in each flavor group, then the number of people in that group who were in the 13-17 age range. Since we want a percentage, let's set each thing up as a ratio:

Cotton Candy $= \frac{14}{135} = 10.37\%$

Moose Tracks $= \frac{60}{156} = 38.46\%$

Vanilla $= \frac{44}{119} = 36.97\%$

Mint Chocolate Chip $= \frac{48}{90} = 53.33\%$

Since Mint Chocolate Chip has the highest percentage, our answer is **D**.

SAMPLE PROBLEM 2: TWO-WAY TABLES

Based on the summary in the table, which of the following is most likely true about the groups sampled in the survey?
  A) A young person who likes Cotton Candy ice cream is more than twice as likely to be age 7 or under than any other age.
  B) A young person is roughly equally likely to prefer one of Cotton Candy or Vanilla as they are to prefer one of Moose Tracks or Mint Chocolate Chip.
  C) A child's preference is most likely to shift from Cotton Candy to Moose Tracks as he grows up.
  D) Because the number of children surveyed in each demographic is not proportional to the number of children in those demographics in the population at large, the survey is not representative of the population it surveys.

Now we have a question that involves a little less computation and a little bit more analysis. Let's start by analyzing each statement:

A) A young person who likes Cotton Candy ice cream is more than twice as likely to be age 7 or under than any other age. – *There are 135 young people who like Cotton Candy, and 87 are between Ages 3 and 7. This amounts to 64.44%—close, but not quite twice as likely.*

B) A young person is roughly equally likely to prefer one of Cotton Candy or Vanilla as they are to prefer one of Moose Tracks or Mint Chocolate Chip. – *The probability of a young person liking Cotton Candy or Vanilla is 254/500, close to 50%. The probability of a young person liking Moose Tracks or Mint Chocolate Chip is $\frac{246}{500}$, also close to 50%. This is our most likely answer.*

C) A child's preference is most likely to shift from Cotton Candy to Moose Tracks as he grows up. – *This table gives us no real basis to judge the preferences of children as they grow older. So, even though older*

children do have a preference for Moose Tracks, we don't know if this is on an individual basis.

D) Because the number of children surveyed in each demographic is not proportional to the number of children in those demographics in the population at large, the survey is not representative of the population it surveys. – *This is pure speculation—we have no information about the population at large, so no way to support this.*

Thus, our answer must be **B**.

WRAP-UP

When dealing with Two-Way Tables, always make sure that all of the information is present. If not, use the surrounding information to fill in the rest of the table. Then read the question or questions associated with each table carefully and analyze each answer choice. Many of the questions will involve probability or percentages, so brush up on the percentages lesson in Lesson 2B if you feel like you need more help.

BLUE MATH LESSON 10B: TWO-WAY TABLES
Learning to Swim

Directions: Answer each question below.

PRACTICE SET 1 (CALCULATOR)

Questions 1 and 2 refer to the following information.

A survey was conducted of the television viewing habits of 2,000 randomly chosen adults. Some of the results are shown below.

Television Habits of Adults of Different Age Groups

	< 1 Hour/Day	1 to 3 Hours/Day	3+ Hours/Day	Total
Age 18-30	180	212	112	504
Age 31-40	58	195	136	389
Age 41-50	70	201	121	392
Age 51+	190	474	51	715
Total	498	1,082	420	2,000

1. According to the table, the highest percentage of which age group watched less than 1 hour per day of television?

2. Of those who answered that they watched at least 3 hours of television per day, 200 were chosen at random and asked if they watched an average of 5 or more hours of television per day. Just 10% said that they did. About how many of the 2,000 people in the overall survey watch 5 or more hours of television per day?

Questions 3 and 4 refer to the following information.

In a recent middle-school election, each student was asked to choose among 3 prospective slogans for the school. The table below shows the results of the election.

Slogan Preference for Each Grade at Hawthorne Middle School

Grade	"Reach for the Stars"	"Live and Learn"	"Be the Best"	Total
6th	251	87	133	471
7th	205	101	66	372
8th	187	55	120	362
Total	643	243	319	1205

3. The "Reach for the Stars" slogan won the election by the highest percentage margin (over the second-most-popular slogan) among students from which grade?

4. After the election, a random sample of 100 6th graders who voted were asked to choose their 2nd-favorite of the 3 slogans. Of these students, 12 chose "Reach for the Stars," 55 chose "Live and Learn," and 33 chose "Be the Best." Based on this data and the table, which slogan was most likely the least favorite of the highest number of 6th graders?

Question 5 refers to the following information.

A city employee counts all of the trees in Haverford Park; she also measures each tree's circumference (in inches) and categorizes the trees as either deciduous or evergreen, as shown in the table below.

Type and Size of Trees in Haverford Park

Circumference	Deciduous	Evergreen	Total
< 12 in.	6	1	7
12 – 23 in.	12	7	19
24 – 35 in.	18	14	32
36+ in.	6	15	21
Total	42	37	79

5. For which circumference range did the ratio of deciduous to evergreen trees most nearly match the ratio of all of the deciduous trees to all of the evergreen trees in the park?

BLUE MATH LESSON 10B: TWO-WAY TABLES
Diving into the Deep End

Directions: Answer each question below.

PRACTICE SET 2 (CALCULATOR)

Questions 6 and 7 refer to the following information.

A laboratory scientist breeds a large number of mice, measuring the lengths of their bodies (in centimeters), including tails, when they reach maturity. The results of these measurements, broken down into male and female categories, are shown below.

Combined Body and Tail Length of Laboratory-Bred Mice

Length	Male	Female	Total
13 – 14 cm	15	12	27
15 – 16 cm	28	29	57
17 – 18 cm	27	34	61
19 – 20 cm	21	19	40
Total	91	94	185

6. A mouse from the study is chosen at random from each of the 4 size categories. A mouse from which category is most likely to be male?
    A) 13 – 14 cm
    B) 15 – 16 cm
    C) 17 – 18 cm
    D) 19 – 20 cm

7. Which statement about the data from the experiment is most accurate, based on the table?
    A) The data show that laboratory-bred mice are longer on average than mice in the wild.
    B) The data show that female mice are, on average, around 2 centimeters longer than male mice.
    C) The data do not show any significant differences in average total length between male and female mice.
    D) The data indicate that most mice have a total length of 15 centimeters or less.

Questions 8 and 9 refer to the following information.

A seismologist tracked all of the earthquakes to occur in California during 2013. The earthquakes were categorized based on their fault zone and their magnitude on the Richter scale, as shown in the table below. Earthquakes of below a 3.4 on the Richter scale were not included. (Stronger quakes have higher magnitudes.)

Earthquakes in California in 2013 by Magnitude and Fault Zone

Magnitude	San Andreas	Sierra Nevada	Gulf of California	Mendocino	Total
3.4 – 3.9	19	61	63	32	175
4.0 – 4.5	7	17	29	13	66
4.6 – 5.1	1	1	1	4	7
5.2 +	2	0	0	1	3
Total	29	79	93	50	251

8. Based on the data in the table, which of the following probabilities is most likely the highest (when considering only earthquakes of at least 3.4 magnitude)?
   A) The probability that an earthquake in the San Andreas fault zone has a magnitude between 3.4 and 3.9.
   B) The probability that an earthquake in the Sierra Nevada fault zone has a magnitude between 3.4 and 3.9.
   C) The probability that an earthquake in the Gulf of California fault zone has a magnitude between 3.4 and 3.9.
   D) The probability that an earthquake in the Mendocino fault zone has a magnitude between 3.4 and 3.9.

9. Based on the trends in the table, if the table is expanded to include an additional category for earthquakes of magnitude 2.8 to 3.3, approximately how many earthquakes from the Mendocino zone would you expect there to be in this group?
   A) Less than 10
   B) Between 10 and 20
   C) Between 20 and 30
   D) More than 30

Questions 10 and 11 refer to the following information.

A high school offers three foreign languages: French, German, and Spanish. Each freshman student is required to take one of these courses; for the higher grades, the foreign language courses are optional. The table below shows how many students in each grade are enrolled in each course.

Foreign Language Course Enrollment among High School Students

Grade	French	German	Spanish	No Foreign Language	Total
Freshmen	108	151	248	0	507
Sophomores	72	56	149	208	485
Juniors	59	59	145	196	459
Seniors	48	27	83	254	412
Total	287	293	625	658	1863

10. According to the data in the table above, among those students taking a foreign language, a student of which grade level would be most likely to take Spanish?
    A) Freshman
    B) Sophomore
    C) Junior
    D) Senior

11. A random sampling of 150 students who were not enrolled in a foreign language course were asked to select which of the 3 languages they would prefer to take if required to do so. Of those, 27% preferred Spanish, 18% preferred German, and 55% preferred French. Based on this information and the table above, which statement is most likely true?
    A) Among seniors, more students either take or prefer French than either of the other two languages.
    B) Among seniors, more students either take or prefer Spanish than either of the other two languages.
    C) Among juniors, more students either take or prefer French than either of the other two languages.
    D) Among juniors, more students either take or prefer German than either of the other two languages.

Questions 12 and 13 refer to the following information.

The 2010 Colorado census asked respondents of Hispanic or Latino origin to identify their ancestral nationality. These ancestries are then grouped into 4 regions: Central American (including Mexican), South American, Caribbean, and European (Spanish or Portuguese). The data is also broken down by age, as shown in the table below. All numbers are rounded to the nearest 1,000 residents.

Nation of Origin among 2010 Hispanic/Latino Colorado Residents

Age	Central American	South American	Caribbean	European	Total
Under 18	167,000	3,000	8,000	23,000	201,000
18 – 39	297,000	5,000	10,000	24,000	336,000
40 – 64	244,000	9,000	10,000	22,000	285,000
65 +	79,000	2,000	3,000	11,000	95,000
Total	787,000	19,000	31,000	80,000	917,000

12. If a Hispanic/Latino Colorado resident is chosen at random from each of the 4 regional origins, a resident who is 65 years or older would most likely be chosen from which region?
    A) Central American
    B) South American
    C) Caribbean
    D) European

13. In addition to the data shown above, 120,000 people identified as Hispanic or Latino but either did not list a nation of origin or listed nations from multiple regions. If these people are added to the table above in amounts proportional to those in the table, approximately how many residents age 40 or older of Central American origin would be in the revised table?
    A) 276,000
    B) 322,000
    C) 365,000
    D) 430,000

Questions 14 and 15 refer to the following information.

Four gardeners in different parts of the country decided to experiment with different tomato plant varieties to see which type would produce the most fruit. Each gardener planted 10 plants of each variety and measured the total weight of tomatoes produced during the season. The results are shown in the table below.

Pounds of Tomatoes Produced by Variety and Location

State	San Marzano	Yellow Oxheart	Purple Russian	Super Sweet 100s	**Total**
Washington	54	46	78	66	244
Illinois	105	83	108	130	426
Georgia	187	155	234	189	765
Connecticut	87	42	83	49	261
Total	433	326	503	434	1696

14. In the state in which San Marzano tomatoes produced the largest proportion of the overall yield, what fraction of the state's overall yield did these tomatoes produce?

15. Gardeners in Texas, California, and Montana repeated the experiment above. After the tomatoes were weighed, 25% of this weight came from the Super Sweet 100s plants. If the 7 states combined to grow 2500 pounds of tomatoes, how many pounds of Super Sweet 100s did Texas, California, and Montana grow, combined?

PRACTICE SET 3 (NO CALCULATOR)

Questions 16 and 17 refer to the following information.

A national survey of 1,000 fast-food restaurant customers was conducted to determine the times of day that customers typically patronize each of several types of restaurant. The results are shown below.

Fast-Food Restaurant Patronage by Time of Day and Type of Cuisine

	Burgers/Sandwiches	Chicken	Tacos/Burritos	Total
Morning	115	76	54	245
Afternoon	109	80	69	258
Evening	144	39	84	267
Night	110	12	108	230
Total	478	207	315	1,000

16. Based on the table, during which time of day do the customers of the burger or sandwich restaurants make up the highest percentage of all customers?
    A) Morning
    B) Afternoon
    C) Evening
    D) Night

17. Another question on the survey found that only 10% of night-dining customers live near a chicken restaurant that is open during the night. Among these customers, approximately what percentage prefers chicken to the other cuisines when dining at night?
    A) 5%
    B) 12%
    C) 52%
    D) 57%

Questions 18 and 19 refer to the following information.

Three hospitals shared their statistics on emergency room admissions during the month of June 2014. The admissions statistics were broken down by the reason for which each patient was admitted.

Emergency Room Admissions by Type, June 2013

	Sacred Heart	County General	Princeton-Plainsboro	**Total**
Car Accident	151	286	221	658
Violence	48	87	60	195
Other Injury	312	281	215	808
Illness	182	245	368	795
Total	693	899	864	2456

18. In which category of reason for admission does the number of admissions to County General Hospital make up the largest proportion of that category's total?
    A) Car accident
    B) Violence
    C) Other injury
    D) Illness

19. The "Other Injury" category includes, among other injuries, burns. A random sampling of 200 "Other Injury" cases used in the study found that 15% were burns. Based on this information and the table, approximately how many patients were admitted for burns to Sacred Heart Hospital during the month of the study?
    A) 27
    B) 32
    C) 42
    D) 47

New SAT Blue Math
Lesson 10B: Two-Way Tables

Version 2.0

Questions 20 and 21 refer to the following information.

In a poll, several groups of people were asked to predict the winner of a 4-team college basketball tournament. The numbers of people who picked each team are shown below.

Basketball Tournament Predictions by Three Groups

Predicted Winner	Media	Students	Other Fans	Total
Southwest University	17	83	168	268
Oklahoma Tech	54	118	192	364
New England State	24	26	88	138
Orlando College	10	51	165	226
Total	105	278	613	996

20. Which of the colleges was predicted to win the tournament by a higher proportion of the Students group than of the other two groups?
    A) Southwest University
    B) Oklahoma Tech
    C) New England State
    D) Orlando College

21. A random sample of 175 people who did not chose Oklahoma Tech to win the tournament were then asked which team would finish second. Of these, 60% chose Oklahoma Tech to finish second. Based on this information and the table, approximately how many in the "Other Fans" group would choose Oklahoma Tech to finish either 1st or 2nd?
    A) 253
    B) 410
    C) 445
    D) 560

Questions 22 and 23 refer to the following information.

Using a powerful telescope, a group of astronomers classifies all of the galaxies visible in a small region of the sky. The galaxies are described by shape—elliptical, spiral, or lenticular (bulging)—and by distance from Earth (in millions of light-years, Mly).

Galaxies Observed by Type and Distance

Distance	Elliptical	Spiral	Lenticular	**Total**
0 – 10 Mly	5	2	1	8
11 – 100 Mly	18	16	5	39
101 – 1000 Mly	54	87	24	165
1001 + Mly	21	65	30	116
Total	98	170	60	**328**

22. If a galaxy from the survey is chosen at random, which of the following is most likely to describe that galaxy?
    A) A galaxy that is more than 1,000 million light-years away.
    B) An elliptical galaxy.
    C) A spiral galaxy 1,000 million light-years away or nearer.
    D) A non-spiral galaxy 1,000 million light-years away or nearer.

23. A fourth type, known as "peculiar" galaxies, is not included in the table above. Peculiar galaxies do not fit into any of the other 3 categories. If 32 peculiar galaxies were observed, and nearly 90% of them were within 100 million light-years, which statement is most likely true?
    A) Peculiar galaxies are more common than lenticular galaxies in the 101 to 1000 million light-year range.
    B) Peculiar galaxies make up over half of all galaxies in the 11 to 100 million light-year range.
    C) Peculiar galaxies are the most common type in the 11 to 100 million light-year range.
    D) Peculiar galaxies are the most common type within 100 million light-years of Earth but the least common type outside of this distance.

Questions 24 and 25 refer to the following information.

A long-running survey measures the shoe size of 1,000 adult male Americans every decade. Below, the results of the survey for the last 4 decades are shown for 4 ranges of shoe size (using the U.S. system; half-sizes are rounded down).

Shoe Size Survey of American Men, 1980 – 2010

	Size 7 & Under	Size 8 or 9	Size 10 or 11	Size 12 & Up	Total
1980	384	366	122	128	1000
1990	314	350	184	152	1000
2000	277	373	181	169	1000
2010	243	365	201	191	1000
Total	1218	1454	688	640	4000

24. If the data are assumed to be normally distributed (spread evenly around the median), in which survey year was the median shoe size most likely to have been size 8?

25. Based on the trends in the survey, approximately how many of the 1000 American men in the 2020 survey would be expected to have a shoe size of 12 or higher? Round to the nearest multiple of 10.

BLUE MATH LESSON 10B: TWO-WAY TABLES
Race to the Finish

Directions: Answer each question below.

HOMEWORK SET (CALCULATOR)

Questions 1 and 2 refer to the following information.

A biologist counts the number of toads of 4 different species in a state park. Two of the species are from genus *Bufo*: *Bufo debilis* and *Bufo punctatus*. The other 2 are from genus *Spea*: *Spea multiplicata* and *Spea bombifrons*. She also identifies the sex of each toad. The resulting data are shown below.

Toads in Conley Woods State Park

	B. debilis	B. punctatus	S. multiplicata	S. bombifrons	Total
Male	22	37	55	18	132
Female	10	56	44	35	145
Total	32	93	99	53	277

1. Based on the data in the table, if a toad in the park is chosen at random, which of the following has the highest probability of being chosen?
    A) A male toad from genus *Bufo*.
    B) A female toad from genus *Bufo*.
    C) A male toad from genus *Spea*.
    D) A female toad from genus *Spea*.

2. Under the right conditions, male toads can change into females. Typically, one of the necessary conditions is a lack of breeding females relative to the number of males. For which species in the park would this phenomenon be most likely to occur in the near future?
    A) *B. debilis*
    B) *B. punctatus*
    C) *S. multiplicata*
    D) *S. bombifrons*

Questions 3 and 4 refer to the following information.

The Census Bureau recently conducted a survey of randomly chosen working adults (age 25 and up) living in the city of Atlanta, Georgia to determine the highest level of education they have completed. The results for 3 age groups are shown below.

Educational Attainment vs. Age Among Adults in Atlanta, GA

Highest Completed Level of Education	Age 25-39	Age 40-54	Age 55-70	Total
Less than High School	55	95	85	235
High School	130	245	310	685
4-Year College Degree	655	905	440	2000
Graduate Degree	340	365	255	960
Total	1180	1610	1090	3880

3. According to the table, which statement is most accurate about the working adults surveyed?
   A) Younger adults (Age 25-39) are the age group most likely to have ended their education before completing high school.
   B) Younger adults (Age 25-39) are the age group most likely to have completed a graduate degree.
   C) Older adults (Age 55-70) are the age group most likely to have at least a 4-year college degree.
   D) Among those who have achieved a 4-year college degree, older adults (Age 55-70) are least likely to have continued their education by getting a graduate degree.

4. A random sampling of 300 adults from the age 25-39 group were asked what type of job they have. Of these, 45% worked in a technical job, 30% worked in a non-technical office job, 15% worked in a service job, and 10% worked as laborers. Approximately how many adults from the age 25-39 group of the larger survey work in a technical job?
   A) 295
   B) 355
   C) 530
   D) 725

Questions 5 and 6 refer to the following information.

A farmer grows 3 types of citrus fruits: oranges, lemons, and grapefruit. The farmer recently examined each tree to determine whether it is actively producing fruit. Inactive trees could be too young, too old, or too diseased to produce fruit.

Citrus Tree Fruit-Producing Status by Type

	Orange	Lemon	Grapefruit	Total
Active	123	75	34	232
Too Young	18	9	2	29
Too Old	21	15	10	46
Too Diseased	38	28	7	73
Total	200	127	53	380

5. According to the table, if the farmer chose a tree at random, which of the following would have the highest probability of being chosen?
   A) An active orange tree
   B) An inactive orange tree
   C) An active lemon or grapefruit tree
   D) An inactive lemon or grapefruit tree

6. A farmer decides to cut down all the trees that are too old or too diseased to produce fruit. Among the remaining trees, which type has the highest percentage of active trees?
   A) Orange
   B) Lemon
   C) Grapefruit
   D) A tie between orange and lemon

Questions 7 and 8 refer to the following information.

The first 500 entrants into a Renaissance Festival are asked to identify their favorite aspect of the festival. The choices are food, shows, shopping, and activities. The results shown below are broken down by gender and by adults (18 years old and up) versus children.

Favorite Aspect of the Renaissance Festival by Age and Gender

	Food	Shows	Shopping	Activities	Total
Girls	24	38	18	22	102
Boys	27	39	13	26	105
Women	41	34	59	34	168
Men	30	11	52	32	125
Total	122	122	142	114	500

7. According to the data in the table, a randomly selected member of which group would be most likely to select shopping as his or her most favorite activity?
   A) Girls
   B) Boys
   C) Women
   D) Men

8. Which statement below most accurately describes a key difference between children and adults, as revealed by the table?
   A) Compared to adults, children are much less likely to rank food as their favorite aspect of the festival.
   B) Compared to adults, children are much less likely to rank shows as their favorite aspect of the festival.
   C) Compared to adults, children are much less likely to rank shopping as their favorite aspect of the festival.
   D) Compared to adults, children are much less likely to rank activities as their favorite aspect of the festival.

Questions 9 and 10 refer to the following information.

An international medical study consulted doctors in 4 countries to determine the heights of 10-year-old children in each country. The results, with heights in inches, are reported below.

Heights of 10-Year-Old Children (Male and Female) in 4 Countries

Height	Indonesia	Norway	Senegal	Panama	Total
< 46 in.	90	13	45	48	196
46 – 49 in.	103	30	70	87	290
50 – 53 in.	44	115	125	81	365
54+ in.	16	160	121	52	349
Total	253	318	361	268	1200

9. Which country reported the highest percentage of 10-year-old children between 46 and 53 inches in height?
    A) Indonesia
    B) Norway
    C) Senegal
    D) Panama

10. A randomly selected sample of 100 children from the study who measured at least 54 inches tall were selected for follow-up screenings at age 12. Of these, 10% grew at least 6 inches in the two years between studies. Which statement is most likely true regarding the children from the study two years later, at age 12?
    A) At least 16 of the 12-year-olds from Indonesia are 60 or more inches tall.
    B) At least 16 of the 12-year-olds from Norway are 60 or more inches tall.
    C) At least 50 of the 12-year-olds from Norway are 60 or more inches tall.
    D) At least 50 of the 12-year-olds from Panama are 60 or more inches tall.

Questions 11 and 12 refer to the following information.

A small movie theater is showing 4 films this week. The theater manager keeps track of the number of tickets sold for each film based on the price paid. There are 3 price levels: child ($5 per ticket), senior or student discount ($7 per ticket), and adult ($9 per ticket). The table below shows the number of tickets sold of each type for each film.

Tickets Sold by Type and Film

Film	Child	Senior/Student	Adult	Total
Flames of Avalon	34	97	155	286
Under the Sea	187	33	152	372
Secret Agents	21	168	180	369
Robot Lawyer	88	122	175	385
Total	330	420	662	1412

11. Based on the data in the table and the ticket prices listed above, which film earned the most money in ticket sales?
    A) *Flames of Avalon*
    B) *Under the Sea*
    C) *Secret Agents*
    D) *Robot Lawyer*

12. The table above does not include midnight screenings of the films; the theater sold 200 tickets to these screenings. Assuming that no children's tickets were purchased for these screenings but that the tickets were otherwise sold in amounts proportional to the results shown above, about how many total senior/student tickets were purchased for *Flames of Avalon* during the week?
    A) 115
    B) 145
    C) 168
    D) 184

Questions 13 and 14 refer to the following information.

An economist reviews survey data from 10-year intervals to determine the changes in Americans' beverage spending over time. She adjusts the amounts spent into 2014 dollars to account for inflation so they can be accurately compared. The data are shown below.

U.S. Per-Capita Yearly Spending on Nonalcoholic Beverages (2014 Dollars)

	Milk	Juice	Soda	Coffee/Tea	**Total**
2014	$59	$28	$100	$288	$475
2004	$64	$36	$113	$256	$469
1994	$72	$32	$125	$196	$425
1984	$81	$30	$88	$150	$349
Total	$276	$126	$426	$890	**$1718**

13. During which year was soda's proportion of the United States' nonalcoholic beverage spending the highest?
    A) 2014
    B) 2004
    C) 1994
    D) 1984

14. In 1984, the U.S. population was 286 million. Approximately how much money did Americans spend on milk in that year (in 2014 dollars)?
    A) $16.9 billion
    B) $20.6 billion
    C) $23.2 billion
    D) $25.2 billion

Questions 15 and 16 refer to the following information.

A corporation that owns many radio stations polls its listeners to determine their favorite genres of music. The results of the poll are shown below, broken down by gender.

Music Genre Preferences Among Adult Men and Women

	Men	Women	Total
Rock	4,023	3,630	7,653
Country	1,909	1,633	3,542
Hip-Hop/R&B	3,006	3,248	6,254
Pop	4,482	4,839	9,321
Other	2,220	2,152	4,372
Total	15,640	15,502	31,142

15. According to the table, which of the following is most likely?
    A) A randomly chosen rock fan will be a man.
    B) A randomly chosen country fan will be a man.
    C) A randomly chosen hip-hop/R&B fan will be a woman.
    D) A randomly chosen pop fan will be a woman.

16. The radio station asked a random sample of 1,000 of those who answered "Other" to name their preferred genre. These responses included 14% for jazz, 6% for classical, 24% for folk, and 31% for dance music. If the station extrapolates these folk responses to the entire poll and combines them with the rock category, how many responses would there be in the combined Rock/Folk genre?
    A) 7,893
    B) 8,265
    C) 8,503
    D) 8,702

Questions 17 and 18 refer to the following information.

A local historian reviews the historical birth registries for 4 nearby towns, adding up the number of births in each town during 4 successive decades in the 19th century. The results are shown below.

Number of Births in Four Towns in the Gloucester-Worchester Area, 1850-1889

Decade	Cradley	Bromyard	Ross-on-Wye	Tewkesbury	Total
1850s	278	418	682	912	2,290
1860s	292	424	700	1,080	2,496
1870s	314	417	757	976	2,464
1880s	352	348	714	1,115	2,529
Total	1,236	1,607	2,853	4,083	9,779

17. How many children were born in Bromyard during the decade in which the percentage of births in Bromyard for the four cities was the largest?

18. The nearby town of Great Malvern is missing its birth records from the 1870s. The historian knows that in the other decades in the table, Great Malvern had about 32% fewer births as Tewkesbury. If the same relationship held true in the 1870s, what would be the best estimate for the number of births in Great Malvern in the 1870s?

Questions 19 and 20 refer to the following information.

A linguist compiled the table below showing the number of people in several European countries who speak a given language as their first language.

First Languages Spoken in Several European Nations (in Thousands of People)

	Belgium	Switzerland	Monaco	Total
French	4,290	1,570	17	5,877
German	96	4,640	2	4,738
Dutch	6,210	12	1	6,223
Italian	2	520	8	530
Total	10,598	6,742	28	17,368

19. The number of Dutch speakers in Belgium has fallen by 10% in the last decade while the number of French speakers has risen by 10% in the same time period. What was the ratio of Dutch speakers to French speakers in Belgium 10 years ago?

20. The official language of Monaco is Monegasque. In a survey of 100 randomly chosen Monacans, 20% spoke Monegasque natively, 60% spoke one of the four languages from the table above, and 20% spoke another language. Based on this information, how many people from Monaco speak Monegasque as their first language? (Round to the nearest thousand.)

BLUE MATH LESSON 11A: ONE- AND TWO-VARIABLE EQUATIONS AND INEQUALITIES
Learning to Swim

Directions: Answer each question below.

PRACTICE SET 1 (NO CALCULATOR)

1. If $x + 17 = 6$, what is $x + 4$?

2. If $\frac{4y(x-2)}{x+2} = 6y$, $y \neq 0$, and $x \neq -2$ or 2, what is $\frac{x+2}{x-2}$?

3. If $5x = 3 - 5y$, what is $x + y$?

4. If $y + 6 = 2 - 3x$, what is $3x + y$?

5. If $\frac{x}{2} + \frac{y}{2} = 2$, what is $3x + 3y$?

BLUE MATH LESSON 11A: ONE- AND TWO-VARIABLE EQUATIONS AND INEQUALITIES
Diving into the Deep End

Directions: Answer each question below.

PRACTICE SET 2 (NO CALCULATOR)

6. If $\frac{3}{x-4} + 1 > 4$, and $x \neq 4$, which of the following is true?
   A) $4 < x < 5$
   B) $x < 4$ or $x > 5$
   C) No real value of x satisfies the inequality.
   D) All real values of x except 4 satisfy the inequality.

$$2x + 3y \geq 4$$
$$x < y$$

7. Which of the following ordered pairs satisfies the system of equations above?
   A) $(-2, 2)$
   B) $(-1, 1)$
   C) $(1, 2)$
   D) $(2, 2)$

8. If $5x + 3y = 12$, what is the value of $\frac{x}{3} + \frac{y}{5}$?
   A) $\frac{1}{5}$
   B) $\frac{4}{5}$
   C) $\frac{5}{4}$
   D) 5

9. If $\frac{4x(y+2)}{y-3} = 2x, y \neq 3$ or -2, and $x \neq 0$, $\frac{y-3}{y+2} =$
   A) $\frac{1}{8}$
   B) $\frac{1}{2}$
   C) 2
   D) 8

$$\frac{1}{2x-5} = \frac{2}{3x+1}$$

10. In the equation above, what is the value of x?
    A) $-\frac{7}{4}$
    B) $\frac{5}{2}$
    C) 6
    D) 11

11. If $16y - 8x = 12$, what is $12y - 6x$?
    A) 3
    B) 6
    C) 9
    D) 12

$$3x + 2y = 11$$
$$x - \frac{y}{2} = 6$$

12. Which of the following points is a solution to the above system of equations?
    A) $(-5, 2)$
    B) $(5, -2)$
    C) $(-2, 5)$
    D) $(2, -5)$

13. If $z^3 = 9z$, which of the following CANNOT be a value of z?
    A) -3
    B) 0
    C) 3
    D) 9

14. If $-3x - 7y + 6 = 2x - (1 + 5x)$, what is y?

15. If $\frac{5}{4} + 2x = \frac{3}{4} + 2y$, what is $2y - 2x$?

PRACTICE SET 3 (NO CALCULATOR)

$$\frac{6}{2c-1} + 2 = -1$$

16. In the equation above, what is the value of c?
    A) -1
    B) $-\frac{1}{2}$
    C) $\frac{1}{2}$
    D) 1

$$x + 4y = 2y - x + 10$$
$$2x = 3y$$

17. Based on the system of equations above, what is the value of y^2?
    A) 4
    B) 9
    C) 16
    D) 36

18. If $\frac{1}{x-6} + 2 = 3$, what is $4x + 2$?
    A) -22
    B) -18
    C) 28
    D) 30

19. If $5x - 20y = 85$, what is $8y - 2x$?
    A) −34
    B) −17
    C) 17
    D) 34

$$\frac{30}{2z+4} = \frac{z-5}{2}$$

23. In the equation above, what is one value of z?
    A) 3
    B) 5
    C) 8
    D) 11

$$2x + 9 = -2(5 + x)$$

20. What is the solution to the equation above?
    A) $-\frac{19}{4}$
    B) $-\frac{1}{4}$
    C) $\frac{1}{4}$
    D) $\frac{19}{4}$

24. If $\frac{2}{5x} < 4$ and $\frac{3}{10x} > 2$, what is a possible value for x?

$$x - 3 = \frac{7}{5}$$

25. In the equation above, what is the value of x?

21. If $16 < 6x + 2 < 20$, which of the following is a possible value for x?
    A) 2
    B) 2.25
    C) 2.5
    D) 3

22. If $\frac{c(2b-1)}{1+b} = 3c, c \neq 0$, and $b \neq -1$ or $\frac{1}{2}$, what is $\frac{b+1}{1-2b}$?
    A) −3
    B) $-\frac{1}{3}$
    C) $\frac{1}{3}$
    D) 3

BLUE MATH LESSON 11A: ONE- AND TWO-VARIABLE EQUATIONS AND INEQUALITIES
Race to the Finish

Directions: Answer each question below.

HOMEWORK SET (NO CALCULATOR)

1. If $\frac{2x}{9} + \frac{5y}{2} = 3$, what is the value of $8x + 90y$?
   A) 12
   B) 54
   C) 108
   D) 216

$$\frac{7-(k+1)}{3} = \frac{2+k}{2}$$

4. In the equation above, what is the value of k?
   A) 0
   B) $\frac{5}{6}$
   C) $\frac{6}{5}$
   D) $\frac{18}{5}$

2. If $15x + 35y = -30$, then $9x + 21y =$
   A) −50
   B) −42
   C) −30
   D) −18

$$2d = \frac{4}{3}(d + 1)$$

5. In the equation above, what is the value of d?
   A) −2
   B) 0.5
   C) 1
   D) 2

$$4x + \frac{y}{9} = 6$$
$$3x - y = -2$$

3. Based on the above system of equations, what is the value of the product xy?
   A) $\frac{4}{3}$
   B) 6
   C) 8
   D) 24

$$5y + 4 = \frac{7}{3}$$

6. In the equation above, what is the value of y?
   A) $-\frac{5}{3}$
   B) $-\frac{1}{3}$
   C) $\frac{1}{3}$
   D) $\frac{5}{3}$

C2 education
be smarter

$$3x - 5y = 17$$
$$10y + 18 = 2x$$

7. Which of the following ordered pairs is a valid solution to the system of equations above?
    A) $(4, -1)$
    B) $(4, 1)$
    C) $(-4, -1)$
    D) $(-4, 1)$

8. If $\frac{2}{x-3} + 2 = -3$, what is $10x$?
    A) 26
    B) 31
    C) 32
    D) 33

9. If $\frac{6}{x-1} + 2 = -3$, then $x =$
    A) $-\frac{11}{5}$
    B) $-\frac{1}{5}$
    C) $\frac{1}{5}$
    D) $\frac{11}{5}$

10. If $\frac{3}{2-x} \geq 3$, which of the following is true?
    A) $1 \leq x < 2$
    B) $1 \leq x \leq 2$
    C) $x \leq 1$ or $x > 2$
    D) $x < 1$ or $x \geq 2$

11. If $-\frac{6y}{x+2} = 3$, then $\frac{-x-2}{y} =$
    A) -2
    B) $-\frac{1}{2}$
    C) $\frac{1}{2}$
    D) 2

12. If $\frac{3y}{z} = 12$, $y \neq 0$, and $z \neq 0$, what is $\frac{z}{y} - 1$?
    A) $-\frac{3}{4}$
    B) $\frac{1}{4}$
    C) 3
    D) 5

13. If $-\frac{2}{x} = \frac{1-y}{4}$ for all nonzero x, what is $xy - x + 3$?
    A) -5
    B) 5
    C) 8
    D) 11

14. If $6x + 18y = 9$, what is $3x + 9y$?
    A) $\frac{9}{4}$
    B) 3
    C) $\frac{9}{2}$
    D) 6

15. If $\frac{(3x+2)y}{y-4} - 4 = 6x$, $y \neq 4$, and $x \neq -\frac{2}{3}$, what is $\frac{y-4}{y}$?

    A) $-\frac{1}{2}$

    B) $\frac{1}{2}$

    C) 1

    D) 2

16. If $(2x + 1)^2 = 25$, then x could equal

    A) 4 or 6

    B) 2 or 3

    C) 4 or –6

    D) 2 or –3

17. If $-3 < 4x - 5 < 11$, and x is an integer, what is one possible value of $3x$?

18. If $16x - 20y = 8$, what is $\frac{x}{2} - \frac{5y}{8}$?

19. If $\frac{1}{2x-1} = 6$, what is $6x$?

20. If $2x - 17 = -y$, what is $6x + 3y$?

BLUE MATH LESSON 11B: INTERPRETING EQUATIONS AND INEQUALITIES
Learning to Swim

Directions: Answer each question below.

PRACTICE SET 1 (NO CALCULATOR)

1. A peanut processing facility packs 18-ounce bags of unshelled peanuts. For consistency, a machine in the facility ensures that all of the bags are within 0.25 ounces of the 18-ounce goal. If the weight of peanuts in a bag is P, write an inequality that models the acceptable range of P, in ounces.

2. A manager at a fast-food restaurant earns $1500 per month, plus 2% of the sales at the restaurant while the manager is on duty. If the manager's sales are given as d dollars, write an equation that can be used to find the total monthly pay, m, of that manager (in terms of d).

3. Atmospheric pressure is dependent on elevation. In order to find the atmospheric pressure for a given elevation, you must subtract 0.8% of the elevation (in meters) from the atmospheric pressure at sea level, which is 101 kilopascals (kPa). Write an equation that can be used to find the atmospheric pressure, P, in kPa, at elevation h meters.

4. Becky must earn at least $2400 dollars each month in order to pay all of her bills. She has two jobs— one that pays a set salary of $x for the month and another that pays $y per hour. If she works 30 hours a month at each job, write an inequality that expresses how much Becky must earn in terms of x and y.

5. A botanist plants r radish plants in a test field. She then tracks q, the number of total radishes produced by these plants in a growing season. If 100 of the plants die (producing no radishes), but the surviving plants produce more than 5 radishes per plant, write an inequality that relates r and q.

BLUE MATH LESSON 11B: INTERPRETING EQUATIONS AND INEQUALITIES
Diving into the Deep End

Directions: Answer each question below.

PRACTICE SET 2 (NO CALCULATOR)

6. As a quick way of estimating a person's body fat percentage, some doctors use Body Adiposity Index (BAI). They begin with 100 times a patient's hip circumference (in meters), and divide that by the patient's height (in meters) raised to the power of 1.5. Finally, they subtract 18 from the result. If c represents hip circumference and h represents height, which expression can be used to calculate BAI?
   A) $100(\frac{c}{h^{1.5}} - 18)$
   B) $\frac{100c}{h^{1.5}-18}$
   C) $\left(\frac{100c}{h}\right)^{1.5} - 18$
   D) $\frac{100c}{h^{1.5}} - 18$

7. To install a wooden fence, a company charges $100 plus $20 per foot of fence. What would be the cost (in dollars) to completely enclose a rectangular yard of length l feet and width w feet?
   A) $100(2l + 2w) + 20$
   B) $20(2l + 2w) + 100$
   C) $20lw + 100$
   D) $20(2l + 2w + 100)$

8. The cost of a decorative stained glass window is equal to $150 per square foot. If the window is a semicircle with a radius r, what is the cost of the window (in dollars) in terms of r?
   A) $75\pi r^2$
   B) $150\pi r^2$
   C) $75\pi r$
   D) $150(\pi r + 2r)$

9. A farmer is trying to calculate how much her crops will earn this year. She has planted 200 acres of corn and 500 acres of soybeans. If each acre of corn earns c dollars and each acre of soybeans earns s dollars in a year, which expression shows how much the farmer will earn in all this year?
   A) $200c + 500s$
   B) $(200 + 500)(c + s)$
   C) $200c \times 500s$
   D) $(200 + 500)cs$

10. The farmer in problem 9 ends up earning $6.6 million from her crops. If the soybean crop earned 25% more per acre than the corn crop, how much did the corn crop earn per acre?
    A) $6,000
    B) $8,000
    C) $10,000
    D) $12,500

11. To get from the Cancun airport to Isla Mujeres, an island off the coast, a traveler must ride in a shuttle bus for 25 miles and a ferry for 8 miles. If the bus's speed is b miles per hour and the ferry's speed is f miles per hour, which of the following gives the time it takes the traveler to get from the airport to Isla Mujeres?

A) $\frac{25+8}{b+f}$

B) $\frac{25}{b} + \frac{8}{f}$

C) $\frac{25}{b} \times \frac{8}{f}$

D) $25b + 8f$

12. A leather craftsman sells two kinds of bags. A large bag costs $\$L$ to make and sells for $\$x$, while a small bag costs $\$S$ to make and sells for $\$y$. If the craftsman sells z large bags and twice as many small bags as large bags, what is an expression of his profit (sales minus costs)?

A) $(L - x) + 2(S - y)$

B) $z(L - S) + 2x(x - y)$

C) $z(x - L) + 2z(y - S)$

D) $z(2Sy - Lx)$

13. A batting cage costs $\$b$ for the first 5 minutes and $\$c$ for each additional minute. If Ernesto spends $\$d$ in one trip to the batting cage, how many minutes did he spend there? (Assume he spent more than 5 minutes in the cage.)

A) $5 + \frac{d-c}{b}$

B) $5 + \frac{b+c}{d}$

C) $5 + \frac{d-b}{c}$

D) $5 - \frac{d+b}{c}$

14. A group of x campers and y counselors are traveling in v vans on a field trip. If one of the vans breaks down, how many more people will have to ride in each van?

A) $\frac{x+y}{v-1}$

B) $\frac{x+y}{v^2-v}$

C) $\frac{xv+yv}{v-1}$

D) $\frac{2x+2y}{v^2-v}$

15. A landscaping company is hired to mow the 500,000 square feet of grass at a large park. If the company owns r large mowers that mow 1500 square feet per minute and s small mowers that mow 500 square feet per minute, which of the following could be used to determine the number of minutes (m) needed to mow the entire park using all the mowers?

A) $500{,}000 = m(1500r + 500s)$

B) $500{,}000 = \frac{1500r+500s}{m}$

C) $500{,}000 = 1500rm + 500s$

D) $500{,}000 = 2000m(r + s)$

PRACTICE SET 3 (NO CALCULATOR)

16. Alita earns K dollars each month at her job as a yoga instructor. If she must pay 20% of this amount in taxes and spend 15% of the remaining amount on supplies, how much does she have left over each month in terms of K after these expenditures?
    A) $0.65K$
    B) $0.68K$
    C) $0.72K$
    D) $0.75K$

17. Two planes simultaneously leave New York City headed to Los Angeles. One plane travels at a miles per hour without stopping. The other travels at b miles per hour and stops in Chicago for an hour before continuing onward. If each planes travels a total of 2500 miles and arrives at the same time in Los Angeles, which equation accurately describes the relationship between a and b?
    A) $2500a = 2500(b - 1)$
    B) $2500a = 2500(b + 1)$
    C) $\frac{2500}{a} = \frac{2500}{b} - 1$
    D) $\frac{2500}{a} = \frac{2500}{b} + 1$

18. A car-repair enthusiast buys a used car for z dollars. He invests an additional 40% of the price he paid for the car into parts to improve the car. Later, he sells the car for a profit of 25% on his total investment. Which expression gives the sale price in terms of z?
    A) $0.75z$
    B) $1.05z$
    C) $1.65z$
    D) $1.75z$

19. Andy and Flo are both selling candy bars for a fundraiser. Andy only has time to sell candy bars for 7 days, but he sells 50 candy bars per day on average. If Flo sells 20 candy bars per day for the first 7 days and 30 candy bars per day after that, which inequality could be used to determine d, the number of days she must sell in order to sell more candy bars than Andy?
    A) $7 \times 20 + 30(d - 7) > 7 \times 50$
    B) $7 \times 30 + 20(d - 7) > 7 \times 50$
    C) $7 \times 20 + 30d > 7 \times 50$
    D) $7 \times 30 + 20d > 7 \times 50$

20. A high school science laboratory has 40% fewer aprons than the number of students in a class, n. If 5 students are absent today, which expression gives the number of students who are present but do not have an apron?
    A) $0.4n - 5$
    B) $0.6n - 5$
    C) $0.4n + 5$
    D) $0.6n + 5$

21. On a normal workday, an office has 30 employees. On weekend days, this number is reduced to 15; on holidays, it is 10. If each employee works 8 hours per day, how many total hours do the employees of the office work during November (which has 20 workdays, 8 weekend days, and 2 holidays)?
    A) 550
    B) 740
    C) 4400
    D) 5920

22. A hotel has s suites ($500 per night), o ocean-view rooms ($1000 per night), and g garden-view rooms ($750 per night) with paying customers for the night. If the hotel must take in at least $50,000 each night to turn a profit, which inequality expresses how many of each type of room must be occupied in order for the hotel to make a profit?
   A) $500s + 1000o + 750g \leq 50{,}000$
   B) $500s + 1000o + 750g \geq 50{,}000$
   C) $500 + 1000 + 750(s + o + g) \leq 50{,}000$
   D) $(500 + 1000 + 750)(s + o + g) \geq 50{,}000$

23. In one state, the first $25,000 of a person's income is not taxed. Any income above $25,000 up to $100,000 is taxed at a rate of $a\%$, and any amount above $100,000 is taxed at a rate of $b\%$. Which expression gives the amount of tax for a person who earns $150,000?
   A) $1000a + 500b$
   B) $750a + 750b$
   C) $750a + 500b$
   D) $250a + 750b$

24. An agricultural researcher is investigating two hybrid corn varieties. Of the a plants from Variety A, 65% survived simulated drought conditions. Of the b plants from Variety B, 45% survived. Which expression gives the percentage of all the plants that survived?
   A) $\dfrac{(0.65a)(0.45b)}{a+b}$
   B) $\dfrac{(0.65a)(0.45b)}{ab}$
   C) $\dfrac{(0.65a)+(0.45b)}{ab}$
   D) $\dfrac{(0.65a)+(0.45b)}{a+b}$

25. As part of a holiday sale, there is a 10% discount on every item in the store. Scarves are discounted an additional 20%. If Magya purchases 3 scarves (original price: $\$s$ each) and a coat (original price: $\$c$), how much does she pay in all?
   A) $0.9c + 2.16s$
   B) $0.9c + 2.4s$
   C) $0.72c + 2.4s$
   D) $2.7c + 0.72s$

BLUE MATH LESSON 11B: INTERPRETING EQUATIONS AND INEQUALITIES
Race to the Finish

Directions: Answer each question below.

HOMEWORK SET (NO CALCULATOR)

1. Gretchen and Carlton each earn $10 per hour as phone salespeople, plus a bonus of $50 for each customer they sign up for a new plan. If Carlton works 42 hours this week and signs up 12 people for new plans, which combination of hours worked and new sign-ups would allow Gretchen to make more money than Carlton?
   A) 20 hours worked, 16 sign-ups
   B) 30 hours worked, 15 sign-ups
   C) 32 hours worked, 14 sign-ups
   D) 36 hours worked, 13 sign-ups

2. When kept in an aquarium, koi fish survive best when the temperature of the water is within 4.7 degrees of 65.2 degrees. Which inequality best models the acceptable temperatures, x, for such an aquarium?
   A) $|x - 4.7| \leq 65.2$
   B) $|x - 4.7| \geq 65.2$
   C) $|x - 65.2| \leq 4.7$
   D) $|x - 65.2| \geq 4.7$

3. A grocery store sells food, which is taxed at only 2%, and other items, which are taxed at 8%. If Ricardo buys a 5-pound turkey at p per pound and a roasting pan for r, how much does he pay in all, after tax?
   A) $4.6p + 0.98r$
   B) $4.9p + 0.92r$
   C) $5.1p + 1.08r$
   D) $5.4p + 1.02r$

4. In a game of horseshoes, a ringer is worth 3 points, a leaner is worth 2 points, and any other throw within 6 inches of the stake is worth 1 point. A total of at least 50 points is needed to advance to the next round. If a player tosses r ringers, l leaners, and n throws within 6 inches, which inequality shows the number of each needed to advance?
   A) $3r + 2l + n \geq 50$
   B) $3l + 2r + n \geq 50$
   C) $3r + 2l + n \leq 50$
   D) $3n + 2l + r \leq 50$

5. A car's speed (in miles per hour) t seconds after the start of a race is given by $s = 20 + 0.2t$. What does the 20 mean in the equation?
   A) The car reaches its maximum speed in 20 seconds.
   B) The car's maximum speed is 20 miles per hour.
   C) The car is accelerating at a rate of 20 miles per hour squared.
   D) The car was already traveling at 20 miles per hour when the race started.

6. Anya types q words per minute for the first 6 hours she is at work. From that point until she goes home, she types 25% slower. If she works for h hours total (where $h > 6$), which expression gives her total number of words typed in terms of q and h?
   A) $360qh + 45q$
   B) $360q + 45qh$
   C) $270q + 60q(h - 6)$
   D) $360q + 45q(h - 6)$

Use the following information to answer Questions 7 and 8.

A car wash currently charges $25 per vehicle for a standard full-service wash. Last month, the business earned $21,250 from these washes. After doing research, the owner of the car wash determines that for each $1 that the price is lowered, the business will attract 20 more cars each month. This is expressed by the function $C(x)$, which gives the money earned for x $1 price lowerings.

7. Which of the following best models $C(x)$?
   A) $C(x) = (25 - x)(850 + 20x)$
   B) $C(x) = (20 - x)(850 + 25x)$
   C) $C(x) = 25(20 - x) + 850$
   D) $C(x) = 20(25 - x) + 850$

8. Which statement is true based on the above information?
   A) Lowering the price will result in more cars and higher total earnings.
   B) Lowering the price will result in more cars but lower total earnings.
   C) It is impossible for the car wash to attract more than 1200 cars in a month.
   D) It is impossible for the car wash to earn more than $22,500 per month.

9. The population of Corpus Christi, Texas rose 10% from 2000 to 2010. In 2010, its population was 304,700. Which linear equation best models the population $P(y)$, where y is the number of years since 2000?
   A) $P(y) = 304,700 - 3047y$
   B) $P(y) = 304,700 + 3047y$
   C) $P(y) = 277,000 - 2770y$
   D) $P(y) = 277,000 + 2770y$

Hours Since Start of Experiment	Number of Bacterial Colonies Present in Sample
0	20
3	110
6	200
....	...
24	740

10. Which function $B(t)$ best models the number of bacteria present in the sample t hours after the start of the experiment, as described by the table above?
    A) $B(t) = 20t + 30$
    B) $B(t) = 30t + 20$
    C) $B(t) = 90t + 30$
    D) $B(t) = 90t + 20$

11. Mordecai is baking a large cake. He has plenty of all the ingredients except for eggs and butter. Eggs cost $3 per dozen and butter costs $5 per pound. The recipe calls for a eggs and b sticks of butter. If each stick of butter is one-fourth of a pound, which equation can be used to determine the cost, C, of the eggs and butter for the cake?
    A) $C = \frac{a}{12} + \frac{5b}{4}$
    B) $C = \frac{a}{12} + 5b$
    C) $C = \frac{a}{4} + \frac{5b}{4}$
    D) $C = \frac{a}{4} + 5b$

12. Abigail sells lemonade and iced tea at a stand in her front yard in order to save money for a new bicycle. She has already made $85, and the bicycle costs $200. If she makes $1 on each glass of lemonade, l, and $1.50 on each glass of iced tea, t, which inequality shows the number of glasses she must sell in order to buy the bicycle?
    A) $85 + l + 1.5t \leq 200$
    B) $85 + l + 1.5t \geq 200$
    C) $85 + t + 1.5l \leq 200$
    D) $85 + t + 1.5l \geq 200$

13. Louisiana's highest point, Driskill Mountain, is 535 feet above sea level. Its lowest point Winrock Quarry, is 68 feet below sea level. Which inequality below best models the possible elevations, h, in Louisiana?

A) $|h - 301.5| \leq 233.5$
B) $|h - 301.5| \geq 233.5$
C) $|h - 233.5| \leq 301.5$
D) $|h - 233.5| \geq 301.5$

14. Tickets to a baseball game cost $\$t$ per person in 2013. Buying each ticket also requires paying a service charge of $2.50. If the team raises ticket prices by 12% in 2014, how much would it cost to buy n tickets?

A) $(2.5t + 1.12)n$
B) $(2.5t)(1.12n)$
C) $(t + 2.5)(1.12n)$
D) $(1.12t + 2.5)n$

15. Renting a ski lodge costs $150 per night, but booking an entire week comes with an 18% discount. Ski lessons at the nearby resort cost $50 per hour. If a family rented L lodges for a week each and took H hours of ski lessons, what would be the total cost, in dollars?

A) $1.18(150)(L) + 50H$
B) $1.18(150)(7L) + 50H$
C) $0.82(150)(L) + 50H$
D) $0.82(150)(7L) + 50H$

16. A business card-printing company charges $10 to design and print the first 100 cards; additional cards can be ordered for $5 per set of 100. What is the cost of c hundreds of cards, assuming an added 5% sales tax?

A) $1.05[10 + 5(c - 1)]$
B) $1.05[5 + 10(c - 1)]$
C) $1.05[5(c - 1)] + 10$
D) $1.05(10 + 5c)]$

Questions 17 and 18 refer to the table below.

Year	Orlando Cougars Average Attendance per Game
1995	8,045
1999	7,277
2003	6,509
2007	5,741

17. If the linear function $A(y) = 8045 - my$ models the average attendance per game for the Orlando Cougars, where y is the years since the team's founding in 1995, what is m?

18. Assuming the trend continued, what was the team's average attendance per game in 2010?

19. The height (in meters) of a rock thrown on Mars can be measured by $h = -3.7t^2 + 8.2t + 0.5$, where t is the time in seconds since the rock was thrown. From what height, in meters, was the rock thrown?

<u>Airport Parking Prices</u>
Hourly Lot: $3 for first hour, $2/hour afterward
Daily Lot: $25 for first day, $20/day afterward

20. Morton and Joanna both park at the airport for exactly 2 days. Morton parks in the Hourly Lot, but Joanna parks in the Daily Lot. How many more dollars does Morton pay compared to Joanna?

BLUE MATH LESSON 12A: INTERPRETING RATIOS, RATES, PROPORTIONS, AND SCALE
Learning to Swim

Directions: Answer each question below.

PRACTICE SET 1 (NO CALCULATOR)

1. A moving truck can be rented by the hour at the rate of d dollars per hour plus c cents per mile driven. Write an equation for the cost C of renting this truck for h hours and driving it for exactly half of the time it is rented at an average speed of 30 miles per hour.

2. Two trains head toward each other in a straight line from starting points 550 miles apart. Train A leaves at noon and travels 70 miles per hour. Train B leaves at 1 p.m. and travels 50 miles per hour. When they meet, how many miles are they from Train A's starting point?

3. A crop fertilizer provides nitrogen, phosphorus, and potassium in the ratio $a : 2a : 3$. How many pounds of potassium are contained in b pounds of the fertilizer?

4. If the straight-line distance from London to Paris (350 kilometers) is represented by j centimeters on a map, how many millimeters represent a distance of k kilometers?

5. Set up an equation for the following scenario: Ron can mow a lawn in r hours, while Stephanie can mow the same lawn in s hours. The two of them, working simultaneously, can mow how many lawns, x, of that size in h hours?

BLUE MATH LESSON 12A: INTERPRETING RATIOS, RATES, PROPORTIONS, AND SCALE
Diving into the Deep End

Directions: Answer each question below.

PRACTICE SET 2 (NO CALCULATOR)

6. A metal alloy is made from nickel, copper, and zinc in the ratio $4 : 3 : 7$ by weight. To make as much of the alloy as is possible with 78 pounds of copper requires how many pounds of nickel?
    A) 58.5
    B) 104
    C) 136.5
    D) 182

7. A machine on an assembly line produces plastic covers for the battery compartment of a children's toy at the rate of 5 per minute. Another machine attaches the covers to the back of the toys at a rate of 144 every half hour. In 8 hours, how many plastic covers will be produced but not attached?
    A) 12
    B) 96
    C) 460
    D) 1248

8. Alvin rides the bus to work at a rate of 12 miles per hour. If the weather is nice, he walks home at a rate of 3 miles per hour. If his home is m miles from his workplace, which of the following equations expresses x, the number of minutes he spends commuting to and from work on a nice day, in terms of m?
    A) $x = \dfrac{m}{144}$
    B) $x = 12m$
    C) $x = 25m$
    D) $x = 144m$

9. To cover the cost of a vacation home rental for a ski trip, each of P people plans to pay D dollars. If N of the P people decide to cancel, but the cost of the house remains unchanged, how many dollars will each attendee now need to pay?
    A) $D - \dfrac{DN}{P}$
    B) $D(P - N)$
    C) $\dfrac{PD}{N}$
    D) $\dfrac{PD}{P-N}$

10. A new energy drink is sold in bottles that have volume V cm³. What is the volume of b of these bottles in cubic meters, in terms of b and V?
    A) $0.000001bV$
    B) $0.0001bV$
    C) $10000bV$
    D) $1000000bV$

11. Two printers are working side-by-side to print the same large document, one starting from the beginning and the other from the end. The first machine can print a pages per hour. The second machine can print b pages per hour. If the document has P pages, which of the following expressions is equal to the number of pages left unprinted after m minutes?
    A) $\frac{(a+b)m}{60}$
    B) $60(a+b)m$
    C) $P - (a+b)m$
    D) $P - \frac{(a+b)m}{60}$

12. If 3 workers can tile a roof in 6 hours, how many hours will it take 2 workers to tile the same roof?
    A) 4
    B) 8
    C) 9
    D) 12

13. A cordless drill is powered by a battery good for 150 minutes of use. Mahmoud can drill 2 holes in one minute with this drill. He is building a wall that requires 180 wooden planks, each of which must have four holes drilled in it. Assuming the battery is fully charged when Mahmoud begins drilling, how many times will he have to recharge the battery?
    A) 0
    B) 1
    C) 2
    D) 3

14. A company divides its executives into junior and senior levels. There are j junior-level executives and s senior-level executives. The ratio of male to female junior-level executives is 2:3. The total number of female executives is f. What fraction of all executives are female and senior level?
    A) $\frac{f - \frac{2}{5}j}{j+s}$
    B) $\frac{f - \frac{3}{5}j}{j+s}$
    C) $\frac{f+s}{j+s}$
    D) $\frac{\frac{3}{5}s}{j+s}$

15. A cylindrical tube has radius r centimeters and height h centimeters. Which of the following adjustments would change the volume of the tube?
    A) Multiplying the radius by 2 and dividing the height by 4.
    B) Multiplying the radius by 2 and dividing the height by 2.
    C) Dividing the diameter by 4 and multiplying the height by 16.
    D) Dividing the radius by 2 and multiplying the height by 4.

PRACTICE SET 3 (NO CALCULATOR)

16. If 12 farmers can churn 96 gallons of butter in 5 hours, how many minutes will it take 10 farmers to churn 12 gallons of butter?

   A) 15
   B) 25
   C) 30
   D) 45

17. If 2.5 inches on a floor plan of a building represent 10 feet in real life, what is the floor area in square feet of a perfectly circular dome whose floor has a diameter of 9 inches on the floor plan, to the nearest integer multiple of π?

   A) 127π
   B) 225π
   C) 324π
   D) 1296π

18. If it takes m minutes to fill a 2-meter deep rectangular swimming pool that measures $l \times w$ meters, at what rate does the pool fill in cubic meters per hour?

   A) $\frac{lw}{30m}$
   B) $\frac{2wl}{m}$
   C) $\frac{120lw}{m}$
   D) $\frac{30lw}{m}$

19. One driver leaves Tampa for Atlanta (a distance of 550 miles) at the same time as another driver leaves Atlanta for Tampa. The second driver travels at 1.2 times the first driver's speed. How many miles from Tampa will the two cars be when they pass each other?

   A) 110
   B) 250
   C) 300
   D) 440

20. Anya runs three laps around a $\frac{1}{4}$-mile track in a seconds, b seconds, and c seconds, respectively. She then attempts to compute the time t it would take her to run a mile based on this average rate. In the equation $\frac{3}{4(a+b+c)} = \frac{1}{t}$ modeling this problem, what does the expression $\frac{3}{4(a+b+c)}$ represent?

   A) The time it takes Anya to run $\frac{3}{4}$ of a mile
   B) The average rate at which Anya runs, in miles per second
   C) The average time it takes Anya to run a lap
   D) The distance Anya runs in three laps

21. Electric power consumption is often measured in *kilowatt hours* (kWh), defined as one kilowatt (1000 watts) of electricity used for a period of one hour. If a 75-watt light bulb is left on for 60 days straight, how many kWh of electricity does it consume?

   A) 4.5
   B) 75
   C) 108
   D) 1250

22. An airplane makes a 3600-mile journey from New York to Amsterdam in 7 hours and 12 minutes with a tailwind. Another plane, flying against the same wind from Amsterdam to New York, makes the trip in 9 hours. How fast is the wind, in miles per hour?

    A) 50
    B) 100
    C) 108
    D) 180

23. Emma and her brother John have both set up lemonade stands near their house. Emma's stand earns a profit of E dollars every day, while John's earns a profit of J dollars every day. In the equation $k = \frac{1000}{E+J}$, what does k represent?

    A) The rate at which Emma and John together earn money, in thousands of dollars per day.
    B) The average price of a lemonade at the two stands if Emma and John together earn $1000 per day.
    C) The number of dollars Emma and John will earn in 1000 days.
    D) The number of days it will take Emma and John to earn a combined profit of $1000.

24. A group of P people in an office form a lottery pool in which each person buys a ticket, and if anyone holds the winning ticket, the entire group will evenly divide the prize of D dollars. If an additional person joins the group, which of the following represents the amount by which each individual's share of the potential winnings will decrease?

    A) $\dfrac{D}{P+1}$

    B) $\dfrac{D}{P(P+1)}$

    C) $D - \dfrac{D}{P+1}$

    D) $\dfrac{DP}{P+1}$

25. Mr. Lin's property measures 132 feet by 66 feet. What area would it take up, in square inches, on a map of his neighborhood in which the scale factor is 8 inches to 1 mile?

    A) 0.02
    B) 0.20
    C) 0.40
    D) 4.85

C2 education
be smarter

BLUE MATH LESSON 12A: INTERPRETING RATIOS, RATES, PROPORTIONS, AND SCALE
Race to the Finish

Directions: Answer each question below.

HOMEWORK SET (NO CALCULATOR)

1. A recipe for a loaf of banana bread calls for 2 teaspoons of baking powder. How many loaves of banana bread can be made if a bakery has ½ cup of baking powder available? (Note: 1 cup = 16 tablespoons; 1 tablespoon = 3 teaspoons.)
   A) 4
   B) 8
   C) 12
   D) 24

2. A bulldozer can remove 3 cubic meters of soil from a construction site in 40 seconds. How many minutes would it take 4 such bulldozers to remove 810 m³ of soil?
   A) 27
   B) 45
   C) 100
   D) 405

3. Two runners start simultaneously around a 400-meter track from the same starting line. They continue to run laps around the track until the faster runner passes the slower one, having gained one full lap on her. The faster runner can complete a lap in a seconds; the slower can complete a lap in b seconds. In the equation $\frac{400}{x} = \frac{1}{a} - \frac{1}{b}$ modeling this situation, what does x represent?
   A) The number of laps the faster runner completes before passing the slower one.
   B) The number of laps the slower runner completes before being passed.
   C) The number of seconds for which the two runners are running.
   D) The rate at which the faster runner pulls ahead of the slower one, in laps per second.

4. In July 2014, one dollar was equal to 0.70 euro. Sarah bought three sweaters in Ireland for 45 euros each. How many dollars were the three sweaters worth all together, to the nearest cent?
   A) $31.50
   B) $64.29
   C) $94.50
   D) $192.86

5. Which of the following will have the effect of doubling the area of a trapezoid? The area of a trapezoid is represented as $A = \frac{1}{2}h(b_1 + b_2)$, where h is its height and b_1 and b_2 are its bases.

   A) Doubling the length of both bases without altering the height.
   B) Doubling the length of the longer base without altering the height.
   C) Doubling the length of both bases and dividing the height by 2.
   D) Doubling the height and the length of the longer base, and dividing the length of the shorter base by 2.

6. A block of solid iron measured at 5 cm × 10 cm × 25 cm has a weight of 9.6 kilograms. What is the density of iron in grams per cm³?

   A) 0.13
   B) 0.77
   C) 7.68
   D) 130.21

7. The shock wave from an earthquake was found to propagate (spread outward) at a rate of 320 meters per second up to a distance of 20 km from the epicenter of the quake. Another measurement found that from 20 km to 40 km from the center, the shock wave traveled at a rate of 240 meters per second. What was its average rate, to the nearest meter per second, over the whole distance?

   A) 270
   B) 274
   C) 280
   D) 288

8. At a guitar store, three-fifths of the guitars in stock are acoustic guitars, and the remaining ones are electric. One-tenth of all guitars in stock are left-handed, as are one-eighth of the acoustic guitars. What fraction of the electric guitars are left-handed?

   A) $\frac{1}{10}$
   B) $\frac{1}{12}$
   C) $\frac{1}{15}$
   D) $\frac{1}{16}$

9. On a map with a scale of 1 inch : 40 yards, what distance in miles is represented by 6 feet and 5 inches, to the nearest hundredth of a mile?

   A) 0.58
   B) 1.48
   C) 1.75
   D) 1.93

10. One oil well produces one barrel of oil every 12 minutes. Another nearby well produces 3 barrels every 50 minutes. Which of the following equations would help determine how many hours, h, it will take to extract x barrels of oil from the two wells combined?

   A) $h = 60x\left(\frac{1}{12} + \frac{3}{50}\right)$
   B) $h = \dfrac{x}{60\left(\frac{1}{12} + \frac{3}{50}\right)}$
   C) $h = \dfrac{60x}{\frac{1}{12} + \frac{3}{50}}$
   D) $h = \dfrac{\frac{1}{12} + \frac{3}{50}}{60x}$

11. If one person can donate a pint of blood in 15 minutes, how many hours will it take to collect 90 gallons of blood, given that the donation center can accommodate 15 donors at a time? (Note: one gallon = 8 pints.)
   A) 6
   B) 12
   C) 30
   D) 45

12. The only factory producing a new model of car can produce 1250 cars per hour. In the first week of sales, 140,000 people sign contracts to buy one of these cars. How many hours per day does the factory have to be in operation for a week (assuming it is open all seven days) to keep up with this rate of sales?
   A) 7
   B) 14
   C) 16
   D) 18

13. If n robots working together can produce w widgets in h hours, which of the following is an expression for the number of hours it will take m robots to produce $2w$ widgets?
   A) $\frac{2hn}{m}$
   B) $\frac{2hm}{n}$
   C) $\frac{2wn}{hm}$
   D) $\frac{2n}{hm}$

14. Two rockets are fired in opposite directions at the same time and the same speed. Their initial positions are m meters apart. After s seconds, they are 500 meters apart. Which of the following equations can be used to find the speed x of each rocket in meters per second?
   A) $x = \frac{500}{s} - m$
   B) $x = \frac{500-m}{s}$
   C) $x = \frac{500-m}{2s}$
   D) $x = \frac{500}{2s} - m$

15. Tyler, Brenda, and Jackie work in a deli. Tyler can make sandwiches twice as fast as Brenda. Jackie makes 5 sandwiches in the time it takes Brenda to make 4. If Tyler makes T sandwiches in an hour, which of the following is an expression for the number of sandwiches the three, working together, will make in five hours?
   A) $\frac{85T}{8}$
   B) $\frac{55T}{4}$
   C) $\frac{85}{T}$
   D) $\frac{15T}{8}$

Use the following equation and information for Questions 16 and 17.

$$P_1 V_1 = P_2 V_2$$

The product of the pressure (P_1) and volume (V_1) of a fixed quantity of a gas at a fixed temperature is constant; if one of them is altered, the other will change (V_2 and P_2) to compensate.

16. A gas in a sealed container of volume V has pressure P. It is pumped into another container of volume Q. Which of the following is an expression for its pressure in this new container?
    A) $\frac{Q}{PV}$
    B) $\frac{QV}{P}$
    C) $\frac{PQ}{V}$
    D) $\frac{PV}{Q}$

17. Which of the following changes would result in reducing the pressure of a gas in a cylinder by one-fourth?
    A) Quadruple the radius of the cylinder and leave the height unchanged.
    B) Double the height and diameter of the cylinder.
    C) Double the radius of the cylinder and leave the height unchanged.
    D) Quadruple the radius of the cylinder and divide the height by 2.

18. If fossils dated to be approximately 70,000,000 years old are found at the base of a 196 meter cliff consisting of sedimentary rock, what was the average rate of rock deposition (the geological process by which material is added to landform or land mass) at this site, in millimeters per century?
    A) 0.0028
    B) 0.028
    C) 0.28
    D) 2.8

19. Mr. Jones receives a weekly paycheck of X dollars. Mrs. Jones receives her paycheck of Y dollars every other week. Which of the following equations can be used to find w, the number of weeks it will take the two of them together to earn $20,000?
    A) $w = \frac{20000}{X + \frac{Y}{2}}$
    B) $w = \frac{20000}{X + 2Y}$
    C) $w = \frac{10000}{2X + Y}$
    D) $w = \frac{2X + Y}{40000}$

20. One construction worker can lay x bricks in 10 minutes. Another can lay 15 bricks in x minutes. In the equation modeling this situation, $60k\left(\frac{x}{10} + \frac{15}{x}\right) = A$, what does k represent?
    A) The number of bricks the two workers together can lay in an hour.
    B) The combined rate of the two workers in bricks per minute.
    C) The number of bricks the two workers together can lay in A hours.
    D) The number of hours it will take the two workers together to lay A bricks.

BLUE MATH LESSON 12B: INTERPRETING PERCENTS
Learning to Swim

Directions: Answer each question below.

PRACTICE SET 1 (CALCULATOR)

1. A jacket costs d dollars on Wednesday. On Thursday it goes on sale for 20% off. On Friday, its price is increased by 20% from Thursday's price. Does the jacket on Friday cost less than, more than, or the same as it did on Wednesday? What is the Friday price in terms of d?

2. A bakery has a 25% profit margin: its profits are equal to 25% of its expenses. Profit (P) is calculated as revenue (R) minus expenses (E), or $P = R - E$. The bakery's expenses are what percent of its revenues?

3. If the bakery in Problem 2 sees its expenses increase by 10% and its revenues decrease by 1%, what will its profit margin be, as a percent of its new expenses?

4. If Evan's hourly wage of W dollars is increased by x%, what is his new hourly wage in terms of W and x?

5. If the width of a rectangular swimming pool is increased by x%, and the length of the same pool is also increased by x%, by what percent will the pool's area increase, in terms of x?

BLUE MATH LESSON 12B: INTERPRETING PERCENTS
Diving into the Deep End

Directions: Answer each question below.

PRACTICE SET 2 (CALCULATOR)

6. After increasing its rate of production by 12%, a soap factory produces 16,800 gallons of soap per day. How many gallons per day did it previously produce?
   A) 2,016
   B) 14,784
   C) 15,000
   D) 15,600

7. One measure of the effectiveness of a person's immune system is her or her T-cell count (a T-cell is a type of white blood cell). A patient's T-cell count is monitored after treatment with an experimental drug for an immunodeficiency disorder; the doctors find that it increases by 20% each day. If on Wednesday it was 375, what is it on Saturday?
   A) 378
   B) 540
   C) 600
   D) 648

8. The product PV of the pressure (P) and volume (V) of a gas at a fixed temperature always remains constant. If the volume of a sealed container full of hydrogen is increased by 28%, by what percent will the pressure decrease, to the nearest tenth of a percent?
   A) 3.6%
   B) 21.9%
   C) 28%
   D) 78%

9. Tim's meal at a restaurant cost $10.88, including a 6.25% sales tax. Tim wishes to tip 20% on the pre-tax amount. How much tip should he leave, to the nearest cent?
   A) 2.00
   B) 2.05
   C) 2.18
   D) 2.31

Problems 10 and 11 use the following information:

Juan, a newly hired car salesman, is given a choice between two compensation plans. He can either earn (Plan A) a guaranteed salary of $50,000 per year plus a commission of 2% of the sale price of each car he sells, or (Plan B) a guaranteed salary of $35,000 per year plus a commission of 3% of the sale price of each car.

10. If Juan sells 140 cars in a year at an average price of $13,000 per car, what percent greater will his total pay be under Plan B than under Plan A?
    A) 0.8%
    B) 3.7%
    C) 4.9%
    D) 6.7%

11. How many cars must Juan sell at an average price of $12,000 to make an equal amount of money under either compensation plan?
    A) 120
    B) 125
    C) 150
    D) 165

12. In a chemical reaction, the number of water molecules increases from 1.02×10^{25} to 1.12×10^{25}. This is equivalent to what percent increase?

    A) 6.0%
    B) 9.8%
    C) 10.8%
    D) 30.0%

$$A = \frac{1}{2}s^2$$

13. The area of an isosceles right triangle is given by the equation above. If the length of a side of the triangle is increased by 30%, the triangle's new area will be what percent of the old area?

    A) 130%
    B) 160%
    C) 169%
    D) 190%

14. The minimum wage in a certain state is set to increase from $9.75 per hour to $10.92 per hour. This is equivalent to what percent increase?

15. If a candidate's share of the prospective vote in pre-election polling increases from 48% of the vote to 54% of the vote, while the estimated total number of votes cast remains the same, the number of votes the candidate is expected to receive increases by what percent?

PRACTICE SET 3 (CALCULATOR)

16. Physicists fired a bullet at a target, having already calculated the theoretical velocity the bullet would travel if there were no air resistance, as well as the number of seconds it would take to hit the target at that velocity. They found that the bullet, in actuality, averaged 93% of its theoretical velocity. The time it took to reach the target was approximately what percent of the theoretically predicted time?

    A) 106.5%
    B) 107.0%
    C) 107.5%
    D) 115.0%

17. Margie bought a coat for $87.44 that was on sale for 15% off. The original price of the coat was

    A) $74.32
    B) $100.56
    C) $102.44
    D) $102.87

18. A prestigious college has an admission rate of 14% of applicants, and 75% of admitted students end up enrolling, filling a total of 1365 spaces in its freshman class. The following year, 20% more students apply. Assuming the number of available spots and the enrollment rate among accepted applicants both remain the same, approximately what should the college's acceptance rate be?

    A) 11.20%
    B) 11.67%
    C) 16.80%
    D) 17.50%

Use the following table to answer Questions 19 and 20:

A study evaluated the effectiveness of a new test for a rare genetic condition by administering the test to patients who already knew whether or not they suffered from the condition. A positive test result means the test indicated the patient had the condition; a negative result means the test did not indicate the condition. The results are as follows:

Patient Status	Pos. Test	Neg. Test	Total
Has Condition	49	1	50
Does Not Have	6	944	950
Total	55	945	1000

19. What percent of patients who suffered from the condition had a positive test result?
    A) 10.9%
    B) 89.1%
    C) 90.9%
    D) 98.0%

20. What percent of patients who had a positive test result did not actually suffer from the condition?
    A) 2.0%
    B) 10.9%
    C) 12.0%
    D) 12.2%

21. Alina paid a restaurant bill that came to $110 before including the 6.5% sales tax, and tipped 20% on the total including tax. If she had instead tipped 20% on the pre-tax amount, how much less would she have paid altogether?

22. Omar buys used furniture, refurbishes it, and sells it at a 25% markup from what he paid. A desk available used at Omar's shop for $85 is on sale new at a large furniture outlet for $100. What percent of the new price did Omar pay to purchase the desk?

23. In question 22, Omar's expenses other than the actual cost of the furniture he buys (tools, supplies, and rent and utilities for his office) cost him an average of 20% of what he spends on furniture. Omar's profit (total revenue minus total expenses) is equal to what percent of his total expenses, to the nearest tenth of a percent?
    A) 3.4%
    B) 4.0%
    C) 4.2%
    D) 5.0%

For Questions 24 and 25, use the information below.

The graph below represents the number of hours of daylight on the 21st of each month in New York City and Miami.

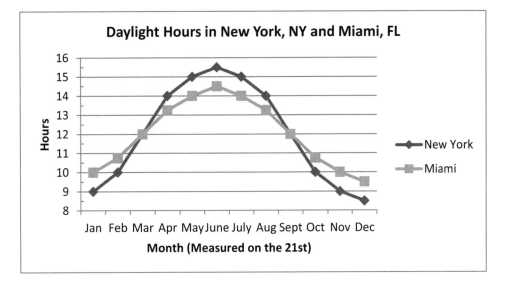

24. New York in September sees what percent more daylight than Miami in January?
    A) 16.7%
    B) 20%
    C) 25%
    D) 33.3%

25. In the month in which the percent difference in daylight hours between the two cities is greatest, the city with less daylight experiences what percent of the number of daylight hours of the city with more daylight?
    A) 89.5%
    B) 90.0%
    C) 90.9%
    D) 93.5%

BLUE MATH LESSON 12B: INTERPRETING PERCENTS
Race to the Finish

Directions: Answer each question below.

HOMEWORK SET (CALCULATOR)

1. A shoe salesman made $31.50 in commission on a sale of a $252 pair of dress shoes. What was his commission rate as a percent of the sale?
    A) 10.8%
    B) 12%
    C) 12.5%
    D) 15%

2. A bicycle on sale for 36% off costs $307.20. What is the normal, non-sale price of the bike?
    A) $196.61
    B) $417.79
    C) $480.00
    D) $503.81

3. Geneticists are studying two rare mutations in rats: one that causes them to have blue eyes, and another that causes colorblindness. They find that all blue-eyed rats are colorblind. If 9% of rats have blue eyes, and 15% of rats are colorblind, what percent of colorblind rats have blue eyes?
    A) 6%
    B) 40%
    C) 60%
    D) Cannot be answered with the given information

4. 40% of what percent of 225 is equal to 144?
    A) 64
    B) 156.25
    C) 160
    D) 360

5. Minyoung scored 40% more goals in last year's soccer season than the next-best player on her team. The two of them together scored 50% of the team's goals. If Minyoung scored 21 goals over the course of the season, how many did the team score?
    A) 30
    B) 66
    C) 72
    D) 105

6. The US–Japan exchange rate, in yen per dollar, increased by 5% on Thursday, decreased by 4% on Friday, and increased by 7.5% on Saturday. If a dollar at the start of Thursday was worth 100 yen, how many yen was it worth at the end of Saturday?
    A) 108.36
    B) 108.50
    C) 108.58
    D) 108.61

Use the following information for Questions 7 and 8:

A soap manufacturer surveyed potential customers about two different brands of hand soap, asking them which brand they preferred in a blind test. The results are displayed below:

Liquid Hand Soap Market Research

Brand	Men	Women	Total
Squeaky Clean	77	78	155
Fresh Feeling	55	90	145
Total	132	168	300

7. What percent of men preferred Squeaky Clean brand soap to Fresh Feeling, to the nearest tenth of a percent?
    A) 41.7%
    B) 49.7%
    C) 51.7%
    D) 58.3%

8. What percent of customers preferred the brand that was NOT favored by a majority of their gender, to the nearest tenth of a percent?
    A) 44.0%
    B) 44.3%
    C) 48.3%
    D) 55.7%

9. The tax rate where Alice lives is 20% of all income up to $40,000, and 30% of all income over $40,000. In 2010, Alice made an annual salary, before taxes, of $36,000. In 2011, she received a 20% raise. By what percent did the amount of income tax owed by Alice increase from 2010 to 2011, to the nearest tenth of a percent?
    A) 20%
    B) 24.4%
    C) 68.9%
    D) 80%

10. A jewelry store employee receives a 2% commission on the value of all jewelry she sells in addition to a flat annual salary of $33,000. Last year, she sold $750,000 worth of jewelry. This year, she sold enough jewelry that her total compensation (salary plus commissions) increased by 10%. What dollar value in jewelry did she sell this year?
    A) $792,000
    B) $825,000
    C) $828,300
    D) $990,000

11. In 2013, Vanessa's company earned a profit margin of 5%; that is, its total profit (total revenue minus total expenses) was equal to 5% of total expenses. In 2014, the company's revenue increased by 10% and its expenses increased by 12%. What was the company's profit margin in 2014?
    A) 3.0%
    B) 3.5%
    C) 4.0%
    D) 4.8%

12. One mole (6.02×10^{23} molecules) of water has a mass of 18 grams. One mole of ethanol has a mass of 46 grams. In a kilogram of a solution that is 40% ethanol and 60% water by mass, approximately what percent of the molecules are ethanol molecules?
    A) 20.7%
    B) 23.5%
    C) 26.1%
    D) 39.1%

13. A used appliance dealer buys lightly used household appliances for 75% of their new retail value and resells them at a 30% markup from the price at which the dealer acquired them. Relative to the retail price of a new appliance, a customer buying a used appliance from this company pays
    A) 5% less
    B) 2.5% less
    C) 2.5% more
    D) 5% more

14. Martin tipped $7.70 on a restaurant bill which came to $47.30 including 7.5% sales tax (but not including his tip). What percent of the pre-tax price of the meal did Martin tip?

15. If A is B% of C, and B is C% of D, then D is what percent of A?
    A) $\dfrac{C^2}{100}$
    B) $\dfrac{C^2}{1{,}000{,}000}$
    C) $\dfrac{100}{C^2}$
    D) $\dfrac{1{,}000{,}000}{C^2}$

16. A box contains 350 raffle tickets, each equally likely to be drawn. Ten winning tickets are added to the box, and the probability of winning increases by a factor of 25%. How many winning tickets were in the box to begin with?

Use the following information for Questions 17 and 18.

Inflation is a decline over time in the value of a unit of currency. It is typically measured as a percent *increase* in prices across the economy—for example, if the U.S. experienced 25% inflation, a loaf of bread that had cost $4.00 would now cost 25% more, or $5.00.

17. If a loaf of bread cost $1.25 in 2020, and the U.S. then experienced 40% inflation every 10 years until 2050, what would the same loaf of bread cost in 2050?

18. If the price of a pound of rice was $0.30 and increased by 60% over the following ten years, by what percent did the value of a dollar *decrease* during this time, in pounds of rice per dollar?

For Questions 19 and 20 use the information below:

A total of 250 students at Ridgemont High School were surveyed as to their favorite school subject among four choices: English, Social Studies, Math, and Science. The results are graphed below:

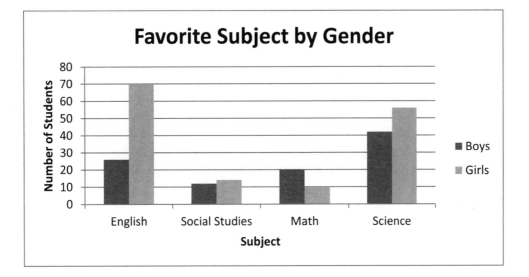

19. What percent of girls responding to the survey cited English as their favorite subject?
    A) 26%
    B) 46.7%
    C) 58.3%
    D) 70%

20. Compared to the percentage of boys whose favorite subject was science, the percentage of girls whose favorite subject was science was
    A) 4.7 percentage points lower.
    B) 11.1 percentage points lower.
    C) 14 percentage points higher.
    D) 25 percentage points higher.

BLUE MATH LESSON 13A: MULTI-STEP UNIT CONVERSIONS
Learning to Swim

Directions: Answer each question below.

PRACTICE SET 1 (CALCULATOR)

1. The speed of light is 3.0×10^8 m/s. If a light-year is the distance light will travel in one year, what is the magnitude of a light-year in miles? (1 mile is equivalent to 1.61 km)

2. Jason is hosting a party and needs to order pizza for everyone. There are 13 people attending the party. Each pizza pie costs $12.50 and can feed 3 people. Assuming Jason must order entire pizza pies, how much will it cost to feed everyone at the party?

3. Emily donates 5% of her income to charity. If Emily donated $2950.20 to charity last year and made $33 an hour, how many hours did she work that year?

4. Mark wants to put tile on his kitchen floor. The floor is 96 square feet with a width of 8 feet and the tile is 12 inches wide and 24 inches long. How many tiles will he need to cover the floor?

5. A printer can print at 300 pixels per square inch. How many pixels are there in an 8.5" x 11" piece of paper?

BLUE MATH LESSON 13A: MULTI-STEP UNIT CONVERSIONS
Diving into the Deep End

Directions: Answer each question below.

PRACTICE SET 2 (CALCULATOR)

6. A top tennis player puts an average of 3300 revolutions per minute of spin on the ball with each strike. A ball traveling the 60 feet from the baseline on one side of the court to the service line on the other side of the net at 90 miles per hour will rotate how many times during its flight?
   A) $\frac{5}{12}$
   B) 25
   C) 50π
   D) 2200

7. A cube measures 10 inches a side, what is its volume in cubic meters? (1 inch is equivalent to approximately 2.54 cm.)
   A) 0.0164
   B) 0.0201
   C) 0.0297
   D) 0.0324

8. Fine silver has a density of 10.5 g/cm³. If the price of silver on a particular day is $21.30 per ounce, what is the value of a rectangular ingot with dimensions 6.75 cm × 3.5 cm × $\frac{2}{3}$ cm? (An ounce is equivalent to 28.35 grams.)
   A) $86.12
   B) $124.25
   C) $220.11
   D) $905.78

9. The density of a certain substance is 5.6 g/mL. If a 1-gallon container is half-full of this substance, what is its mass in lbs? (1 gram is equivalent to 0.035 ounces and 1 gallon is equivalent to 3785 mL)
   A) 22.55
   B) 23.18
   C) 24.15
   D) 24.95

10. If a slug moves at a rate of 2 ft per hour, how many miles does the same slug move in a year's worth of moving?
    A) 2.91
    B) 3.01
    C) 3.32
    D) 3.87

11. Lou is painting her living room, which is 4.5 meters square; the walls are 2.5 meters high. One gallon of paint can cover 350 square feet of surface. If she is going to paint three of the walls in her main color, which is only available in quarts, how many quarts should she buy? (One meter is 3.28 feet.)
    A) 2
    B) 3
    C) 4
    D) 5

12. The unit Pascal (Pa) is a unit of pressure representing newtons (N) per square meter. If the standard atmospheric pressure is 101.3 kilopascals what is that pressure in psi (pounds per square inch)? (1 pound is equivalent to 4.45 newtons.)
   A) 12.34
   B) 13.43
   C) 14.69
   D) 15.23

13. Eric is mowing his ¼-acre lawn. His lawn mower cuts an 18-inch swath, and, including pauses to bag the cut grass, he averages 405 linear feet in every five minutes. How long will it take him to complete the whole lawn (assuming his swaths do not overlap)? (1 acre = 4840 yd²)
   A) 0.67 hour
   B) 1.00 hour
   C) 1.49 hour
   D) 5.98 hour

14. The average person can run about 20 miles per hour, what is this speed in m/s? (1 mile is equivalent to 1.61 km)
   A) 8.89
   B) 9.62
   C) 10.23
   D) 11.98

15. The density of a piece of unknown metal is 12.8 g/cm³. What is the weight in lbs of a 1 L sample of the metal? (1 mL = 1cm³ and 1 ounce is equivalent to 28.35 grams.)
   A) 21.67
   B) 24.56
   C) 26.81
   D) 28.22

PRACTICE SET 3 (CALCULATOR)

16. An acre-inch of rain (i.e. one inch of rain falling on an area of one acre) is 27,154 gallons of water. If rain is falling at a steady rate of 2 inches in 5 hours and a gallon of water weighs 8.33 pounds, what weight of water falls on a 40-acre field in 4 hours?
   A) 181 tons
   B) 1810 tons
   C) 7238 tons
   D) 9045 tons

17. Amanda is sorting through various files. She can sort through 250 files in an hour. There are 300 files in a filing cabinet. How long will it take for her to sort through 4 filing cabinets?
   A) 2.4 hours
   B) 3.3 hours
   C) 4.8 hours
   D) 30 hours

18. A surveyor's wheel is a tool for measuring distances that are too long for a tape measure to be practical; it rolls along the ground and the number of revolutions is counted. If a rectangular field is measured at 200 revolutions by 120 revolutions using a wheel with a radius of 5 ¾ inches, how many acres is the field (assume that the ground is perfectly flat)? (1 acre = 4840 yd²)
   A) 0.127
   B) 4.99
   C) 19.9
   D) 719

19. Roger is currently filling his 3000 gallon pool. He wants to fill it 90% of the way to the top. He fills the pool for three hours each day. With the hose he has, he fills his pool at a rate of 4 gallons per minute. How many days will it take for Roger to fill his pool? Round to the nearest tenth.

20. Samantha is ordering balloons for a party. She needs 108 balloons. She can order in bulk and receive 4 boxes of balloon for $28. Each box contains 4 bundles of balloons. Each bundle of balloons contains 9 balloons. She could also buy each box individually at the cost of $8 per box. How much money would she save if she bought every box individually instead of buying them in bulk?

21. Baljit owes $500 to his friend in India. He wants to transfer this money through a currency exchange agency that charges a $4.99 flat fee and exchanges dollars to rupees (Indian currency) at a rate of 62.4 rupees for every dollar. How much does it cost Baljit, in rupees, to transfer the money through the agency?
A) 504.99
B) 21,430.65
C) 31,200.00
D) 31,511.38

22. The cost of electricity in Philadelphia is 24.5 cents per kWh. A typical central air conditioner uses 5 kWh per day when operated continuously, and a typical fan uses 6 kWh a month when operated continuously. What would be the combined cost of operating a fan for 6 months and a central air conditioner for one year?
A) $447.13
B) $455.95
C) $464.77
D) $471.13

23. Bill takes 45 minutes to build a small guitar and 1 hour to build a large guitar. If Bill made 5 small guitars and 3 large guitars how much money does Bill make if he is paid $12 an hour?

24. A large graduate program in chemistry will award 22 PhDs this year; each degree recipient wrote a dissertation with an average length of 180 pages. The department has available an inkjet printer capable of printing 35 pages per minute, which uses $130 ink cartridges that can print 9200 pages before running out, and a laser printer that prints 42 pages per minute, using $120 cartridges with a 6000 page capacity. If the department uses the cheaper option for printing all 22 dissertations, how will the time to print them compare to the time it would have taken to print using the more expensive option?
A) 28 minutes less
B) 19 minutes less
C) 19 minutes more
D) 28 minutes more

25. A hobby farmer plans to plant 400 radish seeds. Which will yield the lower price per radish: medium quality seeds (75% of the seeds will germinate and grow) that come in packets of 80 seeds for $2.50, or high quality seeds (germination rate 95%) that come in packets of 40 seeds for $1.99?
A) The medium quality is 1.07¢ lower.
B) The medium quality is 1.85¢ lower.
C) The high quality is 51¢ lower.
D) The high quality is 5.24¢ lower.

BLUE MATH LESSON 13A: MULTI-STEP UNIT CONVERSIONS
Race to the Finish

Directions: Answer each question below.

HOMEWORK SET (CALCULATOR)

1. A ball travels 18 meters in 3 seconds. What is it speed in kilometers per hour?
   A) 6.0
   B) 18.0
   C) 21.6
   D) 22.2

2. A large ball of metal is placed in a bathtub. The change in volume is recorded as 500 ml. If the ball is massed at 4 kg what is its density in g/ml?
   A) 2
   B) 4
   C) 6
   D) 8

3. A small cube, 5 cm on a side, has a density of 1kg/m^3. What is it mass in grams?
   A) 0.100
   B) 0.125
   C) 0.150
   D) 125.0

4. Water enters a bathtub at 10 liters per hour. After 10 minutes how many milliliters of water are in the tub?
   A) 10
   B) 1000
   C) 1667
   D) 2500

5. A plane is traveling at a speed of 500 km/hr. How many meters does the plane cover in 180 seconds, rounded to the nearest meter?
   A) 139
   B) 500
   C) 5000
   D) 25,000

6. A gravel pile is being removed at the rate of 25 kg per week. How many milligrams are being removed every hour?
   A) 125,475
   B) 148,810
   C) 165,932
   D) 184,734

7. A large ball of metal is placed in a bathtub. The change in volume is recorded as 12 L. If the ball is massed at 200 lbs, what is its density in g/ml? (1 kg is equivalent to approximately 2.2 lbs)
   A) 6.25
   B) 7.02
   C) 7.58
   D) 8.31

8. The density of aluminum is 2.7 g/cm^3. If a square cube with a side length of 15 mm is made of aluminum what is its mass in mg?
   A) 8123.3
   B) 8796.7
   C) 9112.5
   D) 10,092.8

9. A car is traveling at 70 km/hr, what is its speed in m/s?
   A) 19.44
   B) 23.22
   C) 25.86
   D) 70.00

10. Water is leaking out of a sink at 1 mg per minute. How many grams will leak out after 7.5 hours?
    A) 0.06
    B) 0.42
    C) 0.45
    D) 0.75

11. A carton of strawberries costs $2.99 and contains 24 strawberries. What is the cost, in cents of a single strawberry? Round to the nearest hundredth of a cent.
    A) 10.67
    B) 12.46
    C) 14.23
    D) 15.15

12. If a car averages 28 miles per gallon, what is its gasoline consumption in km/L? (1 mile is equivalent to approximately 1.6 km and 1 gallon is equivalent to approximately 3.785 L)
    A) 10.7
    B) 11.2
    C) 11.9
    D) 12.3

13. If gasoline in the United States costs $3.50 a gallon, what is the cost, in British pounds, of a liter of gas? Assume that the conversion rate is 1 pound per 1.5 U.S. dollars.
    A) 0.11
    B) 0.62
    C) 1.39
    D) 1.62

14. Janice's salary is $5500 a month. She is transferred to France, where she is paid the same amount, but on a bi-weekly (every two weeks) basis. How many euros will she be paid per two-week period? ($1.3 = 1 euro)
    A) 976.33
    B) 1952.66
    C) 2538.46
    D) 3300.00

15. The average toilet uses about 1.6 gallons of water per flush. How many mL is this? (1 gallon is equivalent to approximately 3.785 L)
    A) 1600
    B) 3220
    C) 4570
    D) 6060

16. A car is traveling at the speed of 100 km/hr. If the wheel has a diameter of 1 m what is the value of the wheel's rpm (revolutions per minute)? Round your answer to the nearest tenth.

   A) 106.1
   B) 523.6
   C) 530.5
   D) 5236.0

17. If it takes 30 minutes for a Ferris wheel with a radius of 15 ft to make an entire rotation around, what is its speed in miles per hour? Round to the nearest hundredth.

18. If eggs cost $20 for a gross, what is the cost, in cents, of a single egg? Round to the nearest tenth of a cent. (1 gross is equivalent to 12 dozen)

19. If the density of water is 1 g/mL what is its density in lbs. per gal.? Round to the nearest hundredth. (1 kg is equivalent to approximately 2.2 lbs and 1 gallon is equivalent to approximately 3.785 L)

20. The standard tire pressure of a car is 32 psi (pounds per square inch). What is that pressure in N/cm^2? Round to the nearest tenth. (1 pound is equivalent to 4.45 newtons and 2.54 cm is equivalent to 1 inch.)

BLUE MATH LESSON 13B: DIRECT AND INVERSE VARIATION
Learning to Swim

Directions: Answer each question below.

PRACTICE SET 1 (NO CALCULATOR)

1. If a varies directly as b^2 and inversely as $c + 5$, set up an equation for c in terms of a, b, and k, the constant of variation.

2. Given a constant amount of engine force, the acceleration of a locomotive varies inversely with its mass. If a car with mass m kilograms accelerates at $(a - 2)$ meters per second squared, what will be the acceleration of a car with mass m^2 kilograms?

3. The cost to rent a wedding venue varies inversely with the number of people invited to the wedding. If a p-person wedding costs $\$t$ per person, how many fewer people can attend the wedding if the total price of the wedding remains constant, but the price per person is doubled?

x	y
12	8
6	4
0.5	0.25
0.1	0.5

4. What sort of relationship exists among the variables x and y above?

5. The number of pitches thrown by a pitcher varies directly with the number of innings he pitches. If the pitcher pitches $w + 3$ pitches while pitching $2w$ innings, how many pitches will he throw when he pitches $6w$ innings?

BLUE MATH LESSON 13B: DIRECT AND INVERSE VARIATION
Diving into the Deep End

Directions: Answer each question below.

PRACTICE SET 2 (CALCULATOR)

6. The electric field generated by a charged object varies directly as the charge on the object, and inversely as the square of the distance away from the object. A Van de Graaff generator carrying a charge of 0.28 µC gives a field of 2520 N/C at a point 1.00 meter away. What charge will result in the same field strength at a distance of 0.600 m?
   A) 0.1008 µC
   B) 0.1680 µC
   C) 0.4667 µC
   D) 0.7778 µC

7. When temperature is measured in units of kelvin, it is directly proportional to kinetic energy. At room temperature, 298 K, water molecules are moving with an average KE of 6.17×10^{-21} joules. What is the average energy of water molecules at the boiling point, 373 K?
   A) 4.87×10^{-21} joules
   B) 4.93×10^{-21} joules
   C) 7.72×10^{-21} joules
   D) 4.83×10^{22} joules

8. The time for a pendulum to make one complete swing varies directly as the square root of the length of the pendulum. If the pendulum on a grandfather clock, which swings once per second, is 16 inches long, what would the period be if the pendulum were lengthened to 18 inches?
   A) $\frac{3\sqrt{2}}{16}$ sec
   B) 0.94 sec
   C) $\frac{3\sqrt{2}}{4}$ sec
   D) $12\sqrt{2}$ sec

9. The force of Earth's gravity on any object varies directly as the mass of the object and inversely as the square of its distance from the center of the Earth. If a person whose mass is 59 kg experiences a force of 579 N on the surface of the Earth (radius 6378 km), what is the force on a 79 kg explorer at the Karman line, above which the atmosphere is too thin to support aircraft—100 km above the surface?
   A) 315.3 N
   B) 751.5 N
   C) 775.3 N
   D) 779 N

10. A team of 10 robots can assemble 2500 game consoles in 5 hours. How many more robots will be needed to output twice the number of consoles in 40% of the time?
   A) 30 more
   B) 40 more
   C) 50 more
   D) 60 more

11. The electric force between two point charges varies inversely as the square of the distance between the two charges. If the force between two charges 1 cm apart is 1500 N, what force will be applied to the two charges if their distance is 1 m?
   A) 0.15 N
   B) 15 N
   C) 150 N
   D) 1500 N

12. The volume of a gas varies inversely as the pressure applied on it. If the volume is 300 cm³ under pressure of 50 kg/cm³, what pressure has to be applied to have a volume of 250 cm³?
    A) 50 kg/cm³
    B) 60 kg/cm³
    C) 70 kg/cm³
    D) 75 kg/cm³

13. The force a magnetic field exerts on a charged particle moving perpendicular to the field varies jointly as the charge, its velocity, and the strength of the magnetic field. If the velocity of a particle is decreased by 25% while the field strength is increased by 25%, what is the percent decrease in the total force?
    A) 0%
    B) 6.25%
    C) 56.25%
    D) It cannot be determined from the information provided.

14. The distance an object falls varies directly with the square of the time it falls (ignoring air resistance). If a stone falls 400 m in 4 seconds, how many seconds longer will it take for the stone to fall 900 m?

15. The length of a guitar string varies inversely as the frequency of its vibration. A guitar string 16 inches long vibrates at a frequency of 350 vibrations per second. If another string is 28 inches long, what is its frequency in vibrations per second?

PRACTICE SET 3 (CALCULATOR)

16. The kinetic energy of an object varies directly with the square of the object's velocity. By what percent does the kinetic energy of a car increase when its speed increases from 55 mph to 65 mph?
    A) 18%
    B) 28%
    C) 40%
    D) It cannot be determined from the information provided.

17. Hooke's Law for a spring dictates that the distance a spring stretches varies directly with the force applied to the spring. If a force of 1000 newtons stretches a spring 0.01 m, how much more force will be needed to stretch the spring an additional 2 cm?
    A) 500 newtons
    B) 1000 newtons
    C) 2000 newtons
    D) 3000 newtons

18. The energy of a photon of electromagnetic radiation is directly proportional to its frequency. Given that blue light with a frequency of 1.03×10^{15} Hz (cycles per second) has an energy of 6.82×10^{-19} joules, what is the energy of a radio wave photon with frequency 9.87×10^{7} Hz?
    A) 6.71×10^{-42} joules
    B) 6.62×10^{-34} joules
    C) 6.54×10^{-26} joules
    D) 7.12×10^{-12} joules

x	y	z
3	4	2
0.5	0.5	0.04166

19. Which of the following equations best demonstrates the relationship between x, y, and z?

A) $xyz = k$

B) $\frac{xz}{y} = k$

C) $\frac{zy}{z} = k$

D) $\frac{xy}{z} = k$

20. An object's momentum varies directly as its velocity; for a given object the constant of proportionality is its mass. How much more momentum does a 1400 kg small car have at a highway speed of 26.8 m/sec than it does at a surface street speed of 17.9 m/sec?

A) 26 kg·m/sec

B) 12,460 kg·m/sec

C) 25,060 kg·m/sec

D) 37,520 kg·m/sec

21. The time it takes an ice cube to melt completely varies directly as the volume of the cube. If an ice cube of volume 1000 in³ takes 10 hours to melt, how long would it take a cube of volume 1728 in³ to melt?

A) 12 hrs

B) 14.4 hrs

C) 17.28 hrs

D) 28.8 hrs

22. As the number of people who contribute to purchasing a business increases, the price per person decreases. If the price per person for 10 people to buy the business is $600 more than the price per person for 20 people to buy the business, how much does the business cost?

A) $600

B) $1200

C) $6000

D) $12,000

23. The force of attraction or repulsion between electrically charged objects depends directly on their charges and inversely on the square of the distance between their centers. The charge on an electron is 1.60×10^{-19} coulombs; the charge of the nucleus of a lithium atom is three times that, while the nucleus of a cesium atom is 55 times the charge of an electron. Given that the lithium atom's outermost electron is 167 pm (1.67×10^{-10} meters) away from the nucleus, and the electrical force on it is 2.48×10^{-8} newtons, what is the force on a cesium atom's outermost electron, at 298 pm from the cesium nucleus? (We are ignoring the effects of other electrons in the same atom.)

A) 1.08×10^{-42} newtons

B) 4.26×10^{-17} newtons

C) 1.43×10^{-7} newtons

D) 2.55×10^{-7} newtons

24. The cost per person of sharing a limousine varies inversely as the number of people and directly as the number of hours the limo is rented. The cost of sharing the limousine with 10 people for 2 hours is $40 per person. If five additional people split the cost of the limo and the party rents the limo for 4 additional hours, how much more money will each person need to contribute?

25. The variable a varies inversely with the square of b and directly with c. If $a = 12$ when $b = 3$ and $c = 2$, what is the value of a when $c = 0.5$ and $b = 6$?

BLUE MATH LESSON 13B: DIRECT AND INVERSE VARIATION
Race to the Finish

Directions: Answer each question below.

HOMEWORK SET (CALCULATOR)

1. In an electric circuit, voltage varies jointly as the current and the resistance. What is the relationship between current and resistance?
   A) They are directly proportional to each other.
   B) They are inversely proportional to each other.
   C) They have no consistent relationship.
   D) It cannot be determined from the information provided.

2. The frequency of light is inversely proportional to its wavelength. The blue light with a frequency of 1.03×10^{15} Hz from problem 18 earlier has a wavelength of 292 nm (2.92×10^{-7} m); what is the wavelength of the 9.87×10^7 Hz radio wave?
   A) 2.80×10^{-14} m
   B) 3.05 m
   C) 3.57×10^{13} m
   D) 2.97×10^{16} m

3. The time it takes to travel a distance varies inversely as the speed traveled. If it takes 3 hours travelling at 45 mph to reach a destination. How much longer will it take to travel the same distance if it is traveled at ⅔ the speed?
   A) 30 minutes
   B) 45 minutes
   C) 90 minutes
   D) 135 minutes

4. The amount of simple interest on an investment varies directly with the amount invested, interest rate, and the number of years. If an investment of $1000 yields $35 simple interest in 2 years, how much should be invested to get $105 simple interest in 5 years?
   A) 210
   B) 1200
   C) 2200
   D) 4000

5. The amount of time it takes a piece of fruit to completely decompose varies directly with its mass. If it takes 8 days for an 8 oz. banana to decompose, how long will it take a watermelon that weighs 4 lbs. to decompose?
   A) 21 days
   B) 51.3 days
   C) 64 days
   D) 102.4 days

6. The length of time between seeing lightning and hearing thunder varies directly as the distance from the storm. After Samuel saw lightning and heard thunder 15 seconds later, he knew the storm was approximately 5 km away. If Jeff was 2 km closer to the storm than Samuel, after seeing lightning, how much time should pass before Jeff hears thunder?
   A) 1 second
   B) 5 seconds
   C) 9 seconds
   D) 13 seconds

7. If y varies directly as $\sqrt{x}$, and $y = 5$ when $x = 900$, what is y when $x = 400$?

   A) $2\frac{2}{9}$

   B) $3\frac{1}{3}$

   C) 5

   D) 6

8. The intensity of sound varies inversely as the square of the distance from the source of the sound. Increasing your distance from the speakers at a concert by 50% will have what effect on the sound reaching your ears?

   A) The new intensity will be $\frac{2}{3}$ of the original intensity.

   B) The new intensity will be $\frac{1}{2}$ of the original intensity.

   C) The new intensity will be $\frac{4}{9}$ of the original intensity.

   D) The new intensity will be $\frac{1}{4}$ of the original intensity.

9. Hooke's Law for a spring dictates that the distance a spring stretches varies directly with the force applied to the spring. If a force of 250 newtons stretches a spring 0.1 m, how much additional force will be needed to stretch the spring an additional 2 cm?

   A) 25 newtons

   B) 50 newtons

   C) 100 newtons

   D) 300 newtons

10. The distance an object falls varies directly with the square of the time it fall (ignoring air resistance). If a stone falls 144 m in 4 seconds, how much longer will it take for the stone to fall 900 m?

    A) 6 seconds

    B) 10 seconds

    C) 20 seconds

    D) 25 seconds

11. The weight of an object varies directly with its mass. On Jupiter, an object with a mass of 100 kg has a weight of 253 N. If a structure on Jupiter has a weight limit of 150 N, what is the maximum mass (to the nearest whole number) that can be applied to the structure before it breaks under the weight limit?

    A) 59 kg

    B) 60 kg

    C) 61 kg

    D) 62 kg

12. The intensity of sound varies inversely as the square of the distance from its source. At a rock concert, standing 1 meter from the stage yields a sound intensity of $\frac{1}{10}$ watt per square meter. Approximately how far from the stage should you stand for the intensity of the sound to be $\frac{1}{10^5}$ watt per square meter?

    A) 1 m

    B) 10 m

    C) 100 m

    D) 1000 m

13. According to Kepler's Third Law of Planetary Motion, the square of the time required for a planet to complete a revolution about its sun varies directly with the cube of the average distance of the planet and the sun. Given that the planet Gallifrey is approximately 9 times farther from its sun than a planet that takes a year to revolve about its sun, how many more years will it take to complete a revolution about its sun?
    A) 8 years
    B) 9 years
    C) 26 years
    D) 27 years

14. A capacitor is an electrical component that stores charge on parallel plates of metal; its ability to do so, called capacitance, is measured in units of farads and varies directly as its surface area and inversely as the distance between plates. If a circular capacitor with a radius of 1 cm and plates 2 mm apart has a capacitance of 5.28×10^{-12} farads, what will be the capacitance of a square capacitor 2 cm across, made of identical materials but with the plates spaced 3 mm apart?
    A) 4.48×10^{-12} farads
    B) 6.22×10^{-12} farads
    C) 1.01×10^{-11} farads
    D) 1.41×10^{-11} farads

15. The volume of a cylinder varies directly with its radius squared and its height. If the volume of a cylinder with a height of 2 feet and a radius of 6 feet is 72π cubic feet. What is the radius of the cylinder with a volume 1960π cubic feet and height 10?
    A) 14 feet
    B) 35 feet
    C) 55 feet
    D) 98 feet

16. Jackie's earnings at her summer job vary directly with the number of hours she works. If she makes $111 when she works 12 hours in one week, by what percent will her weekly earnings increase if she works 16 hours?
    A) 25
    B) 33
    C) 37
    D) 148

17. Working at the same rate, it takes a team of 10 painters 3 hours to paint 15,000 square feet. If the team wants to paint an additional 10,000 square feet in 2 hours, how many more painters will need to be hired?

18. The sum of both bases of a trapezoid is inversely related to its height. If a trapezoid's bases measure 6 cm and 8 cm, and its height measures 12 cm, what must be the sum of the trapezoid's bases if its height is tripled?

19. The length of a guitar string varies inversely with the frequency of its vibrations. A guitar's G-string produces a note of frequency of 196 Hz, while the A-string produces a note of frequency of 220 Hz. If the length of the A-string is 20 inches, what is the length of the G-string, to the nearest tenth of an inch?

20. If g varies directly as $\sqrt[3]{f}$, and $g = 8$ when $f = -8000$, what is g when $f = -1000$?

BLUE MATH LESSON 14A: ADVANCED FOILING AND FACTORING
Learning to Swim

Directions: Answer each question below.

PRACTICE SET 1 (NO CALCULATOR)

1. $(2x^2 + 4x + 5) \times (7x^3 - 9x^2 + 3x + 10)$

$$\frac{2x^2+14x+24}{2} \times \frac{x+z}{x+4}$$

2. Write a simplified equivalent to the expression above.

$$6x^3 + x^2 - 2x$$

3. Completely factor the expression above.

4. Write a factored expression equivalent to $x^4 + 7x^2 + 10$.

$$63x^4 + 42x^3 + 7x^2$$

5. Completely factor the expression above.

BLUE MATH LESSON 14A: ADVANCED FOILING AND FACTORING
Diving into the Deep End

Directions: Answer each question below.

PRACTICE SET 2 (NO CALCULATOR)

6. Which of the following expressions is equivalent to $(x + y)(x + 3)$?
   A) $x^2 + 3x + xy + 3y$
   B) $x^2 + 4xy + 3y$
   C) $x^2 + xy + 4y$
   D) $x^2 + 4xy + y^2$

7. Which of the following expressions is equivalent to $(a - b)(b + 2a)$?
   A) $a^2 + 3ab - b^2$
   B) $2a^2 + 3ab - b^2$
   C) $2a^2 - ab - b^2$
   D) $2a^2 - b^2$

8. If $f(x) = x^2 + 3x$ and $g(x) = x - 1$, what is $f(g(x)) - g(x)$?
   A) $x^2 - 1$
   B) $x^2 - 2x + 1$
   C) $x^2 + 5x + 2$
   D) $x^3 + x^2 - 1$

9. Which of the following expressions is equivalent to $(4m - 3n)^2$?
   A) $16m^2 - 9n^2$
   B) $16m^2 - 12mn + 9n^2$
   C) $16m^2 - 24mn - 9n^2$
   D) $16m^2 - 24mn + 9n^2$

10. Which of the following expressions is equivalent to $(x^2 - 2y)(x^2 + 2y)$?
    A) $x^4 - 8x^2y + 4y^2$
    B) $x^4 + 4y^2$
    C) $x^4 - 4y^2$
    D) $x^4 - 2y^2$

11. Which of the following expressions is equivalent to $2j^3 - 20j^2 + 50j$?
    A) $2j(j - 5)^2$
    B) $(2j^2 - 10)(j - 5)$
    C) $(2j - 5)^2$
    D) $2(j - 5)^2$

12. Which of the following expressions is equivalent to $64x^2 + 144xy + 81y^2$?
    A) $(8x + 9y)^2$
    B) $(8x + 12)(9y + 12)$
    C) $(8x + 9y)(8x - 9y)$
    D) $(4x + 3y)(16x + 27y)$

13. Which of the following expressions is equivalent to $(3xy - y^2)^2$?
    A) $9x^2y^2 - y^4$
    B) $9xy - y^4$
    C) $9x^2y^2 - 3xy^3 - y^4$
    D) $9x^2y^2 - 6xy^3 + y^4$

C2 education
be smarter

$$\frac{x^3-2x^2y-2y^2+xy}{2x^3+x^2y+y^2+2xy} \times \frac{2x+y}{x-2y}$$

14. The expression above is equivalent to what?

15. If $(x + y)^2 = 200$, and $xy = 15$, what is the value of $x^2 + y^2$?

PRACTICE SET 3 (NO CALCULATOR)

16. Which of the following expressions is equivalent to $x^4 + 14x^2y + 49y^2$?
    A) $(x + 7y)^2$
    B) $(x^2 + 7y)^2$
    C) $(x + 7y)^4$
    D) $(2x + 7y)^2$

17. Which of the following expressions is equivalent to $(x + 3 - y)(x + 3 + y)$?
    A) $x^2 + 6x + 9 - y^2$
    B) $x^2 + y^2 + 6y + 9$
    C) $x^2 + 2xy + y^2 - 9$
    D) $x^2 - y^2 + 9$

18. Which of the following expressions is equivalent to $(2x - 7)(5x - 3)(x - 4)$?
    A) $10x^3 - 84x^2 + 164x - 84$
    B) $10x^3 - 84x^2 - 164x - 84$
    C) $10x^3 - 81x^2 + 185x - 84$
    D) $10x^3 - 81x^2 + 160x - 81$

19. Which of the following expressions is equivalent to $m^2n^2 - 4m^2 - 9n^2 + 36$?
    A) $(m - 2)(m + 2)(n - 3)(n + 3)$
    B) $(m - 3)(m + 3)(n - 2)(n + 2)$
    C) $(m - 3)(m + 2)(n - 3)(n + 2)$
    D) $(m - 3)(m - 2)(n + 3)(n + 2)$

20. Which of the following expressions is equivalent to $(x - 4)(x + 1) + 3x$?
    A) $(x - 2)(x + 2)$
    B) $(x - 1)^2$
    C) $(x - 2)^2$
    D) $(x - 6)(x + 4)$

21. Which of the following expressions is equivalent to $3x^2 - x - 4$?
    A) $(3x + 2)(x - 2)$
    B) $(3x - 2)(x + 2)$
    C) $(x + 1)(3x - 4)$
    D) $(x - 1)(3x + 4)$

22. Which of the following expressions is equivalent to $16a^2 - 9b^2$?
    A) $(16a - 9b)^2$
    B) $(4a - 3b)^2$
    C) $(16a - 9b)(16a + 9b)$
    D) $(4a - 3b)(4a + 3b)$

23. Which of the following expressions is equivalent to $(a + 3)(b - 4)$?
    A) $ab - a - 12$
    B) $ab - 4a + 3b - 12$
    C) $ab - b - 12$
    D) $ab - 4a + 3b - 1$

24. $(35)^2 + 2(35)(25) + (25)^2 =$

25. What is a positive zero of the function $4x^2 = 15 - 4x$?

BLUE MATH LESSON 14A: ADVANCED FOILING AND FACTORING
Race to the Finish

Directions: Answer each question below.

HOMEWORK SET (NO CALCULATOR)

1. Which of the following expressions is equivalent to $4p^2 - 16p - 180$?

    A) $(2p + 9)(2p - 5)$

    B) $(4p - 15)(p + 12)$

    C) $(4p - 15)(p + 3)$

    D) $4(p - 9)(p + 5)$

2. Which of the following expressions is equivalent to $3(a - 1)(a - 2)$?

    A) $9a^2 - 9a + 2$

    B) $9a^2 - 27a + 18$

    C) $3a^2 - 3a + 2$

    D) $3a^2 - 9a + 6$

3. Which of the following expressions is equivalent to $(3x - 2)(2x - 3)$?

    A) $6x^2 - 13x + 6$

    B) $6x^2 - 13x - 6$

    C) $6x^2 - 5x + 6$

    D) $6x^2 - 5x - 6$

4. Which of the following expressions is equivalent to $2x^2 + x - 15$?

    A) $(2x + 3)(x - 5)$

    B) $(2x + 5)(x - 3)$

    C) $(2x - 5)(x + 3)$

    D) $(2x - 3)(x + 5)$

5. Which of the following expressions is equivalent to $(x + y)(a + 2b)$?

    A) $ax + 2bx + xy + 2by$

    B) $2ax + ay + 2by$

    C) $ax + ay + 2bx + 2by$

    D) $xy + ay + 2bx + 2ab$

6. Which of the following expressions is equivalent to $(p - 3)(p + 4)$?

    A) $-(p + 3)(p - 4)$

    B) $(p + 3)(p - 4) + 2p$

    C) $-(p - 3)(p - 4)$

    D) $(3 - p)(4 - p)$

7. Which of the following expressions is equivalent to $m(m + 1) - 20$?

    A) $(m - 4)(m + 5)$

    B) $(m - 4)(m - 5)$

    C) $(m - 20)(m - 19)$

    D) $m(m - 19)$

8. Which of the following expressions is equivalent to $(x - 3)(x + 2) - 6$?

    A) $(x - 4)(x + 3)$

    B) $(x - 3)(x - 4)$

    C) $x(x - 1)$

    D) $(x - 9)(x - 4)$

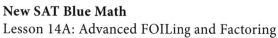
9. Which of the following expressions is equivalent to $(x - 4)(x + 6) + 9$?
   A) $(x + 3)(x - 5)$
   B) $(x - 5)^2$
   C) $(x + 5)(x - 3)$
   D) $(x + 5)(x + 3)$

$$\frac{x^2+3x-18}{x+2} \times \frac{x^2-4}{x-3}$$

10. The expression above is equivalent to which of the following expressions for all values of $x \neq -2, 3$?
    A) $x^2 + 4x - 12$
    B) $x^3 - 18x + 54$
    C) $x^3 + 2x^2 + 4x + 8$
    D) $x^4 + 3x - 72$

11. If $f(x) = x^2 - 3$, and $g(x) = 2x + 1$, what is $f(g(x)) + g(f(x))$?
    A) $2x - 5$
    B) $4x^2 + 4x$
    C) $6x^2 + 4x - 7$
    D) $8x^2 + 4x + 8$

12. Which of the following expressions is equivalent to $(a + 12)^2 - 48a$?
    A) $(a - 12)(a + 12)$
    B) $(a - 12)^2$
    C) $(a - 36)^2$
    D) $a^2 - 48a + 144$

13. Which of the following expressions has zeroes at $x = \frac{2}{3}, x = -\frac{5}{4}$ and $x = \frac{1}{2}$?
    A) $24x^3 - 2x^2 - 27x + 10$
    B) $24x^3 + 2x^2 + 27x + 10$
    C) $24x^3 + 2x^2 - 27x - 10$
    D) $24x^3 + 2x^2 - 27x + 10$

14. Which of the following expressions is equivalent to $(p + 5)(p + 7) + 1$?
    A) $(p + 6)^2$
    B) $(p + 6)(p + 8)$
    C) $(p + 6)(p - 6)$
    D) $(p + 9)(p + 4)$

15. Which of the following expressions is equivalent to $a^4 - 22a^2 + 121$?
    A) $(a - 11)^4$
    B) $(a^2 - 11)^2$
    C) $(a - 11)^2(a + 11)^2$
    D) $a^4 - (a + 11)^2$

16. Which of the following expressions is equivalent to $16x^4 - 81y^4$?
    A) $(2x - 3y)^4$
    B) $(4x^2 + 9y^2)(2x - 3y)(2x + 3y)$
    C) $(4x^2 + 9y^2)^2$
    D) $(2x - 3y)^2(2x + 3y)^2$

17. $(22)^2 + 2(22)(18) + (18)^2 =$

18. If $(a - b)^2 = 150$, and $ab = 15$, then what is the value of $a^2 + b^2$?

19. If $21x^2 - 7x = 14$ and $x > 0$, then what is a possible value of x?

20. What is a positive zero of the equation $12x^2 - 21 = 19x$?

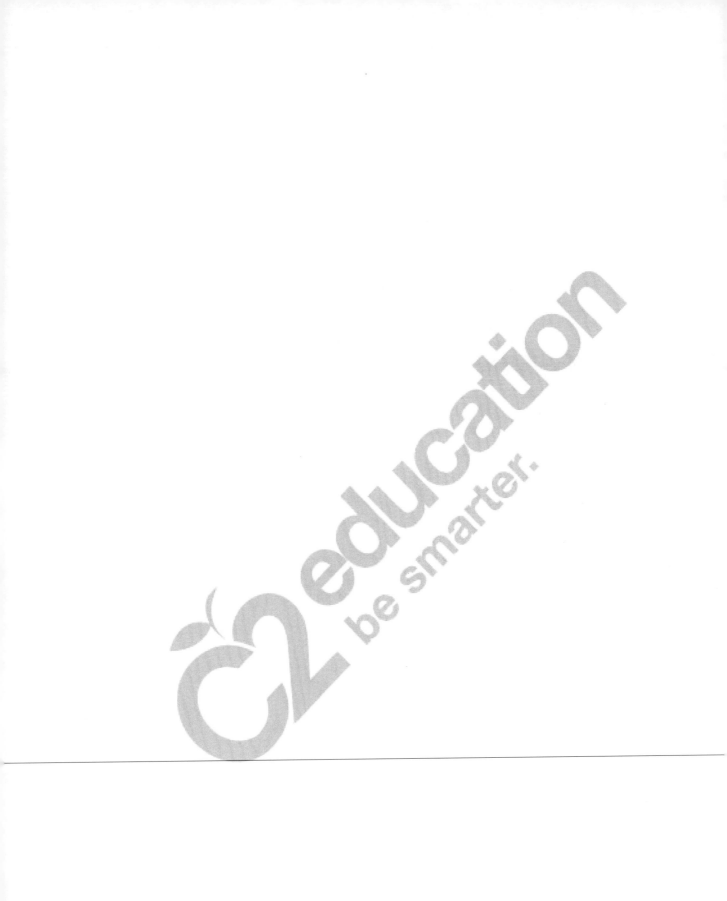

BLUE MATH LESSON 14B: SOLVING QUADRATICS
Learning to Swim

Directions: Answer each question below.

PRACTICE SET 1 (NO CALCULATOR)

1. What are the solutions of the equation $x(2x - 8) = 3(x - 5)$?

2. What are the zeroes of the equation $55x^2 + 64x = 63$?

3. If $5x^2 + 32x = -12$, then x is equivalent to which two values?

4. What values of x will satisfy the equation $3^{x^2+4x} = \frac{1}{81}$?

5. If $18x^2 - 24x = -8$, then x is equivalent to what value?

BLUE MATH LESSON 14B: SOLVING QUADRATICS
Diving into the Deep End

Directions: Answer each question below.

PRACTICE SET 2 (NO CALCULATOR)

6. If $(x + 2)(x + 1) = -1 - x$, what is the least possible value of x?
   A) −3
   B) −2
   C) −1
   D) 0

7. If $m^2 + 3m = 3m - 4m^2 + 5$, what is the difference between the largest and smallest value of m?
   A) −1
   B) 0
   C) 1
   D) 2

8. Which equation has the solutions $\frac{\pi}{2}$ and -2π?
   A) $x^2 + 3\pi x = 0$
   B) $x^2 - 3\pi x - 2\pi^2 = 0$
   C) $2x^2 + 3\pi x - 2\pi^2 = 0$
   D) $2x^2 + 3\pi x + 2\pi^2 = 0$

9. If $x^2 - 81 = 0$ and $2y^2 + 6y - 8 = 0$ what is the greatest product of xy?
   A) −4
   B) 9
   C) 27
   D) 36

10. If $x \neq 0$, what is the greatest solution of x for $\frac{x+7}{2} = -\frac{3}{x}$?
    A) −6
    B) −1
    C) 1
    D) 3

11. If $2x^2 + 4 = 9x$, what is the product of all the solutions for x?
    A) $\frac{3}{2}$
    B) 2
    C) $\frac{9}{2}$
    D) 8

12. The solutions to $x^2 - 4x = 6x - 24$ are distinct and real. Besides the number 1, what factor do both solutions share?
    A) 5
    B) 3
    C) 2
    D) 0

13. What is the sum of the solutions to
$(5x - 7)^2 = 13$?

A) $\dfrac{14}{5}$

B) $\dfrac{\sqrt{13}}{5}$

C) $\dfrac{7+\sqrt{13}}{5}$

D) $\dfrac{28}{5}$

14. What value of a gives only one distinct solution to the equation $x(x - 5) = ax - 49$?

15. What is the only possible value of x that satisfies both equations $8x^2 - x = x + 1$ and $16x^2 - 6x = 1$?

PRACTICE SET 3 (NO CALCULATOR)

16. If $x + 1 - \dfrac{5}{x} = \dfrac{1}{x}$ and $x \neq 0$, what are the possible values of x?

A) −3 and 2

B) −3 and 5

C) 5 and 2

D) Only −3

17. Which of the following equations has the solutions $\sqrt{3}$ and $\sqrt{12}$?

A) $x^2 + 3x + 6 = 0$

B) $x^2 - \sqrt{12}x - 6 = 0$

C) $x^2 - 3\sqrt{3}x + 6 = 0$

D) $x^2 + 9x - 6 = 0$

18. If $3x^2 - 4x - 8 = 0$, what is the sum of all the solutions for x?

A) −1.10

B) −1.33

C) 1.33

D) 3.53

19. What are the solutions to $x^2 + 8x + 20 = 0$?
    A) $-8 + 2i$ and $-8 - 2i$
    B) $-4 + 2i$ and $-4 - 2i$
    C) $4 + 4i$ and $4 - 4i$
    D) $8 + 2i$ and $8 - 2i$

20. If $2x^2 - 8x + 80 = 2(x + 10)$, which integer is half the product of the solutions for x?
    A) 11
    B) 15
    C) 22
    D) 30

21. For which value of c will there be only one solution of $x^2 + 10x = 5(c + 4x)$?
    A) -25
    B) -5
    C) 5
    D) 25

22. Given $x^2 - 6x - 90 = 1$ and $-y^2 - y + 20 = 0$, what is the greatest possible value for $x + y$?
    A) 17
    B) 18
    C) 19
    D) 20

23. Which of the following is one of the solutions to the equation $-2x^2 + 2x + 3 = 0$?
    A) $-\frac{1}{2} + \frac{\sqrt{7}}{2}$
    B) $\frac{1}{2} - \sqrt{14}$
    C) $-1 + \sqrt{28}$
    D) $\frac{1}{2} + \frac{\sqrt{7}}{2}$

24. If $12x^2 + 12x - 128 = 16$, what is the positive difference between the possible values for x?

25. If $-5x^2 + 8x = 5$, what is the sum of the possible values for x?

BLUE MATH LESSON 14B: SOLVING QUADRATICS
Race to the Finish

Directions: Answer each question below.

HOMEWORK SET (NO CALCULATOR)

1. If $8x^2 - 2x - 21 = 0$, what is the product of the two possible values for x?
   A) −2.625
   B) −1.5
   C) 1.75
   D) 2.625

2. If $16x^2 - 8x = -1$, then which of the following is true?
   A) There is only one solution, and that solution is $x = -\frac{1}{8}$.
   B) There are two solutions, and those solutions are $\frac{1 \pm 1\sqrt{2}}{4}$.
   C) There is only one solution, and that solution is $x = \frac{1}{4}$.
   D) There are no solutions to the equation.

3. If $2x^2 + 5x - 12 = 0$, which of the following is a possible value for x?
   A) −4
   B) $-\frac{3}{2}$
   C) $\frac{2}{3}$
   D) There are no solutions to the equation.

4. If $x^2 - 4x + 5 = 0$, what is the product of the possible values for x?
   A) −5
   B) −1
   C) 1
   D) 5

5. If $x > 0$ and $x^2 - 16 = 9$, what is a possible value for x?
   A) −4
   B) $\sqrt{7}$
   C) 4
   D) 5

6. If $2x^2 + 12x - 80 = 0$, what is the product of the solutions for x?
   A) −40
   B) −10
   C) 4
   D) 8

7. If $3x^2 + 4x - 4 = 0$, what is a possible value for x?

A) -4

B) $\frac{1}{3}$

C) $\frac{2}{3}$

D) 4

8. What are the roots for the function $f(x) = -3x^2 + 10x + 3$?

A) $\frac{10 \pm \sqrt{17}}{3}$

B) $\frac{5 \pm \sqrt{34}}{3}$

C) $\frac{1}{3}$ and 3

D) The function has no real roots.

9. If $x^2 + x - 2 = -x + 1$, what is the product of the possible values for x?

A) -3

B) -2

C) 1

D) 3

10. If $x^2 + 2x - 15 = 0$ and $x > 0$, what is a possible value for x?

A) -5

B) -3

C) 3

D) 5

11. If $2x^3 - x^2 - 36x + 4 = 4$, what is the sum of the possible values for x?

A) $-\frac{1}{2}$

B) $\frac{1}{2}$

C) $\frac{15}{2}$

D) The equation has no real solutions.

12. If $6x^2 - 19x + 18 = 8$, what is the product of the possible values for x?

A) $-\frac{10}{9}$

B) $-\frac{3}{5}$

C) $\frac{5}{3}$

D) $\frac{5}{2}$

13. If $-3x^2 + 27 = 0$, then what is the positive difference between the possible values for x?

A) -3

B) 0

C) 3

D) 6

14. If $\frac{7}{4}x^2 + 7 - 7x = 0$, what is the sum of the roots of x?

A) -4

B) -2

C) 1

D) 4

15. If $x^2 - 14x + 13 = 0$, what is one possible value for x?

    A) -1
    B) 2
    C) 13
    D) 14

16. When $x > 0$ and $9x^2 - 45x - 126 = 0$, what is the value of x?

    A) -2
    B) 7
    C) 9
    D) 63

17. If $2x^2 - 16x = -30$, what is the product of the possible values for x?

18. If $x^2 + x - 2 = 4$, what is one possible value of $3x^2$?

19. When $x > 0$ and $2x^2 - 7x = 15$, what is the value for $7x$?

20. If $20x^2 - 40x = -15$, what is a possible value of x?

Blue Math Lesson 15A: Solving Equations with Powers and Roots
Learning to Swim

Directions: Answer each question below.

Practice Set 1 (No Calculator)

1. Gold has a density of 19.3 grams per cubic centimeter. What is the side length of a cube of gold which has a mass is 0.522 grams?

2. Given that $\sqrt{n^3 - 243} = 10$ and $2(nq + 4)^2 = 18$, q could equal

3. If $\sqrt[3]{x + 3} = \sqrt{3}$, then x could equal

4. Given that $\left(\sqrt{x} + 6\right)^3 = 125$, x could equal

5. Given that $(d - 6)^5 - 2^5 = 211$, $d - 8 =$

BLUE MATH LESSON 15A: SOLVING EQUATIONS WITH POWERS AND ROOTS
Diving into the Deep End

Directions: Answer each question below.

PRACTICE SET 2 (NO CALCULATOR)

6. Which values of satisfy x the equation $x - 5 = |\sqrt{1 + x}|$?
    A) 3
    B) 8
    C) 3 and 8
    D) No real values of x

7. How many values of x satisfy the equation $\sqrt{x + 4} + \sqrt{x} = 1$?
    A) One
    B) Two
    C) All real values of x
    D) No real values of x

8. Which values of x satisfy the equation $\sqrt{2x - \sqrt{x^2 - 1}} = 1$?
    A) 0
    B) $\frac{4}{3}$
    C) 0 and $\frac{4}{3}$
    D) No real values of x

9. What value of x satisfies the equation $2^{2x} = 8^{x-1}$?
    A) 0
    B) 1
    C) 2
    D) 3

10. Solve for b: $\left(\sqrt[3]{b + 2} - 1\right)^5 = 243$
    A) 6
    B) 26
    C) 62
    D) 1218

11. The equation $3^x = k5^{x+2}$ has a solution of $x = 1$. What is the value of $5^6 \times k$?
    A) $\frac{3}{125}$
    B) 75
    C) 375
    D) 625

12. What is the solution to $\left(\sqrt{12}\right)^x = 144^{\frac{3}{2}}$?
    A) 3
    B) 6
    C) 9
    D) 12

13. What is the solution to $4x = \sqrt{2x}$?
    A) 0
    B) $\frac{1}{2}$
    C) $\frac{1}{8}$
    D) Both 0 and $\frac{1}{8}$

14. What is the solution to $\sqrt{x-3} = \sqrt{x+2} - 1$?

16. Which value of x satisfy the equation
    $x + 7 = |\sqrt{1-2x}|$?
    A) −4
    B) −12
    C) Both −4 and −12
    D) No solutions exist

15. Let $f(x) = \sqrt{x+1}$ and $g(x) = x + 1$. Given that $f(z) = g(z)$ and $z > -\frac{1}{2}$, what is the value of $g(z)\big(f(z)\big) + z$?

17. What is the solution to $\sqrt{9x+1} - x = 1$?
    A) 0
    B) 1
    C) 7
    D) 0 and 7

18. What value of x satisfies the equation
    $\sqrt[3]{5x-1} = 4$?
    A) 3.4
    B) 7
    C) 11
    D) 13

19. Which value of x satisfies the equation
    $x - \sqrt{-5x+6} = 0$?

    A) −5
    B) −1
    C) 1
    D) 5

20. The equation $\sqrt{4x^2 - 2x - 1} = 1$ is valid for which values of x?

    A) $-\frac{1}{2}$ only

    B) 1 only

    C) Both $-\frac{1}{2}$ and 1

    D) None of these

21. Solve for x: $2\sqrt{\sqrt{x} + 9} = 7$

    A) $\frac{169}{16}$

    B) $\frac{1105}{16}$

    C) $\frac{961}{4}$

    D) $\frac{961}{2}$

22. What values of x satisfy the equation $4^{x^2} = 4^{3x+4}$?

    A) -1 only

    B) 4 only

    C) Both -1 and 4

    D) None of these

23. Find n given that $4\sqrt[3]{2 - n} + 8 = 2^5$.

    A) -1024

    B) -256

    C) -214

    D) 1

24. Given that $a \neq 0$ and $x > 0$, what is a possible value of x in the equation $a^{-x^2-5x} = \frac{1}{a^{24}}$?

25. If $x^3 + 2x^2 - 12x - 41 = (x - 7)(2x + 2)$, then x could equal

BLUE MATH LESSON 15A: SOLVING EQUATIONS WITH POWERS AND ROOTS
Race to the Finish

Directions: Answer each question below.

HOMEWORK SET (NO CALCULATOR)

1. If $9r^3 + 2 = 10$, then r could equal
   A) $-\frac{2}{3}$ or $\frac{2}{3}$
   B) $\frac{2}{3}$
   C) $\frac{2\sqrt{2}}{3}$
   D) $\frac{2\sqrt[3]{3}}{3}$

2. If $x \neq 0$ and $x^{2+q} = 8x^q$, then x could equal
   A) $2\sqrt{2}$ or $-2\sqrt{2}$
   B) $2\sqrt{2}$ only
   C) 8
   D) It cannot be determined from the information provided.

3. If $\frac{3}{2}(n+5)^3 = -12$, then n could equal
   A) -3 or -7
   B) -7 only
   C) $-5 + \frac{2}{3}\sqrt[3]{-12}$
   D) No real values of n

4. Given that $\sqrt[3]{(3-z)^6} = 289$, z could equal
   A) -14 or 20
   B) 14 or -20
   C) -14 only
   D) No real values of z

5. If $(m^2 - 2)(m + 1) = \frac{m^3 - 2m^2 - 2m - 81}{m}$, m could equal
   A) 3 or -3
   B) 3 only
   C) -3 only
   D) No real values of m

6. If $2\left(3 + \sqrt{-2q}\right) = q + 6$, then q could equal
   A) -8 only
   B) 0 only
   C) 8 only
   D) 0 or -8

7. Given that $\sqrt{x^4 + 9} = 3\sqrt{10}$, x could equal
   A) $\pm\sqrt[4]{10}$
   B) -3
   C) $\sqrt{-3 + 3\sqrt{10}}$
   D) No real values of x

8. If $2\left(x + \frac{3}{2}\right)^2 = \frac{7}{2}$, then the solution set for x is
   A) $\frac{-3 + \sqrt{7}}{2}$ or $\frac{-3 - \sqrt{7}}{2}$
   B) $\frac{\sqrt{7} - 3}{2}$ only
   C) $\frac{\sqrt{7} - 6}{2}$ only
   D) $\frac{11}{2}$ only

9. A historian estimates the population of the United States using the function
$$p(y) = 3(2y)^3 + (8y)^2 + 2,500,000,$$
where y is the number of years elapsed since 1776. Using this function, approximately how many more people lived in the U.S. in 1976, compared to 1926?
A) 85 million
B) 110 million
C) 150 million
D) 195 million

10. If $3(2x + 3)^3 = -81$, then $x^3 =$
A) -27
B) -15
C) -3
D) 27

11. If $\sqrt[4]{a^2 - 4} = 2$, then a could equal
A) $-2\sqrt{5}$
B) $6 - 4\sqrt{2}$
C) 6
D) $6 + 4\sqrt{2}$

12. Given that $4x^2 + y^3 - 20 = 0$ and $22 + 2x^2 = \frac{3}{2}y^3$, y is equal to
A) $2\sqrt[3]{2}$
B) 4
C) $\frac{16}{3}$
D) 16

13. Given that $\sqrt{5z} = -3z$ and $3z + 8w = 2$, w is equal to
A) $\frac{1}{24}$
B) $\frac{1}{4}$
C) $\frac{5}{9}$
D) No real values of w exist

Questions 14 through 16 use the following information.

The number of stars in a galaxy, g, is estimated with the function $g(r) = 3\left(\frac{r}{10}\right)^3$, where r is the radius of the galaxy in light years.

14. If the Milky Way galaxy has a radius of 50,000 light years, its estimated number of stars would be:
A) 75 million (75,000,000).
B) 125 billion (125,000,000,000).
C) 375 billion (375,000,000,000).
D) 375 trillion (375,000,000,000,000).

15. Approximately how many more stars are in a galaxy with a radius of 10,000 light years, compared to one with a radius of 9,000 light years?
A) 813 thousand (813,000)
B) 81.3 million (81,300,000)
C) 813 million (813,000,000)
D) 813 billion (813,000,000,000)

16. A "dwarf" galaxy is estimated to have only 192,000 stars. What is its radius?
A) 40 light years
B) 400 light years
C) 800 light years
D) 6400 light years

17. A hemispherical cereal bowl will hold up to 850 cm^3 of oatmeal. To the nearest tenth of a cm, how wide is it at the top?

18. The rate at which the surfaces of an object radiate heat energy, in watts per square meter, varies directly as the fourth power of the object's temperature in kelvin. Given that unprotected human skin at a temperature of 310 K emits 524 W/m^2, a cup of tea that emits at a rate of 1100 W/m^2 has what temperature, to the nearest kelvin?

19. A can of tomatoes has equal height and diameter. If its volume is $\frac{125\pi}{4}$ in^3, what is its height? (The volume of a cylinder is given by $\pi r^2 h$, where r is the radius and h is the height.)

20. Find q given that $3 - \sqrt{q} = \sqrt{q-3}$

BLUE MATH LESSON 15B: BASIC EXPONENTIAL FUNCTIONS
Learning to Swim

Directions: Answer each question below.

PRACTICE SET 1 (CALCULATOR)

1. If $x^3 = y^{12}$, what is x in terms of y?

Questions 2 and 3 use the following information:

Carbon 14 analysis is often used to date dead organisms. The ratio of carbon-14 to carbon-12 is the same in every living organism. When an organism dies, the carbon-12 remains constant, however, it stops taking in carbon-14. Since carbon-14 decays with a half-life of 5700 years, the percent of carbon-14 in a dead sample compared to a living sample is used to determine the age of the dead sample using the following formula:

$$N = e^{\left(\frac{-0.693t}{t_{1/2}}\right)}$$

N = The percent of carbon-14 (in decimal notation) of a dead sample compared to a living one
e = Euler's number (approx. equal to 2.71828)
t = number of years
$t_{1/2}$ = carbon-14 half-life

2. How old, to the nearest integer, is a fossil that has 23% carbon-14 when compared to a living sample?

3. Two fossils were found by a paleontologist. The first had 10% carbon-14 when compared to a living sample and the second had 8% carbon-14 when compared to a living sample. How much older, to the nearest integer, is the second fossil when compared to the first fossil?

4. A certain penny stock doubles every x months. If the stock started at $0.10 and is valued at $6.40 after 12 months, what is x?

5. If $0.04^x = 125^y$, then $\frac{x}{y} = ?$

BLUE MATH LESSON 15B: BASIC EXPONENTIAL FUNCTIONS
Diving into the Deep End

Directions: Answer each question below.

PRACTICE SET 2 (CALCULATOR)

6. What is y when $5^{y-5} = \left(\frac{1}{25}\right)^{y+1}$?
   A) -3
   B) -1
   C) 1
   D) 3

7. A historical biologist modeled the impact of rabbit populations after they were introduced into areas that had never had rabbits before. In Australia, the number of rabbits (r) at a time y years after introduction is given by $r(y) = 9^{y+3}$. In Fiji, the number of rabbits is given by $r(y) = 3^{3y+1}$. After how many years were the two populations equal in number?
   A) 3
   B) 5
   C) 6
   D) 8

8. Alaska's population grew rapidly during the oil boom from 1970 to 1990. If the state's population increased at a 3% annual rate during this span, and the state's population was 300,000 in 1970, what was its population in 1974 (rounded to the nearest thousand)?
   A) 309,000
   B) 328,000
   C) 336,000
   D) 338,000

9. During its early life, a pig's weight increases by 32% per week. If a pig weighs 6 pounds when it is 2 weeks old, how much will it weigh when it is 8 weeks old (rounded to the nearest pound)?
   A) 18 pounds
   B) 32 pounds
   C) 42 pounds
   D) 55 pounds

10. If $4^{18} = 2^{5z+1}$, what is z?
    A) 1.9
    B) 3.4
    C) 5.6
    D) 7.0

11. If $7^b = \left(\frac{1}{343}\right)^a$, what is a in terms of b?
    A) $-3b$
    B) $-\frac{b}{3}$
    C) $\frac{b}{3}$
    D) $3b$

12. The number of zebras in a wildlife preserve declines by 5% each year. If there are 2,808 zebras in the preserve today, how many were there 6 years ago?
    A) 3,629
    B) 3,820
    C) 4,011
    D) 4,388

13. What is x when $\left(\frac{4}{9}\right)^{x-3} = \left(\frac{3}{2}\right)^{x}$?
    A) −3
    B) −1
    C) 1
    D) 2

14. A glacier was 50 miles long 2 years ago, but it is only 40.5 miles long today. If the glacier decreases in length at a constant yearly rate, what will be its length (rounded to the nearest tenth of a mile) in 3 years?

15. An entomologist places n individuals from each of two species of fruit fly in an enclosed area. Each week, the number from Species A increases by 20%, and the number from Species B decreases by 20%. After 7 weeks, the number from Species A is approximately how many times as large as the number from Species B?

PRACTICE SET 3 (CALCULATOR)

16. The number of virus cells observed in a blood culture increases by 12% every 2 hours during an experiment. If b virus cells are observed at the start of the experiment, how many will be observed a day later?
    A) $b(1.06)^{12}$
    B) $b(1.06)^{24}$
    C) $b(1.12)^{12}$
    D) $b(1.12)^{24}$

17. The average weekly pollen count in Atlanta decreases by 18% each week from its peak in mid-April. How many weeks does it take for the average weekly pollen count to drop to below half of its peak value?
    A) 3 weeks
    B) 4 weeks
    C) 5 weeks
    D) 6 weeks

18. Since being introduced to the North American Great Lakes, the non-native zebra mussel has thrived uncontrollably and outcompeted many native species. If the zebra mussel population in Lake Michigan was 1,000 in 1980 and has since grown exponentially at a rate of 28% per year, approximately what was it in 2000?
    A) 6,600
    B) 25,600
    C) 139,380
    D) 877,325

19. Radioactive waste from a certain nuclear power plant is known to decay with a half-life of 13 years; that is, every 13 years, the amount of radioactive substance remaining decreases by 50%. A spent fuel rod from this plant was discovered in 2014 and tests revealed it to contain 22.3 grams of radioactive uranium. If it was disposed of in 1975, how many grams of radioactive uranium did it contain at that point?
    A) 133.8
    B) 178.4
    C) 11,089.6
    D) 48,993.1

20. The number of bacteria in a test colony doubles every 8 days. If the population starts at 2,000 bacteria, after how many days will it first exceed 1 million?
    A) 9
    B) 20
    C) 72
    D) 500

21. From 1995 to 2008, the economy of Ireland grew at a rapid pace. In 1995, the country's GDP (Gross Domestic Product, a standard measure of the size of a national economy) was the equivalent of $67 billion (in 2013 U.S. dollars) and in 2008 it was the equivalent of $186 billion. If Ireland's GDP grew at a constant percentage rate per year during this period, what was it in 2000, to the nearest billion dollars?
    A) $72 billion
    B) $89 billion
    C) $99 billion
    D) $113 billion

Questions 22 and 23 use the following formula for compound interest.

$$A = P\left(1 + \frac{r}{n}\right)^{nt}$$

A = the final amount
P = the principal (starting amount)
r = interest rate
n = number of times the interest is compounded each year
t = number of years

22. A savings bond pays a 5.4% interest rate, compounded quarterly (four times per year). If the principal amount is $2400, how much will the bond be worth in 10 years?
    A) $3696.00
    B) $4060.85
    C) $4103.57
    D) $19,671.42

23. Bill invests $600 in a savings account that pays 4% interest, compounded annually. Steve invests $400 in a mutual fund and it earns 6% interest, also compounded annually. After how many years will Steve first have more money than Bill?
    A) 14
    B) 21
    C) 22
    D) 26

Questions 24 and 25 use the following information.

The portion of sunlight that reaches a given depth (d, in meters) beneath the ocean's surface is equal to $T^{0.1d}$, where T is the transparency constant for that area of ocean. In one area with a T equal to 0.86, about $\frac{1}{20}$ of sunlight reaches an unknown depth.

24. What is the depth for the calculation described above? Round to the nearest ten meters.

25. In the same area described above, what portion of sunlight reaches a depth of 50 meters? Round to the nearest hundredth.

BLUE MATH LESSON 15B: BASIC EXPONENTIAL FUNCTIONS
Race to the Finish

Directions: Answer each question below.

HOMEWORK SET (CALCULATOR)

1. If the volume of a rising loaf of bread increases at a constant percentage rate per hour, and in six hours it increases from 400 cm³ to 1000 cm³, what will its volume be after one more hour?
   A) 1070 cm³
   B) 1100 cm³
   C) 1162 cm³
   D) 1165 cm³

2. A cancer biologist studying HeLa cells notices that the number of cells increases by 25% every two hours. If she begins with 5 cells and ends with 4039 cells, how many two-hour time intervals have passed, rounded to the nearest whole number?
   A) 30
   B) 60
   C) 300
   D) 600

3. If $(2^3)^4(8)^2 = 2^x$, then $x =$
   A) 16
   B) 18
   C) 26
   D) 49

4. A town with a population of 700 people doubles its population every six years. How many people will live in the town after thirty years?
   A) 22,400
   B) 44,800
   C) 1.3×10^8
   D) 7.5×10^{11}

Questions 5 through 8 use the following formula for compound interest.

$$A = P\left(1 + \frac{r}{n}\right)^{nt}$$

A = the final amount
P = the principal (starting amount)
r = interest rate
n = # of times interest is compounded per year
t = number of years

5. A high-risk municipal bond pays a 6% interest rate, compounded every 2 months. If $1000 is initially invested in this bond, how much is the bond worth after 3 years?
   A) $1196.15
   B) $1425.76
   C) $1608.44
   D) $1702.43

6. Li Shu calculates that if she does not pay off her credit card debt, which is compounded twice a year at a 10% interest rate, she will owe $11,524 in 4 years. How much does she owe now (to the nearest ten dollars)?
   A) $5560
   B) $6850
   C) $7800
   D) $8230

7. Mitchell and Hassan each invest $2000 in savings in a savings account that is compounded monthly. Hassan's account, however, earns 3.6% interest, compared to the 2.4% interest of Mitchell's account. What is the difference in the values of the accounts after 2 years?
   A) About $44
   B) About $47
   C) About $49
   D) About $51

8. If a certificate of deposit with an interest rate of 9% is compounded every 4 months, how many years will it take for the money invested in it to increase in value by at least 70%?
   A) 5 years
   B) 6 years
   C) 7 years
   D) 8 years

9. Dylan bought a new house for $275,000. Unfortunately, the house depreciates in value at a rate of 12% every three years. After twenty-one years, how much is Dylan's house worth?
   A) $18,770
   B) $112,386
   C) $607,937
   D) $2,971,058

10. Twenty-three ants invade a picnic. If the number of ants increases by 60% each minute, how long will it take, to the nearest minute, for the number of ants at the picnic to triple?
    A) 2
    B) 3
    C) 4
    D) 6

11. Willow and Xander both invest $750 in a savings account that offers 7% in interest. Willow's account is compounded annually, while Xander's is compounded quarterly. What is the difference between how much money is in their respective accounts after six years?
    A) $11.78
    B) $234.18
    C) $1125.27
    D) $2678.73

12. Nematodes are studied for their genetic simplicity. A colony of nematodes reproduces at a rate of 7.5% a day. After 60 hours, there are 800 nematodes in the colony. Approximately how many nematodes did the colony begin with?
    A) 436
    B) 668
    C) 876
    D) 965

13. A college student drinks four cups of coffee, which contains 400 mg of coffee. If caffeine leaves the bloodstream at a rate of 31% every half hour, how much caffeine will be in the student's bloodstream after six hours?
    A) 0.0003
    B) 0.35
    C) 4.66
    D) 43

14. The Ebola virus can replicate inside a host at a rate of 2% per hour. Once the virus has created 50,000 copies of itself, the host develops symptoms. If a host is infected with 32 virons, how many days, to the nearest day, will it take to develop symptoms?

A) 15
B) 33
C) 40
D) 371

15. Solve for x: $5^{x-3} \cdot 5^{4-2x} = \frac{1}{25}$

A) 1
B) 3
C) 4
D) 5

16. Solve for r: $\left(\frac{4r^2}{r^3}\right)\left(\frac{1}{r}\right)^2 + \left(\frac{2}{r}\right)^3 = \frac{4}{9}$

A) $\frac{5}{9}$
B) $\frac{9}{5}$
C) 3
D) 4

17. In order to model the descent of a spaceship, scientists estimate that after entering the atmosphere the speed of the spaceship doubles every 10 seconds for the first 30 seconds, and then triples every 10 seconds thereafter. If the speed upon entering the atmosphere was 100 miles per hour, what was the speed after 50 seconds?

18. If $3^r = k \cdot 9^r$ and $0.5^r = 16$, then $k = ?$

19. If $4^x = 64$, then $3^{2x} =$

20. In 2001, there were 243 internet subscribers in Montana. As of 2014, there were 10,874 subscribers. Assuming the rate of subscribers joining was constant, by what percentage did customers subscribe to the internet each year?

BLUE MATH LESSON 16A: OPERATIONS ON RATIONAL FUNCTIONS
Learning to Swim

Directions: Answer each question below.

PRACTICE SET 1 (NO CALCULATOR)

1. What is the domain of the rational function $f(x) = \dfrac{x-6}{x^2-1} - \dfrac{x+1}{x-6}$?

2. What are all of the real solutions to the equation $\dfrac{1}{x-3} - \dfrac{5}{x^2-x-6} = 0$?

3. Solve for M in terms of x: $\dfrac{x^2}{x^2+10x+25} - \dfrac{50}{2x^2+20x+50} = \dfrac{M}{x+5}$.

4. Solve for P: $\dfrac{3}{t+2} + \dfrac{4}{t-5} + \dfrac{5}{t} = \dfrac{P}{t^3-3t^2-10t}$.

5. If $\left(\dfrac{y}{3}\right)\left(\dfrac{y+1}{4}\right)\left(\dfrac{24}{-y}\right) = 10$, then $y =$

BLUE MATH LESSON 16A: OPERATIONS ON RATIONAL FUNCTIONS
Diving into the Deep End

Directions: Answer each question below.

PRACTICE SET 2 (NO CALCULATOR)

6. Simplify $\dfrac{x^3-4x}{8x^2-48x+64}$.

    A) $\dfrac{x^2+2x}{8x-32}$

    B) $\dfrac{x^2-2x}{8x-32}$

    C) $\dfrac{x^2-2x}{8x+32}$

    D) $\dfrac{x+2}{8x+32}$

7. What is the product of $\dfrac{3x+9}{x+7}$ and $\dfrac{3x+21}{x+3}$?

    A) 9

    B) $\dfrac{9}{x-7}$

    C) $\dfrac{9x-27}{x+3}$

    D) $\dfrac{9x+63}{x-7}$

8. A regular tabletop has an area of 720 square inches. If the table's length is $\dfrac{v^2+6v-16}{2v-14}$ inches and its width is $\dfrac{3v^2+15v-252}{v-2}$ inches, what is one possible value of v?

    A) 6

    B) 9

    C) 12

    D) 15

9. $\dfrac{5x+10}{x^2-8x+15} \div \dfrac{x^2-3x-10}{x^2+3x-18} =$

    A) $5x+30$

    B) $\dfrac{5}{x+6}$

    C) $\dfrac{x+6}{x^2-10x+25}$

    D) $\dfrac{5x+30}{x^2-10x+25}$

10. If $\dfrac{a^2+5a+4}{a^2+4a+3} \div \dfrac{a^2+2a-8}{2a+6} = -2$, what are all the possible values of a?

    A) 3 and 1

    B) −1 and −3

    C) −3 only

    D) 1 only

11. The equation $\dfrac{x^2+6x+9}{x^2-64} \times \dfrac{x^2+10x+16}{x^2+5x+6} = \dfrac{x+3}{x-8}$ is true for all real values of x EXCEPT:

    A) −8, −3, −2, and 8

    B) −8, 2, 3, and 8

    C) −3, 2, and 8

    D) −8 and 8

12. What is the sum of $\dfrac{x+2}{x-3}$ and $\dfrac{4}{x-2}$?

    A) $\dfrac{4x-12}{x^2-5x+6}$

    B) $\dfrac{4x+8}{x^2-5x+6}$

    C) $\dfrac{x^2-4x+8}{x^2-5x+6}$

    D) $\dfrac{x^2+4x-16}{x^2-5x+6}$

13. If the expression $\frac{4x^2}{2x-1}$ is written in the equivalent form $\frac{1}{2x-1} + A$, what is A in terms of x?

   A) $2x$
   B) $2x - 1$
   C) $2x + 1$
   D) $4x^2 - 1$

14. As part of a science fair project, a student counts the number of pine cones beneath two large trees in a nearby park. There are $p^2 + 7p + 6$ pine cones beneath the 1st tree, an area of $p - 3$ square meters. There are $p^2 + 3p + 2$ pine cones beneath the 2nd tree, an area of $p^2 - p + 6$ square meters. The student finds that the number of pine cones per square meter under the 1st tree is 10 times that of the 2nd tree. What is p?

15. A zookeeper measures the speed of two sloths. The sloth named Janine travels $3z$ feet in $z - 2$ minutes. Another sloth named Egon travels 12 feet in $z - 3$ minutes. The zookeeper determines that Egon travels an average speed of 1 foot per minute faster than Janine travels. What is a possible value of z?

PRACTICE SET 3 (NO CALCULATOR)

16. $\frac{y-2}{y+1} - \frac{y-1}{y-2} =$

   A) $\frac{2y^2-4y+3}{y^2-y-2}$
   B) $\frac{-4y+5}{y^2-y-2}$
   C) $\frac{4y+3}{y^2-y-2}$
   D) $\frac{2y-4}{y^2-y-2}$

17. Simplify $\frac{2x+16}{x^2+7x-8}$.

   A) $\frac{2}{x+1}$
   B) $\frac{2}{x-1}$
   C) $\frac{-2}{x+1}$
   D) $\frac{-2}{x-1}$

18. What is the simplified form of $\frac{x+5}{x-2} \times \frac{3}{x^2+7x+10} \times \frac{x^2-4}{x-5}$?

   A) $\frac{1}{x-5}$
   B) $\frac{3}{x-5}$
   C) $\frac{3x-6}{x^2-3x-10}$
   D) $\frac{3x+6}{x-2}$

19. If $\frac{4y+28}{y^2-4y+4} \times \frac{y^2-5y+6}{y^2+4y-21} = -1$, what is one possible value of y?

A) -7

B) -2

C) 2

D) 3

20. What is $\frac{x-3}{x^2+8x+12}$ divided by $\frac{x^2-x-6}{2x+12}$?

A) $\frac{1}{2x^2+8x+8}$

B) $\frac{2}{x^2+4x+4}$

C) $\frac{2x^2-12x-18}{x^2+12x+36}$

D) $\frac{x^2-6x-9}{2x^2+24x+72}$

21. The domain of the rational function $f(x)$ is all real values of x except 4 and -3. Which of the following could be $f(x)$?

A) $f(x) = \frac{1}{x^2-x-12}$

B) $f(x) = \frac{1}{x^2+x-12}$

C) $f(x) = \frac{1}{x^2-7x+12}$

D) $f(x) = \frac{1}{x^2+7x+12}$

22. $\frac{x}{3x-2} + \frac{x+1}{x+6} =$

A) $\frac{4x^2+7x-2}{3x^2+16x-12}$

B) $\frac{3x^2+7x-2}{3x^2+16x-12}$

C) $\frac{4x^2+7x-2}{3x^2-12}$

D) $\frac{3x^2+7x-2}{3x^2-12}$

23. What is $\frac{2}{x+3}$ subtracted from $\frac{x-1}{x+4}$?

A) $\frac{x+1}{x+3}$

B) $\frac{x^2-11}{x^2+7x+12}$

C) $\frac{x^2+5}{x^2+7x+12}$

D) $\frac{x^2+4x+5}{x^2+7x+12}$

24. A train, traveling at a constant speed, covers the $15x$ miles between two cities in $x + 1$ hours. During the trip, a man walks from the back of the train to the front, a distance of x miles, in $2x - 1$ hours. If the man's combined speed relative to the surrounding countryside is 8 miles per hour, what is a possible value of x?

25. If $\frac{3}{z+8} = \frac{z-3}{3z-4}$, what is a possible real, positive value of z?

BLUE MATH LESSON 16A: OPERATIONS ON RATIONAL FUNCTIONS
Race to the Finish

Directions: Answer each question below.

HOMEWORK SET (NO CALCULATOR)

1. Simplify $\dfrac{6x^2-14x-12}{6x^2-5x-6}$.

   A) $\dfrac{6x+4}{3x-2}$

   B) $\dfrac{x-6}{2x-3}$

   C) $\dfrac{x-3}{2x-3}$

   D) $\dfrac{2x-6}{2x-3}$

4. $\dfrac{x^2-2x-3}{x^2+6x+5} \div \dfrac{x^2-4x+3}{x^2-1} =$

   A) $\dfrac{x-1}{x+5}$

   B) $\dfrac{x+1}{x+5}$

   C) $\dfrac{x^2-1}{x+5}$

   D) $\dfrac{x^2+2x+1}{x+5}$

2. $\dfrac{2}{x^2-5x+4} \times \dfrac{x^2-7x+12}{4x^2-10x-6} =$

   A) $\dfrac{1}{2x^2-x-1}$

   B) $\dfrac{2}{2x^2-x-1}$

   C) $\dfrac{1}{2x^2-7x-4}$

   D) $\dfrac{1}{x^2-4x+3}$

5. What is the sum of $\dfrac{2x+1}{x-3}$ and $\dfrac{x}{2x-1}$?

   A) $\dfrac{2x^2+x}{2x^2-7x+3}$

   B) $\dfrac{3x^2+3x-1}{2x^2-7x+3}$

   C) $\dfrac{5x^2-4}{2x^2-7x+3}$

   D) $\dfrac{5x^2-3x-1}{2x^2-7x+3}$

3. If $\dfrac{x^2-6x+9}{2x+1} \times \dfrac{2x^2+13x+6}{x^2-9} = 14$, what are all the possible values of x?

   A) $3, \dfrac{1}{2},$ and -3

   B) 15 and -4

   C) 3 and -6

   D) -4 only

6. If $\dfrac{x^2-6x+2}{x^2+x-2} + \dfrac{1}{x-1} = B$ for all real x other than $x = -2$ and $x = 1$, what is B in terms of x?

   A) $\dfrac{x-4}{x-2}$

   B) $\dfrac{x+4}{x-2}$

   C) $\dfrac{x-4}{x+2}$

   D) $\dfrac{x+4}{x+2}$

7. What is $\frac{2x+3}{x-1}$ minus $\frac{4x}{2x+1}$?

   A) $\frac{4x+3}{2x^2-x-1}$

   B) $\frac{12x+3}{2x^2-x-1}$

   C) $\frac{8x^2+12x+3}{2x^2-x-1}$

   D) $\frac{8x^2+4x+3}{2x^2-x-1}$

8. Simplify $\frac{6x^2-18x-168}{9x^2+45x+36}$.

   A) $\frac{2x-7}{3x+1}$

   B) $\frac{2x-14}{3x-3}$

   C) $\frac{2x-14}{3x+3}$

   D) $\frac{6x-14}{9x+3}$

9. $\frac{8}{x^2-12x+32} \times \frac{x^2-16}{x^2+12x+32} =$

   A) $\frac{8}{x^2-16}$

   B) $\frac{1}{x+8}$

   C) $\frac{1}{x^2-64}$

   D) $\frac{8}{x^2-64}$

10. What is $\frac{4d^2+12d+9}{d^2+8d+16}$ divided by $\frac{2d^2+5d+3}{d^2+5d+4}$?

   A) $\frac{1}{d^2+5d+4}$

   B) $\frac{2d+3}{d+1}$

   C) $\frac{2d+3}{d+4}$

   D) $\frac{2d+3}{d^2+5d+4}$

11. If $\frac{x^2-5x-14}{x^2-4} \div \frac{x-7}{2x^2-4x} = \frac{5}{4}$, what is one possible value of x?

   A) $\frac{5}{8}$

   B) $\frac{4}{5}$

   C) $\frac{5}{4}$

   D) $\frac{8}{5}$

12. $\frac{6}{x+6} + \frac{2}{x-3} =$

   A) $\frac{2}{x+6}$

   B) $\frac{8}{x+3}$

   C) $\frac{4x-30}{x^2+3x-18}$

   D) $\frac{8x-6}{x^2+3x-18}$

13. $\frac{2x-1}{x-2} - \frac{x+2}{x-1} =$

   A) 1

   B) $\frac{5-x}{x^2-3x+2}$

   C) $\frac{x^2-3x+5}{x^2-3x+2}$

   D) $\frac{-x^2+3x-5}{x^2-3x+2}$

14. What are all the possible real values of x if $\frac{x+3}{x+2} - \frac{2}{x+3} = \frac{2}{x^2+5x+6}$?

   A) -3 and -1

   B) -3 and -2

   C) 3 and -1

   D) -1 only

$$\frac{x^2}{2x-4} - \frac{10}{x-2} = \frac{2x}{8-4x}$$

15. What is the product of the 2 solutions to the above equation?

A) −24
B) −20
C) 24
D) 80

16. $\frac{3x}{x+1} + \frac{3x+3}{x^2+2x+1} =$

A) 3

B) $\frac{3x^2+3}{x^2+2x+1}$

C) $\frac{6x+3}{x^2+2x+1}$

D) $\frac{6x^2+9x+3}{x^2+2x+1}$

17. If $\frac{c^2-9}{c+6} \div \frac{c^2-4c+3}{c^2+5c-6} = 8$, what is c?

18. The gas usage of a hybrid car is 4 miles per gallon better than the standard version of the same car. If the hybrid travels $10x$ miles on $x - 6$ gallons of gas and the standard version travels $6x - 2$ miles on $x - 7$ gallons of gas, what is a possible value of x?

19. A poster has an area of 8 square feet. If its height is $\frac{3b^2-4b+1}{2b^2-7b+6}$ feet and its width is $\frac{b^2-2b}{b-1}$ feet, what is one possible value of b?

20. Two campaign volunteers spend Election Day driving voters to the polls. Dakota drives $2v$ voters over the course of $v - 2$ hours. Vanessa drives $3v - 3$ voters over the course of $v - 3$ hours. Working together at these rates, they combine to drive 8 voters per hour. What is a possible value of v?

Blue Math Lesson 16B: Systems of Equations and Inequalities – Linear and Quadratic
Learning to Swim

Directions: Answer each question below.

Practice Set 1 (No Calculator)

1. While buying groceries Jeff purchased 4 oranges and 4 bananas and paid $2.40. Sarah bought 7 oranges and 4 bananas from the same store for $3.45. Write a system of equations that can be used to solve the situation.

$$(y + 7)^2 + (x + 1)^2 = 36$$
$$x^2 + 2x + y^2 + 14y + 14 = 0$$

2. What best describes the solution to the system of equations above?

$$x^2 + y^2 = 25$$
$$y^2 = x^2 - 2x + 1$$

3. List all of the ordered pairs that solve the system of equations above.

$$x^2 + y^2 = 3$$

$$y = 2x$$

$$y = -2x$$

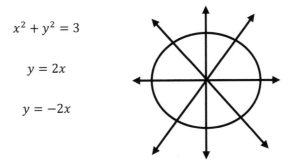

4. A system of three equations and their graphs in the xy-plane are shown above. How many solutions does the system have?

5. The area of an ellipse is given by the equation $A = \pi ab$ and the perimeter of an ellipse is approximated as $P = 2\pi \sqrt{\frac{(a^2 + b^2)}{2}}$. If $a > b > 0$, the area is 45π, and the perimeter is $2\pi\sqrt{53}$ what are the values of a and b?

BLUE MATH LESSON 16B: SYSTEMS OF EQUATIONS AND INEQUALITIES – LINEAR AND QUADRATIC
Diving into the Deep End

Directions: Answer each question below.

PRACTICE SET 2 (NO CALCULATOR)

$$y - 10 = 3(x - 1)^2$$
$$y = x^2 + 4x - 5$$

6. Which of the following values of x satisfy the system of equations above?
   A) $-\frac{1}{2}(5 - i\sqrt{11}), \frac{1}{2}(5 + i\sqrt{11})$
   B) $\frac{1}{2}(5 - i\sqrt{11}), \frac{1}{2}(5 + i\sqrt{11})$
   C) $\frac{1}{2}(5 - \sqrt{11}), \frac{1}{2}(5 + \sqrt{11})$
   D) $5 - \sqrt{11}, 5 + \sqrt{11}$

7. The product and sum of two numbers are 12 and 24.5 respectively. If y is the value of the larger number, what if the value of the expression $(y - 4)^2$?
   A) 20
   B) 24
   C) 400
   D) 576

8. A circle centered at $(3, 1)$ with a radius of 2 and the function $f(x) = x^2 - 4x + 4$ share a solution (x, y), where $x = y$. What is the value of $(4y)$?
   A) 1
   B) 4
   C) 9
   D) 16

9. Which is an approximate point of intersection of the ellipse $\frac{x^2}{4} + \frac{y^2}{9} = 0.5$ and the hyperbola $\frac{x^2}{4} - \frac{y^2}{9} = 0.0001$?
   A) $(1.5, -1)$
   B) $(1.5, 1)$
   C) $(1, 0.5)$
   D) $(1, -1.5)$

10. To earn $200 in a day, Jeffrey can either paint 4 portraits or make 10 hats. Jeffrey sold 7 items and earned $200. How much money did Jeffrey earn today by selling portraits?
    A) $20
    B) $100
    C) $170
    D) $200

11. For $10 one can order 3 slices of pizza and 2 beef hamburgers or 6 beef hamburgers and a slice of pizza. Given that you have $20 and order 5 slices of pizza, how many hamburgers can you order with the remaining money?
    A) 5
    B) 6
    C) 7
    D) 8

12. The square of the difference between two numbers is 16. If the sum of the numbers is 12, what is the value of twice the product of the two numbers?

    A) 4
    B) 8
    C) 32
    D) 64

PRACTICE SET 3 (NO CALCULATOR)

16. The positive quotient of two numbers is 4 and the square of the difference of the numbers is 16. What is triple the sum of the two numbers?

    A) 4
    B) $\frac{20}{3}$
    C) 16
    D) 20

13. A quadratic of the form $f(x) = ax^2 + bx + c$ passes through the points $(1, 1)$, $(3, 1)$, and $(2, 7)$. Which of the following points is also on $f(x)$?

    A) $(-2, -89)$
    B) $(-2, -47)$
    C) $(-2, 47)$
    D) $(-2, 89)$

17. Pears cost $0.45 each, and peaches cost $0.35 each. Given that a customer purchased 20 items and her total came out to $8.50, how many more pears than peaches were bought?

    A) 5
    B) 10
    C) 15
    D) 20

14. Three ounces of hummus and four ounces of peanuts have 66.5 grams of protein. Six ounces of hummus and 3 ounces of peanuts have 93 grams of protein. How much more protein do 3 ounces of peanuts have than 2 ounces of hummus?

18. The square of a number is the sum of another number and 2. Given that the square of the first number is equal to the second number squared, what is a possible value of the sum of the two numbers?

    A) 0
    B) 1
    C) 2
    D) 3

15. The product of two numbers is 4 and their sum is 16.25. If the larger number is divided by the smaller number, how many times larger is the quotient compared to the smaller number?

19. A pair of DJs are planning a one hour setlist. They plan to use only pop and dance tracks. Each pop song is 3 minutes long and each dance track is 2.5 minutes long. If they plan to use 22 songs in total, how many of them will be pop songs?

    A) 4
    B) 10
    C) 12
    D) 20

$$y = (x + 3)(x - 1)$$
$$x = y$$

$$\frac{(x-3)^2}{4} + \frac{(y+2)^2}{9} = 1$$
$$y = x - 5$$

20. Which of the following ordered pairs is a solution that satisfies the system of equations below?

   A) $\left(\frac{1}{2}(-1 - \sqrt{13}), \frac{1}{2}(-1 - \sqrt{13})\right)$

   B) $\left(\frac{1}{2}(-1 - \sqrt{13}), \frac{1}{2}(1 + \sqrt{13})\right)$

   C) $\left(\frac{1}{3}(-1 - \sqrt{13}), \frac{1}{3}(-1 - \sqrt{13})\right)$

   D) $\left(\frac{1}{2}(1 + \sqrt{13}), \frac{1}{2}(1 + \sqrt{13})\right)$

21. The height of a bullet shot from ground level can be modeled as a function of time using the equation $h = 2t - 0.2t^2$ for all $t > 0, h > 0$. The descent of a disk can be modeled as a function of time using the equation $h = -t^2 + 8$ for all $t > 0, h > 0$. At what time does the bullet strike the disk, assuming that they both collide if they reach the same height (h) at the same time (t)?

   A) 1.13
   B) 1.88
   C) 2.15
   D) 4.65

23. Which of the following sets of ordered pairs could possibly satisfy the system of equations above?

   A) $\left(-3 - \frac{6}{\sqrt{13}}, -2 - \frac{6}{\sqrt{13}}\right),$
   $\left(-3 + \frac{6}{\sqrt{13}}, -2 + \frac{6}{\sqrt{13}}\right)$

   B) $\left(3 - \frac{6}{\sqrt{13}}, 2 - \frac{6}{\sqrt{13}}\right),$
   $\left(3 + \frac{6}{\sqrt{13}}, 2 + \frac{6}{\sqrt{13}}\right)$

   C) $\left(3 + \frac{6}{\sqrt{13}}, -2 - \frac{6}{\sqrt{13}}\right),$
   $\left(3 - \frac{6}{\sqrt{13}}, -2 + \frac{6}{\sqrt{13}}\right)$

   D) $\left(3 - \frac{6}{\sqrt{13}}, -2 - \frac{6}{\sqrt{13}}\right),$
   $\left(3 + \frac{6}{\sqrt{13}}, -2 + \frac{6}{\sqrt{13}}\right)$

24. If the product of two numbers is 84 and the sum of their squares is 193, what is the absolute value of the sum of the two numbers?

$$(x + 5)^2 - (y + 5)^2 = 25$$
$$x + y + 10 = 0$$

22. Which of the following best describes the solution to the system of equations above?

   A) No solution
   B) $\left(\frac{45}{8}, \frac{35}{8}\right)$
   C) $\left(\frac{5}{4}, -\frac{35}{4}\right)$
   D) All real numbers

25. Alex is building a rectangular fence around his yard and has a budget of $78. He wants the area of the fence to be 60 square yards. If the fence cost $2.50 a yard, what is the length of the shorter side of the fence, to the nearest integer?

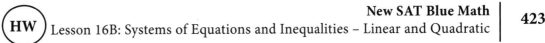
BLUE MATH LESSON 16B: SYSTEMS OF EQUATIONS AND INEQUALITIES – LINEAR AND QUADRATIC
Race to the Finish

Directions: Answer each question below.

HOMEWORK SET (NO CALCULATOR)

1. A bakery sells cakes and cupcakes for different prices. If one order placed for 2 cakes and 12 cupcakes cost $60, and another order placed for 4 cakes and 14 cupcakes cost $85, what is the combined cost of one cake and one cupcake?
   A) $3.50
   B) $8.50
   C) $12.50
   D) $20.00

$$y = 5x^2 + 12x - 6$$
$$y = -x^2$$

2. Which of the following values of x satisfy the system of equations above?
   A) $(-1 - \sqrt{2}), (-1 + \sqrt{2})$
   B) $(-1 - \sqrt{2}), (1 + \sqrt{2})$
   C) $(-1 - \sqrt{8}), (-1 + \sqrt{8})$
   D) $(-1 - \sqrt{8}), (1 + \sqrt{8})$

3. The product of two numbers is 72, and the sum of their squares is 585. What are these numbers?
   A) 1 and 72
   B) 2 and 36
   C) 3 and 24
   D) 4 and 18

4. A customer at an electronics store bought 2 pairs of headphones and 5 new DVDs for a total of $207. Knowing that one pair of headphones costs as much as two DVDs, what is the price of one pair of headphones?
   A) $14
   B) $23
   C) $31
   D) $46

5. A circle is modeled by the equation $x^2 + y^2 = 12$. On which point or points does the line $y = x + 2$ intersect the circle?
   A) $(1 + \sqrt{5}, 3 + \sqrt{5})$
   B) $(1 - \sqrt{5}, 3 - \sqrt{5})$
   C) $(-1 - \sqrt{5}, 1 - \sqrt{5}), (-1 + \sqrt{5}, 1 + \sqrt{5})$
   D) $(1 - \sqrt{5}, 3 - \sqrt{5}), (1 + \sqrt{5}, 3 + \sqrt{5})$

6. A final exam consists of 30 questions and is worth 192 points. If multiple choice questions are worth 4 points each and short essay questions are worth 12 points, how many multiple choice questions are on the test?
   A) 11
   B) 21
   C) 29
   D) 56

7. If $2x - 5y = 42$ and $2x + y = 22$, what is the value of $4x - 4y$?
   A) 23
   B) 44
   C) 53
   D) 64

$$-4x - 3y = 22$$
$$5x + 4y = 13$$

8. For the system of equations above, what is the value of $2x + 2y$.
   A) 35
   B) 70
   C) 105
   D) 140

9. A certain number of high school seniors attend post prom, which costs each student a certain amount for a total cost of $1000. If ten more students had attended post prom, everyone would have paid $5 less. Which system of equations illustrates this problem?
   A) $a + b = 1000$
      $ab = 1000$
   B) $ab = 1000$
      $(a + 10)(b - 5) = 1000$
   C) $ab = 1000$
      $(5ab) = 1000$
   D) $a + b = 1000$
      $(50ab) = 1000$

10. A drama club sells bottles of water and candy bars at intermission. The first night they sold 40 bottles of water and 20 candy bars and made $180. The second night they sold 20 bottles of water and 30 candy bars and made $150. For how much did they sell one candy bar?
    A) $1.50
    B) $3.00
    C) $3.75
    D) $4.00

11. A student spends 105 hours studying for both math and chemistry. The ratio of time the student spends on math to chemistry is 5 to 2. How many hours does the student spend studying math?
    A) 25
    B) 50
    C) 75
    D) 100

$$y = x + 4$$
$$y = \sqrt{x + 6}$$

12. Which of the following ordered pairs satisfies the system of equations above?
    A) $(-5, 1)$
    B) $(-2, 2)$
    C) $(2, 6)$
    D) $(5, 9)$

13. What value of A will cause the line $y = A$ to be tangent to the vertex of the parabola, $x^2 - 26x + 170 - y = 0$?
    A) -2
    B) -1
    C) 0
    D) 1

14. A rock is thrown upward from the bottom of a hill just as the ant starts climbing up the hill. The height of the rock is given by the equation $h = 4.1t - 3.7t^2$ for $t > 0$ and $h > 0$. The height of the ant up the hill is given by $h = 0.64t$ for $t > 0$ and $h > 0$. At what time does the rock hit the ant, assuming that they both collide if they reach the same height (h) at the same time (t)?

A) 0.532
B) 0.935
C) 1.331
D) 2.903

$$y = -7x^2 + 2x - 5$$
$$y + 3x = 1$$

15. Which of the following ordered pairs satisfies the system of equations above?

A) $(-1, -9), \left(\frac{7}{2}, -\frac{45}{2}\right)$
B) $(1, 9), \left(\frac{7}{2}, \frac{45}{2}\right)$
C) $(9, 1), \left(\frac{45}{2}, \frac{7}{2}\right)$
D) The two equations have no points of intersection.

$$\frac{(x-3)^2}{8} - \frac{(y+7)^2}{15} = 1$$
$$\frac{(y+7)^2}{15} + \frac{(x-3)^2}{8} = 1$$

16. Which of the following ordered pairs satisfies the system of equations above?

A) $\left(-3 - 2\sqrt{2}, -7\right), \left(-3 + 2\sqrt{2}, -7\right)$
B) $\left(3 - 2\sqrt{2}, -7\right), \left(3 + 2\sqrt{2}, -7\right)$
C) $\left(7 - \sqrt{15}, -3\right), \left(7 + \sqrt{15}, -3\right)$
D) $\left(-7 - \sqrt{15}, -3\right), \left(-7 + \sqrt{15}, -3\right)$

17. What is the diameter of a Jacuzzi, to the nearest integer foot, if it is in the shape of a right circular cylinder, the volume is 40 cubic feet, and the ratio of the height to radius is 2 to 1?

18. If the product of two numbers is 273 and the difference of their squares is one less than the product, what is the absolute value of the sum of the two numbers?

$$y^2 - 4y + 4 = x^2$$
$$y = 2x - 1$$

19. If (x, y) is a solution to the system of equations above, what is a possible value of the positive difference between y and x?

$$(x - 1)^2 = 9 - (y + 2)^2$$
$$y = x$$

20. If (x, y) is a solution to the system of equations above, what is a positive value of x?

BLUE MATH LESSON 17A: GRAPHS OF NON-LINEAR FUNCTIONS
Learning to Swim

Directions: Answer each question below.

PRACTICE SET 1 (NO CALCULATOR)

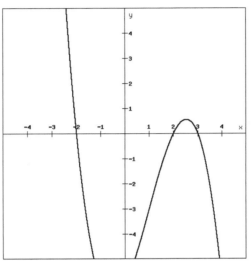

1. Which parent function best describes the graph above?

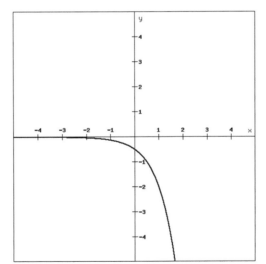

2. Which parent function best describes the graph above?

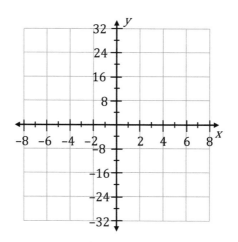

3.   Draw the graph of the equation $y = 16 - 4x^2$ above.

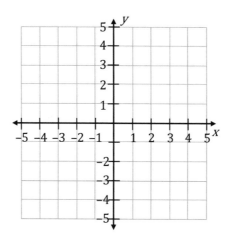

4.   Draw the graph of the equation $y^2 + (x + 2)^2 = 4$ below.

5.   Name the vertical asymptotes of the function $y = \dfrac{1}{(x-2)(x-3)}$.

BLUE MATH LESSON 17A: GRAPHS OF NON-LINEAR FUNCTIONS
Diving into the Deep End

Directions: Answer each question below.

PRACTICE SET 2 (NO CALCULATOR)

6. Which of the following lists all of the x-intercepts of the equation $y = (x + 2)^3 + 1$?
   A) -3 and 3
   B) -3 and -1
   C) -1 only
   D) -3 only

9. Which of the following functions has a vertical asymptote at $x = -5$?
   A) $f(x) = \frac{x^2 - 25}{x - 5}$
   B) $f(x) = \frac{x + 5}{x - 5}$
   C) $f(x) = \frac{x^2 - 25}{x + 5}$
   D) $f(x) = \frac{x - 5}{x + 5}$

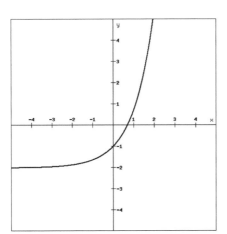

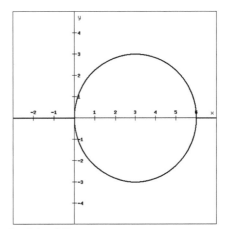

7. Which of the following equations is represented by the graph above in the xy-coordinate plane?
   A) $y = -e^x$
   B) $y = e^x - 2$
   C) $y = -\ln x$
   D) $y = \ln x - 2$

10. Which of the following equations is represented by the graph above in the xy-coordinate plane?
    A) $y = (x - 3)^2 + 9$
    B) $y = (x - 3)^2 + 36$
    C) $(x - 3)^2 + y^2 = 9$
    D) $(x - 3)^2 + y^2 = 36$

8. Which of the following equations for a circle does not pass through Quadrant I?
   A) $(x - 4)^2 + (y - 3)^2 = 16$
   B) $(x + 4)^2 + (y + 3)^2 = 16$
   C) $(x - 4)^2 + (y + 3)^2 = 16$
   D) $(x + 3)^2 + (y - 4)^2 = 16$

11. What is the center of the circle whose equation is represented as $x^2 + 4x + y^2 - 6y = 8$ in standard form?
    A) $(-2, -3)$
    B) $(-2, 3)$
    C) $(2, -3)$
    D) $(2, 3)$

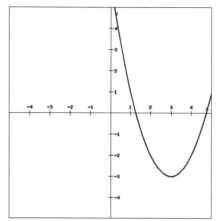

PRACTICE SET 3 (NO CALCULATOR)

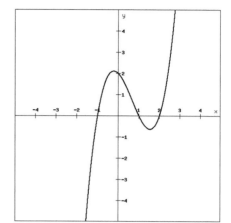

12. Which of the following equations is represented by the graph above in the xy-coordinate plane?
   A) $y = (x - 3)^2 - 3$
   B) $y = (x + 3)^2 - 3$
   C) $y = 2(x + 3)^2 - 2$
   D) $y = 2(x - 3)^2 - 3$

16. Which of the following equations is represented by the graph above in the xy-coordinate plane?
   A) $y = -x^3 + 2x^2 + x - 2$
   B) $y = x^3 - 3x^2 - x + 3$
   C) $y = x^3 - 2x^2 - x + 2$
   D) $y = -x^3 + 3x^2 + x - 3$

13. The graph of $y = x^2 - kx + 8$ has a y-intercept at $4k$. What is the value of k?
   A) -2
   B) 2
   C) 4
   D) 8

17. The graph of a circle in the xy-plane passes through the points $(0, 0)$ and $(0, 4)$. Which of the following could NOT be the coordinates of the circle's center?
   A) $(4, 0)$
   B) $(2, 2)$
   C) $(-4, 2)$
   D) $(0, 2)$

14. What is the value of $x - y$, when (x, y) are the coordinates of the vertex of the equation $y = \frac{1}{2}x^2 - 6x + 14$?

$$f(x) = \frac{3x^4 + 5x^3 - 11x + 2}{(2x^2 + 5)^2}$$

18. Select the equation for the asymptote of the above function:
   A) $y = \frac{3}{4}$
   B) $y - \frac{1}{4}$
   C) $x = \frac{3}{4}$
   D) $x = -\frac{1}{4}$

15. What is the product of the x-intercepts of the equation $y = x^3 - 3x$?

19. The graph of $y = ax^2 + bx + c$ has x-intercepts at –2 and 2. Which of the following MUST be true?
    A) $c = 2$
    B) $b = 4$
    C) The vertex of the graph lies on the y-axis.
    D) The y-intercept of the graph is negative.

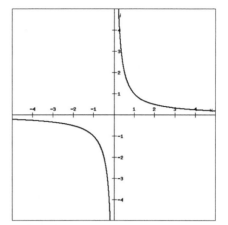

22. Which of the following equations is represented by the graph above in the xy-coordinate plane?
    A) $y = 2^{-x}$
    B) $y = \frac{1}{2^x}$
    C) $y = \frac{1}{x^2}$
    D) $y = \frac{1}{x}$

20. If $a = \frac{1}{2}$, which of the following equations corresponds to the circle with the smallest diameter?
    A) $(x + 1)^2 + (y - 1)^2 = a$
    B) $(x + 2)^2 + (y - 2)^2 = 2a$
    C) $(x - 1)^2 + (y + 1)^2 = a^2$
    D) $(x + 2)^2 + (y + 2)^2 = a^3$

23. The graph of the circle described by $(x + 1)^2 + (y + 3)^2 = 9$ passes through which of the following points?
    A) $(1, 3)$
    B) $(-1, -3)$
    C) $(2, 0)$
    D) $(-1, 0)$

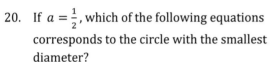

21. Which of the following equations is represented by the graph above in the xy-coordinate plane?
    A) $y = \sqrt[3]{x - 2}$
    B) $y = \sqrt{x - 2}$
    C) $y = \sqrt[3]{x + 2}$
    D) $y = \sqrt{x + 2}$

24. Let $f(x) = \begin{cases} (-x)^2 & \text{for all } x < 0 \\ 9\sqrt{x} & \text{for all } x \geq 0 \end{cases}$
    What is the maximum value that f attains on the interval $-4 \leq x \leq 4$?

25. How many times do the graphs of $y = (x - 1)^4$ and $y = (x - 1)^2$ intersect?

BLUE MATH LESSON 17A: GRAPHS OF NON-LINEAR FUNCTIONS
Race to the Finish

Directions: Answer each question below.

HOMEWORK SET (NO CALCULATOR)

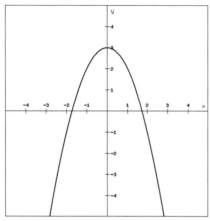

1. Which of the following equations is represented by the graph above in the xy-coordinate plane?

   A) $y = -x^2 + 3$

   B) $y = -x^3 + 3$

   C) $y = x^2 - 3$

   D) $y = x^3 - 3$

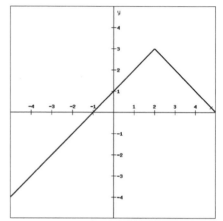

3. Which of the following equations is represented by the graph above in the xy-coordinate plane?

   A) $y = -|x - 2| - 3$

   B) $y = -|x + 2| - 3$

   C) $y = -|x - 2| + 3$

   D) $y = -|x + 2| + 3$

4. What is the y-intercept of the equation $y = \sqrt{x + 4} - 4$?

   A) -2

   B) 0

   C) 4

   D) 12

2. Which of the following graphs represents the equation $y = \frac{1}{x} + 1$?

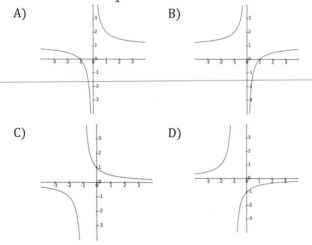

A)

B)

C)

D)

5. Which of the following equations, when graphed in the xy-coordinate plane, would be a circle with a center at $(-3, 3)$ and a radius of 4?

   A) $(x - 3)^2 + (y + 3)^2 = 4$

   B) $(x + 3)^2 + (y - 3)^2 = 4$

   C) $(x - 3)^2 + (y + 3)^2 = 16$

   D) $(x + 3)^2 + (y - 3)^2 = 16$

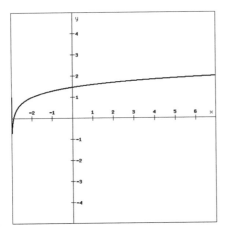

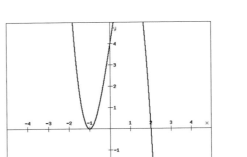

6. Which of the following equations is represented by the graph above in the xy-coordinate plane?

A) $y = \sqrt{x + 3} + 1$

B) $y = 2^{x+3} + 1$

C) $y = \log(x + 3) + 1$

D) $y = \dfrac{1}{x+3} + 1$

9. Which of the following equations is represented by the graph above in the xy-coordinate plane?

A) $y = -2(x - 2)(x + 1)^2$

B) $y = (x - 2)(x + 1)^2$

C) $y = (x - 2)(x + 1)(x - 1)$

D) $y = -(x - 2)(x + 1)$

7. Which of the following is true for the graphs of $f(x) = (x - 4)^2 + 3$ and $g(x) = 2(x + 4)^2 - 3$?

A) The graphs of $f(x)$ and $g(x)$ intersect twice

B) The rate of change of $g(x)$ is negative on the interval $-4 < x < 0$

C) The vertex of $f(x)$ is 8 units to the right of the vertex of $g(x)$

D) The vertex of $f(x)$ is 6 units below the vertex of $g(x)$

10. Which of the following equations would produce an identical graph to the reflection of $y = x^3 + 10$ across the y-axis?

A) $y = x^3 + 10$

B) $y = 10 - x^3$

C) $y = x^3 - 10$

D) $y = \sqrt[3]{x} + 10$

11. The graph of $y = \sqrt{x - 1} - 20$ contains points in which of the following quadrants?

A) I only

B) I and II only

C) I and IV only

D) I, II, and IV

8. The graph of $y = ax^2 + bx + c$ passes through the point $(3, 4)$ and has vertex $(5, -2)$. Which of the following points must also be on the graph?

A) $(0, 13)$

B) $(7, -8)$

C) $(7, -4)$

D) $(7, 4)$

C2 education
be smarter

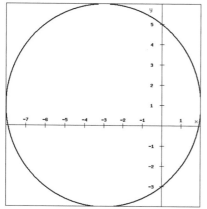

12. Which of the following equations is represented by the graph above in the xy-coordinate plane?
   A) $(y - 1)^2 = (x - 3)^2 + 25$
   B) $(x + 3)^2 + (y - 1)^2 = 5$
   C) $(x - 3)^2 + (y + 1)^2 = 25$
   D) $(x + 3)^2 + (y - 1)^2 = 25$

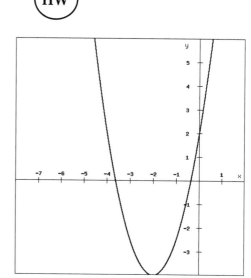

15. The graph depicted above is described by which of the following equations?
   A) $y = 3x^2 + 6x + 2$
   B) $y = 3x^2 + 6x - 2$
   C) $y = 1.5x^2 + 6x + 2$
   D) $y = 1.5x^2 + 2x - 2$

13. The graph of $y = x^2 - x - 2$ intersects the x-axis at which values of x?
   A) 2 and $\sqrt{2}$
   B) 2 and –1
   C) –1 and $\sqrt{2}$
   D) –2 and 1

14. The graph of the equation $y = \dfrac{1}{x^2 - 4}$ has a vertical asymptote at
   A) $x = -2$ only
   B) $x = 2$ only
   C) $x = -2$ and $x = 2$
   D) None of the above

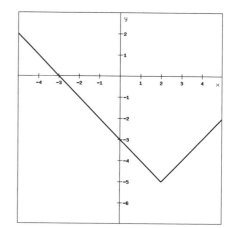

16. Which of the following equations is represented by the graph above in the xy-coordinate plane?
   A) $h(x) = |x - 2| - 5$
   B) $h(x) = |x - 3|$
   C) $h(x) = |x + 2| - 5$
   D) $h(x) = |x - 5| - 2$

17. What is the sum of the x-intercepts of the equation $y = 9x^2 - 6x + 2$?

19. The graph of $y = 2^x$ and the graph of $y = 3^x$ share how many points in common?

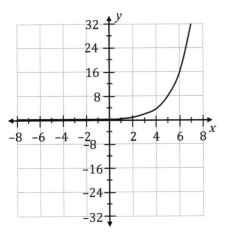

20. The graph of $y = x^2$ and the graph of $y = \sqrt{x}$ share how many points in common?

18. The graph depicted above is that of the equation $y = k \cdot 2^x$, where k is a constant. What is the value of k?

Blue Math Lesson 17B: Solving for a Variable
Learning to Swim

Directions: Answer each question below.

Practice Set 1 (No Calculator)

1. The surface area, S, of a cylinder is equal to $2\pi r^2 + 2\pi rh$, where r is the cylinder's radius and h is the cylinder's height. Solve for h, the cylinder's height, in terms of d and S.

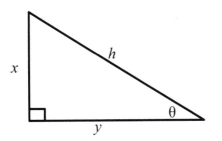

2. The sine of the base angle θ of the 90°-triangle above is equivalent to the ratio of the lengths of side x to side h, while the cosine of the base angle θ is equivalent to the ratio of the lengths of side y to side h. If the tangent of any angle is equal to the ratio of $\sin\theta$ to $\cos\theta$, express $\tan\theta$ in terms of x, y, and h.

3. If $\dfrac{1}{s_i} + \dfrac{1}{s_o} = \dfrac{1}{f}$, then $f =$

4. If $v^2 = v_0^2 + 2a(x - x_0)$, solve for a in terms of v, v_0, x, and x_0.

5. If $K = \dfrac{1}{2}mv^2$ and $U = mgh$, solve for U in terms of K, g, h, and v.

BLUE MATH LESSON 17B: SOLVING FOR A VARIABLE

Diving into the Deep End

Directions: Answer each question below.

PRACTICE SET 2 (NO CALCULATOR)

6. If $\frac{xy-z}{xz-y} = z$, then $x =$

   A) $\frac{z-zy}{z^2-y}$

   B) $\frac{zy-z}{y-z^2}$

   C) $\frac{zy-z}{z^2-y}$

   D) $\frac{z-zy}{y-z^2}$

7. Interest that is compounded continuously can be calculated using the formula $A = Pe^{rt}$. Solve for r in terms of A, P, and t.

   A) $t\ln\left(\frac{A}{P}\right)$

   B) $\frac{1}{t}\ln\left(\frac{P}{A}\right)$

   C) $\frac{1}{t}\ln\left(\frac{A}{P}\right)$

   D) $t\ln\left(\frac{A}{P}\right)$

8. The buoyancy mass of an object, m_b, is defined as the effective mass of an object as can be measured by a gravitational method. This can be found by multiplying the mass of the object, m_o, by the positive difference between 1 and the ratio of the density of the fluid that the object is suspended in, ρ_f, to the density of the object, ρ_o. Which of the following is an equation for the mass of the object in terms of m_b, ρ_o, and ρ_f.

   A) $\frac{m_b\rho_f}{\rho_o-\rho_f}$

   B) $\frac{m_b\rho_o}{\rho_o-\rho_f}$

   C) $\frac{m_b\rho_f}{\rho_f-\rho_o}$

   D) $\frac{m_b\rho_o}{\rho_f-\rho_o}$

9. The enthalpy of a thermodynamic system, H, is the sum of the internal energy of a system, U, and the product of the pressure (P) and volume (V) of the system. Similarly, the product of the pressure and volume of a system is equivalent to the product of the number of moles present in the system (n), the temperature of the system (T), and a constant (R). Solve for the internal energy of a system in terms of n, R, T, and H.

   A) $U = nRT - H$

   B) $U = H - nRT$

   C) $U = \frac{H}{nRT}$

   D) $U = \frac{nRT}{H}$

10. The kinetic energy of an object, K, is equivalent to one-half the product of the mass of the object and the square of its velocity. Which of the following expressions models the velocity of an object of mass 30 kg in terms of its kinetic energy?

    A) $v = \sqrt{\frac{K}{15}}$

    B) $v = \sqrt{\frac{K}{60}}$

    C) $v = \sqrt{60K}$

    D) $v = \sqrt{15K}$

11. If $\frac{x^2-2xy+y^2}{x^2-y^2} = 1$, then $x - y =$

    A) $x + y$

    B) $1 - (x + y)$

    C) $\frac{1}{y}$

    D) $\frac{1}{x}$

12. The population P of a colony of bacteria m minutes after it is placed in an aquarium is given by $P = P_0(1 + r)^m$, where r is the population growth rate per hour and P_0 is the population at the start of the experiment. If a colony that begins with 100 bacteria is observed to grow to a population of x bacteria in 1 hour, which of the following expressions gives the growth rate r in terms of x?

A) $x - 100$

B) $\sqrt[60]{\dfrac{100}{x}} - 1$

C) $\sqrt[60]{100x} - 1$

D) $\sqrt[60]{\dfrac{x}{100}} - 1$

$$P = Xp^k q^{n-k}$$

13. The probability, P, of achieving exactly k successes in n trials of an outcome with exactly two outcomes, success and failure, is shown above. In the formula above, X is a constant value given specific values for both n and k, p is the probability of success, and q is the probability of failure. If the probability of success of a certain outcome is 0.6 and the trial was done 12 times to a total of 4 successes, which of the following equations models X in terms of P?

A) $X = \dfrac{P}{(0.6)^4(0.4)^8}$

B) $X = \dfrac{(0.6)^4(0.4)^8}{P}$

C) $X = \dfrac{P}{(0.6)^8(0.4)^4}$

D) $X = \dfrac{(0.6)^8(0.4)^4}{P}$

14. If $(x + y)^2 = 16$ and $x^2 + y^2 = 12$, then $xy =$

15. The potential energy, U, and kinetic energy, K, of a system are equivalent. If the equations $U = mgh$ and $K = \frac{1}{2}mv^2$ are both relevant, g is a constant equivalent to 9.8 meters per second squared, what is the velocity, v (in meters per second), of an object at a height, h, of 10 meters?

PRACTICE SET 3 (NO CALCULATOR)

16. The distance between two points on a coordinate plane, (x_1, y_1) and (x_2, y_2), can be found by the equation $d = \sqrt{(x_2 - x_1)^2 + (y_2 - y_1)^2}$. Which of the following is a possible point that is 5 units away from the point $(3, 4)$?

    A) $(1, 8)$
    B) $(7, 7)$
    C) $(6, 9)$
    D) $(8, 3)$

17. If $10^x = 100^{x-y}$, then $x =$

    A) $-2y$
    B) $-\frac{2y}{3}$
    C) $\frac{2y}{3}$
    D) $2y$

18. The surface area, S, of a cylinder is modeled by the equation $S = 2\pi r^2 + 2\pi rh$, where r is the radius of the cylinder and h is its height. What is the surface area of the cylinder in terms of its height and the area, A, and circumference, C, of the circles that make up the cylinder's base?

    A) $S = A + Ch$
    B) $S = A + 2Ch$
    C) $S = 2(A + Ch)$
    D) $S = 2A + Ch$

19. If $-\frac{3}{2} < x - \frac{1}{3} < -\frac{9}{8}$, then the value $2 - 6x$ lies between which two values?

    A) -9 and $-\frac{27}{4}$
    B) $-\frac{9}{2}$ and $-\frac{27}{8}$
    C) $\frac{27}{8}$ and $\frac{9}{2}$
    D) $\frac{27}{4}$ and 9

$$\frac{b - (a-b)}{c} = \frac{b - 2(b-c)}{a}$$

20. If $c \neq 0$ and $a \neq 0$, then $b =$

    A) $\frac{a^2 + 2c^2}{2a + c}$
    B) $\frac{2a^2 + c^2}{2a + c}$
    C) $\frac{a^2 + 2c^2}{a + 2c}$
    D) $\frac{2a^2 + 2c^2}{a + 2c}$

21. If $g = h^2 + 4h - 2$, then $h =$

    A) $2 \pm \sqrt{g - 6}$
    B) $2 \pm \sqrt{g + 6}$
    C) $-2 \pm \sqrt{g - 6}$
    D) $-2 \pm \sqrt{g + 6}$

$$x = \frac{-b \pm \sqrt{b^2 - 4ac}}{2a}$$

22. The quadratic formula is shown above. If $a \neq 0$, then $c =$
    A) $ax^2 + bx$
    B) $-ax^2 + bx$
    C) $ax^2 - bx$
    D) $-ax^2 - bx$

24. If $3y^2 - 3x^2 = -15$, $x^2 - y = 2$, and $y > 0$ then
    $y =$

25. If $e = mc^2$ and $\frac{c^2 - e}{e} = 3$, then $m =$

23. Andrew can run a lap around the football field at a rate of a meters per second, while Burns can run a lap at a rate of b meters per second. They start running from the same place, and after t seconds, Burns is 3 meters ahead of Andrew. In terms of a and b, $t =$
    A) $\frac{a - b}{3}$
    B) $\frac{b - a}{3}$
    C) $\frac{3}{a - b}$
    D) $\frac{3}{b - a}$

BLUE MATH LESSON 17B: SOLVING FOR A VARIABLE
Race to the Finish

Directions: Answer each question below.

HOMEWORK SET (NO CALCULATOR)

1. Heat can be calculated using the formula $Q = mc(T_f - T_i)$, where Q is the heat of the substance, m is the mass of the substance, c is the constant of heat capacity of the substance, and T_f and T_i are the final and initial temperatures of the substance, respectively.
$T_f =$

   A) $T_i + \dfrac{mc}{Q}$

   B) $T_i - \dfrac{mc}{Q}$

   C) $T_i + \dfrac{Q}{mc}$

   D) $T_i - \dfrac{Q}{mc}$

2. When given a temperature in degrees Celsius, C, you can find the temperature in degrees Fahrenheit, F, by multiplying C by $\dfrac{9}{5}$ and adding 32 to the total. Which of the following equations can be used to find the temperature in degrees Celsius when given the temperature in degrees Fahrenheit?

   A) $\dfrac{5}{9}(F + 32)$

   B) $\dfrac{5}{9}(F - 32)$

   C) $\dfrac{5}{9}F + 32$

   D) $\dfrac{5}{9}F - 32$

3. If $x = \dfrac{y+xz}{x-z}$ and $x \neq z$, then $z =$

   A) $\dfrac{y-x^2}{2x}$

   B) $\dfrac{(x-y)^2}{2x}$

   C) $\dfrac{(y-x)^2}{2x}$

   D) $\dfrac{x^2-y}{2x}$

4. A cylindrical sewer pipe that is w meters wide and flows at a rate of f meters per second has a flow rate of $F = \dfrac{\pi f w^2}{4}$. In terms of F and f, what is its diameter?

   A) $\sqrt{\dfrac{4F}{\pi f}}$

   B) $\sqrt{\dfrac{4\pi F}{f}}$

   C) $\sqrt{\dfrac{\pi F}{4f}}$

   D) $\sqrt{\dfrac{F}{4\pi f}}$

5. The area of a circle is πr^2, while the circumference of a circle is $2\pi r$. In terms of its area, A, the circumference of a circle, C, can be represented as

   A) $2\pi\sqrt{A}$

   B) $2\pi\sqrt{\dfrac{A}{\pi}}$

   C) $2\sqrt{A}$

   D) $2A\sqrt{\pi}$

6. If $mr^2 + mr = m^2(r + r^2)$, then $m =$

   A) $\dfrac{r-r^2}{r-1}$

   B) $\dfrac{r-1}{r-r^2}$

   C) 1

   D) -1

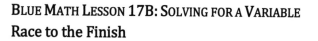

C2education
be smarter

7. The equation of a circle can be represented as $(x - h)^2 + (y - k)^2 = r^2$, where (h, k) is the center of the circle and r is its radius. For a circle centered at $(3, -1)$ with radius 5, $y =$

A) $-1 \pm \sqrt{25 - (x - 3)^2}$

B) $-1 \pm \sqrt{25 + (x - 3)^2}$

C) $1 + \sqrt{25 - (x - 3)^2}$

D) $1 + \sqrt{25 + (x - 3)^2}$

10. If $F_R = \sqrt{F_B^2 + F_V^2}$, then $F_V =$

A) $\sqrt{F_B^2 + F_R^2}$

B) $\sqrt{F_B^2 - F_R^2}$

C) $\sqrt{F_R^2 - F_B^2}$

D) $\sqrt{2F_R^2 + F_B^2}$

$$P = \frac{2St}{D}$$

$$N = e^{\left(\frac{-0.693t}{t_{1/2}}\right)}$$

$N =$ The percent of carbon-14 (in decimal notation) of a dead sample compared to a living one

$e =$ Euler's number (approx. equal to 2.71828)

$t =$ number of years

$t_{1/2} =$ carbon-14 half-life

8. The equation above can be used to find the percent of carbon-14 in a sample of a dead organism. Find an equation for t in terms of N and $t_{1/2}$.

A) $t = \dfrac{t_{\frac{1}{2}} \ln N}{-0.693}$

B) $t = \dfrac{\ln N}{-0.693 t_{\frac{1}{2}}}$

C) $t = \dfrac{-0.693 t_{\frac{1}{2}}}{\ln N}$

D) $t = \dfrac{t_{\frac{1}{2}}}{-0.693 \ln N}$

9. If $f(x) = -\dfrac{1}{2}(x - 2)^4 - 3$, then $x =$

A) $2 + \sqrt[4]{-2f(x) + 3}$

B) $2 + \sqrt[4]{-2f(x) + 6}$

C) $2 \pm \sqrt[4]{-2(f(x) - 3)}$

D) $2 \pm \sqrt[4]{-2f(x) - 6}$

11. Barlow's formula, shown above, relates the internal pressure (P) that a pipe can handle to the strength of the material that it's made out of and the pipe's dimensions ($S =$ allowable stress, $t =$ wall thickness, and $D =$ outside diameter). If wall thickness of a pipe is doubled and its diameter is halved while its allowable pressure remains the same, write a formula for the new allowable stress of the pipe.

A) $S = \dfrac{8PD}{t}$

B) $S = \dfrac{4PD}{t}$

C) $S = \dfrac{PD}{4t}$

D) $S = \dfrac{PD}{8t}$

12. Kimmy can run 1 km at a rate of k meters per second, while Jimmy can run 1 km at a rate of j meters per second. They start at opposite ends of a 3 km street and run towards each other for t seconds. In terms of k, j, and t, how far do they have left to run before they meet each other, d?

A) $d = t(k + j) - 3$

B) $d = t(k - j) - 3$

C) $d = 3 - t(k + j)$

D) $d = 3 - t(k - j)$

13. The surface area of a right regular hexagonal prism can be found by the equation $A = 6ah + 3\sqrt{3}a^2$, where a is the length of its base edge and h is its height. Which of the following equations can be used to find the height of the prism when given its surface area and base edge?

A) $h = \dfrac{3\sqrt{3}a^2 - A}{6a}$

B) $h = \dfrac{A - 3\sqrt{3}a^2}{6a}$

C) $h = \dfrac{6a}{3\sqrt{3}a^2 - A}$

D) $h = \dfrac{6a}{A - 3\sqrt{3}a^2}$

14. If $\dfrac{a^x}{a^y} = a^z$, then $z =$

A) $\dfrac{x}{y}$

B) $x + y$

C) $x - y$

D) xy

15. If $x^2 - \dfrac{yz}{x} = \dfrac{x^2}{yz}$, then $x^3 =$

A) $\dfrac{yz - 1}{y^2 z^2}$

B) $\dfrac{1 - yz}{y^2 z^2}$

C) $\dfrac{y^2 z^2}{1 - yz}$

D) $\dfrac{y^2 z^2}{yz - 1}$

16. One equation of a hyperbola with center (h, k) is $\dfrac{(x-h)^2}{a^2} - \dfrac{(y-k)^2}{b^2} = 1$. Which of the following is equivalent to this expression?

A) $a^2(x - h)^2 - b^2(y - k)^2 = a^2 b^2$

B) $b^2(x - h)^2 - a^2(y - k)^2 = ab$

C) $a^2(x - h)^2 - b^2(y - k)^2 = ab$

D) $b^2(x - h)^2 - a^2(y - k)^2 = a^2 b^2$

17. If $(x - y)^2 = 20$ and $x^2 + y^2 = 32$, then $xy =$

18. If $b^y b^x = b^z$, $\dfrac{b^y}{b^x} = b^z$, and $y = 3$, then z must equal

$$P = Xp^k q^{n-k}$$

19. The probability, P, of achieving exactly k successes in n trials of an outcome with exactly two outcomes, success and failure, is shown above. In the formula above, X is a constant value given specific values for both n and k, p is the probability of success, and q is the probability of failure. If the probability of success of a certain outcome is 0.5 and the trial was done 3 times to a total of 2 successes, what is the value of X if $P = \dfrac{3}{8}$?

20. The Pythagorean theorem states that for a right triangle with side lengths a, b, and c, with c being the hypotenuse, then $a^2 + b^2 = c^2$. If one leg is half the length of the hypotenuse, and the other leg has a length of $3\sqrt{3}$, what is the length of the first leg?

BLUE MATH LESSON 18A: FUNCTIONS – TRANSFORMATIONS AND COMPOSITIONS
Learning to Swim

Directions: Answer each question below.

PRACTICE SET 1 (NO CALCULATOR)

Identify the parent equation and graph the given equation in the space provided.

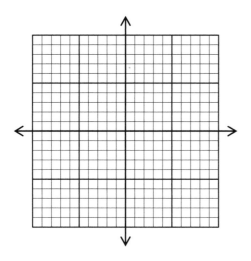

1. $(x - 2)^2 + y^2 = 4$

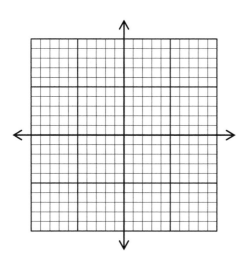

2. $f(x) = -(x + 1)^3 - 2$

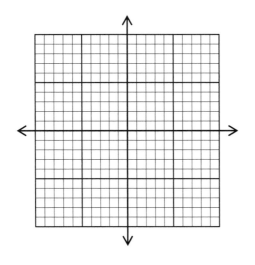

3. $f(x) = \sqrt{-x-2}$

4. If $f(x) = 6x + \dfrac{9}{x}$ and $g(x) = \dfrac{x}{3} - 2$, then $f(g(x)) =$

5. If $f(x) = x^3 + 8$ and $f(g(x)) = x$, then $g(x) =$

BLUE MATH LESSON 18A: FUNCTIONS – TRANSFORMATIONS AND COMPOSITIONS
Diving into the Deep End

Directions: Answer each question below.

PRACTICE SET 2 (NO CALCULATOR)

6. If the function $g(x) = \frac{1}{x-2}$ has a vertical asymptote at $x = 2$ and a horizontal asymptote at $y = 0$, then the graph $f(x) = \frac{1}{x+1} + 2$ has which asymptotes?
   A) $x = 1, y = -2$
   B) $x = 1, y = 2$
   C) $x = -1, y = -2$
   D) $x = -1, y = 2$

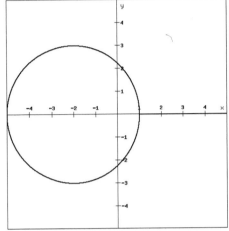

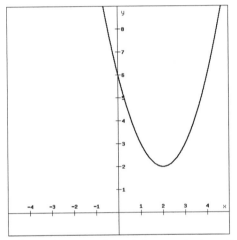

7. What is the equation of the graph above?
   A) $y = (x - 2)^2 - 2$
   B) $y = (x + 2)^2 - 2$
   C) $y = (x - 2)^2 + 2$
   D) $y = (x + 2)^2 + 2$

8. If $f(x) = 3$ and $g(x) = e^{x-3} - 3$, then $g(f(x)) =$
   A) -3
   B) -2
   C) $e - 3$
   D) $e - 2$

9. What is the equation of the graph above?
   A) $(x + 2)^2 + y^2 = 9$
   B) $(x - 2)^2 + y^2 = 9$
   C) $x^2 + (y + 2)^2 = 9$
   D) $x^2 + (y - 2)^2 = 9$

10. What is the resulting function when you shift the graph of $h(x) = \sqrt{x}$ one unit to the right and 2 units down?
    A) $\sqrt{x - 1} - 2$
    B) $\sqrt{x + 1} - 2$
    C) $\sqrt{x - 1} + 2$
    D) $\sqrt{x + 1} + 2$

11. Which of the following transformations will cause the graph of $y = |x|$ to pass through the point $(0, 11)$?
    A) Horizontal shrink by a factor of 3, shift left 2 units, and shift up 5 units.
    B) Horizontal shrink by a factor of 3, shift left 2 units, and shift down 5 units.
    C) Horizontal shrink by a factor of 3, shift right 2 units, and shift up 5 units.
    D) Horizontal shrink by a factor of 3, shift right 2 units, and shift down 5 units.

12. If the graph of $f(x) = -\log x$ is shifted left 3 units, which of the following values is outside of the domain of the function?
    A) –3
    B) –2
    C) 0
    D) 3

14. If the graph of $g(x) = x^2$ is reflected over the y-axis and then rotated 90° clockwise around the origin, the y-coordinate of its vertex is now:

13. The graph of $f(x)$ is transformed to the graph of $f(x + C)$. Which of the following best shows that transformation?
    A) $f(x) = x^2 + 3x,$
       $f(x + C) = x^2 + 3x + C$
    B) $f(x) = 2x^2 - 3,$
       $f(x + C) = 2(x + C)^2 - 3 + C$
    C) $f(x) = \sin x,$
       $f(x + C) = \sin x + C$
    D) $f(x) = \tan x,$
       $f(x + C) = \tan(x + C)$

15. The graph of $f(x)$ above is shifted to form $g(x) = f(x + A) + B$. What is the value of $B - A$?

Practice Set 3 (No Calculator)

16. The graph of the function $f(x) = -2|x - 1| + 1$ can be reflected over the x-axis, then the y-axis, to form which of the following functions, $g(x)$?
    A) $f(x) = -2|-x + 1| + 1$
    B) $f(x) = 2|x - 1| + 1$
    C) $f(x) = 2|-x - 1| - 1$
    D) $f(x) = 2|-x - 1| + 1$

18. The functions $f(x) = x^3 - 1$ and $g(x) = \sqrt[3]{x + 1}$ are inverses of each other. Which of the following statements is always true?
    A) $f(a) = g(a)$
    B) $f(g(x)) = g(f(x))$
    C) $f(g(x)) = -x$
    D) $g(f) = f(g)$

19. What is the resulting function when you stretch the graph of $f(x) = x^2$ vertically by a factor of 2, shift it left 2 units, up 1 unit, and reflect it over the x-axis?
    A) $y = -(2x + 4)^2 + 1$
    B) $y = (-2x + 4)^2 + 1$
    C) $y = -(2x - 4)^2 + 1$
    D) $y = (2x - 4)^2 + 1$

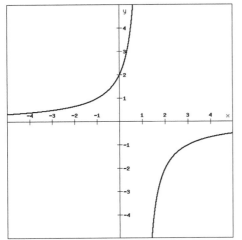

17. Which of the following functions is the best representation of the graph above?
    A) $f(x) = \dfrac{2}{x-1}$
    B) $f(x) = \dfrac{-2}{x-1}$
    C) $f(x) = \dfrac{2}{x+1}$
    D) $f(x) = \dfrac{-2}{x+1}$

20. A circle with diameter 6 is centered on the origin. If its center is shifted 2 units up and 3 units to the right, what is the equation of the new circle?
    A) $(x - 3)^2 + (y - 2)^2 = 36$
    B) $(x + 3)^2 + (y + 2)^2 = 36$
    C) $(x - 3)^2 + (y - 2)^2 = 9$
    D) $(x + 3)^2 + (y + 2)^2 = 9$

21. The parabola $y = 3x^2 + 1$ is shifted 2 units to the left and 2 units down. What is the vertex of the parabola?
    A) $(-2, -2)$
    B) $(-2, -1)$
    C) $(2, -2)$
    D) $(2, -1)$

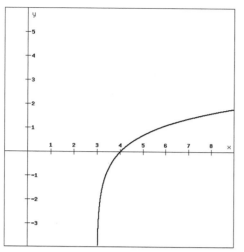

22. Which of the following functions is the best representation of the graph above?
    A) $f(x) = \ln(x + 3)$
    B) $f(x) = \ln(x - 3)$
    C) $f(x) = \sqrt{x + 3}$
    D) $f(x) = \sqrt{x - 3}$

For questions 24 and 25, use the following information:

$$f(x) = (x - 2)^3 + 16$$
$$g(x) = \sqrt{2x - 4}$$
$$h(x) = |x - 2|$$

24. What is the value of $f(g(h(0)))$?

25. What is the value of $f(g(6.5)) - g(h(4.5))$?

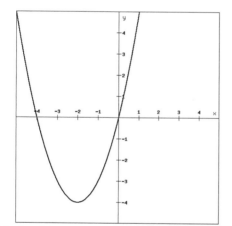

23. Which of the following functions is the best representation of the graph above?
    A) $f(x) = -(x - 2)^2 - 4$
    B) $f(x) = (x + 2)^2 + 4$
    C) $f(x) = (x - 2)^2 - 4$
    D) $f(x) = (x + 2)^2 - 4$

BLUE MATH LESSON 18A: FUNCTIONS – TRANSFORMATIONS AND COMPOSITIONS

Race to the Finish

Directions: Answer each question below.

HOMEWORK SET (NO CALCULATOR)

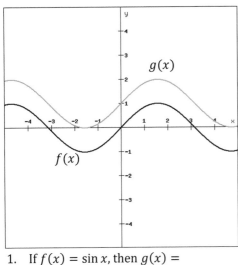

1. If $f(x) = \sin x$, then $g(x) =$
   A) $\sin x + 1$
   B) $\sin(x + 1)$
   C) $\sin x - 1$
   D) $\sin(x - 1)$

2. A circle with radius 4 is centered on the point $(1, 3)$. If the circle is reflected over the x-axis, what is the new equation of the circle?
   A) $(x - 1)^2 + (y - 3)^2 = 16$
   B) $(x + 1)^2 + (y + 3)^2 = 16$
   C) $(x - 1)^2 + (y - 3)^2 = 4$
   D) $(x + 1)^2 + (y + 3)^2 = 4$

3. If the function $f(x) = 3(2)^x$ is shifted 3 units downwards and 1 unit to the right, it's new equation would be:
   A) $f(x) = 3(2)^{x-3} + 1$
   B) $f(x) = 3(2)^{x-1} - 3$
   C) $f(x) = 3(2)^{x-3} - 1$
   D) $f(x) = 3(2)^{x+1} - 3$

4. If $f(x) = -x^2 - x$, and $g(x) = x + 1$, then which of the following is equal to $f(g(x))$?
   A) $x^2 + x + 2$
   B) $-(x^2 + x)$
   C) $-(x^2 + x + 2)$
   D) $-(x + 1)(x + 2)$

5. The function $h(x) = -\dfrac{1}{x-2}$ has an asymptote at $x = 2$. The function $g(x) = \dfrac{1}{x+2}$ must have an asymptote at:
   A) $x = 2$
   B) $x = -2$
   C) $x = 4$
   D) $x = -4$

6. A function $f(x)$ has the form $x^2 + bx + c$. Reflecting $f(x)$ across the y-axis yields the same translation as shifting $f(x)$ 4 units to the right. What value must c hold if $f(x) = 0$ has only 1 solution?
   A) 1
   B) 2
   C) 4
   D) 8

7. Which of the following functions can be reflected over the line $y = x$ to produce the same function?
A) $y = 2$
B) $y = -x + 2$
C) $y = 2x$
D) $y = 2x + 2$

Questions 8 through 10 use the following information:

If a function is an even function, its graph is unchanged after a reflection about the y-axis.
If a function is an odd function, its graph is unchanged after a rotation of $180°$ about the origin.

8. Which of the following functions is an even function?
A) $y = x^3 + x^2$
B) $y = 2x^2 + x$
C) $y = 4x^2 - 6$
D) $y = x^3 - x$

9. Which of the following functions is an odd function?
A) $y = x^3 + x^2$
B) $y = 2x^2 + x$
C) $y = 4x^2 - 6$
D) $y = x^3 - x$

10. Which of the following functions is both an odd function and an even function?
A) $f(x) = x^3$
B) $f(x) = x^2$
C) $f(x) = 1$
D) $f(x) = 0$

11. Which of the following functions is the best representation of the graph above?
A) $f(x) = 3(x + 1)^3$
B) $f(x) = \frac{1}{3}(x + 1)^3$
C) $f(x) = 3(x - 1)^3$
D) $f(x) = \frac{1}{3}(x - 1)^3$

12. The quadratic function $g(x)$ has distinct roots at the points a and b. If the graph of $g(x)$ is shifted 3 units to the right, its roots are now:
A) a, b
B) $3a, 3b$
C) $a + 3, b + 3$
D) $a - 3, b - 3$

13. If the function $f(x) = x^2$ is transformed into the function $-f(-x - 2)$, when $x = 3, y =$
A) -25
B) -9
C) -1
D) 1

14. If the graph of the function $x = 3$ is shifted 2 units to the right and 1 unit down, the new function can be represented as

    A) $x = 2$
    B) $x = 4$
    C) $x = 5$
    D) $x = 6$

17. What is a possible y-intercept of the graph of
    $(y - 2)^2 + (x - 1)^2 = 2$

18. If the graph of $g(x) = |-x - 2| - 1$ is reflected over the y-axis, the x-coordinate of its vertex is now:

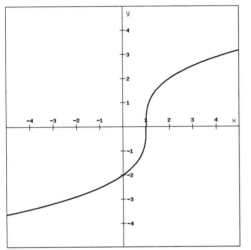

19. The function $f(x) = 2(3)^{x+2} + 6$ has an asymptote at $y =$

15. Which of the following functions is the best representation of the graph above?

    A) $f(x) = 0.5\sqrt[3]{x - 1}$
    B) $f(x) = 0.5\sqrt[3]{x + 1}$
    C) $f(x) = 2\sqrt[3]{x - 1}$
    D) $f(x) = 2\sqrt[3]{x + 1}$

20. If $f(x) = 4^{x-1}$ and $g(x) = -x^2 + 1$, then
    $f\left(g\left(-\frac{\sqrt{2}}{2}\right)\right) =$

16. If $f(x) = g(h(x))$ and $g(x) = x^2 + 1$, then which of the following is true?

    A) $f(x) = x, h(x) = \sqrt{x - 1}$
    B) $f(x) = \sqrt{x - 1}, h(x) = \sqrt{x} - 1$
    C) $f(x) = -x, h(x) = -\sqrt{x - 1}$
    D) $f(x) = -\sqrt{x - 1}, h(x) = \sqrt{x} + 1$

BLUE MATH LESSON 18B: SECTOR AREA AND ARC LENGTH
Learning to Swim

Directions: Answer each question below.

PRACTICE SET 1 (NO CALCULATOR)

1. If the square above has side lengths of 3 and each of its corners is at the middle of a circle, what is the area of the unshaded region above?

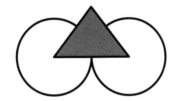

2. The triangle in the image above is equilateral and has a height of $3\sqrt{3}$ units. What is the area of the unshaded region above?

3. A dog is tethered to a pole by a 30-foot leash. If his owner wants to fence the dog in using a square fence, what's the minimum length of fencing the owner will need, assuming that she wants the dog to be able to go to the limits of his leash at all times?

4. What area of the fenced-in enclosure in Problem 3 will the dog be unable to visit because of the constraints of his leash?

5. A circle with radius x and central angle $y°$ has an arc length of what?

BLUE MATH LESSON 18B: SECTOR AREA AND ARC LENGTH
Diving into the Deep End

Directions: Answer each question below.

PRACTICE SET 2 (CALCULATOR)

6. A pie with a 16-inch diameter is cut into 8 equal pieces. If cheese evenly covers 80% of the pizza, how many square inches, to the nearest tenth of an inch, of cheese are on 3 pieces of pizza?
    A) 20.1
    B) 30.2
    C) 60.3
    D) 83.8

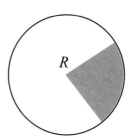

9. Circle R above has a radius of 10 and the shaded region has an area of 25π. What is the perimeter of the shaded region?
    A) $10 + 5\pi$
    B) $20 + 5\pi$
    C) $10 + 10\pi$
    D) $20 + 10\pi$

7. A sector of a circle has an area of 24π. If the circle has an area of 60π, what is the measure of the central angle that is contained in the sector?
    A) 60°
    B) 72°
    C) 120°
    D) 144°

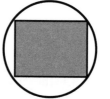

10. A rectangle with side lengths 6 and 8 is inscribed inside of a circle, as shown above. What is the area of the unshaded region above?
    A) $25\pi - 24$
    B) $25\pi - 48$
    C) $50\pi - 48$
    D) $100\pi - 4$

8. A merry-go-round takes 1 minute and 40 seconds to make two complete paths. In 12.5 seconds, a rider on the outer edge of the ride can travel 56 feet. What is the radius of the merry-go-round, in feet?
    A) 35.6 feet
    B) 47.5 feet
    C) 53.4 feet
    D) 71.3 feet

11. Circle A has a radius that is twice as long as that of Circle B. If both circles have sectors of equal area, what is the ratio of Circle A's central angle to Circle B's central angle?
    A) $1 : 8$
    B) $1 : 4$
    C) $1 : 2\sqrt{2}$
    D) $1 : 2$

12. A circle has an area of 36π and a central angle of 80°. What is the difference between the area of the circle and the area of its sector?
    A) 8π
    B) 14π
    C) 28π
    D) 36π

13. A circular room with floor area of 81π square feet needs to have wooden trim put around the border between the wall and the floor. To the nearest foot, how much trim should be used?
    A) 28
    B) 57
    C) 2576
    D) 5153

14. The central angle of a circle measures 100°, while the area of the sector including that angle is 40π. What is the length of the radius of the circle?

15. The ratio between the sector areas of two sectors of the same circle is 4 : 9. What is the ratio between the central angles of those two sectors?

PRACTICE SET 3 (CALCULATOR)

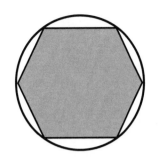

16. The regular hexagon above is inscribed in a circle with radius 6 m. What is the area of the unshaded region above?
    A) $18\pi - 27\sqrt{3}$
    B) $36\pi - 54\sqrt{3}$
    C) $36\pi - 27\sqrt{3}$
    D) $36\pi - 18\sqrt{3}$

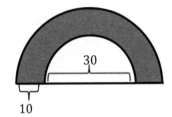

17. What is the area of the shaded region above, which is formed by two semicircles which share the same center?
    A) 100π
    B) 200π
    C) 300π
    D) 400π

18. If the radius of a circle is 4, what is the area of one-sixth of that circle?
    A) $\frac{4\pi}{3}$
    B) $\frac{8\pi}{3}$
    C) $\frac{12\pi}{3}$
    D) $\frac{16\pi}{3}$

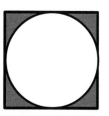

19. A circle with radius 3.5 is inscribed inside of a square, as shown above. What is the area of the shaded region?

A) $\frac{49}{4} - \frac{49\pi}{16}$

B) $\frac{49}{2} - 7\pi$

C) $49 - 14\pi$

D) $49 - \frac{49\pi}{4}$

20. The central angle of a circle is $\frac{\pi}{2}$ radians. If the sector containing that central angle has an arc length of 6π, what is the circumference of the circle?

A) 12π

B) 18π

C) 20π

D) 24π

Questions 21 through 23 use the following information:

Sales by Region (in Millions of Dollars)

■ Northeast - 136
■ Plains - 24
■ Midwest - 80
■ Southeast - 100

21. What is the approximate central angle of the Midwest data of the region above?

A) 25.4°

B) 84.7°

C) 105.9°

D) 144.0°

22. The chart above needs to be reproduced on a square piece of poster board that is 2 meters long. If the pie chart is inscribed inside the poster board, what is the area of the Northeast region, in square meters?

A) 0.52

B) 0.63

C) 0.74

D) 1.26

23. A fifth region, California, is to be added to the pie chart above. If California has sales of $60 million, how big will its central angle be when added to the pie chart?

A) 15.0°

B) 54.0°

C) 63.5°

D) 72.0°

24. If the central angle of a circle is $\frac{\pi}{4}$ radians and the circle's radius is 20. If the area of the sector of the circle containing that central angle is $x\pi$, what is the value of x?

25. How many centimeters does the tip of a $\frac{12}{\pi}$ cm long minute hand of a clock move in 24 minutes?

BLUE MATH LESSON 8B: SECTOR AREA AND ARC LENGTH
Race to the Finish

Directions: Answer each question below.

HOMEWORK SET (CALCULATOR)

1. The diameter of the Earth is 7,918 miles. What is the volume of its Southern Hemisphere, in cubic miles?
    A) 1.30×10^{11}
    B) 2.60×10^{11}
    C) 1.04×10^{12}
    D) 2.08×10^{12}

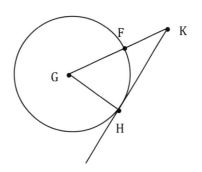

2. A circle has a radius of 12. What is the arc length intercepted by a central angle of 120°?
    A) 8π
    B) 12π
    C) 16π
    D) 48π

4. Line KH is tangent to circle G above. If the length of GF is equal to the length of FK, what is the measure of central angle FGH?
    A) 30°
    B) 45°
    C) 60°
    D) 90°

5. A circle has a diameter of 12 and a sector area of 12π. What is the measure of the central angle of the sector?
    A) 120°
    B) 150°
    C) 180°
    D) 360°

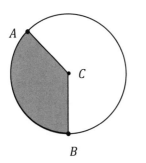

3. Major arc $\widehat{AB}$ above has a length of 12, while minor arc $\widehat{AB}$ has a length of 8. What is the measure of the angle that forms minor arc $\widehat{AB}$?
    A) 96
    B) 144
    C) 240
    D) 270

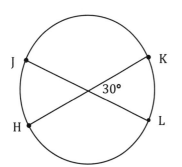

6. If arc *JK* above has a length of 6π, what is the length of arc *KL*?
   A) 1.2π
   B) 1.8π
   C) 3.0π
   D) 3.6π

7. A semicircle is divided into 40 congruent wedge-shaped parts. If the diameter of the semicircle is 10 feet, what is the area of each wedge-shaped part?
   A) $\frac{5}{16}$
   B) $\frac{5}{8}$
   C) $\frac{5}{16}\pi$
   D) $\frac{5}{8}\pi$

8. One revolution of a bicycle wheel propels the bicycle forward a distance equivalent to its circumference. A bicycle with 22-inch diameter wheels travels a distance of 300 feet. Approximately how many revolutions does the bicycle wheel travel?
   A) 26
   B) 52
   C) 104
   D) 163

9. A 16-inch diameter pizza has a cheese-filled end part that is 1-inch wide. If the pizza is divided into 8 equal slices, what is the surface area of one slice of the pizza that can be covered with toppings (i.e. not the end piece)?
   A) 8π
   B) $\frac{63\pi}{8}$
   C) $\frac{49\pi}{8}$
   D) $\frac{35\pi}{8}$

10. The hour hand of a grandfather clock is 8 inches long. How many square inches of the face of the clock will it sweep over in a 45-minute period?
    A) 4π
    B) 6π
    C) 8π
    D) 48π

11. A circular traffic roundabout has a diameter of 100 yards and contains five evenly-spaced exit paths, each of which is 12 feet wide. The local government wants to put a sidewalk around the entire length of the outer edge of the roundabout excluding the exit roads. How long will this sidewalk be, in yards?
    A) 100π − 60
    B) 100π − 20
    C) 100π − 4
    D) 100π

12. A single toilet paper square has a length of 9 cm. If the last square of toilet paper on the toilet paper roll reaches three-fourths of the way around the cardboard tube, what is the diameter of the cardboard tube, in cm?

A) $\frac{6}{\pi}$

B) $\frac{8}{\pi}$

C) $\frac{9}{\pi}$

D) $\frac{12}{\pi}$

15. The infield of a baseball park is a quarter of a circle with a radius of 90 feet. What is the length of the turf, in feet, that separates the infield from the outfield?

A) 22.5π

B) 45π

C) 90π

D) 2025π

13. The graph of a circle is $x^2 + y^2 = 64$. What area of the circle is in Quadrant I?

A) 2π

B) 4π

C) 8π

D) 16π

16. The diameter of a circle is 24 cm. If a sector of the circle has an arc length of 12π cm, what is the area of that portion of the circle in cm²?

A) 36π

B) 48π

C) 72π

D) 144π

14. Line AC is a diameter of the circle above, and $AB = BC$. If AB has a length of $2\sqrt{2}$, what is the area of the unshaded region above?

A) 2π – 2

B) 2π –1

C) 4π – 4

D) 4π – 2

Questions 17 and 18 use the figure of Circle B below:

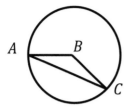

Angle ABC above measures 120°, and the radius of circle B is $\frac{10}{\pi}$.

17. What is the length of minor arc AC?

18. What is the length of major arc AC?

19. What is the circumference of the circle represented by $(x - 2)^2 + (y + 8)^2 = \frac{9}{\pi^2}$?

20. The sector of a circle has an area of 20π, and the circle's radius is 10. What is the angle measure of the sector of the circle?

BLUE MATH LESSON 19A: VOLUME
Learning to Swim

Directions: Answer each question below.

PRACTICE SET 1 (NO CALCULATOR)

1. A box with volume V whose length is twice its width and whose height is twice its length has what width, in terms of V?

2. A pyramid with a square base of area A and a height equal to the length of a diagonal of its base has what volume, in terms of A?

3. A toy company makes two sizes of beach ball. The large ball's diameter is 50% larger than the small ball's diameter. What is the ratio of the large ball's volume to that of the small ball?

4. How much greater is the volume of a cylinder of radius r and height h than the volume of a cone of equal radius and height?

5. If the radius of a sphere is tripled, then its volume is increased by what factor?

BLUE MATH LESSON 19A: VOLUME
Diving into the Deep End

Directions: Answer each question below.

PRACTICE SET 2 (CALCULATOR)

6. A cylindrical can with radius 3 cm and height h cm has approximately the same volume as a cylindrical can with radius 4 cm and height
   A) 0.5625h cm
   B) 0.75h cm
   C) 1.3333h cm
   D) 1.7778h cm

7. A deck of cards has dimensions 0.5 in × 3 in × 2 in. It is possible to pack at least 3000 such decks in a box with any of the following dimensions (length × width × height, in *feet*) EXCEPT
   A) 2' × 1.5' × 2.5'
   B) 2' × 2' × 1.5'
   C) 1.5' × 1.5' × 2'
   D) 3' × 1' × 1.75'

8. A right circular traffic cone has a height of 3 feet and a diameter of 1.5 feet. What is its volume in cubic inches?
   A) 81 in³
   B) 324 in³
   C) 864 in³
   D) 972 in³

9. Steel has a density of 8 grams / cm³. Five thousand spherical steel balls of mass 4.2 grams each, for use as ball bearings, are dumped loose into a cubical box measuring 20 cm on a side. What is the volume of the unused space remaining in the box? (Density is mass divided by volume.)
   A) 1524 cm³
   B) 5375 cm³
   C) 7524 cm³
   D) 8000 cm³

10. The density of iron is 7.87 grams per cm³. An iron nail (above) is a cylinder 3.5 cm long with a radius of 0.05 cm, attached to a head which is a cylinder 0.02 cm thick and has radius 0.2 cm. What mass of iron is required to make 100,000 such nails?
    A) 7.52 kg
    B) 17.90 kg
    C) 23.61 kg
    D) 56.23 kg

11. A 355 mL glass of water is filled all the way to the brim. An ice cube weighing 1.2 grams is placed in the glass. What percent of the water in the glass, by volume, is displaced and spills over the edge? (Note: The density of ice is 0.91 g / cm³. One mL is equal to one cm³.)
    A) 0.31%
    B) 0.37%
    C) 3.88%
    D) 4.68%

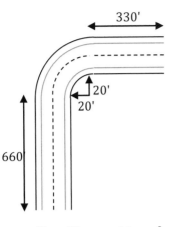

Note: Figure not to scale.

14. A system of storm sewers in a coastal city is designed to capture water runoff during heavy rains and deposit it into the ocean. Engineers have determined that the main outlet should be capable of discharging up to 45 cubic meters of water per second when that water is flowing at a rate of 2.5 meters per second. If the outlet is cylindrical in shape, its diameter must be at least how many meters, to the nearest tenth?

12. To construct a road, asphalt is poured to a thickness of 9 inches. The segment of road being built has two lanes, each 10 feet wide, and 3.5 foot shoulders on either side. It also contains one 90° turn with a radius (measured to the inside edge of the pavement) of 20 feet, as illustrated above. What volume of asphalt is required to pave 990 feet of straight road plus the curved section?

A) 20,048 ft³
B) 20,303 ft³
C) 21,113 ft³
D) 28,151 ft³

15. One soda can has radius r inches and height h inches. Another has a radius 20% greater and a height 25% less. The volume of the second can is what percent of the volume of the first?

13. An unsharpened pencil is a cylinder with diameter 7 mm and length 11.5 cm. A single such pencil is sold in a rectangular box whose interior dimensions are 7.5 mm × 7.5 mm × 12 cm. What percent of the available space inside this box is occupied by the pencil?

A) 48.6%
B) 65.6%
C) 83.5%
D) 99.9%

PRACTICE SET 3 (CALCULATOR)

16. The moon has approximately one-fourth the diameter of the earth, and approximately 2% of the mass. If the earth's density is D, what is the approximate density of the moon in terms of D? (Density is equal to mass divided by volume.)
    A) $0.016D$
    B) $0.02D$
    C) $0.78D$
    D) $1.28D$

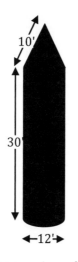

17. An old water tower is a cylinder with a cone-shaped turret on top. Measurements taken from the outside find that the tower has a diameter of 12 feet, the cylindrical portion has a height of 30 feet, and the conical top has a slant height of 10 feet. What is the volume of water that the tower can hold? (Assume the thickness of the walls is insignificant.)
    A) 816π ft^3
    B) 1080π ft^3
    C) 1176π ft^3
    D) 1200π ft^3

18. If a cylinder whose height is six times the radius of its base has volume 384π cm^3, what is its surface area in cm^2?
    A) 160π
    B) 192π
    C) 224π
    D) 256π

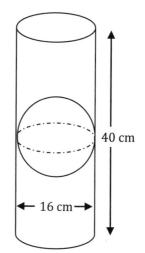

19. If the largest possible solid spherical ball is wedged inside a cylindrical tube of diameter 16 cm and length 40 cm, as depicted above, what is the approximate volume of the air inside the cylinder?
    A) 683π cm^3
    B) 1877π cm^3
    C) 2560π cm^3
    D) 4779π cm^3

20. An 80 kg person climbs into a rectangular bathtub with vertical sides, measuring 3 meters long by 1 meter wide by 70 cm deep. The water level rises 2.7 centimeters. What is the density of this person, in kilograms per cubic meter?
    A) 36.7 kg / m^3
    B) 38.1 kg / m^3
    C) 889.3 kg / m^3
    D) 987.7 kg / m^3

21. An ice cream company is testing a new product: a pre-packaged cone filled to the brim with ice cream (with a flat top, not a rounded one). The cone is to have diameter 16 cm and height 13.5 cm. If the same quantity of ice cream were served in a spherical ball, what would be its diameter?
    A) 6 cm
    B) 8 cm
    C) 12 cm
    D) 16 cm

22. Milk is sold in a rectangular carton with a square base of side length 5 inches and height 13.57 inches. If the same quantity of milk were instead sold in a cylindrical bottle whose height was twice its diameter, approximately what percent less material, by surface area, would be needed? (Assume the thickness of both containers is insignificant.)
    A) 12%
    B) 15%
    C) 18%
    D) 21%

23. A lampshade is made by taking a cone of fabric with a height of 15 inches and a base radius of 10 inches, then cutting off the top 6 inches of the cone. What is the volume of the lampshade?
    A) 300π cubic inches
    B) 360π cubic inches
    C) 468π cubic inches
    D) 500π cubic inches

24. The stone used to construct the Great Pyramid of Giza has an average density of 160 pounds per cubic foot. The pyramid has a square base 756 feet on a side and a height of 455 feet. What is its mass in millions of tons, rounded to the nearest tenth of a million? (1 ton = 2000 lbs.)

25. A cylindrical tank to hold gasoline at a gas station is designed to have a height equal to twice the diameter of its base. What must be the diameter of the base, to the nearest centimeter, if the tank is to hold 1000 liters? (1 L = 1000 cm^3)

BLUE MATH LESSON 19A: VOLUME
Race to the Finish

Directions: Answer each question below.

HOMEWORK SET (CALCULATOR)

1. A cube-shaped crate has a surface area of 1944 square inches. What is its volume?
   A) 1,944 in³
   B) 5,832 in³
   C) 7,776 in³
   D) 11,664 in³

2. A restaurant must dispense 1200 cubic centimeters of soup into a cylindrical to-go container. A container with which of the following dimensions would hold all of this soup with the least remaining leftover volume? (1 inch = 2.54 cm)
   A) Diameter: 6 inches; Height: 15 inches
   B) Diameter: 12 inches; Height: 10 inches
   C) Diameter: 12 inches; Height: 15 inches
   D) Diameter: 15 inches; Height: 10 inches

3. A shipping company must pack a variety of cylindrical cans in cardboard boxes. What is the volume of the largest can that fits into a cube-shaped box with side length of 20 centimeters (rounded to the nearest cubic centimeter)?
   A) 3,142 cm³
   B) 6,283 cm³
   C) 12,566 cm³
   D) 25,133 cm³

4. A skyscraper is a total of 1,300 feet high. Its bottom 1,000 feet of height forms a rectangular prism with a square base of side length 150 feet. The top portion is a pyramid with the same square base. What is the total volume of the skyscraper?
   A) 24,750,000 cubic feet
   B) 27,000,000 cubic feet
   C) 29,250,000 cubic feet
   D) 30,375,000 cubic feet

5. If the surface area of a spherical moon is 3,600π square miles, what is the moon's volume?
   A) 27,000π mi³
   B) 36,000π mi³
   C) 216,000π mi³
   D) 288,000π mi³

6. A wedding cake consists of three cylindrical tiers, each 10 cm high. If the cake's total volume is 3,500π cm³, which of the following could be the diameters of the three tiers?
   A) 5 cm, 10 cm, and 15 cm
   B) 8 cm, 10 cm, and 12 cm
   C) 10 cm, 20 cm, and 30 cm
   D) 16 cm, 20 cm, and 24 cm

7. A desktop globe is a wooden sphere with diameter of 24 inches. To allow for the globe to rotate, a cylindrical hole with a diameter of 2 inches is cut through the globe from the North Pole to the South Pole. What is the remaining volume of the globe?
   A) 1,704π cubic inches
   B) 2,280π cubic inches
   C) 13,800π cubic inches
   D) 18,432π cubic inches

Questions 8 and 9 use the following information.

An anthropologist studying the Inuit sees two buildings: an igloo made of ice and a longhouse made of animal hides. The igloo consists of a half-sphere with radius 9 feet and a 3-foot-long half-cylinder entryway with a radius of 2 feet. The longhouse is a triangular prism 25 feet long with triangle height of 9 feet and base of 7 feet.

8. What is the volume of the igloo?
   A) 492π ft³
   B) 510π ft³
   C) 984π ft³
   D) 996π ft³

9. What is the approximate difference in volume between the two buildings?
   A) 11 ft³
   B) 758 ft³
   C) 1552 ft³
   D) 2340 ft³

10. A group of soldiers digs a rectangular trench 5 meters deep, 4 meters wide, and 20 meters long. If the soldiers then take all the soil that they dug up and form it into a square-based pyramid of side length 10 meters, what is the height of the pyramid?
    A) 4 meters
    B) 12 meters
    C) 24 meters
    D) 36 meters

11. What is the smallest volume of a rectangular prism that can hold three spherical billiard balls, each of which has a volume of 36π cubic inches?
    A) 162 cubic inches
    B) 243 cubic inches
    C) 324 cubic inches
    D) 648 cubic inches

12. A diabolo is a toy made by connecting the points of two identical cones. If the cones have a diameter and a height of 12 centimeters, what is the total volume of the diabolo?
    A) 144π cm³
    B) 288π cm³
    C) 576π cm³
    D) 1152π cm³

13. A dreidel is made from a rectangular solid with a base of 2 cm by 2 cm and a height of 3 cm attached to a half-sphere with a 2 cm diameter. What is the dreidel's volume, to the nearest cm³?
    A) 12 cm³
    B) 14 cm³
    C) 18 cm³
    D) 25 cm³

14. Aluminum has a density of 2.7 g/cm³. A cube of aluminum is carved from the corner of a larger cube, reducing the larger cube's mass by 12.5%. If the smaller cube has a mass of 172.8 grams, what is the side length of the original cube?
    A)   2 cm
    B)   4 cm
    C)   8 cm
    D)   16 cm

15. An aboveground pool is cylindrical in shape, with a radius of 4 meters. If the pool is filled to a depth of 2 meters, what is the approximate mass of the water in the pool? (Water has a density of 1,000 kilograms per cubic meter; density is mass divided by volume.)
    A)   25,100 kg
    B)   50,200 kg
    C)   100,500 kg
    D)   150,700 kg

16. Ritchie has a cube of titanium and a sphere of oak. Titanium has a density of 4.5 g/cm³ and oak has a density of 0.75 g/cm³. The sphere has a radius of 3 cm; the cube has a side length of 2 cm. What is the difference in the masses of the two objects, rounded to the nearest gram?
    A)   0 g
    B)   9 g
    C)   28 g
    D)   49 g

17. There are two sandboxes at a playground. Each is a rectangular prism. If one is 6 feet by 5 feet with a depth of 2 feet of sand and the other is 8 feet by 4 feet with a depth of 3 feet of sand, what is the difference, in cubic feet, between the volumes of sand in the two sandboxes?

18. A right cylindrical traffic cone is 30 inches tall. If its volume is 640π cubic inches, what is its radius in inches?

19. A carpenter constructs a simple shack out of 6 sheets of plywood. Two of the sheets are 2 yards by 3 yards, two others are 3 yards by 5 yards, and the final two are 2 yards by 5 yards. What is the volume of the finished shack in cubic yards?

20. A jumbo-sized rectangular carton full of milk has side lengths of 10 cm, 10 cm, and 30 cm. How many glasses can be completely filled from this carton if each glass is a cylinder with radius of 3 cm and height 10 cm?

BLUE MATH LESSON 19B: COMPLEX NUMBERS
Learning to Swim

Directions: Answer each question below.

PRACTICE SET 1 (NO CALCULATOR)

1. What is the value of $\left(i^{17} - i^{15}\right)^3$?

2. $(3 + i)^3 = ?$

3. $(x - 3 + 2i)(x - 3 - 2i) = ?$

4. Provided that b is a real constant, if $R = b + i$, what is R^2?

5. Simplify $i^{23} \times i^{14}$.

BLUE MATH LESSON 19B: COMPLEX NUMBERS
Diving into the Deep End

Directions: Answer each question below.

PRACTICE SET 2 (NO CALCULATOR)

6. If $x^4 = 25r^4$, then all of the following are possible values of x EXCEPT
   A) $r\sqrt{5}$
   B) $-r\sqrt{5}$
   C) $r\sqrt{5}i$
   D) $r\sqrt{5}i$

7. $i^2(-4 - 4i) = ?$
   A) $4 + 4i$
   B) $4 - 4i$
   C) 0
   D) $16 + 16i$

8. The *magnitude* $|Z|$ of a complex number $Z = a + bi$ is defined as $|Z| = \sqrt{a^2 + b^2}$. What is $|-3 + 2i|$?
   A) $5i$
   B) $13i$
   C) $\sqrt{5}$
   D) $\sqrt{13}$

9. If $Z_1 = 15 + 7i$, $Z_2 = -31 - 9i$, and $Z_1 + 2Z_3 = Z_2$, then $Z_3 = ?$
   A) $8 - 8i$
   B) $-23 - 8i$
   C) $-47 - 11i$
   D) $-1 + 5i$

10. $i^{9253} = ?$
    A) i^{3244}
    B) i^{4219}
    C) i^{4113}
    D) i^{5498}

11. $\frac{1}{5+4i} = ?$
    A) $\frac{4-5i}{20}$
    B) $5 + 4i$
    C) $\frac{5-4i}{9}$
    D) $\frac{5-4i}{41}$

12. If $Z_1 = 1 + i$ and $Z_2 = -1 - 2i,$, which of the following equals $7 - 11i$?
    A) $7Z_1 + 18Z_2$
    B) $25Z_1 + 18Z_2$
    C) $25Z_1 - 18Z_2$
    D) $7Z_1 + 2Z_2$

13. Which of the following is equal to $(-2i)^7$?
    A) 128
    B) -128
    C) $128i$
    D) $-128i$

14. $(7 - 3i)(7 + 3i) =$

16. $\frac{7-i}{7i} = ?$
   A) $i - 1$
   B) $\frac{-1-7i}{7}$

15. If a is a constant and $(5 + ai)^2 = 50i$, what is a?
   C) $49 - 7i$
   D) $\frac{1-7i}{7}$

17. If Z is a complex number and $\frac{Z}{3+i} = 5 - 4i$, what is the value of Z?
   A) $19 - 7i$
   B) $2 - 5i$
   C) $11 - 7i$
   D) $8 + 5i$

18. A complex number in *polar form* is expressed in the form $r(\cos \theta + i \sin \theta)$, where θ is an angle measure and r is a positive real number. Which of the following complex numbers is equivalent to $4(\cos 120° + i \sin 120°)$?
   A) $-2 + 2\sqrt{3}i$
   B) $2 - 2\sqrt{3}i$
   C) $-4 + 4\sqrt{3}i$
   D) $-2\sqrt{3} + 2i$

19. $\dfrac{(3-2i)(4+i)}{3+2i} = ?$

A) $\dfrac{4+i}{13}$

B) $\dfrac{14-5i}{13}$

C) $\dfrac{32-43i}{13}$

D) $52 + 13i$

20. The *magnitude* $|Z|$ of a complex number
$Z = a + bi$ is defined as $|Z| = \sqrt{a^2 + b^2}$.
Which of the following complex numbers has
magnitude 13?

A) $5 - 12i$

B) $-8 + 5i$

C) $12 - i$

D) $-7 + 6i$

21. If k is a real constant, what is the square of the
complex number $k + ki$?

A) k^2

B) $k^2 i$

C) $2k^2$

D) $2k^2 i$

22. If Z is a complex number and $Z^2 = 21 - 20i$,
what is Z?

A) $4 - 2i$

B) $4 + 2i$

C) $5 - 2i$

D) $5 + 2i$

23. $\dfrac{1-i}{1+i} =$

A) 0

B) i

C) $-i$

D) Does not exist.

24. If d is a real number and $\dfrac{d}{4+3i} = 4 - 3i$, what is d?

25. The expression $\dfrac{1}{8-15i}$ simplifies to $\dfrac{8+15i}{k}$, where k
is an integer. What is k?

BLUE MATH LESSON 19B: COMPLEX NUMBERS
Race to the Finish

Directions: Answer each question below.

HOMEWORK SET (NO CALCULATOR)

1. What is the value of $(-i)^3$?
   A) -1
   B) 1
   C) $-i$
   D) i

2. Which of the following is equivalent to $\frac{5}{i}$?
   A) $-5i$
   B) -5
   C) 5
   D) $5i$

3. Which of the following is equal to $i(3 + 2i)$?
   A) $3i + 2$
   B) $3i - 2$
   C) $-3i + 2$
   D) $-3i - 2$

4. $-i(3 - i)$ is equivalent to
   A) $-3 - i$
   B) $-1 - 3i$
   C) $1 - 3i$
   D) $3 - i$

5. Which of the following expressions is $\frac{4}{1+i}$ equivalent to?
   A) $4 - 4i$
   B) $4 + 4i$
   C) $2 - 2i$
   D) $2 + 2i$

6. Which of the following is equivalent to $\frac{i}{2+2i}$?
   A) $\frac{1}{4} - \frac{i}{4}$
   B) $\frac{1}{4} + \frac{i}{4}$
   C) $4 - 4i$
   D) $4 + 4i$

7. Which of the following expressions is $(3i)^2 + (2i)^3$ equivalent to?
   A) $-9 - 8i$
   B) $-9 + 8i$
   C) $8 - 9i$
   D) $8 + 9i$

8. Which of the following expressions is $(3 + 3i)^2$ equivalent to?
   A) $-18i$
   B) -18
   C) 18
   D) $18i$

9. $i^2(7 - i) =$

   A) $-7 + i$

   B) $7 - i$

   C) $-1 + 7i$

   D) $1 - 7i$

The following definition is used in Questions 13 through 15.

The magnitude of a complex number in the form $a + bi$ (where a and b are real constants) is defined as:

$$|a + bi| = \sqrt{a^2 + b^2}$$

10. What is $(5 + 3i)(4 - 3i)$?

    A) $11 - 3i$

    B) $11 + 3i$

    C) $29 - 3i$

    D) $29 + 3i$

13. What is the magnitude of $3 + 4i$?

    A) 5

    B) 7

    C) 12

    D) 25

11. The product $(7 + 2i)(3 + 4i)$ is equivalent to which of the following?

    A) $13 - 34i$

    B) $13 + 34i$

    C) $29 - 22i$

    D) $29 + 22i$

14. What is the magnitude of $-5i$?

    A) -25

    B) -5

    C) 5

    D) 25

15. Which of the following complex numbers has a magnitude of 13?

    A) $3 + 10i$

    B) $4 - 13i$

    C) $-5 + 12i$

    D) $-6 - 9i$

12. Provided that c is a real constant, what is the value of $(c + 2i)(c - 2i)$?

    A) $c^2 - 4$

    B) $c^2 + 4$

    C) $c^2 - 4i$

    D) $c^2 + 4i$

16. What is $\dfrac{ci}{c - ci}$ for any real number c?

    A) $\dfrac{1}{2} + \dfrac{i}{2}$

    B) $-\dfrac{1}{2} + \dfrac{i}{2}$

    C) $-\dfrac{c}{2} + \dfrac{ci}{2}$

    D) $\dfrac{1}{2c} + \dfrac{i}{2c}$

17. Which of the following is equivalent to $\frac{2+i}{2-i}$?

 A) -1
 B) 1
 C) $\frac{3}{5} - \frac{4}{5}i$
 D) $\frac{3}{5} + \frac{4}{5}i$

18. $i^{160} =$

19. $(2i)(-3i)(5i)(-15i) =$

20. $\frac{1-i}{2+i} \times \frac{-i-2}{i-1} =$

BLUE MATH LESSON 20A: NON-LINEAR LINES OF BEST FIT – SCATTERPLOTS
Learning to Swim

Directions: Answer each question below.

PRACTICE SET 1 (CALCULATOR)

Questions 1 and 2 use the following information.

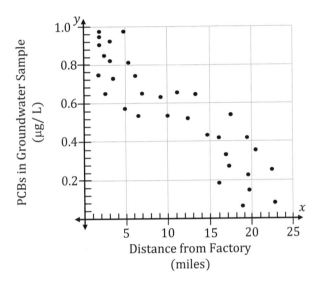

The scatterplot above shows the results of an investigation of PCB contamination in groundwater near a factory that formerly produced heating and cooling equipment. PCBs (polychlorinated biphenyls) are synthetic organic compounds with various industrial uses that were banned by the U.S. Congress in 1979 because of their cancer-causing properties. Groundwater was sampled by boring small holes to extract it at sites within 25 miles of the factory from which the pollution originated. PCB content was measured in micrograms per liter of water.

1. Which type of equation (expressing PCB concentration as a function of distance from the factory) would produce the most appropriate best-fit curve for the data shown?

2. The Environmental Protection Agency has established a standard of 0.5 µg / L as the maximum safe concentration of PCBs in water. For cleanup purposes, the agency will treat as contaminated the largest radius around the site of origin of the pollution inside which *any* samples were taken that exceeded the 0.5 µg / L threshold. Based on this and the results of the study above, the groundwater should be considered contaminated within about how many miles of the factory?

Questions 3 through 5 use the following information.

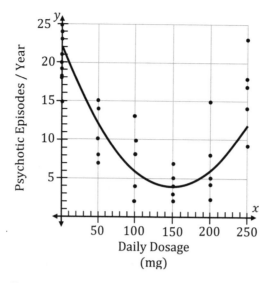

A study was conducted on the effectiveness of a new antipsychotic drug for patients suffering from certain forms of schizophrenia. Patients who agreed to participate were experiencing an average of 30 episodes of psychosis per year prior to enrollment in the study. They were randomly assigned to a dose at which they took the drug for a year, and recorded the number of acute episodes of their disorder that occurred. The results are depicted in the scatterplot above.

3.   The drug is most effective at which daily dosage, in milligrams per day?

4.   Those patients in the study whose dose was 0 mg were given a placebo: a medically ineffective pill that they were told was the drug. (This is a common practice in studies to distinguish the actual effects of the medication from psychological effects resulting from patients' belief that they will get better.) The best-fit curve predicts that, compared to a patient taking nothing, a patient taking a placebo will see their symptoms decrease by what percent?

5.   If the best-fit line continues to accurately predict the drug's effect for doses higher than those tested in this study, then at what dose, in milligrams per day, will patients taking the drug be predicted to have the same level of psychotic symptoms as patients taking a placebo (0 mg dose)?

BLUE MATH LESSON 20A: NON-LINEAR LINES OF BEST FIT – SCATTERPLOTS
Diving into the Deep End

Directions: Answer each question below.

PRACTICE SET 2 (CALCULATOR)

Questions 6 and 7 use the following information.

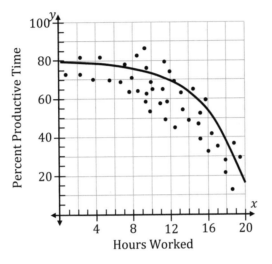

The scatterplot above shows the results of a study conducted of workers in an office environment. The participants tracked their activities and determined what percentage of their time at work was spent doing productive tasks. The results are plotted in relation to the number of hours each employee worked the day of the study.

6. Which type of function describes the best-fit curve shown in the graph above?
   A) Rational
   B) Quadratic
   C) Cubic
   D) Exponential

7. Based on the best-fit curve shown above, if a worker increases her work day from 12 hours to 16 hours, the total amount of productive time she spends at work is predicted to
   A) decrease by 36 minutes.
   B) decrease by 9 minutes.
   C) increase by 24 minutes.
   D) increase by 2 hours and 12 minutes.

Questions 8 through 10 use the following information.

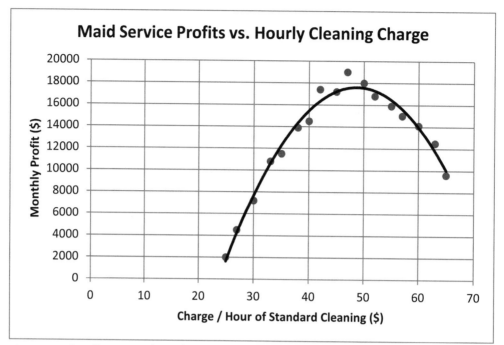

A maid service wanted to figure out the right amount to charge for a standard cleaning in order to maximize profits. Accordingly, the service's owner changed the price of this cleaning once a month, then recorded the company's profits for each month. The resulting data is shown above.

8. The curve of best fit for the graph above can best be described as
   A) quadratic.
   B) cubic.
   C) exponential.
   D) logarithmic.

9. The *x*-intercepts of the best-fit curve shown above represent what real-world scenario?
   A) The maximum amount of profit that the company can earn each month.
   B) The amount of money that the company will lose if it charges $0 per hour for cleaning.
   C) The per-hour charges that will result in the company making approximately $0 in profit.
   D) The per-hour charges that will result in the company maximizing its profit.

10. The service also determines that offering a coupon increases monthly profits by approximately 10%. If the company's profits were $17,600 during a month when a coupon was offered, about how much might the company have charged per hour of standard cleaning during that month?
   A) Either $32 or $64
   B) Either $41 or $56
   C) Either $46 or $51
   D) $48

Questions 11 through 13 use the following information.

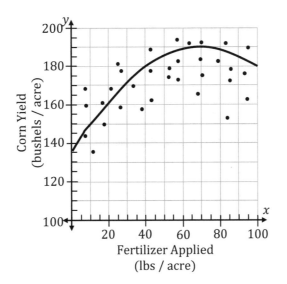

The scatterplot above shows the results of a study on the effectiveness of a new brand of fertilizer. The amount of corn produced in a season (yield) by corn farmers participating in the study is plotted relative to the number of pounds of fertilizer per acre that they applied at the beginning of the growing season.

11. Which of the following equations, where y = yield in bushels per acre and x = pounds of fertilizer used, is closest to that of the best-fit curve shown in the graph above?

A) $y - 70 = -\frac{(x-190)^2}{30}$

B) $y - 70 = -\frac{(x-190)^2}{90}$

C) $y - 190 = -\frac{(x-70)^2}{30}$

D) $y - 190 = -\frac{(x-70)^2}{90}$

12. Which amount (in pounds) of fertilizer is predicted by the best-fit line to yield the same amount of corn as using 10 pounds of fertilizer does?

A) 110

B) 130

C) 150

D) Cannot be answered using the given information

13. Increasing fertilizer use by 33.3% would produce a *decrease* in crop yields for any farmer who was initially using at least how many pounds of fertilizer per acre?

A) 37

B) 45

C) 60

D) 70

Questions 14 and 15 use the following information.

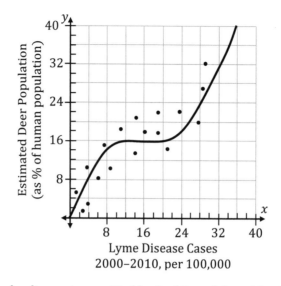

Lyme disease is a neuromuscular disease transmitted by the bites of deer ticks. Deer ticks, as their name indicates, live on deer, and so an analysis was conducted of multiple U.S. states where cases of Lyme disease were reported. The number of cases in a 10-year period in each state was obtained. Naturalists' estimates of the deer population in each state relative to the human population were averaged over the years of the study. The results are depicted in the scatterplot above.

14. The best-fit curve shown above has equation $y - 16 = a(x - 16)^3$, where a is a constant. What is the value of a?

A) $\frac{1}{256}$

B) $\frac{1}{16}$

C) 16

D) 32

15. The state of Minnesota (pop. 5.4 million) is estimated to have 970,000 deer. How many cases of Lyme disease would the best-fit curve above predict were recorded in the state between 2000 and 2010?

A) 24

B) 114

C) 1296

D) 1404

PRACTICE SET 3 (CALCULATOR)

Questions 16 through 18 use the following information.

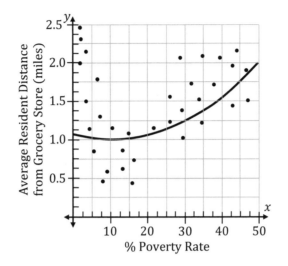

The scatterplot above analyzes a phenomenon that public health and nutrition advocates have called "food deserts." It refers to the observation that some low-income neighborhoods are underserved by grocery stores, making it difficult for their residents to obtain fresh produce or other healthy foods. In the study whose results are plotted above, the poverty rate of a census tract (typically an area of several blocks) was determined, along with the average distance a resident of that tract lived from the nearest full-service grocery store.

16. Which of the following equations is closest to that of the best-fit curve in the graph above?
    A) $y = 0.000625(x - 10)^2 + 1$
    B) $y = 0.025(x - 10)^2 + 1$
    C) $y = 0.025x + 0.75$
    D) $y = 0.0003125(x - 10)^3 + 1$

17. Residents of a hypothetical neighborhood with a poverty rate of 60% would be predicted by this best-fit curve to live an average of how many miles from a grocery store?
    A) 2.00
    B) 2.25
    C) 2.56
    D) 3.00

18. The census tract located farthest from a full-service grocery store had a poverty rate of approximately
    A) 2.5%
    B) 16%
    C) 28%
    D) 44%

Questions 19 through 21 use the following information.

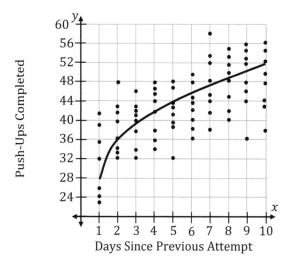

Days Since Previous Attempt

The scatterplot above depicts results from a study on rest and muscle recovery times after exercise. College students who participated did an intensive strength-based workout and then rested for different numbers of days as randomly assigned. The scatterplot shows the number of push-ups (one part of the workout) that students were able to complete relative to the number of days they had taken off since their previous workout.

19. Which of the following equations is closest to that of the best-fit curve depicted in the graph above, where y = number of push-ups completed and x = days of rest since last attempt?

A) $y = \frac{1}{8}(x - 1)^2 + 28$

B) $y = 53 - 2^{\frac{10-x}{2}}$

C) $y = 8\sqrt{x - 1} + 28$

D) $y = \frac{8}{3}x + \frac{76}{3}$

20. A student does the workout from the study on Sunday. He wishes to perform 50% better than he would if he did it again on Monday. On which day should he work out?

A) Tuesday

B) Thursday

C) Friday

D) The following Sunday

21. The best-fit line above would be LEAST likely to result in a reasonable prediction of the number of push-ups done by a student after resting

A) 2 days.

B) 10 days.

C) 24 days.

D) The prediction is about equally likely to be accurate for any of the above.

Questions 22 through 23 use the following information.

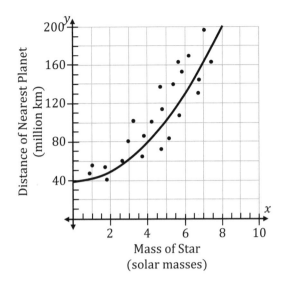

The scatterplot above shows the mass of a number of stars known to have planets orbiting them, plotted relative to the distance from each star of its nearest planet. Masses are given in solar masses; 1 solar mass is equal to the mass of our sun.

22. Which of the following equations is closest to that of the best-fit curve graphed above, where y is the distance from the sun in millions of kilometers and x is mass in solar masses?
    A) $y = 40(1 + 2^{0.25x})$
    B) $y = 1.25x^3 + 40$
    C) $y = (x - 40)^2$
    D) $y = 2.5x^2 + 40$

23. Mercury, the closest planet to our sun, is approximately 58 million kilometers from the sun. Compared to this, the distance the best-fit line would predict it to be from the sun is
    A) about 10% closer.
    B) about 30% closer.
    C) about 10% farther.
    D) about 30% farther.

Questions 24 and 25 use the following information.

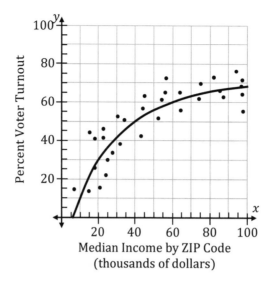

Median Income by ZIP Code
(thousands of dollars)

The scatterplot above shows the percent of eligible voters that voted in various ZIP codes, plotted in relation to the median income of a resident of that ZIP code.

24. A resident of a ZIP code in which the median income is approximately $120,000 would be expected to have a voter turnout of approximately
    A) 50%.
    B) 60%.
    C) 70%.
    D) 85%.

25. A resident of a ZIP code in which the median income is how many dollars is twice as likely to vote as a resident of a ZIP code whose median income is $20,000?
    A) 30,000
    B) 40,000
    C) 60,000
    D) 80,000

BLUE MATH LESSON 20A: NON-LINEAR LINES OF BEST FIT – SCATTERPLOTS
Race to the Finish

Directions: Answer each question below.

HOMEWORK SET (CALCULATOR)

Questions 1 through 3 use the following information.

The scatterplot above shows the sale prices (in thousands of dollars) of homes in a certain neighborhood during the years 2005 to 2013.

1. If sale price is S and years since 2005 is y, which of the following is closest to the equation of the best-fit curve shown in the graph above?
   A) $S(y) = -6y^2 - 56y + 170$
   B) $S(y) = -6y^2 - 56y + 300$
   C) $S(y) = 6y^2 - 56y + 170$
   D) $S(y) = 6y^2 - 56y + 300$

2. Based on the scatterplot and best-fit curve shown above, a resident selling his or her home in this neighborhood during the year 2008 would have been expected to receive a sale price of approximately
   A) $186,000.
   B) $212,000.
   C) $236,000.
   D) $250,000.

3. In a 2013 sale not recorded on the chart above, a homeowner received a $276,000 sale price for her home in the neighborhood. By approximately how much did the homeowner exceed the expected sale price, based on the curve of best fit shown above?
   A) $10,000
   B) $20,000
   C) $40,000
   D) $60,000

Questions 4 through 6 use the following information.

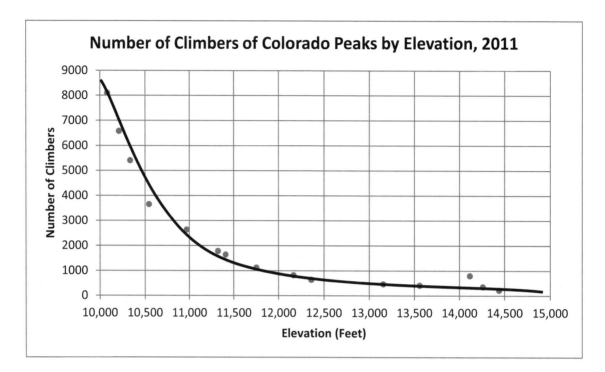

The chart above shows statistics for Colorado's fifteen most popular trails that end at the summit of a mountain peak. The number of people to climb the mountain each year is plotted against the mountain's elevation.

4. Which of the following equations, where N is the number of climbers and L is the elevation, best matches the curve of best fit shown above?
    A) $N(L) = 1000(-0.00085L + 10)^4 + 300$
    B) $N(L) = 1000 \times 4^{-0.00085L+10} + 300$
    C) $N(L) = 1000(-0.00085L + 10)^4 - 300$
    D) $N(L) = 1000 \times 4^{-0.00085L+10} - 300$

5. If, in 2011, one peak received 5,000 climbers and another received 1,000 climbers, which is closest to the predicted difference in elevation between the two peaks?
    A) 750 feet
    B) 1,250 feet
    C) 2,400 feet
    D) 3,100 feet

6. Based on the graph and best-fit curve above, which of the following is true regarding a peak that is 11,500 feet high and that saw 750 climbers in 2011?
    A) The peak had about twice as many climbers as expected.
    B) The peak had about 20% more climbers than expected.
    C) The peak had about 25% fewer climbers than expected.
    D) The peak had about half as many climbers as expected.

Questions 7 through 9 use the following information.

The graph above shows the listed weights and salaries of the players on a professional football team.

7. The best-fit curve for the data shown above suggests that the lowest-paid player on a team would be expected to weigh approximately how many pounds?
    A) 200 pounds
    B) 240 pounds
    C) 280 pounds
    D) 320 pounds

8. Which of the following statements is most strongly supported by the data presented above?
    A) A 175-pound player and a 275-pound player would have roughly the same predicted salary.
    B) A 190-pound player and a 250-pound player would have roughly the same predicted salary.
    C) A 210-pound player and a 290-pound player would have roughly the same predicted salary.
    D) A 225-pound player and a 300-pound player would have roughly the same predicted salary.

9. Based on the best-fit curve to the data shown above, the team's quarterback, whose salary is $9.8 million and who weighs 195 pounds, makes approximately how much more than his predicted salary?
    A) $0.5 million
    B) $2.0 million
    C) $4.5 million
    D) $7.0 million

Questions 10 through 11 use the following information.

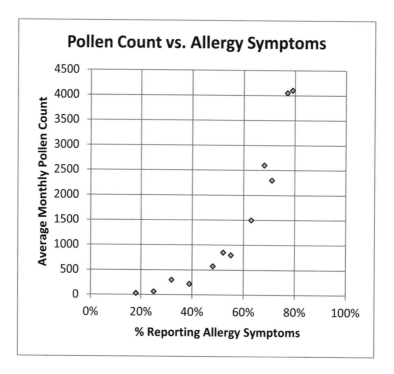

Medical researchers tracked the average monthly pollen count in Montgomery, Alabama, during the year 2013. During each month, they also conducted a phone survey to determine what percentage of the city's residents reported experiencing allergy symptoms (runny nose, sneezing, itchy eyes, etc.) at any point during the month. The results are shown in the graph above.

10. Which type of function provides the most appropriate best-fit line or curve to match the data shown above?
    A) Linear
    B) Quadratic
    C) Exponential
    D) Logarithmic

11. Based on the data shown above, which of the following would be the best prediction for the average monthly pollen count during a month when 60% of the citizens reported allergy symptoms?
    A) 750
    B) 1250
    C) 1750
    D) 2250

Questions 12 through 14 use the following information.

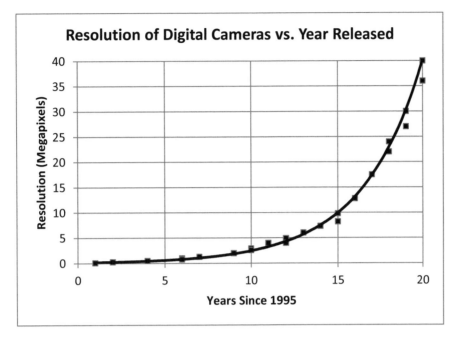

The graph above shows the maximum resolution (in megapixels) produced by a variety of top-end digital cameras released at different times in a 20-year period.

12. Which of the following equations best matches the curve of best fit shown above, given that R represents the resolution of a camera and t represents its release year (in years since 1995, as on the graph above).
   A) $R(t) = 0.2 \times 1.3^t$
   B) $R(t) = 1.3 \times 0.2^t$
   C) $R(t) = 0.2 \times 1.3^{-t}$
   D) $R(t) = 1.3 \times t^{0.2}$

13. In 2010, a company released a top-end camera that produced 13 megapixels. Compared to what would be predicted from the best-fit curve above, the actual resolution of the camera was
   A) about 65% lower.
   B) about 30% lower.
   C) about 30% higher.
   D) about 65% higher.

14. Based on the data above, which of the following is the most accurate estimate for the length of time needed for the maximum resolution of top-end cameras to double?
   A) 1.5 years
   B) 2.5 years
   C) 4 years
   D) 6 years

Questions 15 and 16 use the following information.

Earthquake Strength vs. Property Damage

A scatterplot with y-axis labeled "Magnitude" ranging from 0 to 7, and x-axis labeled "Amount of Property Damage (1,000s of $)" ranging from 0 to 70,000.

A geologist researched all of the earthquakes of magnitude 3.5 or greater that have occurred in her state in the past decade. She plotted this data in the chart above in order to show the relationship between each earthquake and the amount of damage it caused to property in the state.

15. Which type of line or curve of best fit would be most appropriate for the graph shown above?
     A) Linear
     B) Cubic
     C) Exponential
     D) Logarithmic

16. Based on the information above, why might the geologist have excluded earthquakes of magnitude less than 3.5 from the graph?
     A) These earthquakes caused so much damage that they would have required the graph to be far too large.
     B) These earthquakes did not cause enough damage to be visible on the large scale of the graph's *x*-axis.
     C) The damage caused by these earthquakes was too inconsistent to fit with the graph's curve of best fit.
     D) Because earthquakes of lower magnitude are less common, there were not enough of these earthquakes to put them on the graph.

Questions 17 and 18 use the following information.

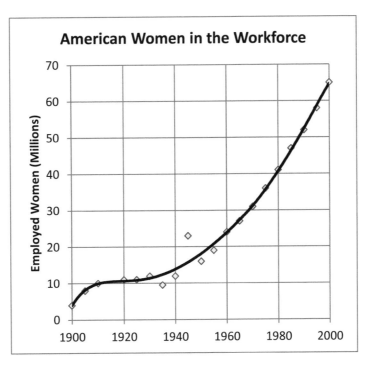

The graph above shows the number of American women ages 23-65 who were employed at least part-time in different years in the 20th century.

17. The curve of best fit above can best be described as
   A) quadratic.
   B) cubic.
   C) exponential.
   D) logarithmic.

18. During World War II, particularly from 1943 to 1945, the number of women in the workforce increased dramatically as they were brought in to take the place of the men who were serving as soldiers overseas. According to the graph and curve of best fit above, about how many more women than expected were working during this time?
   A)   1.5 million
   B)   7 million
   C)   16 million
   D)   23 million

Questions 19 and 20 use the following information.

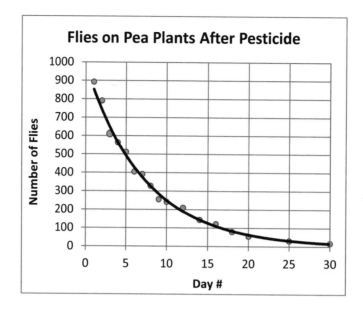

As part of an experiment, the fruit flies on a group of pea plants are counted every day. On the first day of the experiment, a new pesticide is applied to the plants. The graph above shows the results.

19. If d is the day after the start of the experiment and F is the number of flies, which of the following equations most closely matches the curve of best fit shown above?
    A) $F = 100 \times 2^{(2d)}$
    B) $F = 100 \times 2^{(-2d)}$
    C) $F = 100 \times 2^{(0.2d)}$
    D) $F = 100 \times 2^{(-0.2d)}$

20. Which statement about the effectiveness of the pesticide is most accurate based on the data shown above?
    A) The pesticide is very effective in the first 10 days, but after that, it allows the fruit fly populations to go up again.
    B) An equal number of fruit flies are killed each day.
    C) The pesticide's effectiveness increases continually with time.
    D) The pesticide continues to kill an equal percentage of the remaining fruit flies each day.

BLUE MATH LESSON 20B: TWO-WAY TABLES
Learning to Swim

Directions: Answer each question below.

PRACTICE SET 1 (CALCULATOR)

Four zoos combine for a census of their ape populations. The results are shown in the table below.

Ape Census of Four Zoos

	San Diego	Indianapolis	St. Louis	The Bronx	Total
Gorillas	8	4	A	0	17
Chimpanzees	14	B	7	2	23
Orangutans	5	8	11	6	30
Gibbons	16	6	C	0	26
Total	43	18	27	8	96

1. A =

2. B =

3. C =

4. If gibbons were eliminated from the census, which zoo would have the highest percentage of gorillas among its apes?
   A) San Diego
   B) Indianapolis
   C) St. Louis
   D) The Bronx

5. A fifth zoo in Miami, Florida, also took an ape census. One-fourth of these apes were orangutans. If 30% of all the apes at the five zoos are orangutans, how many total apes are at the Miami Zoo?
   A) 18
   B) 24
   C) 29
   D) 36

BLUE MATH LESSON 20B: TWO-WAY TABLES
Diving into the Deep End

Directions: Answer each question below.

PRACTICE SET 2 (CALCULATOR)

Questions 6 through 8 refer to the following information.

A bird-watcher counts the number of visits from birds of five different species (broken down into male and female groups) to a backyard feeder during a month. The results of these observations are shown below.

Feeder Visits by Gender and Species

	Male	Female	Total
Blue Jay	13	11	24
House Sparrow	112	75	187
Cardinal	27	28	55
Goldfinch	18	13	31
Chickadee	80	74	154
Total	250	201	451

6. If a visiting bird of each species is chosen at random, the birds of which species are more likely to be male than the goldfinch?
   A) Chickadee and Blue Jay
   B) House Sparrow and Chickadee
   C) House Sparrow and Blue Jay
   D) House Sparrow only

7. Which statement about the bird-watcher's observations is most accurate, based on the table?
   A) If a female bird of these 5 species was seen, there is an 11% chance that it was a cardinal.
   B) If a male bird of these 5 species was seen, there is a 32% chance that it was a chickadee.
   C) If a male bird of these 5 species was seen, there is a 37% chance that it was a house sparrow.
   D) If a female bird of these 5 species was seen, there is a 45% chance that it was a house sparrow.

8. A male bird is picked at random from all of the birds observed. That bird is least likely to be a
   A) Blue Jay
   B) Cardinal
   C) Goldfinch
   D) Chickadee

Questions 9 through 11 refer to the following information.

An online retailer uses 4 types of box to ship its products: A, B, C, and D (from smallest in volume to largest). The retailer sells 3 classes of product: media (books, movies, and video games), electronics, and clothes. The table below shows the number of products of each type that the retailer has shipped this week, as well as the boxes used to ship each product.

Online Retailer's Weekly Shipping Report

Box	Media	Electronics	Clothes	Total
A	314	47	12	373
B	277	201	99	577
C	88	162	133	383
D	41	66	76	183
Total	720	476	320	1516

9. Based on the table above, which of the following is the highest?
   A) The probability that a media shipment chosen at random is packed in a type A box.
   B) The probability that a media shipment chosen at random is packed in a large (type C or D) box.
   C) The probability that a clothing shipment chosen at random is packed in a small (type A or B) box.
   D) The probability that a clothing shipment chosen at random is packed in a type C box.

10. The retailer decides to split the media category up into 3 sub-categories: books, movies, and video games. There are equal numbers of movie and video game orders. If none of the video game orders are packed in a type D box and only 10% of the movie orders are packed in a type D box, what fraction of the 300 book orders are packed in a type D box?
    A) $\frac{1}{30}$
    B) $\frac{3}{50}$
    C) $\frac{1}{15}$
    D) $\frac{1}{10}$

11. Approximately 10% of all of the Media shipped in A boxes was damaged because it was shipped in a box that was too big. A new box, smaller than box A is going to be used to ship all of these products. Approximately what percentage of all media will be shipped in this new box?
    A) 2.4%
    B) 2.8%
    C) 4.4%
    D) 10%

Questions 12 and 13 refer to the following information.

A recent United Nations census tracked the number of migrants between each of the world's regions during the years 2005 to 2010. The table below describes the portion of this census data related to people migrating from three Asian regions to other parts of the world.

Migrants from Three Asian Regions to Other Regions, 2005-2010 (Thousands)

	from South Asia	from East Asia	from Southeast Asia	Total
to North America	1,506	1,057	971	3,534
to Europe	1,373	455	582	2,410
to Middle East	4,589	37	809	5,435
to Other Regions	994	419	669	2,082
Total	8,462	1,968	3,031	13,461

12. If a migrant from Asia is chosen at random for each of the four destination regions, a migrant headed to which of the following regions would be most likely to be from Southeast Asia?
    A) to North America
    B) to Europe
    C) to Middle East
    D) to Other Regions

13. Approximately 1 million of the migrants included in the "to Other Regions" category migrated from one Asian region to another. These migrants are removed from the data set in amounts proportional to the current data in order to estimate the number of migrants who left Asia. Based on this estimate, approximately how many migrants went from Southeast Asia to other, non-Asian regions?
    A) 218,000
    B) 348,000
    C) 448,000
    D) 517,000

Questions 14 and 15 refer to the following information.

Environmental scientists in four cities track the air quality in those cities during the course of a year. Based on the levels of air pollutants, each day is classified into one of four air-quality groups: Dangerous, Poor, Moderate, and Good. The results are shown in the table below.

Air Quality Ratings in Four Cities During the Year 2012

	Philadelphia	Atlanta	Houston	Los Angeles	**Total**
Dangerous	13	45	62	58	178
Poor	65	102	79	77	323
Moderate	154	131	165	98	548
Good	133	87	59	132	411
Total	365	365	365	365	1460

14. Based on the table, for which air quality category or categories did Houston have the highest proportion of the total number of days in that category?
    A) Dangerous
    B) Poor
    C) Moderate
    D) Dangerous and Moderate

15. Doctors recommend that residents restrict outdoor physical activities on days in which the air quality rating is Poor or Dangerous. Based on the table, a doctor in which of the four cities would be most likely to make such a recommendation on a given day?
    A) Philadelphia
    B) Atlanta
    C) Houston
    D) Los Angeles

PRACTICE SET 3 (NO CALCULATOR)

Questions 16 through 18 refer to the following information.

A private high school offers three music programs: chorus, orchestra, and marching band. To determine how best to allocate resources to these programs, the school examined the number of students in each grade who participated in each program. The resulting data are shown in the table below.

Music Program Participation by Grade Level

Grade	Chorus	Orchestra	Marching Band	Total
Freshmen	13	21	44	78
Sophomores	19	30	56	105
Juniors	28	35	47	110
Seniors	25	41	39	105
Total	85	127	186	398

16. According to the data in the table above, among those students in a program that requires renting or buying an instrument (i.e., orchestra or marching band), a student of which grade level would be most likely to choose marching band?
    A) Freshman
    B) Sophomore
    C) Junior
    D) Senior

17. A random sampling of 200 students not participating in any music program were asked to select which of the 3 programs they would prefer to join if required to do so. Of those, 25% selected chorus, 30% chose orchestra, and 45% chose marching band. Based on this information and the table above, if participating in a music program was required, the percentage of music program participants in which of the program(s) would increase?
    A) Chorus and Orchestra
    B) Chorus and Marching Band
    C) Chorus only
    D) Orchestra only

18. The information from the table above is used to analyze another private school, which had 250 music students with approximately the same grade distributions as the one studied above. Grade-by-grade preferences for music remained unchanged, other than the fact that 50% fewer seniors were in chorus; instead, those seniors were evenly split between the orchestra and the marching band. How many Marching Band members does this school have?
    A) 111
    B) 121
    C) 136
    D) 190

Questions 19 through 21 refer to the following information.

A geneticist breeds three groups of mice: ordinary mice (the control group), mice that have been genetically modified to have extra speed (the "speed" group), and mice that have been genetically modified to be particularly intelligent (the "brains" group). The geneticist tests each group of mice in a maze and records how long the mice take to finish (or if they do not finish at all).

Results of Putting Different Groups of Mice through a Laboratory Maze

Maze Time	Control	Speed	Brains	Total
Under 30 s	6	9	3	18
30 – 90 s	14	4	6	24
90+ s	12	1	5	18
Did not finish	10	5	0	15
Total	42	19	14	75

19. According to the table, which probability is lowest?
   A) The probability that a mouse that finished the maze in less than 30 seconds is genetically modified.
   B) The probability that a mouse that finished the race in between 30 and 90 seconds is in the control group.
   C) The probability that a mouse that finished the race in more than 90 seconds is in the control group.
   D) The probability that a mouse that did not finish the maze is in the control group.

20. Based on the table above, which statement about the experiment is most likely to be accurate?
   A) Modifying a mouse to give it added speed does not improve its likelihood of finishing a maze in less than 90 seconds.
   B) Modifying a mouse to give it added speed does not improve its likelihood of finishing a maze in any amount of time.
   C) Modifying a mouse to give it added intelligence does not improve its likelihood of finishing a maze in less than 90 seconds.
   D) Modifying a mouse to give it added intelligence does not improve its likelihood of finishing a maze in any amount of time.

21. Based on the table above, which probability is highest?
   A) The probability that a mouse with "Brains" finished the race.
   B) The probability that a mouse with "Speed" finished the race.
   C) The probability that a control mouse finished the race.
   D) The probability that any mouse finished the race.

Questions 22 and 23 refer to the following information.

The owner of a coffee shop keeps track of the number of drinks that the shop sells during a week. She breaks this data down in two ways: by type of drink (coffee, tea, smoothie, or other) and by size (small, medium, or large). The data is shown below.

Drinks Ordered in Sue's Café During the Past Week, by Type and Size

	Small	Medium	Large	**Total**
Coffee	151	225	180	556
Tea	48	64	55	167
Smoothie	24	47	89	160
Other	69	78	103	250
Total	292	414	427	1133

22. The coffee shop makes the most profit on large drinks and the least on small drinks. Based on this information and the table, which type of drink is likely the most profitable on a per-order basis?
    A) Coffee
    B) Tea
    C) Smoothie
    D) Other

23. The Other group includes sodas, hot chocolates, and juices. If sodas make up 40% of the orders in this group, and sodas are not offered in the small size, what percentage of the hot chocolate and juice orders were in the small size?
    A) 28%
    B) 40%
    C) 46%
    D) 52%

Questions 24 through 25 refer to the following information.

Atmospheric scientists have many ways of classifying clouds. One is to group them by their "genus," which is based mostly on appearance. Another is to differentiate by height of the cloud. One scientist used these two methods to classify all of the clouds observed above a laboratory during a month-long observation period. The results are shown below.

Clouds Above Atmospheric Sciences Lab, by Genus and Height

Genus	Low Height	Moderate Height	Towering Height	Total
Stratus	158	210	37	405
Cumulus	362	414	103	879
Nimbostratus	63	185	92	340
Cumulonimbus	84	117	212	413
Total	667	926	444	2037

24. Which cloud genus had the highest percentage of clouds that were of moderate height?
   A) Stratus
   B) Cumulus
   C) Nimbostratus
   D) Cumulonimbus

25. A total of 150 clouds from a fifth genus, cirrus, were also observed. Eighty percent of these clouds were of low height, and the rest were of moderate height. If all 5 genera are included, approximately what percentage of the low-height clouds were cirrus?
   A) 8%
   B) 12%
   C) 15%
   D) 20%

BLUE MATH LESSON 20B: TWO-WAY TABLES
Race to the Finish

Directions: Answer each question below.

HOMEWORK SET (CALCULATOR)

Questions 1 through 3 refer to the following information.

A team of astronomers use a high-powered telescope to search for "exoplanets," planets that orbit stars other than the Sun. "Super Earths" are rocky planets significantly larger than Earth but smaller than gas giant planets. They classify each planet they find by size and predicted temperature.

Exoplanet Survey by Size and Temperature

	Earth Size	"Super-Earth" Size	Gas Giant Size	Total
Cold	2	5	94	101
Temperate	1	7	68	76
Hot	8	20	101	129
Total	11	32	263	306

1. The astronomers theorize that in order to sustain life, planets must have a temperate climate and must not be larger than "Super-Earth" size. At current rates, how many total planets must the team find if they want to find at least 20 planets that could potentially sustain life?
   A) 408
   B) 510
   C) 765
   D) 874

2. If a cold planet, a temperate planet, and a hot planet are chosen at random from the planets found in the survey, which of the following is most likely?
   A) The cold planet is in the "Super-Earth" Size group.
   B) The temperate planet is in the Earth Size group.
   C) The temperate planet is in the "Super-Earth" Size group.
   D) The hot planet is in the Earth Size group.

3. Before completing a second survey, the astronomers make improvements to the telescope aimed at being able to better identify Earth-sized planets. If these changes lead to a 20% improvement in the number of Earth-sized planets found relative to the total number of planets found, how many planets will be in the "Earth Size" category if the second survey finds 209 total planets?
   A) 7
   B) 9
   C) 11
   D) 13

Questions 4 through 6 refer to the following information.

A wireless phone provider compiles information about its customers so that it can improve its service. The table below shows some of this information: type of phone and type of service plan. There are three classes of phone: basic phones (meant for primarily making phone calls), feature phones (with cameras and texting capabilities), and smart phones (with apps and internet features).

Phone Type and Service Plan Type for Customers of ABC Wireless (Thousands)

Plan Type	Basic Phone	Feature Phone	Smart Phone	Total
Budget	97	77	59	233
Standard (No Data)	68	80	128	276
Limited Data	0	25	170	195
Unlimited Data	0	0	178	178
Total	165	182	535	882

4. What percentage of the users who do not have a basic phone subscribe to one of the two data plans?
    A) 42%
    B) 52%
    C) 57%
    D) 65%

5. Which probability is highest?
    A) The probability that a randomly selected customer will have a standard plan.
    B) The probability that a randomly selected customer with a basic phone will have a standard plan.
    C) The probability that a randomly selected customer with a feature phone will have a standard plan.
    D) The probability that a randomly selected customer with a smart phone will have an unlimited data plan.

6. The company takes a survey of 500 randomly chosen feature phone-owning customers to determine what would happen if the company stopped supporting feature phones. Eighty percent of these customers said they would stay with the wireless company, while the other 20% would leave. Of the remaining customers, 64% said they would be willing to upgrade to a smart phone, while the rest chose a basic phone. Based on these results and the table, if all of the feature phone supporters were forced to choose between a smart phone, a basic phone, and canceling their service, how many smart phone users would the company have?
    A) 256,000
    B) 452,000
    C) 628,000
    D) 651,000

Questions 7 through 9 refer to the following information.

Doctors in a laboratory are testing several drugs that could potentially help kill cancer cells. The doctors test each drug in a Petri dish with cells from each of several types of cancer. Each drug/cancer cell combination is tested in 25 Petri dishes. A successful test is one in which the drug kills at least half of the cancer cells. The results of the experiment are shown below.

Number of Successful Drug Tests (Out of 25 Tests for Each Combination)

Cancer Type	Drug A	Drug B	Drug C	Total
Carcinoma	12	4	3	19
Melanoma	2	9	6	17
Leukemia	0	18	8	26
Lymphoma	1	7	2	10
Total	15	38	19	72

7. Based on the data in the table, if a Petri dish from a successful test is chosen at random for each of the 4 cancer types, which is most likely?
   A) The test using carcinoma cells will involve Drug A.
   B) The test using melanoma cells will involve Drug B.
   C) The test using leukemia cells will involve Drug B.
   D) The test using lymphoma cells will involve Drug B.

8. The doctors also tried testing combinations of the three drugs. They found that the success rates for these combinations were equal to the average of the individual drugs' success rates. Based on this information and the table, the success rate is highest for which combination?
   A) Drug B & Drug C tested on carcinoma
   B) Drug A & Drug B tested on melanoma
   C) Drug A & Drug C tested on leukemia
   D) Drug B & Drug C tested on lymphoma

9. The three drugs are all tested with a 5th type of cancer, glioma, using the same procedures described above. The success rates in these tests are approximately the same as the total success rates for the carcinoma and melanoma tests. Approximately how many successful glioma tests occurred in all?
   A) 9
   B) 12
   C) 18
   D) 36

Questions 10 through 12 refer to the following information.

Four bodybuilders keep track of the number of exercises they perform during a group workout, as shown in the table below.

Number of Repetitions Performed for Each Exercise During a Workout

	Squats	Deadlifts	Bench Presses	Lat Raises	**Total**
Paula	45	12	30	18	105
Simon	20	18	40	20	98
Randy	36	20	0	12	68
Kelly	50	25	20	15	110
Total	151	75	90	65	381

10. Lat raises make up the highest proportion of which person's workout?
    A) Paula's
    B) Simon's
    C) Randy's
    D) Kelly's

11. Randy forgot to include his bench presses in the table. When his total is included, it makes up 40% of all the bench presses that the group did during the workout. How many bench presses did Randy do?
    A) 36
    B) 44
    C) 52
    D) 60

12. The "Squats" category includes two types of squats: bodyweight squats and barbell squats. None of Kelly's squats used a barbell, and half of both Simon's and Randy's squats used a barbell. If there were 37 barbell squats in all during the workout, approximately what percentage of Paula's total repetitions were bodyweight squats?
    A) 9%
    B) 19%
    C) 26%
    D) 34%

Questions 13 through 15 refer to the following information.

A group of marine biologists observed the number of algal blooms—harmful concentrations of algae and other microorganisms in the Pacific Ocean. The team identified the color and duration of each bloom, as shown in the table below.

Algal Bloom Characteristics in U.S. Waters, by Color and Duration

	1-3 Days	4-6 Days	7+ Days	Total
Green	48	12	2	62
Cyan	16	21	18	55
Yellow-Brown	5	6	10	21
Red	8	13	21	42
Total	77	52	51	180

13. Samples of the water from each algal bloom were taken. If one sample from each of the four colors is chosen at random, which is most likely?
    A) The green sample is from a bloom that lasted 4 days or longer.
    B) The cyan sample is from a bloom that lasted 3 days or fewer.
    C) The yellow-brown sample is from a bloom that lasted 7 days or longer.
    D) The red sample is from a bloom that lasted between 4 and 6 days.

14. The marine biologists discovered that roughly 30% of the blooms from the "1-3 Days" group were mistakenly labeled and should have been put in the "4-6 Days" group. If these blooms are distributed proportionally among the colors, how many cyan blooms actually lasted between 4 and 6 days?
    A) 23
    B) 25
    C) 27
    D) 30

15. The scientists noted that the information from the algal blooms in the Pacific Ocean represented approximately 35% of the world's algal blooms. If the rest of the world's algal blooms mirrored the data above, approximately how many Cyan 7+ Day blooms were there worldwide?
    A) 6
    B) 51
    C) 60
    D) 303

Questions 16 through 18 refer to the following information.

A sports website polled its readers on their favorite sports. Each reader was classified based on age (under 18 or adult) and gender. The results of the poll for the 4 most popular sports are shown below.

SportWorld Survey of Readers' Favorite Sports

	Males Under 18	Females Under 18	Adult Males	Adult Females	Total
Football	91	78	266	281	716
Baseball	43	32	185	154	414
Basketball	48	19	99	71	237
Soccer	65	58	70	62	255
Total	247	187	620	568	1622

16. Which sport had the greatest proportion of its support from female readers?
    A) Football
    B) Baseball
    C) Basketball
    D) Soccer

17. The 5th-most popular sport in the survey was hockey, which was selected by 180 readers. If the age and gender breakdowns for hockey were similar to those for basketball, about how many adult males chose hockey as their favorite sport?
    A) 29
    B) 36
    C) 72
    D) 75

18. The males surveyed had the greatest support for which sport?
    A) Football
    B) Baseball
    C) Basketball
    D) Soccer

Questions 19 and 20 refer to the following information.

A geologist classifies all the volcanic mountains in a mountain range according to two criteria: activity level and height.

Volcanic Mountains in the Domain Range by Size and Activity Level

Height	Active	Dormant	Extinct	Total
Under 2,000 m	8	35	67	110
2,000-2,999 m	4	19	43	66
3,000-3,999 m	7	11	20	38
4,000+ m	2	7	12	21
Total	21	72	142	235

19. If one volcanic mountain is chosen at random from each of the 4 height classifications, the mountain from which classification would be most likely to be a non-extinct volcano?
    A) Under 2,000 m
    B) 2,000 – 2,999 m
    C) 3,000 – 3,999 m
    D) 4,000+ m

20. A follow-up study examined a random sampling of 30 mountains in the "Extinct" group. This study revealed that 30% of those mountains were actually dormant, not extinct. If these results are extrapolated to all the extinct mountains, the new totals for the dormant and extinct groups would be most nearly
    A) 94 dormant, 99 extinct.
    B) 94 dormant, 120 extinct.
    C) 115 dormant, 99 extinct.
    D) 115 dormant, 120 extinct.

Contributors

A *Very Special Thank You* to the following contributors

Ashley Zahn (HQ)

Brian MacNeel (HQ)

Chris Thomas (HQ)

Kyle Hurford (Johns Creek, GA)

Micah Medders (HQ)

Monica Huynh (Johns Creek, GA)

Sarah Plunkett (Cumming, GA)

Abigail Burns (Johns Creek, GA)

Alicyn Henkhaus (Palos Verdes, CA)

Ankit Rawtani (Bridgewater, NJ)

Anne Hellerman (Coppell, TX)

Benjamin Yu (Bridgewater, NJ)

Brent Cash (Germantown, MD)

Brett Vigil (Johns Creek, GA)

Brian Cabana (Paramus, NJ)

Brian Hester (Roswell, GA)

Caitlin Pancarician (Middletown, NJ)

Casey Lynch (Livingston, NJ)

Christopher Muyo (New York)

Christopher Woodside (Edison, NJ)

Danielle McMullin (Clifton, NJ)

David Rutter (Snellville, GA)

Drew McKelvy (Olney, MD)

Edward Helmsteter (Westfield, NJ)

Eli Aghassi (Northridge, CA)

Elizabeth Peterson (Centreville, VA)

Erica Schimmel (West Portal, CA)

Erin Lynch (Coppell, TX)

Erin Short (Palo Alto, CA)

Greg Hernandez (Rancho Cucamonga, CA)

Heather Kelly (Issaquah, WA)

James Kyrsiak (Old Alabama, GA)

James Wagner (Los Angeles, CA)

Jeffrey Pereira (Scarsdale, NY)

Jessica Loud (Palos Verdes, CA)

Jin Park (Frisco, TX)

John F. Callahan (Parsippany, NY)

Kaleab Tessema (Coppell, TX)

Katharine Galic (Palo Alto, CA)

Kyla Bye-Nagel (Sterling, MD)

Kyle Mesce (Chatham, NJ)

Lane D'Alessandro (King of Prussia, PA)

May-Lieng Karageorge (Lorton, MD)

Michael Fienburg (Calabasas, CA)

Michael Lupi (Paramus, NJ)

Morgan McLoughlin (Brentwood, CA)

Nicole Lampl (Calabasas, CA)

Peter Lee (Hamilton Mill, GA)

Rachel Becker (Burke, VA)

Rachel Tucker (Naperville, IL)

Richard Faulk (Fremont, CA)

Robert Jedrzejewski (Timonium, MD)

Sam Anderson (Paramus, NJ)

Sean Llewellyn (Lynnwood, WA)

Thach Do (Monrovia, CA)

Tina-Anne Mulligan (Paramus, NJ)

Qi-lu Lin (Parsippany, NY)

Zack Arenstein (Livingston, NJ)

Zafar Tejani (Little Neck, NY)

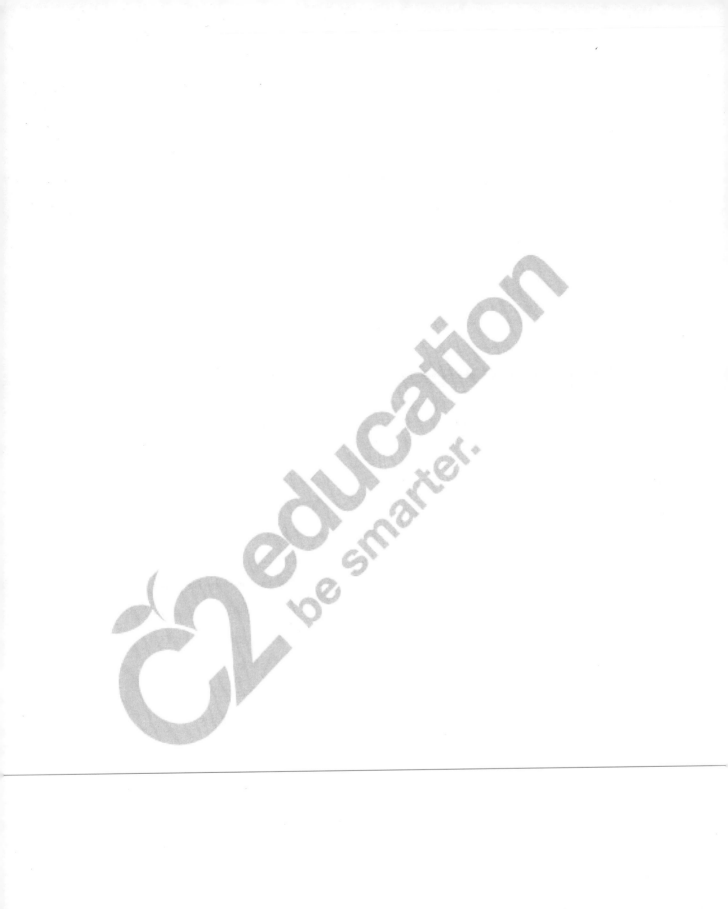